LEADERSHIP, PARTICIPATION, AND GROUP BEHAVIOR

LEADERSHIP, PARTICIPATION, AND GROUP BEHAVIOR

Edited by

L.L. CUMMINGS
University of Minnesota

BARRY M. STAW
University of California, Berkeley

JAI PRESS INC.

Greenwich, Connecticut   London, England

Library of Congress Cataloging-in-Publication Data

Leadership, participation, and group behavior / edited by L.L. Cummings,
 Barry M. Staw.
      p.   cm.
  ISBN 1-55938-220-1
  1. Organization. 2. Leadership. 3. Decision-making, Group. 4. Organizational
behavior. I. Cummings, Larry L. II. Staw, Barry M.
HM131.L37   1990
303.3′4—dc20   90-4529
                                               CIP

CONTENTS

LIST OF CONTRIBUTORS

Mary L. Baetz
University of Toronto

Janice M. Beyer
University of Texas at Austin

Paul S. Goodman
Carnegie-Mellon University

Robert J. House
University of Pennsylvania

Edwin A. Locke
University of Maryland

Elizabeth Ravlin
Carnegie-Mellon University

Marshall Schminke
Creighton University

Helen B. Schwartzman
Northwestern University

David M. Schweiger
University of Maryland

George Strauss
University of California, Berkeley

Harrison M. Trice
Cornell University

PREFACE

The social and interpersonal context of behavior plays a central role in predicting and understanding much of human behavior. This book brings together six essays which focus on subthemes about this context. Two articles focus on the subtheme of leadership; its antecedents, its forms, and its consequences. Two emphasize the related subtheme of the roles of participation in decision making. Two highlight the role of groups in organizations, with particular focus on types of groups that have typically been understudied and on the roles of technology and organizational design influencing the functioning of groups.

Robert House and Mary Baetz begin with a chapter that reviews the leadership literature of a decade ago. Emphasis is given both to theoretical and to methodological issues that need solution if the construct of leadership is to be as useful theoretically as it is popular among executives. Major avenues of needed research are explicated and studies are suggested which were thought to advance leadership scholarship as of 1979. Much of what House and Baetz criticize and advocate still holds true now, more than a decade later.

One avenue of leadership thought that has re-emerged as quite active is that of the role of charisma. Harrison Trice and Janet Beyer review the concept of charisma as it has developed historically. They go beyond definitional and historical foundations by illustrating how charisma became institutionalized and routinized in two different organizational settings. The keys to routinization are summarized and the two cases are used to contrast conditions that facilitate vs. hinder institutionalization of charisma in leadership practices.

Edwin Locke and David Schweiger present a highly controversial chapter cautioning the advocates of participative decision making that the case for participation cannot be made based on productivity and performance improvements. Rather, the case rests on ideological connotations and assumptions and on the frequent, but not consistent, association of participation with enhanced job satisfaction. Evidence is reviewed showing that participation is frequently less effective in enhancing performance than three other managerial tools, i.e., compensation, goal setting, and job enrichment.

George Strauss explores and reviews the scholarship on workers' participation from a global perspective. He articulates the differences in the ways participation is conceived in different countries and the different participative practices associated with these different meanings. He places participation squarely into its sociopolitical context and questions its use as a managerial tool of motivation and control. Strauss's focus is on *formal* arrangements for worker participation in management as these are legally enacted or have come to be accepted in practice through institutional labor–management arrangements. The varying effectiveness of formal participation schemes is attributed to the impact of technology, values, and reward systems across cultures and institutional settings.

Helen Schwartzman provides an insightful analysis for one particular type of *group* setting, i.e., committee meetings. She makes the important point that while such meetings are much maligned, they are understudied in terms of the socialization and symbolic functions they perform in organizations. She takes us well beyond the view of groups as merely communication and decision-making mechanisms. Schwartzman calls for a shift in viewing meetings as *tools* for action to a *topic* of substance worthy of study in their own right.

Finally, Paul Goodman, Elizabeth Ravlin, and Marshall Schminke present a framework for understanding the behavior and *products of groups* in organizations. Their contribution is important for several reasons. The focus is on the productive performance of real groups in real, on-going settings. They also draw upon an unusually wide array of literatures, including but beyond social psychology, important to our knowledge of how groups function and produce. They offer also highly original prescriptions for future scholarship aimed at understanding and facilitating group performance. These prescriptions focus on three concepts: the technologies used by groups, group cohesiveness, and group norms. Suggestions are also made concerning methodological issues needing our attention as the study of groups re-emerges in organizational behavior.

L.L. CUMMINGS
Minneapolis, Minnesota

BARRY M. STAW
Berkeley, California

LEADERSHIP: SOME EMPIRICAL GENERALIZATIONS AND NEW RESEARCH DIRECTIONS[1]

Robert J. House and Mary L. Baetz

ABSTRACT

This paper presents a selective review of the literature concerning leadership. The major empirical generalizations that appear supportable are identified. Theories of leadership enjoying current widespread attention and empirical support are also reviewed and subjected to critical analysis. Major issues in the leadership literature are identified and reviewed. Suggestions for future research are advanced throughout the review of the empirical and theoretical literature.

1

". . . probably more has been written and less known about leadership than any other topic in the behavioral sciences" (Bennis, 1959, p. 259).

"After 40 years of accumulation, our mountain of evidence about leadership seems to offer few clear-cut facts" (McCall, 1976).

"It is difficult to know what, if anything, has been convincingly demonstrated by replicated research. The endless accumulation of empirical data has not produced an integrated understanding of leadership" (Stogdill, 1974, p. vii).

The above quotes suggest the conclusion that despite the fact that leadership has been the subject of speculation, discussion, and debate since the time of Plato and the subject of more than 3000 empirical investigations (Stogdill, 1974), there is little known about it. We disagree with this conclusion. It is our position that there are several empirical generalizations that can be induced from the wealth of research findings concerning leadership. Further it is our position that when viewed collectively these empirical generalizations provide a basis for the development of a theory of leadership—a theory that potentially describes, explains, and predicts the causes of, processes involved in, and consequences of the leadership phenomena. While such a theory is not presently available, it is argued here that it is possible of attainment.

This paper presents a selective review and summary of the major findings resulting from empirical research conducted to date. As the title implies, one of the purposes of this paper is to suggest new directions for leadership research. Identification of research directions is a theoretical endeavor. This paper is such an endeavor. Hopefully, this theorizing will result in some new and fruitful insights about the phenomenon of leadership. These insights, if presented in an empirically testable form, constitute directions for future research.

In reviewing the literature, we were primarily guided by Stogdill's (1974) exhaustive compilation and summary of seven decades of leadership research. In addition to Stogdill's review, we considered several others (Cartwright and Zander, 1968; Filley, House, and Kerr, 1976; Pfeffer, 1977; Fiedler and Chemers, 1974; McCall, 1976; Sims, 1977; Barrow, 1976; and Schriesheim, House, and Kerr, 1976) and approximately 150 studies published since 1972.

Our objective in conducting this review was to identify issues in the leadership literature that we judged to have significant theoretical and practical implications. To identify such issues we searched for:

1. Theories of leadership for which there is empiric support or for which there is current widespread interest.

2. Significant empirical generalizations based on repeatedly replicated findings.

3. Research suggestions by others that we judged to offer significant promise.

4. Discrepancies in results that, if reconciled, we believe would contribute to knowledge about leadership and its effects.

Upon identification of such theories, empiric generalizations, research suggestions by others, or empiric discrepancies, we then consulted the more prominent works and read them in the original. By rereading these works in the original we hoped to gain additional insights about the phenomena in question. These insights constitute the product of our review of the literature and many of the new directions for leadership research that we propose.

We begin with an examination of the construct of leadership and advance a definition of that construct that we hope is both empirically testable and operationally useful. We then discuss the question of how and what kind of effects leadership has on individual and organizational outcomes. Following the discussion of leadership effects, we review research on leadership traits, leadership behavior, and determinants of leadership behavior. This review is intended to identify issues for leadership research that have not been as yet specified, or suggestions for research, although not new to the literature, that seem not to have been adequately pursued. As will be shown, many such suggestions have been advanced earlier and appear to warrant serious reconsideration.

Following the review of the literature concerned with leadership traits, leadership behavior, and determinants of leader behavior, we turn to a consideration of current leadership theories and attempt to identify the most critical research issues raised by these theories. Throughout our review we will attempt to identify the more important research issues associated with each topic and suggest new directions for leadership research where appropriate.

LEADERSHIP AS A SCIENTIFIC CONSTRUCT

Stogdill reviewed seventy-two definitions of leadership advanced by writers from 1902 to 1967. Almost all definitions imply that leadership is a form of social influence. However, as Pfeffer points out, leadership as usually defined is not distinct from other concepts of social influence and ". . . to treat leadership as a separate concept, it must be distinguished from other social influence phenomena" (Pfeffer, 1977, p. 105).

It is the opinion of the authors that because of the unique context in which leadership takes place it is necessary to define it as a specific subset of social phenomena. To define the construct of leadership we will briefly describe the operational methods by which leadership is defined and studied in the social science literature. We will then infer from this description those variables that appear to be the defining characteristics of the leadership phenomena.

Studies commonly falling under the descriptive term "leadership research" can be grossly divided into two classifications: The first classification of studies consists of those that concern the traits, behavior, and impact of individuals who are assigned formal or legal authority to direct others. These individuals are referred to in these studies as *formal leaders*.

The second class of studies falling under the descriptive term "leadership research" consists of those studies concerned with the traits, behavior, and impact of individuals who exert significant influence over others in task groups for which there is no formally allocated authority. Individuals who are observed to exert such influence are referred to in this literature as *emergent leaders*.

For the first category of studies the independent variables are usually the specific traits or behaviors of the "formal leader." The formal leader is assumed to engage in behavior intended to influence those reporting to him or her. Further, the formal leader is assumed to have a legal or jurisdictional right to influence subordinates.

For the second category of studies—those concerned with emergent leaders—the independent variables are usually the traits or behaviors of the individuals to whom social influence is attributed. This attribution is usually measured by group member responses, after some period of interaction, to such questions as "who was the real leader?" or "who exerted most influence in the group?" The dependent variable is usually the degree to which others voluntarily comply with the influence attempts of the emergent leader. Voluntary compliance is taken by the researchers as an indication that the group members perceived the influence attempts of the emergent leader as acceptable.

Note that both formal and emergent leaders are implicitly defined in this literature in terms of two dimensions. These dimensions are: the degree to which behavior is intended to influence others and the degree to which such influence attempts are viewed as acceptable to the person who is the target of the influence attempt.

It is not assumed that group members and subordinates are consciously aware of another's intention to influence them or of the acceptability of such influence attempts at the time that the attempts occur. Rather, it is assumed for purposes of leadership research that members of a group or subordinates of a formal leader are able to report the degree to which they attribute to the leader the intention to influence them and the degree to which they view the leader's influence attempts as acceptable after some period of interaction.

Thus, the construct of leadership is defined as the degree to which the behavior of a group member is perceived as an acceptable attempt to influence the perceiver regarding his or her activity as a member of a particular group or the activity of other group members.[2] To qualify as a leader behavior it is necessary that the behavior is both perceived as an influence attempt and that the perceived influence attempt is viewed as acceptable. An action by a group member becomes an act of leadership when that act is perceived by another member of the group as an acceptable attempt to influence that person or one or more other members of that group. Thus, as Calder (1977) has pointed out, leadership is an attribution that one person makes about other persons.

It is argued here that leadership is an attribution made about the intentions of others to influence members of a group and about the degree to which that influence attempt is acceptable. The term leadership will be used throughout the remainder of this paper to refer to the construct of leadership as defined above, that is as an attribution.

In the literature to be reviewed in the remainder of this paper leadership is not explicitly defined as it is here. However, as argued above, leadership researchers seem to operationalize the construct of leadership in a manner that is implicitly consistent with our definition. Therefore, for the studies we review, we will proceed on the assumption that this implicit definition holds.

JUSTIFICATION FOR DEFINING LEADERSHIP AS A SCIENTIFIC CONSTRUCT

It was asserted above that because of the unique context in which leadership occurs it is necessary to define it as a scientific subset of social influence phenomena. Leadership takes place in groups of two or more people and most frequently involves influencing group member behavior as it relates to the pursuit of group goals. The nature of the goals, the task technology involved in achieving the goals, and the culture or broader organization in which the group exists frequently have a direct effect on the attitudes and behavior of group members. These variables frequently serve to direct, constrain, or reinforce follower attitudes and behavior. Thus they frequently moderate the relationship between leader behavior and follower responses. The moderating effect of these variables is discussed in more detail later in this paper.

Considering leadership as a scientific subset of the social influence phenomena and defining leadership as a separate construct calls attention to the unique characteristics of the environment in which it occurs. Without such attention important antecedents to leadership and moderator variables are likely to be overlooked and thus result in a less complete understanding of the phenomenon that when the construct of leadership is separately defined.

Research Implications of the Proposed Construct of Leadership

The above proposed construct of leadership has significant implications for leadership research.

First, it is possible to measure the degree to which the leadership construct is associated with outcome variables traditionally studied in leadership research. Some of these outcome variables are the subordinate's compliance with influence attempts, motivation, satisfaction, and individual or group productivity. If the proposed construct is shown to be causally implicated with such outcomes, it would be of significant theoretical and practical interest to identify the functional relationship between the attribution of leadership and the specific traits and behaviors of those to whom leadership is attributed. Further, the moderating effects of situational factors and group member characteristics on this relationship would also be of interest. Identification of such associations would permit prediction of the specific person or persons who emerge as leaders within groups. Further, identification of such associations would help explain how formal leaders gain and maintain influence over subordinates.

If specific behaviors or traits of individuals are found to be associated with the leadership construct, and if the construct is shown to be associated with significant group or individual outcomes, these findings would provide information for the design of leadership selection and training efforts.

Finally, it is possible to conduct an empirical test to determine if group members or observers of groups attribute responsibility for group outcomes to those group members whose behaviors are high on the two leadership dimensions. If this indeed is the case, we would have an understanding of how credit or blame for group outcomes is assigned to group members. Such findings have significant implications for predicting performance appraisal ratings, individual advancement in organizations, and assignment of rewards and punishments to group members.

The Effects of Leadership

Pfeffer (1977) states that "literature assessing the effects of leadership seems to be equivocal" (p. 105) and that "given the resources that have been spent studying, selecting and training leaders, one might expect that the question of whether or not leaders matter would have been addressed earlier" (p. 106).

Following is a brief review of some of the literature concerned with the question of whether leadership does or does not cause variance in organizational effectiveness or other relevant outcomes. To establish that leader behavior causes variance in outcomes it is necessary to show that: *(a)* a change in leader behavior precedes a change in the outcome and *(b)* that the relationship between leader behavior and the outcome is not caused by a third variable. While most leadership studies do not meet both of these requirements, there are several studies that do. Following is a brief summary of these studies.

Specific leadership styles, or combinations of leader behaviors, have been demonstrated as causing significant amounts of variance in: *(a)* the effort level of subordinates when not under the direct surveillance of the leader (Lewin, Lippitt, and White, 1939), *(b)* adaptability to change, and performance under conditions of change (Coch and French, 1948; Fleischman, 1965; Day and Hamblin, 1964; Schachter et al., 1961; DeCharms and Bridgeman, 1961), *(c)* levels of follower's turnover (Dansereau, Graen, and Haga, 1975; Graen and Ginsburgh, 1977; Coch and French, 1948), *(d)* absences (Coch and French, 1948), *(e)* subordinate productivity (Lawrence and Smith, 1955; Tomekovic, 1962; Delbecq, 1965; Shaw and Blum, 1966; Campion, 1968; Cammalleri et al., (1972); Wexley, Singh, and Yukl, 1973; Calvin, Hoffmann, and Hardin, 1957), *(f)* degree of subordinates learning from supervisory training efforts (Fleischman, Harris, and Burtt, 1955), *(g)* the quality of subordinates' decisions and the degree to which subordinates accept these decisions (Maier, 1963, 1970), and *(h)* subordinates' motivation (Graen et al., 1973a).

Most of the above evidence comes from field longitudinal studies at lower levels in the organizations or from laboratory studies. While these studies demonstrate that changes in leader behavior preceded changes in relevant outcomes and controlled for extraneous variables either statistically or by the use of control groups, very few of them were conducted at middle or higher levels in the organization. Notable exceptions to this statement are the findings of Meyer (1975) and Lieberson and O'Connor (1972).

Meyer found that organizational structures change as a result of selection of new leaders for middle management positions in a government bureaucratic organization. To identify the impact of changes in leadership on organizational structure Meyer measured the number of organizational structural changes made in government finance offices from 1966 to 1972. He found significantly more organizational changes occurred during that period after new leaders were selected as compared to the number of changes in offices in which there were no changes in leadership. Lieberson and O'Connor (1972) found that 31 percent of the variance in net profit on sales over 20 years for 167 large companies in thirteen industries is directly attributable to changes in top leadership in these companies. However, this finding held only when measured 2 and 3 years after the appointment of new chief executives. Thus, leadership alone accounted for approximately one-third of the variance in profit on sales in the sample studied. While other factors were also shown to contribute to measures of economic performance, such an effect of leadership is indeed profound and can hardly be dismissed as insignificant.

The studies reviewed in this section, when viewed collectively, demonstrate unequivocally that leadership can potentially influence significant variables related to organizational effectiveness and individual member satisfaction. However, there have also been longitudinal and experimental studies that show that leader behavior has little or no effect on subordinates' performance (Lowin, Hrapchek, and Kavanagh, 1969), or satisfaction (French, Israel, and As, 1960). Further, there are several studies that show that leader behavior is *caused by* the performance of subordinates (Herold, 1977; Lowin and Craig, 1968; Farris and Lim, 1969; Greene, 1976).

The above findings suggest that leadership has an effect under some conditions and not under others and also that the causal relationships between leader behavior and commonly accepted criteria of organizational performance is two-way.

Thus, the current prevailing paradigm in leadership research is a contingency paradigm. That is, it is now commonly accepted that the most fruitful approach to the study of leadership is a "situational" or contingency approach. According to this view it is necessary to specify the conditions or situational parameters that moderate the relationship between leader behavior and criteria. Further, it has also been found that the traits associated with leadership have differential impact on the behavior and effectiveness of leaders, depending on various aspects of the situation. We now turn to a consideration of these leader traits.

Trait Theory Revisited

Early leadership research is primarily concerned with the identification of traits that discriminate between leaders and nonleaders, effective leaders and noneffective leaders, or leaders at high echelons in organizations as opposed to those at lower echelons. A trait is defined as any distinctive physical or psychological characteristic of the individual to which the individual's behavior can be attributed. Traits are thus inferred from observation of an individual's behavior or from self-reported data provided by the individual in interviews or pencil and paper questionnaires or psychological tests.

Stogdill (1948, 1974) reviewed 70 years of trait research. The review covers approximately 280 published and unpublished studies and review articles. Certain traits have been consistently found to correlate positively with leadership. From his review Stogdill concludes that there is a cluster of personality traits that differentiate *(a)* leaders from followers, *(b)* effective from ineffective leaders, and *(c)* higher-echelon from lower-echelon leaders.

While none of the traits reviewed by Stogdill were found in all studies to be associated with leadership, the consistency with which some traits were found to be associated with leadership and the magnitudes of these associations is impressive. For example, the traits which show the most consistently high correlations with leadership are:

1. Intelligence.
2. Dominance.
3. Self-confidence.
4. Energy, activity.
5. Task-relevant knowledge.

The correlations between leadership and these traits have generally been in the range of .25 to .35. Frequently, the correlations have been much higher. For example, self-confidence, intelligence, and task-relevant knowledge often have correlations with leadership in the range of .40 to .50.

Consider Table 1. The number of times the traits listed in this table were found to be significantly positively associated with leadership prior to 1948 was 346. The number of times their associations were found to be either nonsignificant or negative was 57. Clearly, viewed collectively, these findings are impressive. Stogdill reports a review of 163 trait studies between 1948 and 1974. The number of times these studies revealed positive associations between the traits and leadership are shown in the third column of Table 1. Several abstractors were involved in recording the results of studies between 1948 and 1970. Stogdill states that ". . . it cannot be safely assumed that all negative findings were recorded on the abstracts. For this reason, only positive findings are reported . . ." (p. 73). Since only the positive findings are reported, it is not possible to determine the total number of studies in which a given trait is measured. Consequently, while Stogdill's later survey is suggestive, the reader cannot determine the relative number of positive versus negative findings with respect to a particular trait. For example, twenty-four studies showed that an individual's activity or energy level was related to either a measure of leader effectiveness or to discriminate leaders from followers. However, since the total number of studies concerned with this trait is not reported, one cannot judge the importance of this statistic.

Several of these findings reviewed by Stogdill (1948, 1974) are given further support from studies of emergent leaders. The traits of intelligence

Table 1.   Characteristics of Leaders (Number of Findings)

	1948		1970
	Positive	Zero or Neg.	Positive Only
	1	2	3
Physical Characteristics			
Activity, energy	5		24
Age	10	8	6
Appearance, grooming	13	3	4
Height	9	4	
Weight	7	4	
Social Background			
Education	22	5	14
Social status	15	2	19
Mobility	5		6
Intelligence and Ability			
Intelligence	23	10	25

(Mann, 1959; Bass and Wurster, 1953a, 1953b; Rychlak, 1963); dominance (Dyson, Fleitas, and Scioli, 1972; Mann, 1959; Megargee, Bogart, and Anderson, 1966; Rychlak, 1963), self-esteem (Bass, 1961), task ability (Bass, 1961; Marak, 1964; Palmer, 1962), sociability (Kaess, Witryol, and Nolan, 1961) have all been found to be associated with emergent leadership.

Note that it is only for the traits of age, appearance, height, weight, education, intelligence, ascendance or dominance, and emotional balance that there are sufficient negative or nonsignificant findings to consider disregarding these traits as predictors of leadership.

Yet, several of these latter traits that were nonsignificantly or negatively related to leadership have more recently been found to be associated with leadership under certain well-defined conditions. For example, physical prowess is found to be correlated with leadership under conditions requiring physical abilities such as in boys gangs and groups. Stogdill (1974) reports correlations of .38, .62, and .40 between athletic ability and leadership in three studies of boys' groups.

IQ was reported by Stogdill (1948) to have an insignificant or negative relationship to leadership in 10 of 33 studies. However, five studies show that leaders whose IQ is higher than that of subordinates have a significant advantage, but that extreme discrepancies between the IQ of leaders and followers mitigate against the exercise of leadership. Korman (1968) found intelligence differentiates effective first-line supervisors from ineffective ones, but that at high levels in the hierarchy there are not significant differences in intelligence between effective and ineffective managers. He attributes this inability of intelligence to differentiate among these managers to a restriction in the range of intelligence scores at high levels. Thus consideration of the discrepancy in intelligence between leader and follower and of range restriction helps to reconcile the conflicting findings with respect to this trait.

Leader dominance, a trait that had positive, negative, and nonsignificant associations to leadership in the studies reviewed by Stogdill has been found in the emergent leadership literature (Rohde, 1951) and in experimental studies (Berkowitz and Haythorn, Note 1; Borgatta, 1961) to be rather consistently predictive of leadership. The mixed findings concerning dominance as a trait associated with leadership can be explained by consideration of the measures used and the leadership situations. Several of the findings reviewed by Stogdill are based on measures of the degree to which the leaders were observed as being bossy or domineering. However, when dominance is defined as the leader's predisposition to be ascendant or assertive, as measured by the Dominance scale of the California Personality Inventory, and when the situation calls for one person to assume the role of leadership, this trait is highly predictive of individuals who exhibit behavior that is perceived by other members of the group to be acceptable attempts to influence their behavior. Megargee, Bogart, and Anderson (1966) asked pairs of high- and low-dominance subjects to work together on a manual task requiring one person to verbally communicate instructions to the other. When leadership was emphasized in the experimental instructions to the subjects, the dominant subjects assumed the leadership role in 14 of 16 pairs. When the task was emphasized and leadership was deemphasized, there was no association between dominance and the assumption of the leadership role. Subsequent studies by Megargee (1969) showed that when subjects are paired with members of their own sex, high-dominance subjects are significantly more likely to assume the leadership role. When women who are high in dominance are paired with men who are low in dominance, the women are found to make the decisions as to who should assume the leadership role. However, these women who asserted leadership in the decision-making phase of the experiment requested the male partner to assume the leadership role in the communications of instructions to complete the tasks. It was inferred from these findings that the women preferred the follower role in the instruction phase because of the cultural norm that women should be more submissive than men. Whether such findings would hold today among women with more "liberated" attitudes is yet to be established. However, the findings do suggest that cultural norms are capable of moderating the effects of personality variables on behavior.

Thus, the mixed feelings concerning leadership traits reported by Stogdill (1948, 1974) can be reconciled by consideration of the populations studied, the measures used, or the results of more recent research. This interpretation lead us to conclude that the study of leadership traits should not be abandoned. Not only are the mixed findings reconcilable, but the magnitude of the correlations between leader traits and criteria of leadership are as high and often higher than correlations between leader behavior and leadership criteria. While we agree that traits or personality variables alone account for a small amount of behavioral variance, and that the interaction of personality variables and situational variables is a more promising approach to leadership, we speculate that there are certain properties of *all* leadership situations that are present to a significant degree and relatively invariant, and that there are likely to be somewhat specific traits required in most if not all leadership situations. Following are some speculations about these possible invariant characteristics of the leadership situation.

First, leadership always takes place with respect to others. Therefore, social skills are likely always to be needed if attempted influence acts are to be viewed as acceptable by followers. Such skills as speech fluency and such traits as personal integrity, cooperativeness, and sociability are thus prime candidates for the status of leadership traits.

Second, leadership requires a predisposition to be influential. Therefore, such traits as dominance or ascendance, need for influence (Uleman, 1972), and need for power (McClelland, 1961) are also hypothesized to be associated with leadership.

Third, leadership most frequently takes place with respect to specific task objectives or organizational goals. Consequently, such traits as need for achievement, initiative, tendency to assume personal responsibility for outcomes, desire to excel, energy, and task-relevant ability are also hypothesized to be associated with leadership.

Conclusions: New Directions for Trait Research

The above brief review of leadership trait literature suggests several promising avenues for trait research.

First, it would be worthwhile to classify the studies Stogdill reported in his two reviews (1948, 1974) according to the following topics: *(a)* populations studied: sex, approximate age, other reported demographic variables; *(b)* type of tasks performed: routine vs. nonroutine, intellectual, mechanical, discussion, manual labor, athletic, etc.; *(c)* method used to measure traits: test and questionnaire responses, observation of behavior, analysis of biographical and case studies; *(d)* criterion variables: leaders vs. nonleaders, high- vs. low-echelon leaders, effective vs. ineffective leaders.

While such an endeavor would be very time-consuming and is beyond the scope of the present paper, we believe the payoff for such a secondary analysis would be very high. Based on such a classification one could analyze the findings and likely find some of the following: *(a)* those traits correlated with leadership regardless of how they are measured, *(b)* those traits correlated with leadership for only subjects of a given type of population classification or with certain demographic characteristics, *(c)* those traits correlated with leadership for only a given type task, *(d)* those traits correlated with leadership when leadership is measured by only a given kind of criterion.

To illustrate the potential payoff of such a secondary analysis, consider the differences in findings resulting from studies of children as compared to adults. Almost all of the negative or conflicting findings reported by Stogdill (1948) are based on studies of children. Thus, there is very little discrepency with respect to studies of adult leaders.

A second promising avenue for leadership trait research concerns the development of standardized scales designed *specifically* to identify and predict leadership on the basis of traits. This would require factor and item analysis of a large number of items administered to a large population. Studies by Ghiselli (1971) and Goodstein and Schrader (1963) support this suggestion. Ghiselli (1971) administered a number of personality scales to 336 middle managers performing a variety of jobs in nineteen different firms. Ratings for each manager's performance were provided by one other person, generally the manager's superior, who knew him and his work record well. Managerial responses to the personality inventory were compared with responses from 111 first-level supervisors and 238 nonsupervisory employees. Ghiselli found that the traits of intelligence, supervisory ability, initiative, self-assurance, and individuality were significantly related to the manager's organizational level and ratings of their performance. These traits differentiated between middle managers on the one hand, and first-level supervisors and nonsupervisory employees on the other. Secondly, successful managers possessed the traits to a greater degree than did less successful managers. Finally, the relationship between the trait and success was higher for managers than it was for supervisors and employees. The correlation between managerial success and the traits of supervisory ability and intelligence were .42 and .27, respectively. The correlations between initiative, self-assurance, and individuality were in the .20 range. While Ghiselli did not compute a multiple correlation of the traits and supervisory success, these correlations suggest that such a multiple correlation coefficient would be in the magnitude of .5 to .6. Clearly, if this is indeed the case, such a correlation is higher than most behavioral predictors of leadership criteria. In fact, the correlation between supervisory ability and managerial success ($r = .46$) is as high as one generally finds between behavioral variables and leadership criteria.

A study by Goodstein and Schrader (1963) is also revealing. Chi-square comparisons of the responses of 603 managers and supervisors with those of 1748 "men-in-general" indicated that 206 of the 480 California Psychological Inventory (CPI) items reliably differentiated the two groups ($p < .01$). Protocols of the respondents were then scored using the twenty items as a managerial key. This key not only reliably differentiated the total managerial group from the "men-in-general" group, but also differentiated personnel at three different levels of management: top management, middle management, and first-line supervision (all p's < .01). This scale also significantly correlated ($r = .23$) with ratings of success within the total management group and within the top and middle management subgroups (r's = .25 and .27, respectively).

These studies by Ghiselli (1971) and Goodstein and Schrader (1963) show significant promise and suggest that leadership traits might account for a significant proportion of unique variance in leadership.

Third, it would be useful to identify the unique interactions, or combinations of traits, that are most predictive of leadership. For example, it is very likely that dimensions of leader competence (such as intelligence, speech fluency, knowledge of task) interact with measures for one's tendency to attempt leadership behavior such as dominance or need for influence. One would expect measures of a person's tendency to attempt leadership behaviors to be positively correlated with leadership when the person is competent, but that such correlations would be nonsignificant or even negative when the person is not competent.

Fourth, upon identification of a standard set of leadership traits, one could begin to determine the behaviors correlated with the scales. Stogdill's findings indicate that several of the scales used in prior research are positively correlated with the criteria of leadership. However, little is known about the behavioral correlates of these traits. A knowledge of such correlates is necessary if we are ultimately to go beyond statistical associations between traits and leadership and to understand the processes involved.

LEADERSHIP BEHAVIOR

Having reviewed the evidence and advanced some research directions relevant to leadership trait research, we now turn to a consideration of leadership behaviors. By leadership behaviors we mean those behaviors of the group member or of the formally appointed leader that are perceived by subordinates as acceptable attempts to influence their behavior. Here we review in some detail prior experimental findings concerned with task-oriented and socioemotional-oriented leadership and field study findings associated with leader Initiating Structure and Consideration. In addition, both the experimental and field study research concerned with participative decision making is reviewed. The research relevant to these leader behaviors are reviewed in some depth because they have been most frequently found to be the major kinds of behaviors in which leaders engage (Yukl, 1971).

Of interest are the following questions:

1. Is there a well-defined set of behaviors that falls within the above definition of leadership behaviors?

2. What are the effects of such behaviors on others? What are the effects of such behaviors on group performance and organizational effectiveness?

3. Under what conditions do such behaviors constitute a contribution to individual or group performance and individual well-being?

To answer the above questions and suggest further research directions, we will review three independent bodies of literature. The first, concerned with role differentiation of group member behavior, comes primarily from the sociological literature. The second, concerned with subordinates' perceptions of formally appointed leaders, comes primarily from industrial psychology. The third, concerned with emergent leadership, comes primarily from social psychology. As will be shown, the findings resulting from these independent literatures are complementary and in many cases mutually reinforcing.

Role Differentiation in Groups

This section reviews early research concerned with the emergence of leadership roles under conditions where the group has no formally appointed leader. This research was primarily concerned with the following questions:

1. What are the important problems that a group must solve to be effective, cohesive, and to have satisfied members.

2. What are the behaviors of group members who are most likely to be attributed leadership status by others?

3. To what extent are those behaviors that are required to solve group problems divided into specialized roles, or kinds of behaviors, such that different members perform different roles?

4. Under what conditions can these different roles be performed by one member and when will they be divided among two or more members?

5. Will groups be more effective when their roles are divided or integrated?

Leader Role Differentiation

Early research by Bales and his associates (Borgatta, Bales, and Couch, 1954; Bales and Slater, 1955; Bales, 1958) clearly demonstrated that there are generally two functions to be accomplished by the small experimental discussion groups they observed: *(a)* the achievement of some specific group task, and *(b)* the maintenance or strengthening of the social relations group itself. Thus, it was suggested that leadership in a group can be described in terms of an individual's contributions to the accomplishment of these functions.

Group members' behaviors, while primarily addressed to group achievement or group maintenance functions, tend to be factor analytically divided among three distinct dimensions. These dimensions were identified from a number of studies in which members of small groups were asked to rate or choose each other on a wide variety of descriptive criteria, or in which members were assessed by observers.

Carter (1954) reviewed a series of these factor-analytic studies and described the most frequently occurring three factors as follows:

Factor 1: Individual Prominence and Achievement: Behaviors of the individual related to his or her efforts to stand out from others and individually achieve various personal goals.

Factor 2: Aiding Attainment by the Group: Behaviors of the individual intended to assist the group in achieving its goals.

Factor 3: Sociability: Behaviors of the individual related to his or her efforts to establish and maintain cordial and socially satisfying relations with other group members.

Bales (1958) refers to the three factors as "activity," "task ability," and "likeability." He concludes that ratings on these dimensions should be treated as three distinct factors, since over a large population of members, meetings, and groups, they tend to be uncorrelated with each other. Further, he concludes that a member who is high on all three of the factors corresponds to the traditional conception of a good leader, or the "great man." Bales refers to individuals who are high on activity and task-ability ratings but less high on likeability ratings as the "task specialist." Task specialists contribute primarily to leadership of the task function of the group. A member who is high in likeability but less high in activity and task-ability is referred to as the "social specialist." Social specialists contribute to leadership of the group maintenance function.

Thus, it can be concluded from the above studies that the behavior of group members can be measured along three independent dimensions. Two of these dimensions, activity and task ability, combine to influence task achievement while likeability or sociability contribute to group maintenance.

An early study by Carter, Haythorn, Shriver, and Lanzetta (1951) sheds light on the conditions under which individual prominence behavior is required. Carter et al. observed behavior of group members as they performed three different kinds of tasks: a reasoning task, a mechanical assembly task, and a discussion task. For approximately half of the groups a leader was appointed by the experimenter. For the other half no leader was appointed but individuals receiving the highest leadership ratings from group observers were considered "emergent leaders." Comparisons between the emergent leaders and appointed leaders showed that the emergent leader engages more frequently in the following behaviors: "supports or gives information regarding his proposal," "defends himself (or own proposal) from attack," "provides expression of opinion," and "argues with others." Appointed leaders were significantly lower on the above behaviors. While the appointed leaders engaged in significantly less such behavior, they were equally as effective as the emergent leaders.

These findings suggest that under conditions where there is no institutional factor that legitimatizes leader behavior such as formal appointment or title, an individual will have to engage in what Carter et al. (1951) describe as individual prominence and achievement behaviors and what Bales refers to as "activity." However, when leadership is legitimatized through the appointment process, such behavior is not as likely to occur. Thus, in terms of the leadership construct advanced in this paper, it appears that a necessary but not sufficient condition for the attribution of leadership is that the individual distinguish himself or herself from the group by engaging in behaviors intended to establish individual prominence. However, under conditions of appointed leadership, such behaviors are not required and may even be dysfunctional.

Surprisingly, this interpretation has not been tested in field research where appointed leaders have been studied. However, a study by Wofford (1970) is relevant to this interpretation. Wofford factor analyzed responses to a questionnaire consisting of 219 items. Respondents were asked to describe their immediate supervisor's behavior. The analysis yielded four factors: two concerned with task orientation, one concerned with group maintenance, and one concerned with personal enhancement. All factors except the personal-enhancement factors correlated positively with indices of morale and perceived organizational effectiveness.

The personal-enhancement factor correlated negatively $-.51$ and $-.32$ with perceived effectiveness and morale, respectively, thus suggesting support for the hypothesis that personal prominence seeking behavior of appointed leaders is likely to be negatively associated with the attribution of leadership as defined in this paper. This hypothesis is suggested for future field study research.

Are both task-oriented and socioemotional leadership always required for effective group performance? If not, when are they required and when are they not?

The answer to the above questions was found to depend upon whether the group is committed to the task or finds the task to be intrinsically satisfying (Gustafson, 1968; Gustafson and Harrell, 1970; Burke, 1967). Under conditions where the tasks are intrinsically satisfying to group members or members are committed to task accomplishment, task-oriented leadership is viewed as instrumental to group success, but there is less need for socioemotional leadership. Verba (1961) has argued that where tasks are not interesting or are not important to members such leadership is necessary to provide some form of social satisfaction. Task-oriented leadership under such conditions is likely to be resented. Therefore, socioemotionally oriented leadership is required to offset this resentment. A study by Bales (1958) is especially relevant to this issue. Task-oriented leaders tended to be disliked. This finding held most strongly among groups that were not cohesive. However, for the task-oriented leader who made it possible for members to give feedback, raise objections, qualifications, questions, and counter questions, there was no relationship between task orientation and liking. For those task-oriented leaders who did not permit such feedback, the relationship between task orientation and liking was negative.

The question of whether these two roles can be performed by one member or whether they must be divided by two or more members is also of importance. Borg (1957) found that in some groups the roles were integrated and performed by a single member while in other groups the roles were divided. Teams with two leaders made significantly lower effectiveness scores than teams with one leader. When the two leaders were mutually supportive, their groups performed more effectively than when the leaders were in competition with each other, but still not as effectively as groups with leaders who integrated both roles. Thus, it appears that groups with leaders who integrate the two roles will have what Bales and Slater (1955) refer to as "great men" as leaders. They found that when members of a group designated particular individuals as "leader," ". . . the individual is perhaps found to possess those qualities that best serve to solve both the task and social-emotional problems of the group" (p. 291.). ". . . Leadership . . . [is] attributed to that member . . . who best symbolizes the weighted combination and integration of the two more specialized functions [of task orientation and group maintenance]" (p. 298). Further support for this interpretation was found by Borgatta, Couch, and Bales (1954). These authors selected eleven "great men" out of 126 who scored high on three factors: task ability (leadership ratings received on a prior task and IQ score), individual assertiveness (activity rate received on a prior task), and social acceptability (sociometric choice on a prior task). These "great men" were each assigned to four tasks. Two new coparticipants participated in each of the four tasks. Groups led by "great men" were compared with groups led by men who were not high on all three of the above dimensions. Groups led by "great men" had higher rates of giving suggestions and agreements, lower tension, higher positive social and emotional behavior. The authors concluded ". . . thus, it may be said that great men tend to make 'great groups' in the sense that both major factors of group performance—productivity and satisfaction of the members—are increased" (p. 759). There is also evidence that when formally appointed group leaders fail to perform task-oriented behaviors, an informal leader will emerge and perform the task-oriented behaviors required for group success (Crockett, 1955; Berkowitz, 1953).

From the above findings the following empirical generalizations can be drawn:

1. Task-oriented leadership is necessary for effective performance in all working groups.

2. Acceptance of task-oriented leadership requires that the task-oriented leader allows others to respond by giving feedback, making objections, and questioning the task-oriented leader.

3. Socioemotionally oriented leadership is required in addition to task-oriented leadership when groups are not engaged in satisfying or ego-involving tasks.

4. Groups requiring both kinds of leadership behavior will be more effective when these leader behaviors are performed by one person rather than divided among two or more persons.

5. When the leadership roles are differentiated, groups will be most effective if those assuming the roles are mutually supportive and least effective when they are in conflict with each other.

6. When formally appointed leaders fail to perform the leader behaviors required for group success, an informal leader will emerge and will perform the necessary leader behaviors, provided success is desired by the group members.

These findings from the sociological literature concerned with leadership in small groups help us understand some of the conflicting findings resulting from field research. We now turn to a review of these studies.

FIELD STUDIES OF LEADER ROLE DIFFERENTIATION: CONSIDERATION AND INITIATING STRUCTURE

Studies conducted by the Leadership Group at Ohio State University suggest two dimensions of leader behavior that can be interpreted as task-oriented leadership and socioemotionally oriented leadership. These are leader Initiation of Structure and leader Consideration. Leader Initiation of Structure has been measured by three different scales. These scales are intended to measure the degree to which the leader clarifies and defines his or her own role and lets followers know what is expected of them. The Consideration scale is designed to measure the degree to which the leader pays regard to the comfort, well-being, status, and satisfaction of the followers.

These scales have been widely used for purposes of leadership research. Over fifty studies have been reported that assess the relationship between the leader's score on these two scales and subordinates' satisfaction, expectations, performance, turnover, and grievances. The findings resulting from this research are very mixed. All of the scales have been shown to be positively, negatively, or nonsignificantly related to such dependent variables. Much of the confusion with respect to correlates of the initiating structure construct has been traced to the particular scales used to measure this dimension. Initiating structure has most often been measured by one of the following instruments:

1. The Supervisory Behavior Description Questionnaire (SBDQ, Fleishman, Note 1), consisting of twenty items that inquire of subordinates about their leader's actual structuring behavior. Structure as measured by the SBDQ is intended to reflect the extent to which the leader organizes and defines relationships between himself and his group, defines interactions among group members, establishes ways to get the job done, schedules, criticizes, etc. (Fleishman, Note 2, p. 1).

2. The early Leader Behavior Description Questionnaire (LSDQ, Halpin, Note 3), containing fifteen items that ask subordinates to describe the actual structuring behavior of their leader. As measured by this instrument, Structure refers to the leader's behavior in delineating relationships between himself or herself and group members and in trying to establish well-defined patterns of communications and ways to get the job done (p. 1).

3. The revised LBDQ (Stogdill, Note 4), with ten items measuring Structure. As measured by this instrument, Structure is concerned with the actions of the leader in clearly defining his or her own role and letting followers know what is expected (p. 3).

As pointed out by Schriesheim, House, and Kerr (1976), the items comprising the three scales differ in content. The LBDQ forms consist largely of items describing a leader who actively communicates with subordinates, facilitates information exchange, and designs and structures his own work, the work of group members, and relationships among group members in their performance of work. In contrast, the SBDQ consists mainly of items describing a highly production-oriented leader who is autocratic and punitive.

Schriesheim, House, and Kerr (1976) reviewed the studies concerned with Initiating Structure and considered the results obtained from each version of this scale separately. Notice was also taken of the task and environment context in which respondents worked. As a result, apparent discrepancies and findings were reduced and three empirical generalizations were derived.

The findings from the small group research reviewed above helps to explain these empirical generalizations. Schriesheim et al. (1976) concluded that, when measured by the SBDQ, leader Initiating Structure is generally positively related to performance ratings by superiors of manufacturing first-level supervisors and to ratings of the work group performance. However, it is negatively related to satisfaction of the supervisors' subordinates. This generalization also held with regard to non-commissioned infantry officers and air force officers. A similar, although much weaker, pattern ofrelationships was found concerning non-manufacturing supervisors of clerical workers doing routine tasks.

Since the SBDQ scale reflects task-oriented leadership, it is not surprising that leaders high on this scale obtain higher performance ratings by superiors. However, since the items on the scale suggest that leaders who are high on it are arbitrary and punitive, it is reasonable to assume such leaders do not permit subordinates opportunities to react to the leader's Initiation of Structure. Recall that Bales (1958) found that individuals who are task oriented but do not permit others to react to them tend to be disliked by others. Thus, in the light of the above findings by Bales, it is not surprising that such leaders cause subordinates to be dissatisfied.

The differential strength of this pattern of relationships between manufacturing employees and clerical employees is also consistent with the findings from small-group research. Recall that socioemotional leadership was required to offset the negative effects of task-oriented leadership in the small group experiments when subordinates found the task intrinsically dissatisfying. Since it is likely that persons engaged in manufacturing tasks find less satisfaction with these tasks, there will be more resentment of leader Initiating Structure than among persons engaged in clerical tasks, which are likely not as dissatisfying.

Schriesheim et al. (1976) also concluded that when the revised LBDQ

Initiating Structure scale is used to measure leader behavior of first-level supervisors of nonmanufacturing employees performing routine tasks, correlations with subordinate satisfaction are positive although generally so low as to be, at best, only marginally significant. The revised LBDQ Initiating Structure scale does not include the autocratic and punitive items of the SBDQ. Thus, it is less likely that supervisors high on this scale will prevent subordinates from reacting to task-oriented behaviors. Recall that for task-oriented leaders who permit such reactions there was no relationship between task orientation and liking. Thus, the consistently low correlations between Initiating Structure and Satisfaction, as measured by the revised scale, are consistent with the above findings from small group research.

Finally, Schriesheim et al. (1976) found that high occupational level employees consistently react more favorably to leader Initiating Structure regardless of the instrument used. This generalization is consistent with the finding that task-oriented leadership is viewed as acceptable when the task is satisfying to subordinates.

Thus, the findings from the field studies using the Initiating Structure scales are consistent with those of small group research concerned with task-oriented leadership.

The mixed findings with respect to correlates of leader Consideration are also readily interpretable in the light of the small group research findings. House (1971) hypothesized that leader Consideration will have its most positive effect on satisfaction of subordinates who work on stressful, frustrating, or dissatisfying tasks. This hypothesis has been tested in ten samples of employees (House, 1971; House and Dessler, 1974; Szilagyi and Sims, 1974; Stinson and Johnson, 1974; Schuler, 1973; Downey et al., 1975; Weed, Mitchell, and Smyzer, Note 5). In only one of these studies was the hypothesis disconfirmed (Szilagyi and Sims, 1974). In addition, there are experimental studies that show that the effects of considerate leadership on performance are most positive when subordinates have previously been denied some source of satisfaction. For example, in experiments by Day and Hamblin (1964) and DeCharms and Bridgeman (1961) in which leader supportiveness resulted in increased productivity, subjects were first exposed to threatening, irritating, or frustrating treatment, and then to considerate and helpful treatment. In both studies subjects responded favorably to the considerate leader behavior.

These findings are consistent with the results of small group research, which demonstrated the need for socioemotional leadership under conditions where subordinates are neither committed to the task nor find it to be intrinsically satisfying.

Further, while leader Consideration is almost always positively associated with subordinates' satisfaction on dissatisfying tasks, it is not always associated with subordinate performance. Recall that small group research demonstrated that task-oriented leadership is required in small groups. It can be speculated that the failure of leader Consideration to be associated with subordinates' performance under conditions of dissatisfying tasks may be due to the absence of concurrent leader task-oriented behavior. This speculation, if found supported in future research, would serve to reconcile the conflicting findings with respect to performance correlates of leader Consideration.

Participative Leader Behavior

Participative leadership has been the source of significant concern and controversy. Participative leadership takes two forms: participative decision making (PDM) and participative supervision (PS).

PDM refers to efforts by leaders to ensure that all parties for whom a decision is relevant have an opportunity to influence the final decision. A decision is considered relevant to an individual if the individual is ego involved in the outcome of the decision, if the individual possesses significant information that pertains to the decision, or if the individual must be relied on to implement the decision once it has been made. Whereas PDM concerns specific decisions, PS concerns the manner of interaction between superior and subordinate or leader and follower on a continuing, day-to-day basis. When PS is practiced, the leader encourages subordinates to make suggestions concerning what work should be done and how it should be carried out. Further the leader encourages subordinates to engage in independent thinking and action with respect to such factors as problem analysis, selection of means, and planning and scheduling the work process.

While the distinction between PDM and PS is conceptually clear, the studies we review in this section do not distinguish between these two forms of participative leadership. However, it appears that the laboratory studies generally operationalize participative leadership by varying the degrees of PDM as an independent variable. In contrast, field studies generally use questionnaire responses of subordinates. These responses appear to represent the degree to which their formally appointed leader is perceived to engage in both PDM and pS, and PDM and PS are treated as a global measure of participative leadership. As will be seen, the results of both studies are quite consistent, regardless of how participative leadership is operationalized.

Contrary to some conceptions of participative leadership, participative leaders do *not* abdicate the leadership role by becoming a member of the group, *except* insofar as they contribute substantive (as opposed to process) guidance. Maier's research (Maier, 1970) on effective group problem solving serves as the basic paradigm for participative decision making. His work demonstrates that effective participative leaders exert substantial control over the interaction process among subordinates during the decision-making process. The specific behaviors in which effective participative leaders engage are:

- Share information with the participants.
- Prevent dominant personalities from having disproportionate influence.
- Solicit opinions, facts, and feelings from reticent participants.
- Assist participants in communicating with one another.
- Protect deviant opinions from being rejected prior to fair evaluation.
- Minimize blame-oriented statements.
- Redirect unfocused discussion back to the problem at hand.
- Encourage the generation of alternative solutions.
- Delay evaluation of alternatives until all have been presented.
- Guide the process of screening alternatives and selecting the solution.

Maier's work demonstrates that the above skills required to be an effective participative leader are trainable (Maier, 1949, 1963).

Mitchell (1973) recently described at least four ways in which participative leadership style can have an impact upon subordinate attitudes and performance. First, a participative climate should lead to greater clarity of the paths to various goals. Second, it enables subordinates to select goals they value, thus increasing commitment to goal attainment. Third, participants can increase their control over what happens on the job. If subordinate motivation is higher (as a result of points one and two), then having greater autonomy and the ability to carry out their intentions should lead to increased effort and performance. Finally, when people participate in the decision process, the decisions are made in the presence of others. Thus these others know what is expected, causing social pressures to have a greater impact. Thus motivation to perform will stem from internal and social factors as well as from formal external ones.

Maier (1970) has argued that participation should improve decision making, because it is through the participative process that subordinates' knowledge and expertise can be brought to bear. That is, participative decision making is an effective means of obtaining relevant information or expertise from subordinates, and thus of improving the objective quality of decisions. Further, he argues that when decisions require subordinate acceptance for their implementation, participation will increase such acceptance, because subordinates will have an opportunity to influence the decision-making process, and consequently their feelings are more likely to be expressed and respected. Thus, according to these theoretical perspectives, participation is predicted to increase productivity, quality, emotional orientation of subordinates toward their work setting (the job, the decision makers, and the organization), and subordinates' acceptance of decisions.

Filley, House, and Kerr (1976) reviewed thirty-three studies concerned with the effects of participative leadership. Nineteen of twenty laboratory experiments, correlational studies, or field experiments in which satisfaction of subordinates was measured demonstrated a positive relationship between participation and satisfaction. The single study not showing such a relationship had an unclear and uninterpretable result. Seventeen of the twenty-two studies in which productivity of subordinates was measured showed a positive relationship between participation on productivity and seven showed no relationship. In addition, over thirty laboratory studies concerned with the degree with which participative leadership results in effective decisions have been conducted by Maier (1963; 1970) and his associates. Maier defines decision effectiveness as a function of the degree to which *(a)* the decision meets the objective economic and physical requirements of the problem (the quality criterion) and *(b)* the decision is acceptable to subordinates (the acceptance criterion). Maier argues that some problems demand high-quality solutions, some demand high-acceptance solutions, and some both.

Maier and his associates required subjects to role play the part of a person who was in conflict with other group members. In these roles each person possessed critical information about the problem that no other member possessed. For the problem to be solved it was necessary that the information be shared and accurately evaluated. As might be expected under these conditions, participation resulted in higher decision quality and acceptance in *all* of the studies.

Filley, House and Kerr (1976) concluded that when subordinates task demands are clear and routine to the subordinate, participative leadership is not likely to have an effect, because there is little to participate about. These authors segregated the studies on participative leadership for which the task characteristics were controlled. These studies are reported in Table 2. From this table it can be seen that there are rather dramatic differences in the effects of participation, depending largely on the nature of the task performed. Simple tasks with nonambiguous demands do not lend themselves to participative leadership, whereas tasks that are more complex and ambiguous do. House and Mitchell (1974) have hypothesized that on such tasks subordinates are more ego involved in their task and therefore have a desire to influence decisions that affect the work they do and the manner in which they are required to do it. We recommend further tests of this hypothesis in future research.

In addition to being ego involved, subordinates performing such tasks are likely to have been assigned such tasks because of their intelligence

Table 2. Participative Leadership: Studies Controlling for Task Characteristics

Investigators	Type of Study	Type of Task	Performance[a]	Attitude[b]
Argyle, Gardner, and Coiffi (1957)	Field Correlational	Machine paced, paid by piece rate-Males	No relationship	No relationship
		Man paced, salary payment-Males	Positive	Positive
Vroom and Mann (1960)	Field Correlational	Independent-non-cooperative tasks		Negative
		Interdependent-cooperative tasks		Positive
Shaw and Blum (1966)	Lab Experiment	Low structure	Positive	
		Medium structure	Positive	
		High structure	Negative	
Phillipsen (reported in Lammers, 1967)	Field Correlational	Low mechanization	Low positive	Low positive
		High mechanization	Higher positive	Higher positive
Delbecq (1965)	Lab Experiment	Routine	Negative	
		Nonroutine	Positive	

[a] Performance based on objective indices of costs or productivity.
[b] Attitudes measured by questionnaire responses.
Source: Filley, House and Kiot, (1976).

and/or because they have some specialized knowledge relevant to task performances. Thus, it can be hypothesized that subordinates' intelligence or task-relevant knowledge will also moderate the relationship between participative leadership and its effects.

Filley et al. (1976) reviewed the empirical evidence concerned with the moderating effect of subordinate intelligence and knowledge level. Their findings are presented in Table 3. These studies show clearly that when subordinates' knowledge level or intelligence is high, participation has a positive effect. However, where subordinates' intelligence level or knowledge is low, participation generally has an insignificant effect on subordinates' performance and sometimes has a negative effect on their satisfaction.

Viewed collectively, the results of the studies reported in the prior two tables clearly indicate that knowledgeable subordinates or intelligent subordinates working on tasks that impose ambiguous, nonroutine demands perform more effectively under conditions of participative leadership. However, it is not clear whether subordinates performing such tasks respond more positively to participative leadership because they are more ego involved in their work or because they have higher competence (task knowledge and/or intelligence) or both. We recommend further research to clarify this issue.

A number of studies have shown that the effects of participation are also moderated by the predisposition of subordinates to participate or to gain satisfaction from the participative process. Subordinates who have high needs for independence, are nonauthoritarian, and have respect for nonauthoritarian behavior have been hypothesized to be more satisfied and to be more effective under conditions of participative leadership. The evidence supporting this argument is impressive (Delbecq, 1965; Vroom, 1959; Campion, 1968; Tannenbaum and Allport, 1956; Jacobson, 1953).

However, House (Note 6) argued that the moderating influence of subordinate personality upon relationships between participative leadership, satisfaction, motivation, and performance should not be expected to be strong when tasks are ego-involving. House (Note 6) hypothesized that the subordinates' personality will become an important moderator only when the task is not ego-involving. His reasoning is that subordinates performing non-ego-involving tasks who are not predisposed toward participative leadership will not find participation to be either intrinsically satisfying or instrumental to task success, whereas subordinates predisposed toward participation will find the task more satisfying and motivating, due to the opportunities to participate. However, when the task is ego-involving, the subordinates will have a desire to influence decisions *regardless* of whether they are predisposed by personality to participate

Table 3. Studies Testing the Hypothesis That Subject's Intelligence and Level of Knowledge Moderates the Effects of Participation

Investigators	Type of Task	Method	Individual Difference Controlled	Effects Without Controlling for Subject's Characteristics	Effects When Controlling for Subject's Characteristics	Direction of Effect of Controlling for Subject's Characteristics
Calvin, Hoffman, and Hardin (1957)	Complex Decision	Lab Experiment	Subordinate Intelligence		Positive[a]	As Predicted
Mulder and Wilke (1970)	Influence over Other in Complex Problem Solving	Lab Experiment	Leader Knowledge	Not Measured	Positive[b]	As Predicted
Cammalleri et al. (Note 5)	Complex Problem Solving	Lab Experiment	Leader Knowledge	Not Measured	Positive[a]	As Predicted
Kolaja (1965)*	Participative Yugoslav Workers' Council	Field Observation	Desire to Participate and Expertise	Not Measured	Positive	As Predicted
Brockmeyer (1968)*	Participative Yugoslav Workers' Council	Field Observation	Desire to Participate and Expertise	Not Measured	Positive	As Predicted

*Cited in Mulder and Wilke, measurement of effectiveness of participation on workers' committees.
[a] Performance measured in terms of laboratory task completion or accuracy.
[b] Performance measured in terms of amount of attitude change of subjects induced by confederate.
Source: Filley, House and Kerr (1976)

or not. To date, one major investigation (Schuler, 1976) has tested this prediction. Subjects were 354 employees in an industrial manufacturing organization. Personality variables, the amount of participative leadership, task characteristics, and job satisfaction were assessed. As predicted, in nonrepetitive, ego-involving tasks, employees (regardless of their personality) were more satisfied under participative leaders than nonparticipative leaders. In repetitive tasks that were less ego-involving, however, the amount of authoritarianism of subordinates moderated the relationship between leadership style and satisfaction, as hypothesized. Specifically, low authoritarian subordinates were more satisfied under participative leaders than under nonparticipative leaders. This study, together with the theoretical hypothesis advanced by House, appears to explain why findings by Tosi (1970) and Wexley, Singh, and Yukl (1973) did not find a moderating effect of subordinate personality on the relationship between participative leadership and subordinate satisfaction and performance. In both studies the subjects were performing rather routine simple tasks that are not likely to be ego-involving.

Unfortunately, Schuler's study only dealt with subordinate satisfaction as an outcome. Future research directed at replicating Schuler's study and incorporating measures of subordinate motivation and performance is required before the hypothesis can be claimed to be strongly supported.

In summary, research on participation suggests a rather parsimonious set of empirical generalizations that explain and predict the conditions under which participation leads to increased decision effectiveness and increased satisfaction, motivation, and performance of subordinates.

The above research strongly supports the hypothesis that such leadership will be most effective under conditions where tasks are ego-involving, ambiguous, and nonroutine. Further, participative leadership is most effective when subordinates have sufficient competence to contribute to the participative process. Specifically, subordinates' level of intelligence and knowledge about the issue at hand will determine whether the process can result in improved decision making. When task demands are not ego-involving, subordinates' predisposition to participate is hypothesized to moderate the degree to which the participative process will be satisfying to subordinates. On such tasks only for subordinates with a positive disposition toward participation is participation predicted to enhance satisfaction. A similar interaction is hypothesized to occur with respect to subordinate performance, but additional research is needed to test this hypothesis.

In addition to the research on the three dimensions of leader behavior reviewed above (leader initiating structure, consideration, and participation), there is an emerging literature concerned with the degree to which the leader administers rewards and punishment, contingent on subordi-nate performance. This literature will be reviewed in a later section, along with the discussion on Operant Leadership Theory.

DETERMINANTS OF LEADER BEHAVIOR

There are several studies that show that leader behavior is determined by several individual characteristics in interaction with variables in the envi-ronment. Specific measures of individual predispositions to assume the leadership role have been shown to predict emergence of leader behavior, that is, influence attempts that are accepted by group members in leader-less groups. These measures are the Dominance scale of the California Personality Inventory (Megargee et al., 1966); the Need for Influence scale (Uleman, 1972); and the Guilford Zimmerman Ascendance scale (Guetzkow, 1968). In addition, the Leadership scale of the California Personality Inventory developed by Goodstein and Schrader (1963) has been shown to discriminate leaders from others, to correlate positively with level in the organization and not to suffer from range restriction at higher levels.

The essential ingredient that appears to be measured in the Dominance, Ascendance, and Need for Influence scales appears to be the individual's desire or willingness to assert control over others in pursuit of task ac-complishment.

Studies by Megargee et al. (1966), Zdep (1966), and Zdep and Oakes (1967) illustrate how this predisposition on the part of individuals interacts with cues in the environment to predict leader behavior. Megargee et al. (1966) found that the dominance scale of the CPI did not predict the emergence of leader behavior under conditions where the need for leader-ship was deemphasized. However, when the need for leadership was emphasized, fourteen of sixteen high-dominance subjects in pairs of high- and low-dominance subjects assumed the leadership role.

Zdep (1969) found that in an experimental situation high-dominance subjects increased their rate of participation in response to reinforcement administered privately by the experimenter. As participation increased, so did group leadership ratings. Low-dominance subjects exhibited such little participation that Zdep found it impossible to administer the neces-sary reinforcements to increase their rate of participation.

Zdep and Oakes (1967) administered the CPI leadership scale in a re-peated measures design to determine whether the questionnaire has a reactive effect, thereby influencing the behavior of the people who com-plete the questionnaire. While it was not reactive in the usual sense, it appeared to have a differential effect. Only the more ascendant participants increased thier rate of participation after having been exposed to the questionnaire. Thus, the questionnaire likely served as a stimulus to leadership for high-ascendance subjects in the same manner that the experimental instructions by Megargee et al. (1966) served to elicit leader behavior by high-dominance subjects only.

These studies by Megargee et al. (1966), Zdep (1969) and Zdep and Oakes (1967) suggest that a high need for dominance or ascendance in interaction with the environmental cues or reinforcements results in increased acts of leadership.

A study by Guetzkow (1968) shows that individuals who are high on the Guilford Zimmerman Ascendance scale were more likely to assume the leadership role in small group network studies. Individuals who assumed the leadership role in this study established themselves by having more adequate perceptions of the organizational situation than others did and by nominating themselves as leaders. Guetzkow (1968) found that such persons did not force their way into the leadership role even though they were in a position to do so by withholding strategic information from other members of the group.

Smelser (1961) found that when groups composed of pairs in which the dominant subject was assigned a dominant role and a submissive subject a submissive role groups were most productive. The least productive groups were those in which the role assignments were reversed.

Stogdill (1974) describes a study by Rohde (1951) that sheds further light on the behavior of persons high on dominance or ascendance. In five member groups, dominant members were chosen as leaders more often than submissive members and exhibited significantly more controlling behavior. In addition, they agreed and cooperated more often than submissive members.

These studies suggest that individuals with a high need for dominance or ascendance, or individuals who are high on the CPI leadership scale, are not only more likely to take the initiative in seeking a leadership role but are *not* more likely to engage in autocratic or domineering behavior. Rather, these studies suggest that such persons are likely to be helpful to others and to be instrumental in the pursuit of group goals.

Other individual characteristics associated with effective and emergent leadership were reviewed in the earlier section concerning leadership traits. The traits of self-confidence and strength of conviction likely free individuals of inhibitions to assert leadership. In addition, the trait of achievement drive, or desire to excel, likely operates as a motivator to assert leadership in task situations.

In addition to the above characteristics of individuals, it has also been shown that leader behavior is determined by factors in the environment. Crowe, Bochner, and Clark (1972) administered a leadership belief scale to 400 lower- and middle-level managers. Based on their responses, these managers were classified as either autocratic or democratic. The managers then participated in an experimental simulation in which they managed confederate subordinates who behaved either autocratically or democratically. The results showed that subordinates' influence were strong enough to bring about the response from the manager that is opposite to their own preference. Both types of managers behaved democratically with democratic subordinates and autocratically with autocratic subordinates.

There is also evidence that leaders model the behavior of their superiors and adapt to their superiors' expectations. Fleishman, Harris, and Burtt (1955) found that cahnges in supervisory behavior resulting from a training program occurred when the supervisors reported to a leader who engaged in the kind of behavior stressed in the program but did not occur when the supervisor reported to the leader who did not engage in such behavior. Weiss (1977) found that managers who are low in self-esteem described their behavior as similar to behavior of their superiors, whereas managers who are high in self-esteem show no such similarity.

Pfeffer and Salancik (1975) asked supervisors to indicate the performance expectations that their superiors and subordinates held for them. Subsequently, the same supervisors completed a questionnaire indicating how they allocated their time. The findings indicated that whether the supervisor attends more to the expectations of his superior or to those of his subordinate is a function of the following factors: *(a)* the demands to produce coming from the superior, *(b)* percent of time the superior actually engages in supervision rather than in routine tasks, *(c)* the number of persons supervised, *(d)* whether the sex of the supervisor is the same as that of the superior, and *(e)* whether task decisions are made primarily by the supervisor. Pfeffer and Salancik (1975) interpret these findings in terms of role theory. They argue that:

> organizations are composed of interdependent positions and interlocking behaviors. Occupants of these positions are exposed to expectations and social pressures of other organizational members with whom they are interdependent. With experience, the expectations and demands become known, resulting in a collective structure of behavior, and stabilize to predictable patterns. In any given position, the occupant's behavior is influenced and constrained by the social pressures immediately from other persons in the role set (p. 141).

Salancik and Pfeffer (1977) also analyzed the variance in budgets for thirty U.S. cities over a 17-year period to determine how much of that variance is attributable to the budget year, the characteristics of the city, or the behavior of the mayor. The amount of variance explained by the city, year, and mayor was 59.1 percent, 2.5 percent, and 19.5 percent, respectively. The mayor, while having little discretion, was found to have the greatest effect over expenditures that were not as involved with political interests and had most discretion over capital outlays, which were one-time allocation decisions. Thus these findings indicate that the impact of the leader (mayor) is significantly constrained by cultural and historical factors associated with the particular organizational (city) setting. While this study did not include measure of variance in the behavior of the mayors, it is likely that such variance is also significantly determined by these same situational factors.

Salancik, Calder, Rowland, Leblebici, and Conway (1975) provide further evidence to support this position. They found that the amount of influence of power or political leadership of peers in an organization derives from their positions in the social structure. The perceived influence or leadership of members was found to be a linear combination of their position on measurements specifically derived to reflect the social structure of the organizations. In one organization the major dimension of social structure was the professional status and activity of the people involved. In the other organization the major dimensions of social structure consisted of job prestige, job variety, and social similarity to the top managers of the organization. It was also found that the effective leader is one who is responsive to the demands and social system with whom he or she must interact and coordinate his or her behavior. Specifically, the supervisor's coordination with other supervisors was negatively related to a tendency to behave as the subordinate desires ($r = .91$). This study clearly indicates support for the position of Pfeffer and Salancik (1975) that a major determinant of leader behavior is the pattern of expectation and social pressures of other organizational members with whom leaders are interdependent.

Another situational factor that has been found to determine leadership is the amount of stress and ambiguity experienced by the leader and the group. Korten (1968) has argued that:

> The greater the stress and the less the clarity and general agreement on goals and paths, the greater the compulsion among the group members to give power to a central person who in essence promises to remove the ambiguity and reduce the stress (p. 357).

There are several findings that support Korten's position. For example, a leader Initiating Structure scale that included several items describing autocratic behavior of leaders (Hemphill, Note 7) has been found to be positively related to procedural clarity, but not related to performance or satisfaction of subordinates (Halpin, 1954, 1957; Halpin and Winer, 1957), performance ratings of the leader by superiors (Halpin, 1957), or team cohesiveness (Halpin, 1954, 1957; Rush, 1957) under noncombat conditions. In contrast, under combat conditions this scale was found to be positively related to the above variables (Halpin, 1954; Rush, 1957). Other studies also show that under conditions where there is a high degree of external threat, such as that experienced by air crews in combat, individuals have been shown to prefer strong (high structured, assertive, or autocratic) leaders (Mulder and Stemerding, 1963; Mulder, Rietsema, and de Jong, 1970; Sales, 1972; Torrance, 1954; Ziller, 1955). Thus these studies suggest that stress and ambiguity serve to stimulate a desire on the part of subordinates for highly structured leader behavior. Coupled with the finding by Crowe et al. (1972) that leaders responded to subordinates' preferred leader behavior, these studies suggest that stress and ambiguity for subordinates causes leaders to become more structure and more autocratic.

However, Fiedler and his associates (Fiedler and Chemers, 1974, cf. pp. 58–60 below) have argued that a leader's reaction to stress will be determined by the trait measured by the LPC scale. As discussed earlier, persons high on this scale tend to respond to stress by engaging in socioemotional leadership behavior, whereas persons low on this scale respond to stress by engaging in task-oriented, controlling, and somewhat authoritarian behavior.

The theoretical explanation offered by Korten (1968) for findings such as those cited above is that under ambiguous and stressful conditions structured or autocratic leader behavior reduces anxiety by clarifying goals and paths to goals. These behaviors result in a reduction of ambiguity and are essential to successful purposeful actions to reduce anxiety.

There is at present no systematic conceptualization of leadership environments. Moos (1973) reviews the current conceptualizations of human environments and argues for further research in this area. The same may be said for the environments of leaders. Clearly research is needed to develop a theoretical conceptualization of the leaders' environment and to determine those variables in the leader's environment that serve as cues, constraints, and reinforcers of leader behavior.

THEORIES OF LEADERSHIP

In this section we review several theories of leadership. These theories represent deductive frameworks consisting of sets of conceptual propositions from which several specific operational hypotheses can be derived.

These theories purport to describe, explain, and predict the effects of certain kinds of leader behavior and the conditions under which such behaviors will be effective. The theories reviewed here were selected for inclusion in this paper because they have received significant empirical support or because there is current widespread interest in them.

Each theory raises specific issues worthy of future research. These issues are described after a brief description and review of the evidence relevant to each theory.

Idiosyncrasy Credit Theory

This theory, advanced by Hollander (1969), attempts to explain the emergence of leadership and the determinants of leader effectiveness within groups. Leadership is considered to be an influence process. This process is considered to be effective where the leader is able to muster willing group support to achieve certain clearly specified group goals. According to the theory, group members continually evaluate the adequacy of the behavior of other group members. These evaluations are based on whether the group members have conformed to expectations.

There are two kinds of expectations. First are norms, which are expectations that are common to all group members for all other group members. Second, there are expectations that are specific to individuals or defined positions in the group. These are referred to as roles.

Group members' judgments about the individual will be positive to the extent that that individual conforms to expectations and contributes toward the group's goal. Member evaluations in terms of expectancies determine the individual's role and status in the group. Status is defined in terms of "idiosyncrasy credit." This represents an accumulation of positively disposed impressions residing in the perceptions of relevant others; it is defined operationally in terms of the degree to which an individual may deviate from the common expectancies of the group. For an individual to assert leadership, he or she must deviate from the expectations that members have for other group members. This deviant behavior is characterized as being unique or innovative and as contributing to attainment of group goals.

Early in interaction, conformity to group norms serves to maintain or increase credit, particularly as it is seen to be combined with manifest contributions to the group. At a later phase, the credits thus generated permit greater latitude for idiosyncratic behavior. Thus individuals who conform to group norms early in their exposure to the group and also show characteristics of competence will accrue credit. If one continues to amass credits, he or she attains a threshold permitting deviations from norms. However, such high-status persons are constrained by newly differentiated expectancies. These newly differentiated expectancies are those that are associated with the leadership role—expectancies that the high-status member will be innovative in helping the group attain important goals. Thus leaders conform to group norms and yet may act to alter them by an exercise of influence through this sequential process.

Hollander states that while an individual may have established sufficient credits to display idiosyncratic behavior, he or she may not choose to do so and therefore not necessarily become a leader. Thus the theory implies that the individual emergence of leadership depends partly on the individual's predisposition to lead.

Leadership status demands conformity to the group's expectancies regarding the role, but still leaves the leader with sway in the sphere of common expectancies associated with members at large. The leader may deviate from these or bring about the reconstruction of the perceptions of his or her prior activities after generating an appropriately high level of credit. Thus Hollander implies that with continued interaction individuals in a group change their attributions about the intentions of members' behavior.

One of the implications of the theory is that a person who breeches a group norm and in the process succeeds in helping the group to achieve its goal will be judged differently from one who fails to do so. Though the nonconforming behavior of a group with high idiosyncracy credit may be perceived more readily, it is likely to be interpreted in terms of certain positive outcomes, given the development of a history of past deviations that have proven to be fruitful and innovative.

Hollander notes that high-status people are likely to be perceived more favorably than low-status people. Their motives are likely to be viewed as more benevolent and more in the interests of the group. One implication of this hypothesis is that once a strong attribution of leadership has taken place the behavior of the person to whom leadership is attributed is likely to reinforce the attribution. Consequently, high-status people are likely to have significantly more opportunities to earn idiosyncracy credits than low-status people because of this attribution process. Thus the theory implies that, other factors remaining equal, status begets status.

The theory stresses the attribute of competence in those tasks that are of importance to the achievement of the group's goals. Unlike other theories, Hollander's is the only theory that explicitly places such a stress on competence. Various kinds of competence are relevant. They may be specific technical skills or social skills, depending on what is required if the group is to operate effectively. Therefore, the individual's functional value for the group is determined by a wide variety of situational demands for varying kinds of attributes. Also, redefinitions of competence may occur periodically. What may be important in securing a goal at one time may no longer be as important after the goal is achieved.

Another attribute required of the leader is that he or she be seen by potential followers as having an identification with the group, in the sense of a close involvement in the group's activities. It is important that the leader have those attributes that suggest such identification and also that his or her behavior manifest a loyalty to the needs and aspirations of the group members.

In addition to the two attributes of competence and identification with the group, there are three behavioral processes that are hypothesized to be important in determining the effectiveness of leadership: first, providing the group with structure and goal setting; second, maintaining flexibility and adaptability in handling changing requirements as new situations develop; and third, establishing productive social relationships that manifest themselves in emotional stability, dependability, and fairness in distribution of rewards.

Specific behaviors that are hypothesized to be associated with effective leadership are: *(a)* fostering communication within the group by providing mechanisms for participation and for informing members in advance if decisions or actions will affect them, *(b)* restraint in the use of power and impulsiveness, *(c)* rewarding actions that are in the interest of the group and judiciously avoiding the rewarding of behaviors that are contrary to the group's best interests, and *(d)* communicating to other groups and to higher authority the particular desires and needs of the group.

Hollander (1964) reports three studies conducted to test specific predictions of the Idiosyncrasy Credit theory. The first study demonstrated that high-competence people who violate group norms will be tolerated more than low-competence people, and that if one violates the norms *after* having demonstrated competence that the person's influence will be sufficiently higher than if the norm violation occurred earlier.

In a second study a brief description of a person was given to 151 subjects. They were to imagine that this person belonged to any group to which the subjects belonged. Competence and length of time in the group were the major attributes varied in the description. Subjects were asked to indicate their willingness to have that person in a position of authority in the group. A rising mean score of acceptance was found for increasing degrees of competence, and the mean for "new to the group" was uniformly lower than for "in group for some while" at each degree. Subjects were also provided a description of eight possible ways the hypothetical person may behave in the group. According to prediction, two behaviors reflecting innovative action were found to be disapproved significantly less the higher the status attributed to the innovator.

A third study was conducted in which subjects worked with coworkers who characteristically either conformed to the subject's judgments in the task, anti-conformed to their judgments, or behaved independently, that is, were evidently unaffected by the subject's judgment. The effect of these three modes of coworker behavior were studied in combination with each of three competence conditions in which the subject believed: *(a)* he alone was competent on the task, *(b)* that the coworker alone was competent, or *(c)* that both were competent. The proposition that nonconforming behavior is perceived differentially by the group, depending on the amount of credit the individual has built up through previous conformity and demonstrated competence was tested. It was hypothesized that the more the credits the individual has at his or her disposal, the more positively will his or her "nonconformity" be evaluated by the rest of the group. However, credit was expected to be put to use by the facilitation and independence behavior, not for an actual negation of normative prescriptions as in anticonformity behavior. As predicted, highest perceived coworker influence occurred under the condition where the coworker behaved independently and was perceived as competent.

Idiosyncrasy Theory stresses the importance of competence as a determinant of leadership. There is abundant evidence that the leaders' ability to contribute to the achievement of group goals is a characteristic associated with leadership emergence and effectiveness (Evan and Zelditch, 1961; Hollander, 1960; Hollander, Julian, and Perry, Note 8; Julian and Hollander, Note 9) and that this ability is largely determined by the leader's intellectual, interpersonal, administrative, and technical competence.

This statement has been found to hold in a wide variety of experimental (Hamblin, Miller, and Wiggins, 1961; Julian, Hollander, and Regula, 1969) and field studies (Comery, High, and Wilson, 1955a, and 1955b; Kahn and Katz, 1960; Baumgartel, 1956; Goodacer, 1951; Greer, Gallanter, and Nordie, 1954), and it has been demonstrated in such diverse field settings as manufacturing operations, forest ranger stations, railroad operations, research endeavors, and military combat operations.

Stogdill (1974, pp. 92–93) reports a comparative analysis of fifty-two factor-analytic studies published between 1945 and 1974. He found the following to be the most frequently occurring factors associated with leadership. These are presented in order of frequency of occurrence:

1. Social and interpersonal skills.
2. Technical skills.
3. Administrative skills.
4. Leadership effectiveness and achievement.
5. Social nearness and friendliness.
6. Intellectual skills.

The studies reported above are consistent with the prediction of

Idiosyncracy Theory. Further, they indicate that there are many kinds of leader competence. To date, there is no systematic method whereby a particular kind of leader competence can be deduced from an analysis of the leadership situation. Clearly, one would expect the formal role of the leader, the tasks of subordinates, subordinates' ability level, and their needs and expectations to determine the particular kind of competence that would lead to effective leadership.

One promising research direction concerns the need for a better conceptualization for the kinds of competence that a leader needs and a method for deducing the specific kinds of competence required for specific situations. The task remains for research to identify the situational factors that determine the intellectual, interpersonal, administrative, and technical competence requirements associated with leadership.

Prior evidence is consistent with Hollander's hypotheses that individuals who have idiosyncratic credit are more likely to engage in leadership behaviors, i.e., acceptable influence attempts, and that attributions about these behaviors are more likely to be positive than for individuals who do not have idiosyncratic credit. Individuals with high status attempt to influence others more often (Knapp and Knapp, 1966; Bass, 1963) and are generally perceived as more attractive (Pepitone, 1964) and more able (Sherif, White, and Harvey, 1955; Gardner, 1956; Hamblin, Miller, and Wiggins, 1961). Group members have a greater tendency to accept disruptive and inconsistent behavior and to accept changes introduced by high-status individuals (Hollander, 1961; Sabath, 1964; Goldberg and Iverson, 1965).

However, Jacobs (1971) discusses findings from two studies that are not in accord with the theory. These suggest boundary conditions with respect to the hypothesis that the behavior of high-status individuals is generally viewed positively. In both studies high-status confederates who violated group norms *at the expense of the attainment of group goals* were found to have suffered status losses more than the theory would predict (Alvarez, 1968; Wiggins, Dill, and Schwartz, 1965). Thus it appears that deviant behavior on the part of high-status people will be tolerated only insofar as those deviations result in either positive or insignificant consequences for group well-being. These studies suggest that when deviations of high-status persons result in negative consequences for the group, such deviatior will not be tolerated and the high-status members will lose influence v .th the group. Research designed to test this boundary condition is thus recommended.

On balance, the theory enjoys inferential support from prior studies and support from three studies designed to test its explicit hypotheses. The theory is potentially capable of predicting the emergence of leaders and the processes in which leaders engage to maintain leadership status once they have emerged or are appointed in formal organizations. Clearly additional tests of the theory are warranted.

Contingency Theory

Fiedler (1967) and Fiedler and Chemers (1974) advance a theory of formal leadership that uses the interaction of leader personality (as measured by the Least Preferred Coworker scale (LPC) and situation favorability (leader-member relations, task characteristics, and leader position power) to predict effective and ineffective leaders.

Leaders who describe their least preferred coworker in favorable terms (high LPC leaders) are assumed to be relations oriented and those who describe their least preferred coworker in negative terms are assumed to be task oriented. The orientation refers to which of two needs is dominant in that leader's personality. The two needs are need for good leader-subordinate relations and need for task success.

The dimension of situation favorability is seen as a stress continuum that, in interaction with the leader orientation, elicits leader behavior that is consistent with the hierarchical need pattern of the leader. This interaction between the leader's orientation, is measured by LPC and situational favorability, will be referred to here as the need-hierarchy hypothesis. According to this hypothesis, the leader's orientation determines which leader behaviors will be exhibited when the eader is in a stressful situation (low situation favorability). Under such conditions it is assumed that the leader must sacrifice either control over task completion or pleasant relations with subordinates.

Fiedler hypothesizes that leaders have little control over the behaviors exhibited in stressful situations. According to the theory, the low LPC leader, who concentrates on task completion, is the more effective leader in the unfavorable situation because at least the job gets done. In the situations of medium favorability, research has shown that the high LPC leader is more effective, though it is not clear why. In very favorable situations, the low LPC leader is also most effective. In this situation the leader can concentrate on secondary goals, because his or her more basic needs are met. Consequently, in very favorable situations the low LPC leader exhibits considerate behavior while the high LPC leader exhibits task-relevant behaviors. Since task-relevant behaviors are redundant in highly favorable situations (characterized by low task ambiguity, high position power, and good leader-member relations), the low LPC leader is more effective and the high LPC leader is less effective in such situations.

To date there are only three published complete tests of the model. Graen, Orris, and Alveres (1971) failed to support this model. The findings by Chemers and Skrzypek (1972) supported the model in seven of eight octants. And the most recent, most complete study by Vecchio (1977) failed to support the model. All other supporting and disconfirming evidence has been based on partial tests of the model or inferred from studies not intended to test it. The conclusions that follow rest primarily on the three complete studies.

There seems to be no clear reconciliation of the findings. The Graen, Orris, and Alvares (1971) failure to support the model may be due to methodological errors as described by Fiedler (1971). However, both the by Chemers and Skrzypek (1972) and the Vecchio (1977) studies appear to meet Fiedler's suggested requirements for a rigorous test of the theory. Vecchio presents his nonsupporting findings as a clear disconfirmation of the Contingency Model. He suggests that the theory is either task or population bound. If he is correct, then it is not a theory of leadership, but rather a theory of behavior on specific tasks or a theory of the behavior of specific populations and thus is of little value because of its lack of generalizability.

However, Vecchio's acceptance of the null hypothesis seems rather hasty. The contradictory findings resulting from these three studies suggest the need for further studies. The large number of partial tests of the theory that support the theoretical predictions for various octants suggest that the theory has some predictive power and should not be cast aside lightly.

Two main difficulties arise in considering the Contingency Model. First, there is no unambiguous interpretation of the LPC measure. Second, there is no explanation presented to account for the demonstrated effectiveness of high-LPC leaders in situations of medium favorability. Each of these problems is considered below.

Future Research Directions: Contingency Theory

The meaning of LPC There are two approaches to interpreting the LPC measure. The first is to relate this measure directly to other personality measures. Despite numerous studies attempting to relate LPC to other personality measures, none has been consistently correlated with it. A second approach is to relate the scale to observables such as expressed leader behavior and to infer from this behavior the underlying personality dimensions that are being tapped. The need-hierarchy explanation uses this approach.

Schmidt (Note 10) reviewed the research on LPC and offered a reinterpretation of the LPC measure. He noted that the hierarchy definition has received mixed support. The behavioral studies do indicate that as the situation changes, behaviors of low- and high-LPC leaders change in a pattern consistent with the predictions of the theory (see, e.g., Green,

Nebeker, and Boni, 1976). However, he noted that the reason for the behavioral change has not been demonstrated.

If the need-hierarchy explanation is correct, it should be possible to demonstrate changes in motivation consistent with changes in the favorability of the situation. Schmidt argued that one way to demonstrate these changes in motivation would be to measure changes in the correlation between leader job satisfaction and (a) the quality of group interpersonal relations and (b) the degree of task accomplishment. For example, for the high-LPC person in an unfavorable situation, Schmidt would expect a positive relationship between the leader job satisfaction and the quality of interpersonal relations (the primary need) while under favorable conditions the high-LPC leader's satisfaction should be positively related to the task accomplishment (the secondary need). However, his review of the evidence shows that the results are in agreement only with regard to the existence of a primary need for each LPC type. Under unfavorable conditions, leader job satisfaction (or affect) was shown to be positively related to the task accomplishment for low-LPC persons and to interpersonal relations for high-LPC persons. But under favorable conditions there was neither a positive relationship between leader job satisfaction and the task accomplishment for high-LPC persons nor a positive relationship between leader job satisfaction and interpersonal relations for low-LPC persons. Thus, these studies do not clearly demonstrate the emergence of a secondary goal under favorable conditions.

From this evidence Schmidt concluded that it is questionable whether there exists a multiple goal hierarchy that is tapped by the LPC measure and that the motivational hypothesis is supported only for the primary need. Schmidt reviews eight relevant studies. In the eight studies reviewed by Schmidt, the motivational explanation was not tested directly. Consequently, Schmidt's conclusions could be viewed as tentative at this stage.

Schmidt offers an alternative explanation of the LPC measure. He hypothesizes that LPC is an individual difference variable that measures the way an individual defines the job. That is, LPC is an index of which organizational functions and goals the leader identifies as relevant and important. Schmidt argues that an individual's behavior is determined by his or her primary orientation. Four studies are cited to support his hypothesis that low-LPC leaders are ". . . clearly oriented toward the task" (p. 25). Schmidt is more equivocal with respect to the evidence about the orientation of high-LPC leaders.

. . . Some studies have shown clear evidence for an interpersonal orientation for high LPC leaders . . . other studies have produced counter or null results . . . Schmidt and

Fiedler (unpublished) demonstrated that high LPC leaders are concerned with all of the elements of the general situation, including interpersonal relations with subordinates. Similarly Mitchell (1970) found a tendency for high LPC subjects to more evenly weigh the elements of the situation in their judgments, although the group's interpersonal atmosphere was clearly the more salient factor. However, a more complete explanation of the high LPC leader's orientation will require additional research. (pp. 25–26)

Schmidt hypothesizes that the difference between high- and low-LPC leaders concerns their choice of what means will help them meet their needs, not in the needs themselves. Thus, the evidence with respect to the need-hierarchy hypothesis is mixed and the hypothesis with respect to the leader's cognitive orientation remains untested. Schmidt's alternative hypothesis also warrants explicit testing.

The medium favorability situation   To date there has been no explanation offered to account for the findings that groups led by high-LPC leaders perform more effectively in moderately favorable situations. One possible explanation may be that high-LPC individuals experience less stress than low-LPCs in response to the same level of objective stressors. There is evidence that low-LPC leaders respond to stress differently than high-LPC leaders. Low-LPC leaders become more assertive, task oriented, directive, and controlling. These behaviors suggest that low-LPC leaders become more rigid than high-LPC leaders in response to the same objective level of stress induction. Further, low-LPC leaders exhibit significantly less variability in behavior than high-LPC leaders, given the same objective high level of stress (Graen and Nebeker, 1977). Since low variability is a common response to the experience of a high degree of subjective stress (Lazarus, 1966), it can be hypothesized that low-LPC leaders subjectively experience more stress in response to a given level of objective stressor than high-LPC leaders. In the medium favorability situation, either of two conditions prevail: *(a)* leader-member relations are good, the task is unstructured, and position power is weak or *(b)* leader-member relations are poor, the task is structured, and position power is strong. Different leader behaviors are likely to be required in these two situations. Yet high-LPC leaders have been found to be more effective in both situations (Sample and Wilson, 1965; Fiedler, O'Brien, and Ilgen, 1969; Fiedler and Chemers, 1974). These findings suggest that high-LPC leaders need to be and are more flexible in the medium favorability condition. If it can be assumed that high-LPC people perceive less stress than low-LPC people in the same situation, it is likely that high-LPC people will have greater flexibility and thus be able to choose the appropriate leader behaviors for the situation. Feeling less negative effects from the stress, the high-LPC individual can use the contemplative mode to diagnose situation demands and analyze what is needed. For that part of the Situation Favorability continuum under which tasks are structured and leader-member relations are poor, one would expect more considerate, less task-oriented behavior to be accepted more readily by subordinates. It is this kind of behavior that is predicted by high-LPC leaders under low stress conditions. In contrast, if low-LPC individuals perceive the same situation as highly stressful, they would be predicted, according to Contingency Theory, to engage in highly assertive, task-oriented, directive leader behavior. Such behavior is likely to be resented by those for whom the task is highly structured, especially if their relations with the leader are poor.

It is also possible that under the medium situational favorability condition leader behavioral flexibility is required. If low-LPC leaders perceive such situations as stressful, it is doubtful that they would be able to exhibit such flexibility. In contrast, high-LPC leaders experiencing less stress, would be expected to be more flexible and adapt as the situation demands.

Thus, it can be seen that, using the hypothesis of differential perception of and response to stress, an explanation for the superior performance of high-LPC leaders under conditions of medium situational favorability can be provided.

This explanation suggests the following hypotheses for future research:

1. Given a fixed amount of objective stressors, the amount of subjective stress experienced by an individual is negatively related to that individual's LPC score.

2. Leaders can consciously identify the appropriate behaviors for effective leadership under conditions of low perceived stress.

3. Leaders are less able to vary their behavior to meet situational demands as the amount of stress experienced increases.

It is necessary to distinguish between challenging a theory because it fails to predict and because it fails to explain its prediction. The Vecchio study demonstrates the need for further research into whether the Contingency Theory has predictive power. The Schmidt review and reinterpretation of LPC clearly shows a need to further explain LPC measures. Without such an explanation the Contingency Theory is method bound. That is, neither predictions nor prescriptions can be made without reliance on the LPC measure. This prevents multimethod verification of the theory and severely limits its usefulness under conditions that do not permit administration of the LPC scale.

Comparison of Idiosyncracy Theory and Contingency Theory   Idiosyncracy Theory offers a possible explanation as to why low-LPC leaders are effective in highly favorable conditions. First, assume that low-LPC leaders do in fact behave under these conditions as predicted by the theory. That is, low-LPC leaders are dominantly task oriented, assert strong control, and are very directive under unfavorable conditions. Further, assume that under favorable conditions, low-LPC leaders are dominantly relations oriented and considerate of subordinates.

According to the theory, under favorable conditions, leader-member relations are very good. In terms of Idiosyncracy Theory, good relationships would imply that the leader has high status as a result of having accumulated idiosyncracy credits. Thus, subordinates would respond favorably to such high-status leaders. Assuming that the leader is competent, the leader's requests would be readily followed by subordinates and thus the group would perform effectively.

However, Idiosyncracy Theory would make a prediction contrary to Contingency Theory with respect to the low-favorability situation. In such a situation, leader-member relations are poor, subordinate's tasks are unstructured, and the leader has low position power. In terms of Idiosyncracy Theory, poor leader-member relations imply that the supervisor would have low status as a result of not having accumulated idiosyncratic credits. According to Contingency Theory, it is necessary for the supervisor to assert strong control in a highly directive manner under unfavorable conditions. Contingency Theory would also predict this kind of behavior of the supervisor in unfavorable situations. However, since the supervisor has a low idiosyncracy balance, Idiosyncracy Theory would predict that such influence attempts by the supervisor would be rejected by group members. Further, since the supervisor has low power over group members in the unfavorable situation, the supervisor would be in no position to force his will on the group. Thus, such influence attempts by the supervisor would be ineffective. Therefore, the two theories make contrary predictions for the unfavorable situation.

Path-Goal Theory

The Path-Goal Theory of leadership is a situational theory that is deliberately phrased so that additional variables (such as personality variables) can be added as the effects of these new variables become known. The theory is based on theoretical work by Evans (1960) and has been formulated and extended by House (1971) and House and Mitchell (1974). A concise discussion of the theory appears in Filley, House, and Kerr (1976).

> Briefly, the theory consists of two propositions. The first proposition is that leader behavior is acceptable and satisfying to subordinates to the extent that they see it as either an immediate source of satisfaction or as instrumental to future satisfaction.
>
> The second proposition of the theory is that leader behavior will be motivational to

the extent that (1) it makes satisfaction of subordinate needs contingent on effective performance, and (2) it complements the environment of subordinates by providing the coaching, guidance, support, and rewards which are necessary for effective performance and which may otherwise be lacking in subordinates or in their environment.

These two propositions suggest that the leader's strategic functions are to enhance subordinates' motivation to perform, their satisfaction with the job, and their acceptance of the leader . . . The strategic functions of the leader consist of (1) recognizing and/or arousing subordinate's needs for outcomes over which the leader has some control; (2) increasing personal payoffs to the subordinates for goal attainment; (3) making the path to those payoffs easier to travel by coaching and direction; (4) helping subordinates clarify expectancies; (5) reducing frustrating barriers; and (6) increasing opportunities for personal satisfaction, contingent on effective performance. Two classes of situational variables are asserted to be contingency factors; these are *(a)* personal characteristics of subordinates, and *(b)* environmental pressures and demands which subordinates must deal with (p. 254).

Personal characteristics in part determine how subordinates react to leader behavior. Several personality characteristics of subordinates are hypothesized to moderate the relationship between the effects of leader behavior and the satisfaction of the subordinates. For example, Runyon (1973) and Mitchell, Smyser, and Weed (1974) show that a subordinate's score on the Locus of Control Scale (Rotter, 1966) moderates the relationship between participative leadership style and subordinate satisfaction. These studies showed that individuals who are low on the scale, i.e., individuals who believe that their rewards are contingent on their own behavior are more satisfied with a participative leadership style while individuals who are high on the Locus of Control Scale, i.e., individuals who believe their rewards are the result of luck or another's behavior are more satisfied with a directive style.

Another characteristic of subordinates hypothesized to moderate the effect of leader behavior is the subordinate's tendency to be authoritarian. Highly authoritarian subordinates are hypothesized to be less receptive to participative leadership and more receptive to directive or even authoritarian leadership.

A third subordinate characteristic hypothesized to moderate the effect of leader behavior is the subordinates' perceptions of their own abilities with respect to their assigned tasks. The higher the degree of perceived ability relative to task demands, the less the subordinates will view their leader directiveness, closeness of supervision, and coaching behavior as acceptable. Where the subordinate's perceived ability is high, such behavior is likely to have little positive effect on subordinate motivation and to be perceived as excessively close control.

The second aspect of the situation is the environment. The theory asserts that effects of leader behavior on the psychological status of subordinates will be contingent on other aspects of the subordinate's environ- ment that are relevant to motivation. Three broad classifications of contingency factors in the environment are the subordinate's task, the formal authority system of the organization, and the primary work group.

Assessment of the environment conditions makes it possible to predict the kind and amount of influence that specific leader behaviors will have on the motivation of subordinates. Each of the environmental factors mentioned above could act upon subordinates in any of three ways. First, they may serve as stimuli that motivate and direct subordinates to per- form necessary task operations. Second, they may act to constrain varia- bility in behavior. Constraints may help subordinates by clarifying their expectations that efforts lead to rewards or by preventing subordinates from experiencing conflict and confusion. Constraints may also be coun- terproductive to the extent that they restrict initiative or prevent increases in effort from being positively associated with rewards. Third, environ- mental factors may serve to clarify and provide rewards for achieving desired performance. For example, it is possible for subordinates to re- ceive the necessary cues to do their jobs and the needed rewards for satisfaction from sources other than the leader (e.g., coworkers in the primary work group). The amount of variance in subordinate motivation accounted for by leader behavior is thus hypothesized to be a function of how deficient the environment is with respect to motivational stimuli, constraints, or rewards.

With respect to the environment, the theory asserts that when goals and paths are apparent because of the routine nature of the task, clear group norms, or objective controls of the formal authority system, attempts by leaders to clarify paths and goals will be redundant and will be seen by subordinates as an imposition of unnecessarily close control. Although such control may increase performance by preventing malingering, it will also result in decreased satisfaction. The theory also asserts that the more dissatisfying the task, the more subordinates will resent leader behavior directed toward increasing productivity or enforcing compliance with or- ganizational rules and procedures.

Finally, the theory states that leader behavior will be motivational to the extent that it helps subordinates cope with environmental uncertain- ties, threats from others, or sources of frustration. Such leader behavior is predicted to increase subordinate satisfaction with their job context, and to be motivational to the extent that it increases subordinate expectations that their efforts will lead to valued rewards.

This theory and the research it has generated has helped reconcile previous findings regarding relationships between managerial style and subordinate responses. For example, House (Note 6) has utilized Path Goal theory in an attempt to explain field study data by Tosi (1970) and experimental data by Wexley, Singh, and Yukl (1973) that failed to show that any differences in the effects of participation could be attributed to subordinate characteristics. House argued that the task may have an overriding effect on the relationship between leader participation and subordinate responses and that individual predispositions or personality characteristics of subordinates may have an effect only under some tasks. He assumed that when task demands are ambiguous, subordinates will have a need to reduce the ambiguity and that participative problem solving between subordinates and leaders will result in more effective decisions than when the task demands are clear. He further assumed that when subordinates are ego-involved in a task, they will be more likely to want to have a say in the decisions that affect them than when they are not ego-involved. House reasoned that whenever participation is instrumental in reducing ambiguity, or whenever subordinates are ego-involved in the task, participative leadership will be instrumental to both need satisfaction and productivity, regardless of the personality or predispositions of the subordinates. However, when subordinates are not ego-involved in their tasks and the demands are clear, participation will have no instrumental or intrinsic value, unless the subordinates are generally predisposed toward having a high degree of independence and toward respecting nonauthoritarian behavior.

Thus House hypothesized that only when tasks are unambiguous and not ego-involving will subordinate's personality or predispositions moderate the effect of participative leadership. On such tasks, subordinates not predisposed toward participative leadership will not find it either instrumentally or intrinsically satisfying. Subordinates who are predisposed toward participation will find it intrinsically satisfying and motivating. The study by Schuler (1976) described in the above section on participative leader behavior was designed to test this hypothesis. Schuler's findings were as hypothesized.

The second proposition of the theory states that leader behavior will be motivational to the extent that it complements the environment of subordinates by providing the coaching, guidance, support, and rewards that are necessary for effective performance that may otherwise be lacking in subordinates or in their environment. Environmental factors such as intragroup conflict, task characteristics, organizational size, and organizational structure have been shown to moderate the relationship between leader behavior and subordinate satisfaction and performance in a manner consistent with the theory.

Path-Goal theory advances the hypothesis that the effects of leader consideration on performance and satisfaction of subordinates will be most positive when subordinates are engaged in dissatisfying tasks, fatigued, frustrated, or under stress. The literature reviewed above in the section on leader role differentiation concerning the effects of socioemotional leadership and leader consideration is consistent with this hypothesis, as are the findings from more recent tests of this hypothesis reported in the above section concerned with leader behavior.

A recent study by Katz (in press) incorporates intragroup conflict into the theory. Katz distinguished affective intragroup conflict from substantive intragroup conflict and argued that as the different kinds of conflict vary in strength and importance the leader behavior required would also change. Specifically, he hypothesized that increasing affective conflict will precipitate the desire by group members for more considerate and less structuring leader behavior in order to satisfy the needs of group members. Similarly, increasing substantive conflict was hypothesized to evoke a desire by group members for more structuring and less considerate leader behavior.

Finally, Katz argued that either kind of conflict will generate tension and stress, as well as hinder subordinate's perceived path-goal relationships. Thus, he hypothesized that overall effectiveness will be more positively related to leader Initiating Structure and less positively related to leader Consideration under conditions of either high affective or substantive conflict.

Katz tested this hypothesis in a field study, using correlational methods and in two laboratory studies using confederate leaders, questionnaires, and objective measures of performance. His major findings were: (a) the need for or desire for structuring leader behavior is significantly positively related to the degree of substantive or affective conflict, and (b) the relationship between leader structuring and group performance was significantly higher under high-conflict conditions. Only slight evidence was in favor of a similar conclusion for leader consideration. Thus Katz's hypotheses with respect to Initiating Structure were strongly supported. However, he did not find support for the hypothesis that affective conflict will be positively related to the desire for increased leader consideration. To explain his failure to confirm the hypothesized relationship between affective conflict and desired leader consideration Katz speculates that preferences for leader Consideration may be invariably positive. Katz states that an alternative explanation may lie in the Path Goal theory in that Consideration is simply not as relevant or as meaningful a dimension as Initiating Structure for individuals who have jobs with considerable intrinsic satisfaction. Clearly this hypothesis warrants testing.

Reasoning from the second proposition of the theory has also resulted in the identification of organizational size as a variable that can be incorporated into the theory. Miles and Petty (1977) reviewed the evidence on the relationship between organization size and degree of bureaucratization and concluded that there is a strong positive relationship between these two variables. That is formalization, routinization, standardization, and specialization were concluded to be higher in large organizations. From this conclusion they reasoned that social service professionals in large organizations would view leader initiating structure as redundant with the high degree of formalization found in such organizations. They reasoned that leader consideration would be an alternative source of satisfaction or relief from the presumed dissatisfaction that occurs as a result of bureaucratization in large agencies. As predicted, these authors found the correlations between (a) leader Initiating Structure and (b) employee work satisfaction, satisfaction with coworkers, and motivation were significantly higher in small agencies than in large agencies. In the smaller agencies, the correlations were all positive, whereas in the larger agencies they were either nonsignificant or negative. Further, they found the correlations between consideration and employee satisfaction tended to be higher in large agencies than in small agencies. However, these differences were not statistically significant.

Schuler (Note 11) extended the Path Goal theory of leadership by incorporating the moderating effects of organizational structural variables into the predictions of the theory. He found that subordinate role conflict and role ambiguity are lower and expectations that performance will result in desired rewards are higher among employees doing complex tasks in an organic organizational environment than among employees doing simple tasks in mechanistic environments. He reasoned that under complex tasks in organic organizations leader Initiating Structure will not be needed. He also reasoned that under opposite conditions, leader Initiating Structure will be positively related to satisfaction. Schuler's findings supported these hypotheses indicating that when organizational or task variables provide the subordinate with the necessary role clarity and direction, leader Initiating Structure will have little effect.

Recently, the methodologies used to test the theory have been questioned. Sheridan, Downey, and Slocum (1975) and Dessler and Valenzi (1977) have argued that path analysis should be used to test the Path Goal theory when relying on correlation data. Dessler and Valenzi argue "that the use of path analysis procedures may help explain (the conflicting findings regarding the moderating effect of task structure on the relationship between Initiating Structure and satisfaction) by focusing directly on the underlying expectancy motivation linkage specified in the Path Goal theory" (p. 252).

Using path analysis, Sheridan et al. (1975) did not find support for the direct causal relationships hypothesized in Path Goal theory. Dessler and Valenzi (1977) did not find support for the hypothesis that occupational level moderates the relationship between initiation of structure and intrinsic job satisfaction. However, Dessler and Valenzi did find support for the hypothesized linkages between leader behavior and subordinates' expectancies. This contradiction in findings will need to be resolved through future research. Green (1975) attributes the disconfirming finding of Sheridan et al. (1975) to methodological deficiencies of their research design.

Path Goal theory also offers an explanation as to why low-LPC leaders are effective in conditions of either very high or very low situation favorability. Again, if we assume that low-LPC leaders do behave under these conditions as predicted by the theory, then we would expect such leaders to exhibit considerate-relations-oriented behavior under favorable conditions and controlling assertive directive behavior under unfavorable conditions. According to Contingency Theory, under favorable conditions the jobs of subordinates are highly structured. According to Path Goal theory, task-oriented–directive-path–clarifying-leader behavior is unnecessary under these conditions and would be viewed as redundant with the situation by subordinates. Further, if highly structured jobs are assumed to be more routine and thus less satisfying, supportive-relations-oriented leader behavior would be required to offset the boredom and frustration resulting from such jobs. Under such conditions, influence attempts by supportive leaders are more likely to be accepted by subordinates. Assuming the leaders are competent, if their influence attempts are accepted, the groups are likely to be more effective.

Under unfavorable conditions, the task of subordinates are unstructured. According to Path Goal theory, task-oriented leader behavior that clarifies task requirements and paths to goals is likely to be more effective. Thus, under this condition, task-oriented leadership would be seen as instrumental to subordinate goal achievement. Again, assuming that the leader is competent, such task-oriented leader behavior is likely to be more readily accepted and the group is thus likely to be more effective.

Future research directions: Path goal theory. Path Goal theory is rich with opportunities for refinement and extension. There are many variables that have been the subject of other leadership research that are not yet included in the Path Goal model. For example, as mentioned earlier, substantial research has shown that leader task competence is an important variable in predicting leader effectiveness. The theory in its present form assumes the leader to have the task competence when engaging in clarifying behaviors. Leader competence thus constitutes a boundary variable of the theory. It is hypothesized here that the predictions of the theory concerning leader path clarifying behaviors will not hold under conditions where the leader does not have the competence to clarify subordinates' task demands, or where the leader's intelligence is either below or too far above the intelligence of subordinates.

Other leader personality variables might be incorporated into the theory. For example, the traits of dominance and self-confidence are likely predictive of leaders who will initiate path-clarifying behaviors. The traits of sociability, interpersonal skills, and social participation were found by Stogdill (1948, 1974) to be related to criteria of leader effectiveness in a large number of studies (see Table 1). These traits may be used as surrogates for measures of supportive leader behavior.

Subordinate personality variables that might be investigated in addition to authoritarianism and locus of control include subordinate need for achievement, need for affiliation, and tolerance for ambiguity.

A recent study by Graen and Ginzbergh (1977) suggests another variable that might be incorporated into the theory. These authors found that when subordinates perceive their job as relevant to their future career objectives, leader supportiveness was unrelated to their subsequent tendency to resign. However, when the subordinates peceived their jobs as not relevant to career objectives, leader supportiveness had a strong negative relationship to a subsequent tendency to resign. This perception of the employee, which Graen and Ginzbergh (1977) refer to as Role Orientation, thus interacts with leader supportiveness as task satisfaction is hypothesized to interact with leader supportiveness according to Path Goal theory. It thus appears that subordinate role orientation may be a better moderator of the relationships between leader behavior and the dependent variables of the theory than the task characteristics originally specified in the theory. Research to test the relative importance of Role Orientation and task characteristics is called for.

Recent research and theorizing by Kerr (Note 12) suggests additional variables that are hypothesized to moderate relationships between leader behavior and subordinate motivation, satisfaction, and performance. Kerr has advanced a notion of "substitutes for leadership." According to this notion, there are factors in the environment that serve as sources of psychological structure or support for subordinates such that leader behavior is irrelevant to the satisfaction or performance of subordinates. Such "substitutes for leadership" are hypothesized to *negate* the leader's ability to either improve or impair subordinate satisfaction or performance. Kerr argues that what is needed, then, is a taxonomy of situations where we should not be studying leadership in the formal hierarchical sense at all. Kerr advanced a preliminary taxonomy of such substitutes. These are presented in Table 4. In addition, Kerr has developed a questionnaire designed to measure the existence of such substitutes in hierarchical field settings. While the questionnaire is still in its developmental stage, there is evidence that it is useful for its proposed purpose (Kerr, Note 7).

Kerr (note 7) distinguishes between "substitutes" and "neutralizers."

Table 4. Substitutes for Leadership

Characteristic	Will Tend to Neutralize	
	Relationship-Oriented, Supportive, People-Centered Leadership: Consideration, Support, and Interaction Facilitation	Task-Oriented, Instrumental, Job-Centered Leadership: Initiating Structure, Goal Emphasis, and Work Facilitation
of the subordinate		
1. Ability		X
2. Experience		X
3. Training		X
4. Knowledge		X
5. "Professional" orientation	X	X
6. Indifference toward organizational rewards	X	X
of the task		
7. Unambiguous and routine		X
8. Methodologically invariant		X
9. Provides its own feedback concerning accomplishment		X
10. Intrinsically satisfying	X	
of the organization		
11. Formalization (explicit plans, goals, and areas of responsibility)		X
12. Inflexibility (rigid, unbending rules and procedures)		X
13. Highly-specified and active advisory and staff functions		X
14. Closely-knit, cohesive work groups	X	X
15. Organizational rewards not within the leader's control	X	X
16. Spatial distance between superior and subordinates	X	X

A substitute is defined to be a "person or thing acting or used in place of another." In the context of leadership, Kerr uses the term to describe characteristics that render leader behavior unnecessary.

Kerr argues that the effect of neutralizers is therefore to create an "influence vacuum" from which a variety of dysfunctions may emerge. Kerr hypothesizes that the variables listed in Table 4 have the capacity to counteract leader influence. Consequently, all of these variables may be termed neutralizers. Additional research is needed to determine which are neutralizers and which are substitutes or the conditions under which each variable is a neutralizer, a substitute, or neither. There may well be specific conditions under which leadership is necessary but neutralized by environmental factors. Under such conditions the "influence vacuum" will likely result in dysfunctional consequences such as lower performance and satisfaction, increased turnover, conflict, and grievances. Clearly, a better understanding of how environmental factors operate as substitutes or neutralizers of leadership is required.

The Rational Decision Making Theory[4]

Vroom and Yetton (1973) have advanced a prescriptive theory intended to help managers meet the two criteria of effective decision solutions suggested by Maier (1963). That is, the theory is intended to help managers ensure a high quality of solutions to problems they must deal with and also obtain solutions that are acceptable to subordinates, if acceptability of solutions is important to effective implementation.

The theory is intended to be a diagnostic tool with which leaders can choose the appropriate decision-making methods for a given problem. The decision-making method prescribed by the theory ranges from autocratic decision making by the manager alone to various degrees of participation with subordinates, to joint decision making between the manager and his or her subordinates as a group. The model specifies seven properties of problems that Vroom and Yetton believe to have relevance to the determination of appropriate methods of decision making. Various combinations of the seven properties result in twenty-three problem types.

The model specifies seven decision rules that are intended to guide a leader in selecting the most appropriate decision method. A combination of seven decision rules, seven problem attributes, and twenty-three problem types constitute the normative (prescriptive) model.

Application of the seven rules permits the leader to determine the decision-making approaches that are feasible. Once the set of feasible approaches has been identified, the leader is instructed to select the single most suitable approach for a particular situation. Vroom and Yetton state, "When more than one method remains in the feasible set, there are a number of alternative decision rules which might dictate the choice among them'' (p. 37). Vroom and Yetton illustrate how additional rules are developed using the number of man hours required to solve the problem as the basis for choice. Other alternative rules for narrowing the choice among the feasible set are alluded to but are not made explicit.

The Vroom and Yetton theory is the first systematic integration of prior research findings concerning participative decision making. It represents an advance in conceptualizing about situtional factors that determine the degree to which various degrees of participative decision making will be effective. Consequently, the model represents an advance in the literature concerning participative decision making, and it is the opinion of the authors that further research on the model will result in a significant improvement of our understanding of the conditions under which the five decision-making approaches prescribed by the model are effective.

Vroom and his associates have conducted a substantial amount of research on the properties of the theory. Vroom and Yetton (1973) present a substantial amount of data concerning the decision-making approaches managers report having used in various situations, and the approaches they say they would use for hypothetical problems. These self-reports provide some indication of how well managers are able to diagnose situations in terms of the concepts of the model. These data show:

> On both standardized and recalled problems, leaders tend to use participative processes when they lack the necessary information to solve the problem by themselves and when their subordinates have a high probability of possessing that information. This use of participation is a means of protecting the quality of the decision by insuring that the decision making system contains the information needed to generate and evaluate the alternatives. The results from both methods also indicate that acceptance considerations enter into the choice of decision process. Managers tend to employ more participative styles when it is critical for their subordinates to accept the decision in order to get it effectively implemented and when the likelihood of selling an autocratic decision is low (p. 118).

Vroom (1976) and Vroom and Jago (Note 13) report tests of the theory using managers' reports of recalled successful and unsuccessful decisions. After describing the decisions and the decision method they used, the managers were trained in coding problem attributes according to the theory. The percentage of successful decisions based on a decision style within the feasible set was significantly greater than the percentage of unsuccessful decisions not within the set. The percentage of unsuccessful decisions outside the feasible set was significantly greater than successful decisions that were ouside the set. The results of the two studies were very similar, indicating agreement with the predictions of the theory in approximately 67 percent of the cases. This level of agreement is approximately twice that which would be expected by chance alone.

There were several other findings of interest as well. On both standardized and recalled problems, it was found that the model's normatively prescribed behavior exhibited substantially greater variety in decision processes than did the managers' recalled or hypothetical behavior. Thus managers describe themselves as being less flexible than the model prescribes. Further, the model makes more extensive use of the two extreme decision processes than do the managers, in that the model is both more autocratic and more participative than the managers described themselves as being.

While the evidence reported by Vroom (1976) and Vroom and Jago (Note 13) shows rather strong support for the model, there are several reservations that should be considered when evaluating its validity.

Self-report data have been shown in prior research to be biased; that is, self-reports tend to disagree with the observations of others (Bass, 1957; Besco and Lawshe, 1959; Campbell, 1956; and Graham and Gleno, 1970). Jago and Vroom (1975) collected descriptions of managers' decision behavior using self-report data from the managers and data collected from subordinates. The descriptions from the two sources did not correlate significantly, thus raising a serious question about the validity of the managers' self-report data used to test the model.

Filley, House and Kerr (1976) point out that one of the problems in applying the model is likely to be its lack of parsimony.

> The model requires the decision maker to choose one of five kinds of decision-making styles by analyzing a problem in terms of seven attributes and applying it requires a decision about how a particular decision is to be made. Application of the model in this way assumes that the choice of decision style can be made deliberately. If this is true it would probably be very time consuming to apply the model to any new decision. Consequently, the more varied the situations in which managers make decisions the more time will be required to decide how decisions are to be made.
>
> While Vroom & Yetton present evidence that training improves managers' abilities to apply the model appropriately to hypothetical case problems, it is possible that managers are not sufficiently rational or cognitively complex to apply such a complex decision-making model under pressures of time and stresses of work. Even if such a rational selection of decision-making methods is possible, it is questionable whether managers would or could take the time required to apply the model to normal day-to-day problems. Only additional research can answer whether or not managerial attempts to apply the model will result in more effective decision making (p. 252).

This criticism that the model lacks parsimony is primarily concerned with the prescriptive applications of the model. It may well be that such a complex model is necessary to *explain* the conditions under which various kinds of decision-making methods are appropriate, but it is questionable whether the prescriptive applications of the model can be made because of its complexity.

Field (Note 14) analyzed the feasible sets given in the Vroom-Yetton model and concluded that based on the decision rules, a more parsimonious model would suffice. Field noted that the decision style C2 (consultative—the subordinates and manager as a group share ideas, then the manager makes the decision) is in the feasible set for nineteen of the twenty-three problem situations. Of the four situations where C2 is not in this set, G2 (total group decision making with manager as a group member) is found in the feasible set. Thus Field concluded that a simple rule to guarantee a decision method in the Vroom-Yetton feasible set is as follows:

> If acceptance of the decision by subordinates is critical to effective implementation and it is not reasonably certain that subordinates would accept an autocratic decision, but they share organizational goals (or decision quality is not important) use G2, otherwise use C2 (page 27).

This simple model uses four situation attributes instead of the seven used by the Vroom-Yetton model and uses only two decision styles rather than the five of the Vroom-Yetton model.

For prescriptive purposes, Field's suggested rule is much easier to apply and results in the selection of decision methods consistent with the intent of the Vroom-Yetton model. That is, it results in decision methods that, according to the model, will protect the quality of decisions and insure that they are accepted by subordinates.

While it is argued here that the model is likely to be too complex for managers to systematically apply it, it also suffers from omission of decision rules relevant to characteristics of subordinates. In the initial development of the model, a decision rule was included for managers to consider whether subordinates had sufficient information to result in a high-quality decision. Subsequently, this decision was eliminated, because it was found by Vroom and Yetton (1963) that managers almost always assumed subordinates would have additional information, and if the additional information needed to be gathered, then any one of the other decision processes might result in a decision to do so (Vroom and Yetton, 1963, p. 187).

However, as discussed in the previous review of research on participative decision making, subordinates' knowledge relevant to the decision is a significant moderator of the relationship between participative decision making and decision effectiveness (see Table 3 for a summary of studies relevant to this issue). Further, the model does not consider the subordinates' predisposition toward engaging in the participative decision process. Again, there is substantial evidence that such predispositions moderate the relationship between participative leadership and decision effectiveness (cf. pp. 38–40 above for a review of this evidence).

The decision rule that instructs managers to determine whether subordinates can be trusted to base solutions on organizational considerations appears to result in a logical inconsistency. Purportedly, the model applies at all levels of the organization. Thus, when a manager is in the position of making a decision, he must judge subordinates according to this rule in order to determine the appropriate decision method to be used. However, when the manager at the next level above makes a decision, he must also apply the same rule. This assumes that in the first instance the manager can be trusted to base solutions on organizational considerations and in the second instance his superior must question whether he can be so trusted. Thus, there appears to be a logical inconsistency in the model in that the manager who is applying the decision rules is instructed to judge trustworthiness of subordinates, but he or she might not be trustworthy to base solutions on organizational considerations. Consequently, if the model were valid, it would maximize the interests of the manager applying it but would not necessarily maximize organizational effectiveness. In fact, the resulting decision could be contrary to the interests of the organization.

Another limitation of the model concerns the decision styles it makes available to the manager. Field notes that the field model does not provide for delegation in that the leader is actively involved in all decision styles specified by the model.

Field (Note 8) also notes that in some situations managers may wish to use a mixed strategy, such as having each individual generate alternatives and then using the entire group to evaluate the alternatives and reach agreement on one of the alternatives as the solution. There is evidence that such a process results in more alternatives and higher-quality alternatives being generated than when individuals generate alternatives in interaction with each other (Vroom, Grant, and Cotton, 1969).

In conclusion, while the Vroom and Yetton model represents the first systematic attempt to integrate participative decision making with situational variables, both the methods used to test it and the assumptions on which it is based remain to be validated. Additional tests of the model are recommended, using laboratory methods or field research methods that do not rely exclusively on self-report data.

Charismatic Theory of Leadership

Charisma is the term commonly used in the sociological and political science literature to describe leaders who by force of their personal abilities are capable of having profound and extraordinary effects on followers. These effects include commanding loyalty and devotion to the leader and of inspiring followers to accept and execute the will of the leader without hesitation or question or regard to one's self-interest. The term "charisma," whose initial meaning was "gift," is usually reserved for leaders who by their influence are able to cause followers to accomplish outstanding feats. Frequently, such leaders represent a break with the established order and through their leadership major social changes are accomplished.

Most writers concerned with charisma or charismatic leadership begin their discussion with Max Weber's conception of charisma. Weber describes as charismatic those leaders who ". . . reveal a transcendent mission or course of action which may be in itself appealing to the potential followers, but which is acted on because the followers believe their leader is extraordinarily gifted" (Dow, 1969, p. 307). Transcendence is attributed implicitly to both the qualities of the leader and the content of his mission, the former being variously described as "supernatural, superhuman or exceptional" (Weber, 1947, p. 358).

Several writers contend that charismatic leadership can and does exist in formal complex organizations (Dow, 1969; Oberg, 1972; Shils, 1965). House (1977) has explicitly advanced such a theory of charismatic leadership within organizations. The theory is based on a review of the political science, sociological, and social psychological literature. House found that many of the propositions advanced in the sociological and political science literature are implicitly testable. In addition he found several findings from the social psychological literature that help to understand the nature of charismatic leadership.

The dependent variables for the theory are: follower trust in the correctness of the leader's beliefs, similarity of followers' beliefs to those of the leader, unquestioning acceptance of the leader, affection for the leader, willing obedience to the leader, identification with and emulation of the leader, emotional involvement of the follower in the mission, heightened goals of the follower, and the feeling on the part of followers that they are able to accomplish or contribute to the accomplishment of the mission.

House argues that scores of followers on scales designed to measure these variables could serve as a basis for identifying leaders who have charismatic effects. Personality characteristics and behaviors of these leaders could be compared with those of other leaders who do not have such effects to identify characteristics and behaviors that differentiate the charismatic leaders from others.

The theory consists of seven propositions, which, collectively, are intended to explain the conditions under which charismatic leaders emerge and their personality characteristics and behavior. While none of the propositions have been explicitly tested, they all have some inferential support from prior empiric studies. Following are the seven propositions:

1. Characteristics that differentiate leaders who have charismatic effects on subordinates from leaders who do not have such charismatic effects are dominance and self-confidence, need for influence, and a strong conviction in the moral righteousness of their beliefs.

2. The more favorable the perceptions of the potential follower toward a leader, the more the follower will model: *(a)* the valences of the leader, *(b)* the expectations of the leader that effective performance will result in desired or undesired outcomes for the follower, *(c)* the emotional responses of the leader to work-related stimuli, and *(d)* the attitudes of the leader toward work and toward the organization.

3. Leaders who have charismatic effects are more likely to engage in behaviors designed to create the impression of competence and success than leaders who do not have such effects.

4. Leaders who have charismatic effects are more likely to articulate ideological goals than leaders who do not have such effects.

5. Leaders who simultaneously communicate high expectations of, and confidence in, followers are more likely to have followers who accept the goals of the leader and believe that they can contribute to goal accomplishment and are more likely to have followers who strive to meet specific and challenging performance standards.

6. Leaders who have charismatic effects are more likely to engage in behaviors that arouse motives relevant to the accomplishment of the mission than are leaders who do not have charismatic effects.

7. A necessary condition for a leader to have charismatic effects is that the role of followers be definable in ideological terms that appeal to the follower.

Several of the variables of the theory are operationalizable with existing instruments. For example, the personality traits of dominance, self-confidence, and need for influence have been frequently measured by use of psychological tests. Role modeling and its effects have been studied in the laboratory (Bandura, 1968) and field settings (Weiss, 1977). Valence and expectations are frequently measured by researchers of motivation. Motive arousal is frequently measured and also experimentally induced.

Throughout the paper on charisma, House offers suggestions for operationalizing the variables and testing the propositions. Tests of these propositions are recommended for future research. House stated "admittedly tests of the theory will require the development and validation of several new scales. However it is hoped that the propositions are at least presently testable in principle" (p. 24).

An Attribution Theory of Leadership

Calder (1977) has advanced a theory intended to explain the process by which the attribution of leadership occurs. According to this theory, leadership is a label that can be applied to behavior. Certain inherent qualities of the actor are taken as causing both the behavior and its intended effects. Judgments about leadership are made on the basis of observed behavior. Thus leadership is an inference based on behavior accepted as evidence of leadership. Leaders are not in fact leaders until there is some basis for distinguishing their behaviors. These evidential behaviors may differ from group to group. The behaviors accepted as evidence of leadership depend on the particular set of actors involved. At the very least, the predominant social class composition of a class of actors and the purpose of the group renders some behaviors more appropriate than others for leadership inferences. Members of a street-corner gang obviously focus on behaviors that are very different from those that are salient to the corporation board room. Thus, evidential behaviors must be *typical* of a class of behaviors that are *different* from those of most group members. In terms of Hollander's (1964) theory described above, this assertion would mean that one must meet the expectations that the observer has for group leaders and that these expectations are different from the expectations held of other group members.

Calder's theory is diagrammed in Figure 1. The first stage in the attribution of leadership is therefore the observation of behavior by another and the effects of this behavior. If an effect is not in actuality due to a person, it is a source of attributional error. Observed actions and effects may imply entirely different behaviors that have no basis at all in actual observation. These "inferred observations" supply indirect evidence to the attribution process.

In the second stage of the attribution process, actual and inferred observations are either accepted or rejected as evidence of leadership. Observations are first examined for distinctiveness. By definition, leadership cannot describe everyone in the group; its very meaning calls for distinctive behavior. Once distinctive behavior is observed, it is matched against expectations about how leaders should act. The observer has an implicit theory of leadership. This theory is used to interpret potential evidential behaviors and effects. The observed behavior must be consistent for a leader attribution to be made. If an observation, either actual or inferred, is made of behavior and effects that fit the observer's leadership theory;

Figure. 1   Flow diagram of the attribution model.

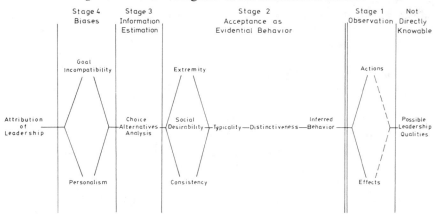

Source: Calder, B.J. An attribution theory of leadership. In Staw & Salancik (1977).

if the evidence for this holds up over time and across relevant situations; and if it is supported by the opinion of other relevant actors, it meets the requirement of consistency and thus will be attributed to the personal disposition of the observer. Coupled with this evaluation of consistency is the evaluation of extremity. First, the evidence must be judged extreme or sufficiently important to imply leadership qualities. The extremity evaluation is also important as a possible by-pass for consistency requirement. Thus, in Figure 1 extremity is depicted as operating in parallel with consistency and social desirability. Any behavior or effect that is sufficiently extreme can override alternative explanations. The requirements of distinctiveness and extremity for the attribution of leadership are consistent with Hollander's (1964) assertion that the leader must engage in idiosyncratic behavior and that this behavior must be seen as a unique or innovative contribution to group goals.

The next stage postulated in the attribution process involves what is termed "information estimation." Evidence may be acceptable and still not specifically informative about leadership qualities. An observer evaluates the evidential worth of an observed behavior and effects by comparing them to what he construes to be the *personal* alternatives to the actor. Here the observer compares the behavior performed with other things the actor might have done. The question is whether there is any evidence for "leadership" qualities causing the observed behavior versus other, perhaps, unsuspected, qualities. If the observed behavior could be explained by nonleadership (externally caused) variables as well as possible leadership (personally caused) qualities, the attribution of leadership will be weaker. Finally, if the goals of the observed person are compatible with those of the observer, there will be a stronger tendency for the attribution of leadership. Again, Hollander (1964) arrives at a similar prediction by asserting that the leader must be perceived as having a high degree of identification with the group values and goals.

The attribution theory of leadership potentially explains the psychological intraperson process of members of leaderless groups that results in the attribution of leadership to one member of the group. As described above, through the process of sociometric choice or questionnaire response, such members indicate who they believe to be the "real leader" of the group or whom they would most prefer to have as their leader.

While the theory has not been tested empirically, several of its assertions are consistent with those of Hollander's (1964) Idiosyncracy Theory of Leadership. Interestingly, the idiosyncratic propositions with which the Attribution Theory are consistent are also the propositions of Hollander's theory that have received the strongest empirical support. Further, the theory is clearly testable. If it is shown that the process described in the theory predicts the attribution of leadership, and that the attribution of leadership is associated with follower satisfaction, motivation, and performance, the theory will have made a significant contribution to the understanding of the leadership phenomena.

Operant Conditioning Theory

Scott (1977), Sims (1977), and Mawhinney and Ford (1977) have argued that behavior is predominantly determined by the contingencies of reinforcement in the environment. Thus, these authors agree that since leaders are a significant source of reward contingencies and a significant source of reward administration, leadership can best be explained in terms of the principles of operant conditioning.

According to this perspective, leadership can be regarded as a process of managing reinforcement contingencies in the work environment. Sims suggests that the supervisor can be instrumental in defining the occasion of appropriate responses such as when and how the task is to be accomplished. In the terms of reinforcement literature, the supervisor would be establishing discriminative stimuli (S^D). Sims interprets the traditional leader behavior dimension of Initiating Structure as a somewhat imprecise measure of the degree to which the leader specifies discriminative stimuli. Similarly, goal specifications by the leader specifies the "occasion for a response" of subordinates and these are therefore interpreted as discriminative stimuli. It is further argued that administration of rewards, contingent upon performance, is also necessary to specify the contingency reinforcement. Thus Initiating Structure and goal specification serve to specify "what comes before" subordinate behavior, while leader reward behavior serves to specify "what comes after" subordinate behavior.

Scott (1977) also argues for the operant perspective of leadership. Scott defines leadership as human operant behavior reinforced by its effect on the behavior of others. Scott points out that an interesting implication of his definition of leader behavior is that individuals other than those formally appointed to lead will be "leading" from time to time and that two or more individuals within a group can be simultaneously leading though possibly not the same followers, if different and incompatible follower responses are reinforcing to the several leaders. Another implication of Scott's definition of leadership is that in the typical case, the behavior of the leader, whether emergent or appointed, is under the control of certain variables in addition to the behavior of followers, whereas the behavior of followers is almost exclusively under the control of the behavior of the leader.

Mawhinney and Ford (1977) also intepret leadership within the operant paradigm. They argue that hypotheses of the Path Goal Theory of Leadership may be better explained by the principles of reinforcement and that the resulting interpretation supports the basic propositions of the Path Goal theory without supporting the validity of the motivational model on which that theory rests. These authors argue that the operant interpretation of leader effectiveness has several advantages when compared to the Path Goal theory. First, it is based on a set of empirically derived generalizations. Second, they argue that the assumption of mental activities on the part of subordinates need not be postulated to explain their behavior. Third, explanation in terms of observable behavior permits remedial action by leaders more easily. Fourth, they argue that from this paradigm conditions in formal organizations requiring leadership can be determined. Finally, they argue that using this paradigm it will be possible to predict the relative influence of leader on follower and follower on leader and thus explain reciprocal influence processes.

Stogdill (1974, Ch. 19) reviews a wide variety of evidence from the operant reinforcement literature. His review indicates that when attempts at leadership are reinforced, a higher rate of leadership acts ensue and that the leadership status of the person involved increases in the eyes of the group members. Possessing the ability to offer rewards or to reinforce the expectations of other group members constitutes an advantage toward emerging as a leader. Leadership attempts are made more frequently under high than under low probabilities of reinforcement and positive reinforcement is more effective than punishment.

In addition, Sims (1977) reviews a number of laboratory studies that demonstrate rather unequivocably that when rewards are administered contingent on performance subsequent performance is improved.

Several field studies concerning the leader's use of reward and punishment contingencies are relevant to the operant theory of leadership.

Leader reward behavior　The degree to which leaders are seen by subordinates as engaging in rewarding and punitive behavior has been investigated in five studies. This research employs a questionnaire developed by Reitz (1971) entitled "The Leader Reward Behavior Questionnaire" (LRBQ). Responses to this questionnaire indicate the degree to which the leader is likely to reward effective performance and punish ineffective performance. The questionnaire is designed to identify the degree to which leaders engage in reward and punishment contingent on performance rather than noncontingent reward and punishment behavior.

Several authors have found positive relationships between leader contingent reward behavior and satisfaction of subordinates (Reitz, 1971; Sims and Szilagyi, 1975; Keller and Szilagyi, 1976). Keller and Szilagyi also found a positive relationship between leader contingent reward behavior and subordinate expectancies that their performance will lead to valued outcomes. Leader contingent punitive behavior has also been found to be positively related to subordinate's satisfaction (Reitz, 1971; Sims and Szilagyi, 1975). Sims and Szilagyi (1975) interpret these findings to mean that when role demands are ambiguous to subordinates, leader contingent punitive behavior can serve to reduce subordinates' role ambiguity, thus increasing their satisfaction. This hypothesis warrants further testing.

Contingent reward behavior has also been found to be positively related to measures of subordinate performance (Sims and Szilagyi, 1975; Hunt and Schuler, Note 15).

Two longitudinal studies have shown that positive reward behavior causes subordinate performance (Greene, Note 16; Sims, 1977). Greene also found that the relationship between punitive reward behavior and performance was reciprocal. Punitive reward behavior caused performance and a lack of performance caused the leader to use punitive reward behavior. In this study, punitive reward behavior caused dissatisfaction among low performers.

The correlations between leader contingent reward behavior and subordinate performance generally range between .40 and .50. Sims (personal communication) has found that this correlation is highest when performance measures are taken approximately 6 months after subordinates described their leaders' reward behavior. Sims found a correlation of .51 after a 6-month interval between the two measures. He found a slight decrease after 9 months and negligible correlations between leader reward behavior and performance after 18 months.

These findings based on the LRBQ, together with the laboratory experiments reviewed by Sims (1977), make an impressive case for the argument that leaders will be more effective to the extent that they administer rewards contingent on performance rather than administer rewards noncontingently, i.e., without respect to performance level of subordinates.

While the above findings concerning the leader contingent reward and punishment are consistent with the operant paradigm, they are also consistent with Path Goal theory. Leader behavior that functions as discriminative stimuli can also be considered path-clarifying behavior. As stated above, such behavior is positively correlated with subordinates' satisfaction and their expectancies of reward for performance and negatively correlated with subordinates' experience of role ambiguity. Thus the evidence clearly suggests the importance of leader contingent reward and punishment behavior. The theoretical interpretation of this evidence is a matter of substantial controversy (Scott, 1977; Evans, Note 17) and is only likely to be resolved through continued research. The major issue in this controversy concerns the use of intervening cognitive variables such as intentions, role perceptions, or expectations. The specific question is whether or not such variables, when treated as intervening variables between leader behavior and subordinate responses, account for more variance in responses of subordinates than a more parsimonious stimulus-response relationship.

Sims specifies many research questions that emerge from the operant leadership paradigm.

First, several questions are appropriate to a closed system, considering *only* the superior/subordinate dyadic relationship:
- How does Initiating Structure and goal specification by the leader (S^D) relate to the behavior of the subordinate?
- How does behavior of the subordinate relate to subsequent Initiating Structure and goal specification (S^D) by the leader?
- How does reward administration by the leader relate to subsequent behavior by the subordinate?
  —Positive versus negative reinforcers?
  —Reinforcing rewards versus nonreinforcing rewards?
  —Externally controlled versus internally controlled rewards?
  —The interaction effect of various types of reinforcers?
  —Effect of *different* schedules of reinforcement?
  —Effect of *changing* schedules of reinforcement (e.g., "Stretching the ratio")?
- What are the interaction effects between various types of discriminative stimuli and various types of reward administration?

Once we have insight into these *basic* questions, the model can be expanded to an open systems approach that includes consideration of contingencies of reinforcement stemming from nonleader sources in the work setting. The operant paradigm would still be appropriate, and would open new perspectives and new questions to be answered. For example:

- What is the result of discriminative stimuli from the leader when adequate S^P is presented from non-leader sources?
- What is the result when discriminative stimuli from the leader contradict S_Ds from other sources?
- What is the result when discriminative stimuli *must* stem from non-leader sources, but reinforcement administration is controlled by the leader?
- What is the result when rewards administered by non-leader sources reinforce behaviors that contradict those behaviors reinforced by the leader?
- What is the result when discriminative stimuli are specified by the leader, but administration of reinforcers is controlled by non-leader sources?

Even in a closed system the fundamental question yet to be answered is this: What leader behaviors serve to define effective contingencies of reinforcement at work? This is indeed a challenging question, principally because contingencies of reinforcement in the work setting are complex structures.

Once insight has been provided into this basic question, an open systems perspective would be appropriate. That is, how do leader behaviors complement, supplement, and interact with other non-leader contingencies of reinforcement? Answers to this question will go far toward building a truly comprehensive contingency theory of leadership that is based on a functional analysis of the relevant contingencies of reinforcement (Sims, pp. 82–84).

Thus, Operant Leadership theory together with the empirical evidence concerning the leader's management of reward contingencies clearly suggest another important class of leader behavior in addition to leader Consideration, Initiating Structure, and Participating. Further, the research issues raised by Sims (1977) and Scott (1977) call for a functional analysis of leader behavior in terms of the operant paradigm are suggested for future leadership research.

Finally, Mawhinney and Ford's (1977) assertions of the relative merits of the operant paradigm over Path Goal theory deserve testing in future research.

OTHER RELEVANT RESEARCH

In addition to the studies and topics reviewed above, several studies were identified that suggest additional new directions for leadership research. Since these studies do not fit together cohesively, nor do they logically fit within any of the above topics, they are reviewed here for the readers' consideration.

Graen and his colleagues (Graen, Dansereau, and Minima, 1972; Dansereau, Cashman, and Graen, 1973; Dansereau, Graen, and Haga, 1975; Graen, Dansereau, Minami, and Cashman, 1973a; Graen, Orris, and Johnston, 1973b; Graen and Cashman, 1975; Graen, 1976; and Graen and Ginsburgh, 1977) have conducted a series of studies that suggest several important directions for future research.

One series of studies concentrated on employees who had been with the organization of a period of time. Graen et al. (1972) found that the amount of structuring by the leader (as perceived by the subordinate) moderated the correlation between the amount of consideration shown by the leader (again as perceived by the subordinate) and the leader's evaluation of the subordinate's performance. It was found that under both high and low structure there was a positive correlation between perceived consideration and performance evalution. Under moderate structure there was no correlation between these two variables.

Dansereau et al. (1973) hypothesized that the findings of the moderating effect of the structuring on the correlation between consideration and performance could be used to predict differential rates of turnover when Instrumentality and Equity theories were considered. High and low structuring leaders were assumed to be consistent in their behaviors toward particular individuals. It was also assumed that this consistency clarifies the relationship between subordinate's performance and the resulting outcomes. Finally, it was assumed that medium structure leaders do not unambiguously establish for their subordinates the contingencies between performance and outcomes. Therefore:

> . . . in the high and low structure group, if increased performance leads to increased rewards, then a lack of these rewards can be attributed in part to the individual's *own* performance level. In this situation, if the individual receives relatively unattractive outcomes, instrumentality theory predicts that he will be motivated toward leaving (perhaps moving to an organization where his same performance level will gain more attractive outcomes). In contrast, in the medium structure group a lack of rewards can not be attributed as clearly to the individual's performance level. As a result, the individual may look at the situations of his colleagues as references to help him determine if he is being treated fairly (p. 192).

Accordingly, under medium structure high performers would feel inequitably treated, since they would be contributing more than lower performers but not receiving higher rewards. Thus it was hypothesized that under medium structure high performers would leave. However, under high and low structure only low performers were hypothesized to leave. The study supported these hypotheses.

Dansereau et al., 1975, and Graen and Cashman, 1975, examined the extent to which a supervisor "is willing to consider requests from a member concerning role development" (Dansereau et al., 1975, p. 51). This willingness on the part of the leader is referred to as negotiating latitude. These studies showed that leaders very early differentiated unit members into "cadre" (with greater negotiating latitude) and "hired hands" (with less latitude). Subordinate subsequent satisfaction, turnover rates, performance, and kind and amount of superior/subordinate interaction were found to be a fucntion of the subordinate's membership in either the "cadre" or "hired hand" group.

Graen (1976) has advanced an integration of the previous studies and proposed an interpretation of the findings. Graen suggests that very early in the relationship between supervisors and subordinates the supervisor differentiates subordinates into cadre and hired hands. The basis of differentiation may be the supervisor's perception of the subordinate's incoming role orientation, i.e., the degree to which the subordinate perceives the job as contributing to a long-term career. The differentiation is necessary, because there is too much work for the supervisor to handle alone and so some of the work must be delegated to those subordinates perceived as most compatible with the leader in terms of skills, orientation, and trust. These subordinates may then become the cadre. To reward the cadre for taking on extra duties, the supervisor provides extra attention, support, and negotiating latitude to these members. Over time the hired hands come to feel rejection and respond by leaving or performing less effectively.

Support for this interpretation was presented by Graen and Ginsburgh (1977). They found that the subordinate's role orientation (the degree to which the subordinate perceives the present job relevant to a long-term career) and leader acceptance interact such that there was a decreased tendency for resignation of employees who were high on role orientation, leader acceptance, or both. Employees low on both variables had an increased tendency to resign.

These studies by Graen and his associates suggest many significant research questions.

Concerning findings on leader Initiating Structure, it is inferred that leaders who are high or low in structuring behavior more effectively communicate expectations to subordinates. Studies designed to test this inference directly would be useful. Such a study would involve determining whether subordinates of high and low structuring leaders have a clearer understanding of their leader's expectations than do subordinates of moderate structuring leaders. It is also not clear what the moderate structuring leaders do or do not do. Is it that they do not distinguish between good and bad performers? Or is it that they do not effectively communicate expectations?

The finding that subordinates are divided into cadre and hired hands has significant implications for group cohesiveness and performance.[5] When this division occurs, under what conditions does it result in a lower amount of cohesiveness among all of the people reporting to a given supervisor? Is there a higher level of cohesiveness within each of the two groups? If so, does the cohesiveness among the hired hands serve to help them in thwarting the objectives of the leader and the organization?

It is not clear what behaviors on the part of subordinates and on the part of the leaders result in the subordinates becoming members of each of these groups. Is it the behavior of the subordinates that causes the leader to be alienated from them or is it the behavior of the leader that causes the subordinates to be alienated?

It is not clear how the subordinates' role orientation is affected by the leader. Is role orientation an effect of initial leader behavior or is it a stimulus that causes leaders to treat subordinates differently?

There is not yet a clear definition of the construct of negotiating latitude. Nor is it clear whether leaders or subordinates are the best source of information for measuring this construct.

These questions raised by the research of Graen and his associates offer many fruitful areas for future research. They are especially important because they are based on one of the few systematic cumulative research efforts based on field study data. Clearly such research efforts should be extended and encouraged.

Ronan, Latham, and Kinne (1973) report a field study based on a questionnaire administered to 292 pulpwood producers. They found that goal setting is correlated with high productivity and a low number of injuries only when it is accompanied by supervision. Goal setting without immediate supervision was related to employee turnover. Supervision alone did not correlate with any performance criteria. Here supervision was measured by the number of hours the producer was on the job with his employees. This measure was in turn found to be correlated significantly with responses to questions related to giving the men instructions and explanations, providing training, using varied methods of employee payment, and having military experience; and negatively related to a response to the question "Do you have a key man in your operation?" These behaviors correlated positively with productivity and negatively with injury rate.

Supervisory behavior that was exclusively production centered, consisting of goal setting only and not related to working with the employees, correlated positively with compulsory and voluntary employee terminations. Supervisory behavior consisting of working with the men but not setting production goals and using key men did not correlate with any performance criterion. In a second study, these authors tested the hypothesis that supervision, as defined by staying on the job with men and setting a daily or weekly production goal, results in higher productivity than supervision that does not include goal setting or goal setting that is not accompanied by supervision. A questionnaire was administered to 1,000 independent producers and 892 responded. Questionnaire responses were related to the amount of cord produced per day by each producer. Based on the questionnaire responses, producers were classified according to whether they provided on-the-job supervision and engaged in goal setting. Goal setting and supervision were found to have a significant interaction effect on daily production. Thus the hypothesis was accepted.

Surprisingly, little attention has been given to supervisory goal setting in prior literature. Goal setting as a supervisory behavior has generally been included in, or implied by, questionnaire items or experimental observational categories designed to measure task-oriented leadership but not dealt with as a separate variable. The study by Ronan et al. (1973) warrants replication. If the findings continue to hold, then supervisory goal-setting behavior should be included as an explicit variable in future leadership research.

A study by Oldham (1976) also suggests several additional leader behaviors that warrant further research. Oldham developed questionnaire scales designed to measure the degree to which leaders engage in personally rewarding and personally punishing behavior contingent on performance, goal setting, designing feedback systems, placing personnel on existing jobs that challenge their skills and designing job systems that are motivational. The scales were found to have moderate independence of each other, and with the exception of the Punishment scale, were all found to be significantly related to the motivational effectiveness of middle managers as rated by store managers and assistant managers. These findings support the validity of a conceptualization of supervisory behavior consistent with present theories of motivation. Clearly the findings reported by Oldham deserve replication and extension.

A study by Stein, Geis, and Damarin (1973) suggests a methodological improvement for research concerning emergent leadership. The research by Stein et al. (1973) concerned the accuracy with which observers perceive emergent task and socioemotional leadership in small groups. One hundred and forty-nine undergraduates viewed a videotape of a group and guessed the order in which the group would rank its members on five leadership test items. Subjects were individually and collectively accurate beyond chance. Subjects' accuracy correlated .82 with the actual group members' rankings of each other. Further research using the methodology developed by Stein et al. (1973) is likely to permit a more precise identification and definition of the particular verbal and nonverbal behaviors of group members that result in leadership emergence. Earlier observation methods used in studying emergent leadership were based on a priori categories developed by the researchers. The methodology used by Stein et al. makes it possible to identify the criteria used by group members to attribute leadership to others within the group.

Finally, a methodological suggestion by Motowidlo (Note 18) deserves serious consideration. Motowidlo argues that the most commonly studied dimensions of leader behavior, mainly leader Initiating Structure, Consideration, and Participative Decision Making, may not result in increased effectiveness under certain conditions, because situational factors may cause leaders to behave in particular ways with respect to these three dimensions, thus resulting in little or no variance in behavior in these situations. Yet it is argued that there still might be wide variance in effectiveness in these situations accounted for by other dimensions of leader behavior not under the causal influence of the situational circumstance. Thus it may well be that other dimensions of leader behavior, which have not as yet been conceptualized, are related to effectiveness. Further, given that leader effectiveness is determined jointly by the leader's behavior and the situation, it is necesary to identify the leader behavior variables *in combination* with the situational variables that will account for the most variance in effectiveness. Thus Motowidlo argues that variables of leader behavior should be defined with full recognition of the situations in which they occur and variables of situations should be defined with full recognition of the leader behaviors that occurred in them. Motowidlo recommends a systematic accumulation of a large number of incidents portraying actual examples of specific leader behaviors observed in a broad range of leadership situations. Each example would include a full description of both the observed leader behavior as well as the situational context in which it occurred. The descriptions should be sufficiently complete to enable persons familiar with leadership processes in these situations to estimate reliably the degree of leader effectiveness reflected in each episode of situational leader behavior. Such situational/behavioral episodes might be gathered by "critical incident" techniques portraying highly effective and ineffective leadership. Motowidlo recommends that the episodes then be rated by another group of knowledgeable persons for level of effectiveness they reflect. The resulting descriptions of specific leader behaviors together with particular situations in which they occurred and informed esimates of the degree to which each situational leader behavior is effective could be used to conceptualize inductively combinations of behavioral and situational variables that may account for variance in estimated leader effectiveness. The conceptualizations and the specific incidents should result in speculations and hypotheses about interaction effects of behavioral situational variables, thus leading to an empirically derived and testable contingency theory of leadership. Motowidlo argues that this approach has several advantages over existing methodology.

Since it does not assume a priori leader behavior variables, it offers a means of avoiding what threatens to be an overly narrow emphasis on the three leader behavior dimensions identified through earlier main effects research . . . While research exploring situationally contingent effects on these three behavioral dimensions may indeed yield much useful information about leadership processes, there is a need for other contingency leadership research that is not confined to these particular behavioral dimensions . . . The strategy outlined here illustrates a broad approach that appears to circumvent the difficulties and promises to enrich leadership research by introducing new variables which may yield interestingly colorful explanations of leadership effectiveness (pp. 10–11).

CONCLUSION

The purpose of the present paper is to identify important empirical generalizations that have been established through replicated research and critical research issues for future investigation. While the literature review was necessarily selective, it is believed by the authors that the material covered is representative of the broad range of leadership research. It is hoped that this paper will be helpful to others in conceptualizations about leadership and in formulations of future research endeavors concerning leadership issues.

FOOTNOTES

1. The authors are indebted to Hugh J. Arnold, Martin G. Evans, Federico Leon, Jack Ito, and Barry Staw for their helpful critiques and suggestions for revision of the first draft of this paper.
2. For purposes of this discussion a group may consist of two or more people.
3. The authors are indebted to Martin G. Evans for calling to our attention the comparisons between Contingency Theory and Idiosyncratic Credit Theory and between Attribution Theory and the Idiosyncracy Theory discussed below.
4. The model analyzed in this section is that for group problems presented in Vroom and Yetton (1973, Chapter 9) and Vroom and Jago (1976).
5. This issue of cohesiveness was suggested to the authors by Martin G. Evans.

REFERENCES

1. Alverez, R. (1968) "Informal Relations to Deviants in Simulated Work Organization: A Laboratory Experiment," *American Sociological Review 33:* 895–912.
2. Bales, R. F. (1958) "Task Roles and Social Roles in Problem-solving Groups," in Eleanor E. Maccoby, T. M. Newcomb, and E. L. Hartley, *Readings in Social Psychology,* New York: Holt, Rinehart & Winston, Inc.
3. ———, and P. E. Slater (1955) "Role Differentiation in Small Decision-making Groups," in T. Parsons et al., *Family, Socialization, and Interaction Processes,* Glencoe, Ill.: The Free Press.
4. Bandura, A. (1968) "Social Learning Theory of Identificator Process," in David A. Goslin (ed.), *Handbook of Socialization Theory and Research,* Chicago: Rand McNally & Company.
5. Barrow, J. C. (1976) "Worker Performance and Task Complexity as Causal Determinants of Leader Behavior Style and Flexibility," *Journal of Applied Psychology 61,* (4) 443–440.
6. Bass, B. M. (1957) "Leadership Opinions and Related Characteristics of Salesmen and Sales Managers," in R. M. Stogdill and A. E. Coons (eds.), *Leader Behavior: Its Description and Measurement,* Columbus: Ohio State University, Bureau of Business Research.
7. ———. (1961c) "Some Aspects of Attempted, Successful, and Effective Leadership," *Journal of Applied Psychology 45:* 120–122.
8. ———. (1963) "Amount of Participation, Coalescence, and Probability of Decision Making Discussions," *Journal of Abnormal and Social Psychology 67:* 92–94.
9. ———, and C. R. Wurster (1953a) "Effects of the Nature of the Problem on LGD Performance," *Journal of Applied Psychology 35:* 96–99.
10. ———, and ———. (1953b) "Effects of Company Rank on LGD of Oil Refinery Supervisors' Performance," *Journal of Applied Psychology 37:* 100–104.
11. Baumgartel, H. (1956) "Leadership, Motivations, and Attitudes in Research Laboratories," *Journal of Social Issues 12,*2: 24–31.
12. Bennis, W. G. (1959) "Leadership Theory and Administrative Behavior: The Problems of Authority," *Administrative Science Quarterly 4:* 259–301.
13. Berkowitz, L. (1953b) "Sharing Leadership in Small, Decision-making Groups," *Journal of Abnormal and Social Psychology 48:* 231–238.
14. ———, and W. Haythorn (1955) "The Relationship of Dominance to Leadership Choice," Crew Research Laboratory, AF Personnel & Training Reserve Center, Randolf AF Base, CRL-LN-55-8.
15. Besco, R. O., and C. H. Lawshe (1959) "Foreman Leadership as Perceived by Superiors and Subordinates," *Personnel Psychology 12:* 573–582.
16. Borg, W. R. (1957) "The Behavior of Emergent and Designated Leaders in Situational Tests," *Sociometry 20:* 95–104.
17. Borgatta, E. F. (1961) "Role-playing Specifications, Personality, and Performance," *Sociometry 24,*3: 218–233.
18. ———, S. Couch, and R. F. Bales (1954) "Some Findings Relevant to the Great Man Theory of Leadership," *American Sociological Review 19:* 755–759.
19. Burke, P. J. (1967) "The Development of Task and Social-emotional Role Differentiation," *Sociometry 30:* 379–392.
20. Calder, B. J. (1977) "An Attribution Theory of Leadership," in B. Staw and G. Salancik (eds.), *New Directions in Organizational Behavior,* Chicago: St. Clair Press.
21. Calvin, A. D., F. K. Hoffmann, and E. D. Harden (1957) "The Effect of Intelligence and

Social Atmosphere on Group Problem-solving Behavior,'' *Journal of Social Psychology* 45: 61–74.

22. Cammalleri, J. R., H. W. Hendrick, W. C. Pittman, Jr., H. D. Blout, and D. C. Prather (1972) "Differential Effects of Democratic and Authoritarian Leadership Styles on Group Problem Solving and Processes," Research Report 72-1, United States Air Force Academy.

23. Campbell, D. T. (1956) "Leadership and Its Effect upon the Group," Columbus: Ohio State University, Bureau of Business Research.

24. Campion, G. E., Jr. (1968) "Effects of Managerial Style on Subordinates' Attitudes and Performance in a Simulated Organizational Setting," unpublished Doctoral Dissertation, University of Minnesota.

25. Carter, L. F. (1954) "Evaluating the Performance of Individuals as Members of Small Groups," *Personnel Psychology* 7: 477–484.

26. ———, W. Haythron, B. Shriver, and J. T. Lanzetta (1954) "The Behavior of Leaders and Other Group Members," *Journal of Abnormal and Social Psychology* 46: 589–595.

27. Cartwright, D., and A. Zander (1968) *Group Dynamics: Research and Method,* third ed., New York: Harper & Row, Publishers.

28. Cashman, J., F. Dansereau, Jr., G. Graen, and W. J. Haga (1976) "Organizational Understructure and Leadership: A Longitudinal Investigation of the Managerial Role Making Process," *Organizational Behavior and Human Performance* 15, 2: 278–296.

29. Chemers, M. M., and G. J. Skrzypek (1972) "Experimental Test of the Contingency Model of Leadership Effectiveness," *Journal of Personality and Social Psychology* 24: 172–177.

30. Coch, L., and J. R. P. French (1948) "Overcoming Resistance to Change," *Human Relations* 1: 512–532.

31. Comrey, A. L., W. S. High, and R. D. Wilson (1955a) "Factors Influencing Organizational Effectiveness. VI. A Survey of Aircraft Supervisors," *Personnel Psychology* 8: 79–99.

32. ———, ———, and ———. (1955b) "Factors Influencing Organizational Effectiveness. VII. A Survey of Aircraft Supervisors," *Personnel Psychology* 8: 245–257.

33. Crockett, W. H. (1955) "Emergent Leadership in Small, Decision-making Groups," *Journal of Abnormal and Social Psychology* 51: 378–383.

34. Crowe, B. J., S. Bochner, and A. W. Clark (1972) "The Effects of Subordinates' Behavior on Managerial Style," *Human Relations* 25: 215–237.

35. Dansereau, F., Jr., J. Cashman, and G. Graen (1973) "Instrumentality Theory and Equity Theory as Complementary Approaches in Predicting the Relationship of Leadership and Turnover among Managers," *Organizational Behavior and Human Performance* 10, 1: 184–200.

36. ———, G. Graen, and W. J. Haga (1975) "A Vertical Dyad Linkage Approach to Leadership within Formal Organizations: A Longitudinal Investigation of the Role-making Process," *Organizational Behavior and Human Performance* 13, 1: 46–78.

37. Day, R. C., and R. L. Hamblin (1964) "Some Effects of Close and Punitive Styles of Supervision," *American Journal of Sociology* 69, 5: 499–510.

38. DeCharms, R., and W. Bridgeman (1961) "Leadership Compliance and Group Behavior," Technical Report, Contract N ONR 816 (11), Washington University.

39. Delbecq, A. L. (1965) "Managerial Leadership Styles in Problem Solving Conferences," *Journal of Academy of Management* 8: 32–44.

40. Dessler, G., and E. R. Valenzi (1977) "Initiation of Structure and Subordinate Satisfac-

tion: A Path Analysis Test of Path-Goal Theory," *Academy of Management Journal* *20*, 2: 251–259.

41. Dow, T. E. (1969) "The Theory of Charisma," *Sociological Quarterly 10:* 306–318.

42. Downey, H. K., J. E. Sheridan, and J. W. Slocum, Jr. (1975) "Analysis of Relationships among Leader Behavior, Subordinate Job Performance, and Satisfaction: A Path-Goal Approach," *Academy of Management Journal 18:* 253–262.

43. Dyson, J. W., D. W. Fleitas, and F. P. Scioli (1972) "The Interaction of Leadership Personality and Decisional Environments," *Journal of Social Psychology 86:* 29–33.

44. Evan, W. M., and M. Zelditch (1961) "A Laboratory Experiment on Bureaucratic Authority," *American Sociological Review 26:* 883–893.

45. Evans, M. G. (1970) "The Effects of Supervisory Behavior on the Path-Goal Relationship," *Organizational Behavior and Human Performance 5:* 277–298.

46. Farris, G. F., and F. G. Lim (1969) "Effects of Performance on Leadership, Cohesiveness, Influence, Satisfaction, and Subsequent Performance," *Journal of Applied Psychology 53:* 490–99.

47. Fiedler, F. E. (1967) *A Theory of Leadership Effectiveness,* New York: McGraw-Hill.

48. ———. (1971) "Notes on the Methodology of the Graen, Orris, and Alvares Studies Testing the Contingency Model," *Journal of Applied Psychology 55:* 202–204.

49. ———, and Chemers, M. M. (1974) *Leadership and Effective Management,* Glencoe, Ill.: Scott, Foresman and Company.

50. ———, G. E. O'Brien, and D. R. Ilgen (1969) "The Effect of Leadership Style upon the Performance and Adjustment of Volunteer Teams Operating in a Stressful Environment," *Human Relations 22:* 503–514.

51. Filley, A. C., R. J. House, and S. Kerr (1976) *Managerial Process and Organizationsl Behavior,* Glenview, Ill.: Scott, Foresman and Company.

52. Fleishman, E. A. (1965) "Attitude versus Skill Factors in Work Group Productivity," *Personnel Psychology 18:* 253–266.

53. ———, E. F. Harris, and H. E. Burtt (1955) "Leadership and Supervision in Industry," Columbus: Ohio State University, Bureau of Educational Research.

54. French, J. R. P., J. Israel, and D. As (1960) "An Experiment on Participation in a Norwegian Factory," *Human Relations 13:* 3–19.

55. Gardner, G. (1956) "Functional Leadership and Popularity in Small Groups," *Human Relations 9:* 491–509.

56. Ghiselli, E. E. (1971) *Exploration in Managerial Talent,* Goodyear Publishing Co. Inc., Pacific Palisades, Calif.

57. Goldberg, H., and M. A. Iverson (1965) "Inconsistency in Attitude of High Status Persons and Loss of Influence: An Experimental Study," *Psychological Reports 16:* 673–683.

58. Goodacre, D. M. (1951) "The Use of a Sociometric Test as a Predictor of Combat Unit Effectiveness," *Sociometry 14:* 148–152.

59. Goodstein, L. D., and W. J. Shrader (1963) "An Empirically-derived Key for the California Psychology Inventory," *Journal of Applied Psychology 47:* 42–45.

60. Graen, G. (1976) "Role Making Processes within Complex Organizations," in M. D. Dunnette (ed.), *Handbook of Industrial and Organizational Psychology,* Chicago: Rand McNally & Company, Ch. 28.

61. ———, and J. F. Cashman (1975) "A Role-making Model of Leadership in Formal Organizations: A Developmental Approach," in J. G. Hunt and L. L. Larsn (eds.), *Leadership Frontiers,* Kent, Ohio: The Comparative Administration Research Institute, Graduate School of Business Administration, Kent State University.

63. ———, F. Dansereau, Jr., and T. Minami (1972) "Dysfunctional Leadership Styles," *Organizational Behavior and Human Performance 7,* 2: 216–236.

63. ——, ——, ——, and J. Cashman (1973a) "Leadership Behaviors as Cues to Performance Evaluation," *Academy of Management Journal 16*, 4: 611–623.
64. ——, J. B. Orris, and K. M. Alvares (1971) "Contingency Model of Leadership Effectiveness: Some Experimental Results," *Journal of Applied Psychology 55:* 196–201.
65. ——, ——, and T. W. Johnson (1973b) "Role Assimilation Processes in a Complex Organization," *Journal of Vocational Beahvior 3*, 4: 395–420.
66. ——, and S. Ginsburgh (1977) "Job Resignation as a Function of Role Orientation and Leader Acceptance: A Longitudinal Investigation of Organizational Assimilation," *Organizational Behavior and Human Performance 19:* 1–17.
67. Graham, W. K., and T. Gleno (1970) "Perception of Leader Behavior and Evaluation of Leaders across Organizational Levels," Experimental Publication System Ms. 144A, Issue 4.
68. Green, S. G., and D. M. Nebeker (1977) "The Effects of Situational Factors and Leadership Style on Leader Behavior," *Organizational Behavior and Human Performance 19:* 368–377.
69. ——, ——, and M. a. Boni (1976) "Personality and Situational Effects on Leader Behavior," *Academy of Management Journal 19*, 2: 184–194.
70. Greene, C. N...(1975) "Limitations of Cross-lagged Correlational Designs and an Alternative Approach," in J. G. Hunt and L. L. Larson (eds.), *Leadership Frontiers,* Kent, Ohio: Kent State University Press, pp. 121–126.
71. Greer, F. L., E. H. Galanter, and P. G. Nordlie (1954) "Interpersonal Knowledge and Individual and Group Effectiveness," *Journal of Abnormal and Social Psychology 49:* 411–414.
72. Guetzkow, H. (1968) "Differentiation of Roles in Task-oriented Groups," in D. Cartwright and A. Zander, *Group Dynamics,* Evanston, Ill.: Row, Peterson.
73. Gustzfson, D. P. (1968) "The Effect of Commitment to the Task on Role Differentiation in Small Unstructured Groups," *Academy of Management Journal 11:* 457–458.
74. ——, and T. W. Harrell (1970) "A Comparison of Role Differentiation in Several Situations," *Organizational Behavior and Human Performance 5:* 299–312.
75. Halpin, A. W. (1954) "The Leadership Behavior and Combat Performance of Airplane Commanders," *Journal of Abnormal and Social Psychology 49:* 19–22.
76. ——. (1957) "The Leader Behavior and Effectiveness of Aircraft Commanders," in R. M. Stogdill and A. E. Coons, *Leader Behavior: its Description and Measurement,* Columbus: Ohio State University, Bureau of Business Research.
77. ——, and B. J. Winer (1957) "A Factorial Study of the Leader Behavior Descriptions," in R. M. Stogdill and A. E. Coons, *Leader Behavior: Its Description and Measurement,* Columbus: Ohio State University, Bureau of Business Research.
78. Hamblin, R. L., K. Miller, and J. A. Wiggins (1961) "Group Morale and Competence of the Leader," *Sociometry 24:* 295–311.
79. Herold, D. M. (1977) "Two-way Influence Processes in Leader-Follower Dyads," *Academy of Management Journal 20*, 2: 224–237.
80. Hollander, E. P. (1960) "Competence and Cofnormity in the Acceptance of Influence," *Journal of Abnormal and Social Psychology 61:* 365–369.
81. ——. (1961) "Emergent Leadership and Social Influence," in L. Petrullo and B. M. Bass, *Leadership and Interpersonal Behavior,* New York: Holt, Rinehart and Winston, Inc.
82. ——. (1964) *Leaders, Groups, and Influence,* New York: Oxford University Press.
83. House, R. J. (1971) "A Path Goal Theory of Leader Effectiveness," *Administrative Science Quarterly 16:* 321–338.
84. ——. (1977) "A 1976 Theory of Charismatic Leadership," in J. G. Hunt and L. L.

Larson (eds.), *Leadership: The Cutting Edge*, Carbondale, Ill.: Southern Illinois University Press.

85. ———, and G. Dessler (1974) "The Path-Goal Theory of Leadership: Some Post Hoc and A Priori Tests," in J. G. Hunt and L. L. Larson (eds.), *Contingency Approaches To Leadership*, Carbondale, Ill.: Southern Illinois University Press.

86. ———, and T. R. Mitchell (1974) "Path-Goal Theory of Leadership," *Journal of Contemporary Business 5:* 81–94.

87. Hunt, J. G., and R. S. Schuler (1976) "Leader Reward and Sanctions Behavior Relations with Criteria in a Large Public Utility," Carbondale, Ill.: Southern Illinois University, Working Paper.

88. Jacobs, T. O. (1971) "Leadership and Exchange in Formal Organizations," Alexandria, Va.: Human Resources Research Organization.

89. Jacobson, J. M. (1953) "Analysis of Interpersonal Relations in a Formal Organization," unpublished Ph.D. Dissertation, University of Michigan.

90. Julian, J. W., E. P. Hollander, and C. R. Regula (1969) "Endorsement of the Group Spokesman as a Function of His Source of Authority, Competence, and Success," *Journal of Personality and Social Psychology 11:* 42–49.

91. Kaess, W. A., S. L. Witryol, and R. E. Nolan1961) "Reliability, Sex Differences, and Validity in the Leadership Discussion Group," *Journal of Applied Psychology 45:* 345–350.

92. Kahn, R., and D. Katz (190) "Leadership Practices in Relation to Productivity and Morale," in D. Cartwright and A. Zandza (eds.), *Group Dynamics Research Theory* New York: Harper and Row, Publishers.

93. Katz, R. (in press) "The Influence of Group Conflict on Leadership Effectivensss," *Organization Behavior and Human Performance.*

94. Keller, R. T., and A. D. Szilagyi (1976) "Employee Reactions to Leader Reward Behavior," *Academy of Management Journal, 19,* 4: 619–627.

95. Knapp, D. E., and D. Knapp (1966) "Effect of Position on Group Verbal Conditioning," *Journal of Social Psychology 69:* 95–99.

96. Korman, A. K. (1968) "The Prediction of Managerial Performance: A Review," *Personnel Psychology 21:* 295–322.

97. Korten, D. C. (1968) "Situational Determinants of Leadership Structure," in D. Cartwright, and A. Zander, *Group Dynamics: Research and Theory,* 3rd ed., New York: Harper and Row Publishers.

98. Lawrence, L. C., and P. C. Smith (1955) "Group Decision and Employee Participation," *Journal of Applied Psychology 39:* 334–337.

99. Lazarus, R. (1966) *Psychological Stress and the Coping Process,* New York: McGraw-Hill.

100. Lewin, K., R. Lippitt, and R. K. White (1939) "Patterns of Aggressive Behavior in Experimentally Created Social Climates," *Journal of Social Psychology 10:* 271–301.

101. Lieberson, S., and J. F. O'Connor (1972) "Leadership and Organizational Performance: A Study of Large Corporations," *American Sociological Review 37:* 117–130.

102. Lowin, A., and J. R. Craig (1968) "The Influence of Level of Performance on Managerial Style: An Experimental Object-Lesson in the Ambiguity of Correlation Data," *Organizational Behavior and Human Performance 3:* 440–458.

103. ———, and W. J. Hrapchak, and M. J. Kavanagh (1969) "Consideration and Initiating Structure: An Experimental Investigation of Leadership Traits," *Administrative Scientific Quarterly 14:* 238–253.

104. McCall, M. W., Jr.7)1976) "Leadership Research: Choosing Gods and Devils on the Run," *Journal of Occupational Psychology 49:* 139–153.

105. McClelland, D. C. (1961) *The Achieving Society,* Princeton, N.J.: D. Van Nostrand.

106. Maier, N. R. F. (1949) "Improving Supervision through Training," in A. Kornhauser (ed.), *Psychology of Labor-Management Relations*, Industrial Relations Association.

107. ———. (1063) *Problem Solving, Discussions and Conferences: Leadership Methods and Skills*. New York: McGraw-Hill.

108. ———. (1970) *Problem Solving and Creativity in Individuals and Groups*. Belmont, Calif.: Brooks-Cole.

109. Mann, R. D. (1959) "A Review of the Relationships between Personality and Performance in Small Groups," *Psychological Bulletin 56*, 4: 241–270.

110. Marak, G. E. (1964) "The Evolution of Leadership Structure," *Sociometry 27:* 174–182.

111. Mawhinney, T. C., and J. D. Ford (1977) "The Path Goal Theory of Leader Effectiveness: An Operant Interpretation," *The Academy of Management Review 2:* 398–411.

112. Megargee, E. I. (1969) "Influence of Sex Roles on the Manifestation of Leadership," *Journal of Applied Psychology 53:377–382*.

113. ———, P. Bogart, and B. J. Anderson (1966) "Prediction of Leadership in a Simulated Industrial Task," *Journal of Applied Psychology 50:* 292–295.

114. Meyer, M. W. (1975) "Leadership and Organizational Structure," *American Journal of Sociology 81:* 514–542.

115. Miles, R. H., and M. M. Petty (1977) "Leader Effectiveness in Small Bureaucracies," *Academy of Management Journal 20,* 2: 238–250.

116. Mitchell, T. R. (1970) "Cognitive Complexity and Leadership Style," *Journal of Personality and Social Psychology 16:* 166–173.

117. ———. (1973). "Motivation and Participation: An Integration." *Academy of Management Journal 16:* 160–79.

118. ———, C. R. Smyser, and S. E. Weed (1974) "Locus of Control: Supervision and Work Satisfaction," unpublished, Technical Report No. 74-57, University of Washington.

119. Moos, R. H. (1973) "Conceptualizations of Human Environments," *american Psychologist 28,* 8: 652–665.

120. Mulder, M., J. R. Ritsema van Eck, and R. D. de Jong (1970) "An Organization in Crisis and Non-crisis Situations," *Human Relations 24:* 19–51.

121. ———, and A. Stemerding (1963) "Threat, Attraction to Group, and Need for Strong Leadership," *Human Relations 16:* 317–334.

122. Oberg, W. (1972) "Charisma, Commitment, and Contemporary Organization Theory," *Business Topics 20:* 18–32.

123. Oldham, G. (1976) "The Motivational Strategies Used by Supervisors: Relationships to Effectiveness Indicators," *Organizational Behavior and Human Performance 15:* 66–86.

124. Palmer, G. J. (1962) "Task Ability and Successful and Effective Leadership," *Psychological Reports 11:* 813–816.

125. Pepitone, A. (1964) *Attraction and Hostility,* New York: Atherton Press.

126. Pfeffer, J. (1977) "The Ambiguity of Leadership," *Academy of Management Journal 2:* 104–112.

127. ———, and G. R. Sanancik (1975) "Determinants of Supervisory Behavior: A Role Set Analysis," *Human Relations 28,* 2: 139–153.

128. Reitz, H. J. (1971) "Managerial Attitudes and Perceived Contingencies between Performance and Organizational Response," *Academy of Management Proceedings 31st Annual Meeting.*

129. Rohde, K. J. (1951) "Dominance Composition as a Factor in the Behavior of Small Leaderless Groups," Evanston, Ill.: Northwestern University, Doctoral Dissertation.

130. Ronan, W. W., G. P. Latham, and S. B. Kinne, III. (1973) "Effects of Goal Setting and

Supervision on Worker Behavior in Industrial Situations," *Journal of Applied Psychology 58,* 3: 302–307.

131. Rotter, J. B. (1960) "Generalized Expectancies for Internal versus External Control of Reinforcement," *Psychological Monographs* 80. (1, whole No. 609).

132. Runyon, K. E. (1973) "Some Interactions between Personality Variables and Management Styles." *Journal of Applied Psychology 57:* 288–294.

133. Rush, C. H. (1957) "Leader Behavior and Group Characteristics," in R. M. Stogdill and A. E. Coons, *Leader Behavior: its Description and Measurement,* Columbus: Ohio State University, Bureau of Business Research.

134. Rychlak, J. F. (1963) "Personality Correlates of Leadership among First Level Managers," *Psychological Reports 12:* 43–52.

135. Sabath, G. (1964) "The Effect of Disruption and Individual Status on Person Perception and Group Attraction," *Journal of Social Psychology 64:* 119–130.

136. Salancik, G. R., B. J. Calder, K. M. Rowland, H. Leblebici, and M. Conway (1976) "Leadership as an Outcome of Social Structure and Process," in J. G. Hunt and L. L. Larson (eds.) *Leadership Frontiers,* The Comparative Administrative Research Institute, Kent State University.

137. ———, and J. Pfeffer (1977) "Constraints on Administrator Discretion," *Urban Affairs Quarterly 12:* 474–498.

138. Sales, S. (1972) "Authoritarianism: But as for Me, Give Me Liberty, or Give Me Maybe, a Big, Strong, Leader I Can Honor, Admire, Respect, and Obey," *Psychology Today 8:* 94–143.

139. Sample, J. A., and T. R. Wilson (1965) "Leader Behaviors, Group Productivity, and Rating of Least Preferred Co-worker," *Journal of Personality and Social Psychology 13:* 266–270.

140. Schachter, S., B. Willerman, L. Festinger, and R. Hyman (1961) "Emotional Disruption and Industrial Productivity," *Journal of Applied Psychology 45:* 201–213.

141. Schriesheim, C. S., R. J. House, and S. Kerr (1976) "Leader Initiating Structure: A Reconciliation of Discrepant Research Results and Some Empirical Tests," *Organization Behavior and Human Performance 15:* 197–321.

142. Schuler, R. S. (1973) "A Path-Goal Theory of Leadership: An Empirical Investigation," Michigan State University Doctoral Dissertation.

143. ———. (1976) "Participation with Supervisor and Subordinate Authoritarianism: A Path-Goal Theory Reconciliation," *Administrative Science Quarterly 21:* 320–325.

144. ———. (1977) "Task Design and Organizational Structure as Contingencies for Leader Initiating Structure Effectiveness: A Test of the Path-Goal Theory," unpublished Mimeo. The Ohio State University.

145. Scott, W. C. J. (1976) "Leadership: a functional analysis," in J. G. Hunt and L. L. Larson (eds.) *Leadership: The Cutting Edge,* Carbondale, Ill: Southern Illinois University Press.

146. Shaw, M. E., and J. M. Blum (1966) "Effects of Leadership Style upon Group Performance as a Fucntion of Task Structure," *Journal of Personality and Social Psychology 3:* 238–242.

147. Sheridan, J. E., H. K. Downey, and J. W. Slocum, Jr. (1975) "Testing Causal Relationships of House's Path-Goal Theory of Leadership Effectiveness," in J. G. Hunt and L. L. Larson (eds.), *Leadership Frontiers,* Kent, Ohio: Kent State Unviersity Press.

148. Sherif, M., B. J. White, and O. J. Harvey (1955) "Status in Experimentally Produced Groups," *American Journal of Sociology 60:* 370–379.

149. Shils, E. A. (1965) "Charisma, Order, and Status," *American Sociological Review 30:* 199–213.

150. Sims, H. P., Jr. (1977) "The Leader as a Manager of Reinforcement Contingencies: An Empirical Example and a Model," in J. G. Hunt and L. L. Larson (eds.), *Leadership: The Cutting Edge,* Carbondale, Ill.: Southern Illinois University Press.
151. Sims, H. P., and A. D. Szilagyi (1975) "Leader Reward Behavior and Subordinate Satisfaction and Performance," *Organizational Behavior and Human Performance 14:* 426–438.
152. Smelser, W. T. (1961) "Dominance as a Factor in Achievement and Perception in Cooperative Problem Solving Interactions," *Journal of Abnormal and Social Psychology 62:* 535–542.
153. Stein, R. T., F. L. Geis, and F. Damarin (1973) "Perception of Emergent Leadership Hierarchies in Task Groups," *Journal of Personality and Social Psychology 28,* 1: 77–87.
154. Stinson, J. E., and T. W. Johnson (1974) "The Path-Goal Theory of Leadership: A Partial Test and Suggested Refinement," proceedings of the 17th Annual Conference of the Mid-West Division of the Academy of Management, Kent, Ohio; pp. 18–36. April.
155. Stogdill, R. M. (1948) "Personal Factors Associated with Leadership: A Survey of the Literature," *Journal of Psychology 25:* 35–71.
156. ———. (1974) *Handbook of Leadership: A Survey of Theory and Research.* New York: The Free Press.
157. Szilagyi, A. D., and H. P. Sims (1947) "An Exploration of the Path-Goal Theory of Leadership in a Health Care Environment," *Academy of Management Journal 17:* 622–634.
158. Tannenbaum, A. S., and F. H. Allport (1956) "Personality Structure and Group Literature: An Interpretative Study of Their Relationships through Event-Structure Analysis," *Journal of Abnormal and Social Psychology 53:* 272–280.
159. Tomekovic, T. (1962) "Levels of Knowledge of Requirements as a Motivation Factor in the Work Situation," *Human Relations 15:* 197–216.
160. Torrance, E. P. (1954) "The Behavior of Small Groups under Stress Conditions of Survival," *American Sociological Review 19:* 751–755.
161. Tosi, H. (1970) "A Reexamination of Personality as a Determinant of the Effects of Participation," *Personnel Psychology 23:*191–99.
162. Uleman, J. S. (1972) "The Need for Influence: Development and Validation of a Measure and Comparison with the Need for Power," *Genetic Psychology Monographs 85:* 157–214.
163. Vecchio, R. P. (1977) "An Empirical Examination of the Validity of Fiedler's Model of Leadership Effectiveness," *Organizational Behavior and Human Performance 19:* 180–206.
164. Verba, S. (1961) *Small Groups and Political Behavior: A Study of Leadership,* Princeton, N.J.: Princeton University Press.
165. Vroom, V. H. (1959) "Some Personality Determinants of the Effects of Participation," *Journal of Abnormal and Social Psychology 59:* 322–327.
166. ———. (1976) "Can Leaders Learn to Lead?" *Organizational Dynamics* 17–28.
167. ———, B. D. Grant, and T. S. Cotton (1969) "The Consequences of Social Interaction in Group Problem Solving," *Organizational Behavior and Human Performance 4:* 477–95.
168. ———, and E. W. Yetton (1973) *Leadership and Decision Making,* Pittsburgh: University of Pittsburgh Press.
169. Weber, M. (1947) *the Theory of Social and Economic Organization,* New York: Oxford University Press.
170. Weiss, H. M. (1977) "Subordinate Imitation of Supervisor Behavior: The Role of

Modeling in Organizational Socialization," *Organizational Behavior and Human Performance 19:* 89–105.
171. Wexley, K. N., J. P. Singh, and G. A. Yukl (1973) "Subordinate Personality as a Moderator of the Effects of Participation in Three Types of Appraisal Interviews," *Journal of Applied Psychology 58:* 54–59.
172. Wiggins, J., F. Dill, and R. D. Schwartz (1965) "On Status Liability," *Sociometry 28:* 197–209.
173. Wofford, J. C. (1970) "Factor Analysis of Managerial Behavior Variables," *Journal of Applied Psychology 54:* 169–173.
174. Yukl, G. (1971) "Toward a Behavioral Theory of Leadership," *Organization Behavior and Human Performance 6:* 411–440.
175. Zedp, S. M. (1969) "Intragroup Reinforcement and Its Effects on Leadership Behavior," *Organizational Behavior and Human Performance 4:* 284–298.
176. ———, and W. F. Oakes (1967) "Reinforcement of Leadership Behavior in Group Discussion," *Journal of Experimental Social Psychology 3:* 310–320.
177. Ziller, R. C. (1955) "Leaders Acceptance of Responsibility for Group Action under Conditions of Uncertainty and Risk," *American Psychologist 10:* 475–476.

REFERENCES NOTES

1. Berkowitz, L., and W. Haythorn (1955) "The Relationship of Dominance to Leadership Choice," unpublished Report CRL-LN-55-8, Crew Research Laboratory, AF Personnel & Training Reserve Centre, Randolf AF Base.
2. Fleishman, E. A. (1972) *Manual for the Supervisory Behavior Description Questionnaire,* Washington, D.C.: American Institutes for Research.
3. Halpin, A. W. (1959) *Manual for the Leader Behavior Description Questionnaire,* Columbus: Bureau of Business Research, Ohio State University.
4. Stogdill, R. M. (1973) *Manual for the Leader Behavior Description Questionnaire—Form XII,* Columbus: Bureau of Busienss Research, Ohio State University.
5. Weed, S. E., T. R. Mitchell, and C. R. Smyser (1974) "A Test of House's Path Goal Theory of Leadership in an Organizational Setting," paper presented at the Western Psychological Association Meeting.
6. Cammalleri, J. R., H. W. Hendrick, W. C. Pittman, Jr., H. D. Blout, and D. C. Prather (1972) "Differential Effects of Democratic and Authoritarian Leadership Styles on Group Problem Solving and Processes," unpublished Research Report 72-1, United States Air Force Academy.
7. House, R. J. (1974) "Notes on the Path Goal Theory of Leadership," unpublished Manuscript. University of Toronto.
8. Hemphill, J. K. (1950) *Leader Behavior Description,* Columbus: Personnel Research Ohio State University.
9. Hollander, E. P., J. W. Julian, and F. A. Perry (1960) "Leader Style, Competence and Source of Authority as Determinants of Actual and Perceived Influence," unpublished Technical Report (No. 5), State University of New York at Buffalo.
10. Julian, J. W., and E. P. Hollander (1966) "A Study of Some Role Dimensions of Leader-Follower Relations," unpublished Technical Report, State University of New York at Buffalo.
11. Schmidt, D. E. (1976) "The Least Preferred Coworker (LPC) Measure: A Review and Reinterpretation of the Research," unpublished Manuscript. (Available from Donald E. Schmidt, Department of Psychology, University of Washington, Seattle, Washington, 98195).

12. Schuler, R. S. (1977) "Task Design and Organizational Structure as Contingencies for Leading Initiating Structure Effectiveness: A Test for the Path Goal Theory," unpublished Manuscript.

13. Kerr, S. (1976) "Substitutes for Leadership," unpublished Manuscript, Ohio State University.

14. Vroom, V. H., and A. G. Jago (1976) "On the Validity of the Vroom-Yetton Model," unpublished Manuscript.

15. Field, G. (1977) "Analysis of the Vroom and Yetton Leadership and Decision Making Model," unpublished Manuscript, University of Toronto.

16. Hunt, J. G., and R. S. Schuler (1976) "Leader Reward and Sanctions Behavior Relations with Criteria in a Large Public Utility," unpublished Working Paper, Southern Illinois University.

17. Greene, C. N. (1976) "A Longitudinal Investigation of Performance Reinforcing Behavior and Subordinate Satisfaction and Performance," paper presented at Midwest Academy of Management Meetings.

18. Evans, M. J. (1977) "Point and Counterpoint in OB," paper presented at Academy of Management Meeting.

19. Motowidlo, S. J. (1976) "Needed: New Variables for the Contingency Paradigm of Leadership Effectiveness," paper presented at Canadian Psychological Association, Toront, (June).

CHARISMA AND ITS ROUTINIZATION IN TWO SOCIAL MOVEMENT ORGANIZATIONS

Harrison M. Trice and Janice M. Beyer

ABSTRACT

This paper integrates concepts of charismatic leadership and its routinization, offering an enumerative definition of both, combined with a review of the few relevant empirical studies. It reports participant observation data, collected recently and over a 20 year period, on two charismatic leaders, one whose leadership was routinized and one whose was not. Reasons for the pronounced differences in routinization—even though their charisma was similar—come from the field data. Where charisma was routinized (1) an administrative apparatus, apart from the charismatic, had developed for putting his mission into practice; (2) rites and ceremonials had acted to transfer and transform the charisma to others in the organization; (3) his message and mission became incorporated into written and oral tradition; (4) the organization selected a successor that served as a "reincarnation" of the charismatic; and (5) it continued to cohere around the charismatic's mission. These factors were largely absent relative to the second charismatic. Reasons for these contrasts were different missions, different reasons for belonging to the organization, different demands for resources, and the different sex of the two founders.

Although the term *charisma* occurs frequently in social conversation, and increasingly in journalistic accounts of business and other organizations, the organizational literature offers little concrete knowledge or even discussion of this phenomenon. Empirical studies of charisma are sparse, and there is little agreement among them on conceptual and operational definitions. There are several compelling reasons why this relative neglect and the resulting confusion about this phenomenon should be remedied, especially through empirical studies of charisma in organizations.

First, in many sectors of U.S. business, and in other organizations as well, the need for organizational change is generally recognized and grows more pressing every day. To inform efforts directed at change, organizational scholars need to explore all possible levers that can help to produce needed change. The literature on the topic suggests that charisma can be a powerful force for change. Inexplicably, in drawing upon the seminal work of Max Weber (1947), organizational researchers have focused primarily on his analyses of bureaucracy and overlooked his central and pervasive concern with social and organizational change. But Weber balanced his analyses of social forms that maintain social order—the rational–legal and traditional systems of authority—with analyses of charismatic leadership as a prominent impetus for social change (Shils, 1965b).

Second, when the concept of charisma has been introduced into organizational theory—largely by sociologists (Bacharach & Lawler, 1980; Blau & Scott, 1962; Scott, 1981; Zald & Ash, 1966)—it has been treated as an isolated phenomenon and left relatively unexplored. Exceptions are Etzioni (1961), who incorporated charisma as a notable part of a more general theory, and House (1977) and Friedland (1964), who have advanced organizational theories of charisma. This benign theoretical neglect is reflected in a paucity of empirical research. A careful search of the social science literature revealed 19 empirical efforts that dealt with charisma, only 11 in organizational settings (see Table 1). Until recently, these efforts have been scattered and not cumulative; House's relatively recent (1977) theory has stimulated 2 empirical studies. Only 8 of these studies have included any analysis of routinization—the processes by which the social changes introduced by the charismatic leader are institutionalized and projected into the future. Only about half of these are more than a brief discussion. A greater volume of empirical work would probably stimulate more thorough theoretical analysis, and vice versa.

Third, the existing evidence and everyday observations suggest that charisma occurs in all arenas of social life, including complex organizations (Blau & Scott, 1962), and has important consequences. Thus, it is not so rare or so inconsequential as to be irrelevant to organizational theory. Perhaps the most widely recognized modern charismatic leaders, people like Gandhi and Martin Luther King, have been founders of social movement organizations (SMOs) that promulgated and tried to bring about radical, large-scale change. But charismatics also have played important roles in other types of organizations—founding colleges, political parties, unions, and business organizations. Analyses of such instances document how charismatic leaders emerged from the general social milieu outside existing organizations to found and lead new organizations that embodied their visions and values. But charismatic leadership can emerge also in organizational offices (Etzioni, 1961; Miller, 1966; Shils, 1965a) that are "located at the center of the institutional fabric, [creating] a power of 'radicalization' from within rather than a challenge from without" (Berger, 1963, p. 949). Lee Iacocca of Ford and Chrysler (Holusha, 1983; Mitroff, Kilmann, & Saxton, 1983) is a current prominent example of a charismatic leader who has reoriented and revitalized an existing organization.

Fourth, charisma should be studied because it represents one facet of the expressive, nonrational side of organizational behavior. By creating new sets of meanings and beliefs for their followers, charismatic leaders—in effect—create new cultures (Pettigrew, 1979). Thus, the study of charisma should be an integral part of the recent rediscovery of the importance of culture in organizations (Trice, 1985).

This paper is intended to contribute both theoretically and empirically to the literature on charisma. We first provide a more systematic and comprehensive definition and review of the existing literature on charisma than is available elsewhere. At the end of that review, we focus on how charisma produces lasting effects on organizations. Because charisma is inherently unstable (Blau & Scott, 1962), it must be transformed into institutional patterns for managing the routine in order to achieve organizational permanence and stability. Weber called this process the *routinization of charisma* (Gerth & Mills, 1946). We review past work on routinization and develop five criteria for assessing routinization processes empirically. We then use data obtained from participant observations over a 20-year period and from various other sources to compare the routinization of charisma of the founders of two social movement organizations.

The overall purposes of the paper can be summarized as follows: (1) to review and discuss the literature on charisma with particular attention to any empirical findings, (2) to review and discuss the literature on the routinization of charisma in order to develop useful empirical indicators, (3) to describe in organizational terms two cases in which routinization occurred more and less successfully, (4) to identify and discuss factors in each case that may help to account for why charisma was routinized successfully in one case but not the other, (5) to draw lessons from these cases for other types of organizations.

Table 1. Empirical Studies Dealing with Charisma

Author	Focus	Setting	Approximate Time Period
Cantril (1941)	Contextual factors giving rise to Hitler and Nazi party	German society	Post World War I–1930s
Constas (1961)	Emergence of Lenin as political leader and routinization of his charisma	Bolshevik Revolution in Russia	1910s–1930s
Drachkovitch (1964)	Political crisis that led to emergence of Tito	Yugoslav society	Late—1940s
Friedland (1964)	Founding of labor unions and supporting social context	*Labor unions in Tanganyika	Late 1950s–1960s
Miller (1966)	Problems of succession and routinization of charismatic leadership	Chippewa Indian tribe in Minnesota	1900–1950
Kanter (1968, 1972)	Commitment of members to utopian communities	*30 utopian communities in U.S.	1780s–1960s
Carden (1969)	Founding and history of the Oneida community	*Utopian community in upstate New York	1850–1970
Clark (1970, 1972)	Radical change and its institutionalization	*Three U.S. colleges	Early 1900s–1970s
Dubofsky & Van Tine (1977)	Radicalization of the American Federation of Labor (AFL) and the founding of the Congress of Industrial Organizations (CIO)	*U.S. labor unions	1930s–1960s
Geertz (1977)	Central location of charisma in social order	Royalty in England, Java, and Morocco	1200s–1890s

88

Salaman (1977)	Case study of problems inherent in moving from personal, charismatic authority to organizational leadership during planned change	*Medium-size manufacturing company in English Midlands	1960s–1970s
Day (1980)	Charismatic reformer in a small organization	*Maternity home in U.S.	1960s–1970s
Smith (1982)	Developing measures to discriminate charismatic from noncharismatic leaders	*U.S. work organizations in business, industry, and government	Late 1970s–1980s
Yukl & Van Fleet (1982)	Elective patterns of leadership (including inspirational leadership)	*U.S. Air Force units in combat and noncombat situations	1950s–1970s
Madsen & Snow (1983)	Social and psychological factors associated with the routinization of the charisma of Juan Peron in Argentine	Argentine society	1955–1965
Schwartz (1983)	Heroic, but uncharismatic, leadership of George Washington	Emergence of U.S. Revolutionary Army and federal government	Colonial period, 1774–1803
Van de Ven et al. (1983)	Case study of failed attempt to guide succession of a charismatic leader	*Black capitalist movement in U.S.	1960s–1970s
Bradley (1984)	Charisma and social structure, including power and communion	57 urban communes	1974–1975
Roberts (1984)	Case study of superintendent's role in a turbulent change	*Suburban public school system	1983

Note:
* Organizational settings, broadly defined

89

THE CONCEPT OF CHARISMA

Because all other writers on charisma use Weber's work as a reference point, we will begin with a fairly thorough review of his use of this concept. To gain an overall perspective on his conception of charisma, it is necessary to begin with his more inclusive conceptions of the origins of authority (Weber, 1947). Briefly stated, he argued that authority emerges when a common value system legitimates its use. When members of a collectivity come to share beliefs that it is right, or somehow is in their best interest, to suspend their own judgments and obey voluntarily, a common value system has emerged to provide a basis for authority. Authority could then take three ideal-typical forms. First, it could be traditional authority, obeyed because the present social order is seen as sacred and not to be violated. Second, it could be charismatic authority, obeyed because of faith in a leader believed to be endowed with exceptional qualities. Third, it could be legal–rational authority, obeyed because of beliefs in the inviolability of formal norms—in the government of laws, not of men.

Weber saw interrelationships between all three forms of authority. These interrelationships are important in the context of this paper because it focuses on those social processes that make it possible for charismatic authority to continue over time. Because charisma is attached to particular persons, its manifestation is inherently unstable, and it will dissipate over time unless forces that can bring about its routinization become attached to it. In effect, unless charismatic authority is either embodied in traditional authority or becomes routinized within a framework of rational–legal authority, it is destined to disappear as a briefly influential historical oddity. In this paper, traditional authority will not be considered as an outcome of charisma, because in recent times the major outcomes of charismatic leadership have involved its routinization into rational–legal authority of some type.[1]

But before we can look at routinization processes intelligently, we must consider what charisma is. The concept has been defined a number of different ways by well-respected scholars. Without first deciding what charisma is and what it is not, we cannot trace its transformation into something else.

An Enumerative Definition Based on Weber

Weber's conception of charisma includes five components: (1) an "extraordinarily gifted" person (1947, p. 358), (2) a social crisis or situation of desperation, (3) a set of ideas providing a radical solution to the crisis, (4) a set of followers who are attracted to the exceptional person and come to believe that he or she is directly linked to transcendent powers, (5) the validation of that person's extraordinary gifts and transcendence by repeated successes. Weber himself did not provide such a concise enumerative definition; we have extracted these five components from a variety of his writings (Weber, 1947) and those of his analysts (Eisenstadt, 1968; Gerth & Mills, 1946; Shils, 1965a, 1965b). As in his discussion of bureaucracy, Weber described *charisma* as an ideal type (Weber, 1949) that includes several elements that can be extracted from empirical observations, counted, and summarized in various ways.[2]

For Weber, charisma emerges when supernatural, superhuman, or exceptional powers are attributed to an individual because of the unusual—almost magical—transcendental qualities some people see in that individual. Followers experience a magnetism and a power of attraction that goes beyond their usual experience and knowledge. Also going beyond their experience and knowledge is the charismatic's mission. This exceptional person espouses radical innovations that challenge established practices and generate excitement and a vision for what the future should be. In direct contrast to the usual, recurrent practices that maintained the order of the social system, the charismatic mission is "explosively novel" (Shils, 1965, p. 199) and radical. It gains acceptance because it is directly aimed at, relevant to, and meaningful for collective definitions of distress, trouble, and agitation arising from perceptions of emergency or crisis. Charismatics and their missions tend to be seen by followers as providing solutions for these out-of-the-ordinary troubles, and also as being possessed by or acting as an agent for miraculous transcendental forces.

Personal Qualities of Charismatics

In popular usage, the term *charisma* usually refers to some individuals' persuasiveness and magnetism; charisma is treated as a property of the person who has it. Popular conceptions of charisma thus resemble trait theories of leadership. This component of charisma also provides a common thread that runs through all of the scientific treatments of charisma. However, as already indicated, Weber's use of the term incorporated much more than the extraordinary gifts of the charismatic person. "In actuality, the 'gift' is likely to be a complex interaction" of several factors (House, 1977, p. 193), which we have already enumerated. Each of these factors receives varying degrees of emphasis in the empirical studies and theoretical discussions of charisma, but there is no disagreement that exceptional personal qualities are one defining characteristic of charisma.

Which personal qualities are charismatic? A central issue for the study of charisma is thus to decide which personal qualities are charismatic and which are not. But what criteria are available to sort out the charismatic from the non-charismatic qualities? One way is to rely on the extant the-oretical literature, especially the original formulations of Weber. This is largely the approach we have taken. Another is to look for charismatic effects—presumably radical social changes associated with certain lead-ers—and to retrospectively infer what personal qualities of the leaders helped to produce those effects. This empirical approach presents obvious tautological pitfalls, but it may nevertheless help to inform theory and conceptualization. A third approach is to infer the qualities of charismatics from what people, in general, have observed in leaders they think are charismatic. The primary difficulties with this last approach are (1) even if provided with a sound definition, people's assessments of who is char-ismatic are likely to differ; (2) it is not clear that charismatic leaders are so prevalent that most people have observed any, except from a distance; (3) given the first two difficulties, the qualities derived are likely to reflect something more mundane and everyday than Weber intended with his conception of charisma.

House (1977, p. 193) derived the following three characteristics from both the literature and his students' reports of charismatic leaders they have known: "extremely high levels of self-confidence, dominance, and a strong conviction in the moral righteousness of his/her beliefs." He also hypothesized that charismatic leaders have "a high need to have influence over others" (House, 1977, p. 194). Considering leader behaviors, House (1977, pp. 194–203) found hints in the existing sociological and political science literatures of five sets of behaviors that distinguish charismatic leadership: (1) effective role modeling; (2) behaviors creating impressions of competence and success; (3) articulation of ideological goals; (4) com-munication of high expectations plus confidence in followers; and (5) mo-tive-arousing behaviors. The list clearly includes more than behaviors; certain effects on subordinates are specified.

One empirical study using House's theory has appeared in the literature. Smith (1982) tested "a fundamental formulation of House's theory; that charismatic leaders can be differentiated based on scaled subordinate re-sponses" (p. iv) reflecting expected charismatic effects upon them. Eigh-teen constructs and 38 individual scales were developed on the basis of the theory and initial field research to measure subordinate reactions to leaders. The scales were then used to try to discriminate persons nominated as charismatic from those nominated as equally effective but noncharis-matic leaders by a different group of respondents. Results were somewhat disappointing; only one of the seven variables that best discriminated the "charismatic" from other leaders—leader dynamism—seems descriptive of exceptional personal qualities. Two others—self-assurance of subor-dinates and self-disclosure to leaders—might be effects of charisma, but also could clearly be effects of something less—perhaps a likeable, trust-worthy leader. The remaining variables (work week length, performance ratings of subordinates, and felt back-up for self) could be relevant to any theory or study of leadership. Overall, the Smith study does not appear to differ in any very substantial ways from other studies of leadership style.

Another group of studies have some similarity to House's general ap-proach. In four studies of the effectiveness of military leaders, Yukl and Van Fleet (1982) included a measure of leader behaviors they called *in-spiration,* defined as "the extent to which a leader stimulates enthusiasm among subordinates for the work of the group and says things to build their confidence in their ability to successfully perform assignments and attain group objectives" (1982, p.90). They found that inspiration was related to leader effectiveness in all four studies, which included both combat and noncombat situations. The consistency of these results was especially impressive because all four studies used somewhat different measures in different situations, thus reducing the likelihood that the results obtained were produced spuriously by uncontrolled variables. However, their variable of inspiration seems but another dimension of leader style, and a rather pale version of what Weber had in mind. To be fair, they did not claim to test Weber; we are making the connection in an attempt to be as inclusive as possible in looking at a concept that has received scant empirical attention.

Curiously, these psychological studies are an empirical realization of the much earlier arguments of Friedrich (1961), a political scientist who criticized Weber, arguing that his types of authority, including charisma, should be discarded because they confuse what Friedrich calls *rulership* and *leadership,* generalize a religious concept to secular situations, and thus lump together different types of behavior as charisma. He particularly objected to the fact that Weber's conceptions could lead to considering two such different men as Martin Luther and Hitler as charismatic. Arguing for more careful distinctions, Friedrich defined power as both a possession and a relation. When the first type of power is dominant, he called it rulership, which, he argued, tends to be coercive. When the relational side of power is dominant, he called it leadership, which, he argued, tends to be consensual. In short, he advanced something very like the demo-cratic–autocratic dichotomy current at about the same time in psycho-logical discussions of leadership style. His most relevant and interesting contribution to the current debate over charisma is his insistence that true charisma is just one form of inspirational leadership—one that rests on the charismatic being "called" by a divine being (1961, p. 22). Thus, he argued, "charismatic leadership is of minor importance, simply because the faith in a transcendent being is not sufficiently strong or general to provide an adequate basis for legitimizing any political leadership." (1961, p. 23). The flowering of various religious cults during the 1970s in the United States and the current political clout of evangelical religions shows how mistaken such generalizations can be for even the near future.

Another normative theory was advanced by Berlew (1979), who argued that just as leadership theory has advanced beyond the custodial mode that engenders anger and resentment to the managerial mode that engenders satisfaction, it should now move to a charismatic mode that engenders excitement. He discussed three ingredients of charismatic leadership: developing a common vision, creating value-related opportunities and activities that can become sources of meaning to members, and making other members feel stronger. The focal needs or values he identified for this mode of leadership are meaningful work, self-reliance, community, excellence, service, and social responsibility (1979, p. 346). It is not clear how he derived these ingredients or values from others' concepts of charisma or from empirical data, except that he implied that many younger organizations in this society incorporate such values (1979, p. 348). Again, Berlew's ideas are really about leadership style, and although they somewhat resemble the basic Weberian conception of charisma, his new conception seems rather incomplete and pale in comparison to the original.

Similarly, although Salaman (1977) labeled a leader he observed as being charismatic, the connection with Weber's definition or any other accepted definition is far from clear. He apparently equates any sort of "highly personal authority" (1977, p. 376)—in this case, an autocratic style—with charisma (1977, p. 374). His article is more valuable for its analysis of routinization, which will be addressed later in this paper.

Sociologists have tended to follow Weber more closely, but several have modified or extended his conception of charisma. Shils (1965a), in his article on charisma in the *International Encyclopedia of the Social Sciences,* argued that charisma is a property not only of persons, but also of institutions, roles, norms, or symbols that "are perceived or believed to be connected or infused with . . . transcendent powers" (p. 386). According to his analysis, persons who "possess an intense subjective feeling of their own charismatic quality, and who have it imputed to them by others . . . [are] charismatic persons" (p. 386). But why should people impute charisma to themselves or to certain other persons and not to others? According to his argument, both charismatic leaders and their followers are more aware of and experience their charisma more than the general population. His definition of charisma thus emphasized that charisma is a product of self and follower attributions.

Shils also emphasized that charismatic leaders derive their authority from personal contact with what is most vital, most powerful, and most authoritative in the universe or in society. They simultaneously can be creators of a new order and breakers of the routine order. The new order is discovered through "inspiration from transcendent powers," (1965a, p. 387) and stands in contrast to routine, uninspired actions, which are linked more closely to practical and immediate demands than to a concern with transcendent matters. Shils's conception of charisma is more circumscribed than Weber's. His emphasis on transcendence and his generalizing charisma to be a property of groups, institutions, and even inanimate objects effectively limits its manifestation to leaders of religious or other moral movements.

Kanter (1968, p. 514) used a similar conception of charisma in her study of utopian communities, in which she emphasized the diffusion of charisma throughout the community into something she called "institutionalized awe" (1972, p. 116). She viewed charisma as more a potential than a property or set of traits possessed by some leaders; only when these leaders were invested with awe-inspiring qualities by their followers did they become charismatic.

In the same vein, Etzioni defined charisma as "the ability of an actor to exercise diffuse and intense influence over the *normative* orientations of other actors" (1961, p. 203). According to his definition, influence over specific matters—such as most managers exercise—is not charisma. Charisma involves a much more diffuse kind of influence—one that is more characteristic of political and religious leaders than of men of practical affairs. Etzioni also distinguished between what he called *personal charisma* and *office charisma*. Because the latter is obtained automatically by virtue of moving into a certain office, office charisma is an ascribed status. All popes of the Roman Catholic Church have what he means by office charisma. But personal charisma is an achieved status; usually it must be achieved again and again by the charismatic redemonstrating his or her power. Some persons have both personal and office charisma; the current Pope Paul is a good example.

Which personal qualities are not charismatic?   Another stream of research has helped to clarify the personal qualities that are part of charisma by observing and analyzing its antithesis. By being explicit about what is *not* charisma, a more trenchant definition is possible. The best example of this approach is provided by Schwartz's recent analysis (1983, p. 30) of the leadership style of George Washington as a "polar" opposite to Weber's ideal–typical charismatic. Washington's leadership and career was directly opposite to Weber's conception of charisma in several ways: Washington showed little, if any, confidence in his ability to lead the colonial forces in their rebellion against England. There is good evidence that he actually sought to avoid leadership even though subsequently appointed to it. In addition, Schwartz observed, Washington displayed few, if any, extraordinary talents, or the superhuman or supernatural qualities usually associated with charisma, nor did he accomplish any unusual military or political triumphs of personal heroism or magnetism. Weber's ideal-type charismatic leaders used their unusual talents to perform near-miraculous undertakings and to put forward innovative beliefs in the form of an explicit mission; Washington did none of these. Also, rather than eschewing bureaucracies, as a charismatic would, Washington held formal positions in military and governmental bureaucracies where he used "universalistic" standards (Schwartz, 1983, p. 31). In contrast, charismatic leaders use their authority in "particularistic" ways, expressing personal and mission-oriented biases and interests. Finally, Washington played a direct role in the creation of bureaucratic forms. Typically, charismatics remain aloof from the processes of institutionalization.

Despite his lack of charismatic qualities, considerable evidence shows that Washington was "virtually deified" by his generation (Schwartz, 1983, p. 21). Schwartz explains this veneration by suggesting that Washington was a collective representation of "the values and tendencies of his society rather than a *source* of these values and tendencies" (1983, p. 30). Also, of course, the American Revolution was not really a time of social crisis in the sense that radical changes in social values or the prevailing social order were seen as necessary to deal with severe problems internal to American society. Changes in the political system were seen as necessary largely because of the loss of previously enjoyed freedoms. Most analysts see the ensuing American government as providing substantial continuity for political, economic, and social structures and practices firmly rooted in the English tradition (Padover, 1955). Schwartz concluded that "the republican leader and the charismatic leader represent two polar forms of heroic leadership" (1983, p. 30). This analysis is valuable for reminding us that the charismatic is not a leader who is the symbolic embodiment of *prevailing* ideologies.

Other scholars have identified other types of heroic or inspirational leadership that are not charismatic. Zaleznik and Kets de Vries (1975, p. 232) contrasted the "consensus leader" with the charismatic leader. The consensus leader negotiates among diverse interest groups and, through bargains, trade-offs, and the use of rewards, incorporates as many as possible into decision making. By contrast, the charismatic leader "is simply followed [because] he is their leader" (1975, p. 241). Other noncharismatic examples of heroic leadership arise in situations in which personal heroism is an inherent characteristic of the collectivity. Dornbusch (1955) concluded from his study of the Coast Guard Military Academy that "there is a complete absence of charismatic veneration of heroes of the past and present. Stirring events are recalled, not as examples of the genius of a particular leader, but as part of the history of the great organization which they will serve" (p. 319).

Social Context of Crisis

Gerth and Mills (1946, p. 62) argued that Weber believed that charisma required not only exceptional individual qualities—which he called the "gift of grace"—but that the gift had to be relevant to the crises and agitations present in the social context from which the charismatic person emerged.

Later sociologists disagreed on the extent to which charisma is a product of the social situation within which the charismatic figure operates. Three empirical studies concluded that context is the primary determinant of charisma; none specified situations of acute crisis as part of the context. On the basis of his observations of the founding of several labor unions in Tanganyika, Freidland (1964) concluded: "In any social situation, there can be found incipient charismatics. Before incipient charismatics can emerge as genuine, the social situation must exist within which their message is relevant and meaningful to people" (p. 25). It follows that charismatic qualities may occur in many social situations but go unheeded.

From his study of communes in urban centers, Bradley (1984) concluded that the emergence of charisma results from organizational context and structure rather than from the personal qualities of an individual. He defined charisma as a structural phenomenon, arguing that structural features such as intense communal bonds are more determinative of charisma than are followers' beliefs that an individual leader initially possesses unusual qualities.

> For Weber, charismatic beliefs are a prerequisite for charismatically based social change. Without the existence of beliefs acknowledging the continued possession of charisma by a leader, there is no longer a basis for charismatic rule . . . [and] the possibility of radical social change that it enables, ceases to exist. (1984, p. 245)

In contradiction to Weber, Bradley concludes that "the causal priority lies at the structural level, and that charismatic beliefs are not needed to account for social change under charismatic conditions." In effect, Bradley argues that certain structural features such as intense cohesiveness cause groups to endow certain individuals with exceptional qualities.

In her field study of a school superintendent, Roberts (1984) observed that contrary to Weber's description, "charisma co-existed with a rational bureaucratic authority structure in a large school system in the throes of turbulent change" (p. 34). From her observations she argued that "more than just an exceptional individual is required to create a charismatic effect. Recognition of a charismatic may be the consequence of a complex set of factors that depend more on a context and structure than they do on the personal qualities of an individual" (1984, p. 35).

In substantial disagreement, Dow (1969) interpreted Weber as showing the "relative independence [from the context] of both the exceptional [charismatic] individual and his ideas," and went on to point out that social disorders "have not uniformly produced a revolutionary departure, a transcendent ideal, and have as often resulted in noncharismatic as charismatic solutions" (p. 309). He argued that Friedland had given too little recognition to the truly exceptional nature of charisma, the relative autonomy of the charismatic, and the fact that "revolutionary change . . . is always—in rational terms—an improbable course of action, which is pursued because of the followers' faith in the 'supernatural, superhuman, or exceptional' qualities of the leader" (1969, p. 309).

There is some merit in both sides of this agrument. Friedland correctly pointed to the fact that charismatic qualities may be distributed more generally than is commonly recognized; Dow was correct in underscoring Weber's insistence on the exceptional and transcendental qualities of the charismatic individual. Thus, times of crisis, distress, and agitation will not necessarily spawn charisma; nor is it realistic to argue that charismatics, no matter how potent their endowments, can generate relevancy and cogency for their mission without some fit with the social situation. When the two coincide, the likelihood that genuine charisma will emerge will increase. *On the other hand, to argue that charisma is primarily a structural variable is, in effect, to define away the concept and to deny the phenomenon Weber was seeking to explain.* If certain structural situations produce radical change without the presence of exceptionally endowed leaders, why call these instances of charisma?

Clark's study of three distinctive liberal arts colleges provides examples of different levels of crisis and exceptional personal qualities triggering organizational changes. In the 1910s, Antioch College was in a "crisis of decay" (1972, p. 180). A sense of failure pervaded the organization and there was a general consensus that incremental changes were insufficient. In 1919, a "charismatic utopian reformer" took over as president and instituted a radical program that "overturned everything" (Clark, 1972, p. 180). Antioch appears to be a clear-cut example of context and charismatic leader coming together to produce lasting and radical change. At another college, Swarthmore, the situation was less clear. Although "ready for evolutionary change" (1972, p. 181), there was no crisis in 1920 when Swarthmore's new president displayed such personal magnetism, enthusiasm, and flair that he stimulated processes that eventuated in profound change in that college—although more gradually than at Antioch. The third leader, who founded Reed College, was a "high-minded reformer" who "did not want to be limited by established institutions, all of which were, to his mind, corrupt in practice" (1972, p. 180). Clark concluded: "Charisma is a function of the social situation and the perspectives of the rank and file as well as a man's personal qualities" (1970, p. 241).

Other analysts have identified more generalized social situations of crisis, chronic agitation, and distress in which charisma emerged. Drachkovitch (1964, p. 57) described the profound intensity of the conflict and the schism between indigenous political forces in Yugoslavia and Stalinist power in the half-decade following World War II. Because orthodox Stalinism was not acceptable to the population, innovation was needed. Tito emerged as a charismatic with a radical program to modify Stalinism to include independence of individual enterprises, profits on capital investments, and merit pay. More recently, the art, literature, music, and drama originating in the United States during the mid-1960s has been seen as reflecting widespread societal "disintegration, decay, and despair" (Kenniston, 1965, p. 3). This milieu provided fertile ground for charismatics to found such youth-oriented religious cults as the Unification Church or "Moonies" (Bromley & Shupe, 1979; Galanter, 1982) and the Divine Light Mission (Galanter, 1981).

Perhaps the most convincing and classic example of the part played by social context in the emergence of charisma is the rise of Hitler to authority in Germany in the 1930s. Cantril (1941), who followed Hitler's rise to power through careful analysis of journalistic and other accounts of the period, described the sense of desperation, frustration, anger, and disgrace that gripped post–World War I Germany in the decade prior to Hitler's ascendance.

The Charismatic Mission

Political demagogues like Adolph Hitler provide clear, if frightening, examples of the prominant part the charismatic mission plays in the charismatic's success. Hitler proclaimed a dream of the future; his was a self-proclaimed "sacred" mission. He envisioned a new social order in which a strong central authority would swiftly and efficiently deal with the sources of Germany's problems—trade unions, communists, and Jewish minorities; provide small businessmen with political protection, financial support, and government pensions; and provide an elite military force that would restore Germany's lost prestige and power in the world. "Visions of a great Pan-Germanic state were held before the eyes of the people by Hitler and Nazi spellbinders" (Cantril, 1941, p. 242).

Similarly:

Bolshevism had the typical features of a charismatic movement, and its founder, Lenin, played the role of charismatic leader. . . . [It] specifically envisaged a universal salvation in this world on the basis of developed technology . . . a this-worldly version of Christian eschatology so that outside the party there is no salvation. The final days are at hand. The new kingdom is imminent, as it were. (Constas, 1961, 284)

Like the personal qualities of the leader, the charismatic mission must go beyond the limits of usual experience and knowledge. As Schwartz (1983) pointed out, this was not true for George Washington. Far from being radical in his orientation and program, he "was totally committed to existing traditions." His mission was to protect a status quo from the encroachments of the Crown, and, as such, his role was as a "protector of the central institutions of his society" (1983, p. 30).

John L. Lewis, on the other hand, clearly had a mission that went beyond and departed from the experiences and traditions of the American Federation of Labor (AFL). The most succesful U.S. unions until that time had joined together to form the AFL; these unions represented only skilled workers and were organized along craft lines. He proposed to organize unskilled, mass-production workers into industrially based unions (Dubofsky & Van Tine, 1977, p. 226).

Characteristics of Followers

Willing followers are essential for the emergence of any authority. For charisma to emerge, the leader's message must be accepted by some group of followers. From their study of the "Moonies," Bromley and Shupe (1979) concluded that charisma "is, in fact, largely a socially constructed attribute" (p. 143). As Friedland (1964) expressed it, charisma must be "validated by social groups" (p. 21). Madsen and Snow (1983) are perhaps most emphatic on this point:

> Charisma . . . requires the meshing of the special qualities of the leaders with a complementary set of equally special qualities in the following. Put somewhat differently, charisma is never simply the result of the magnetism of a leader; it depends equally upon the "magnetizability" of the followers . . . an individual is not charismatic when separated from the audience receptive to his particular appeal. (p. 338)

At the same time, the charismatic does not derive his or her authority from the consent of the followers in a democratic sense; rather, it is their duty to obey because of the moral authority with which they endow the charismatic leader. Parson's (1947) analysis of Weber succinctly expressed this idea:

> The authority of the leader does not express the "will" of his followers, but rather their duty or obligation. Furthermore, in the event of conflict there can in principle be only one correct solution. Majorities, if employed at all, are given authority only because they are thought to have *the* correct solution, not because a greater number have as such a greater right to prevail. And the leader does not compromise with his followers in a utilitarian sense. Recognition by them is interpreted as an expression of the moral legitimacy of his claim to authority. (p. 65)

This analysis also points out how far from Weber's original ideas are such conceptions as consensus leaders (Zaleznik & Kets de Vries, 1975).

Weber also implied that the followers of the charismatics may be the emotionally disturbed, the alienated, or others who feel helpless to take action on their own. Recent empirical data supports his position. In her study of persons attracted to the "Moonies," Lodahl, (1982, pp. 39–40) found that they had greater feelings of helplessness, cynicism, distrust of political solutions, and less confidence in their own values, their own sexual identity, and the future in general, than did members of the anti-nuclear movement or a sample of Cornell students. Galanter (1982) summarized clinical literature to the effect that "psychological distress is a frequent antecedent to joining a [charismatic] sect" (p. 1539). One study described followers of charismatics as depressed, inadequate, or borderline antisocial youths (Etemad, 1978). Another found they had felt lonely, rejected, and sad prior to becoming a follower (Levine & Salter, 1976). In another set of data, Galanter (1981) found a decrease in neurotic distress and an increase in group cohesiveness among such persons after they joined a charismatic sect. In modern societies, alcoholics and other drug addicts comprise a relatively large group of persons who are likely to experience strong feelings of alienation, anomie, and helplessness. Trice and Roman (1970a) found that alcoholics who affiliated successfully with Alcoholics Anonymous (AA) were attracted to the cohesive social relations and conformity to norms evident in AA groups.

Others have looked at followership in psychoanalytic terms. For McIntosh (1970), Weber's emphasis on a sense of duty and obligation to the leader "indicates that we are dealing with an aspect of superego functioning" that "represents an advance to the Oedipal level" (p. 903). According to his view, charisma can operate at this level, acting out the universal Oedipal fantasy of the sons rising to overthrow their father through the rebellious qualities of both leader and follower. Within the infamous Manson "family" (Fine, 1982), such unconscious forces were evident in the family's preoccupation with the "breaking of the 'fear force' " (p. 52). The charismatic leadership of Manson succeeded in imposing a strange and distorted superego that demanded unconventional sexual practices, torture, and eventually horrible butchery and murder.

The results of empirical studies, however, suggest that factors other than their personal emotional disturbances or psychic drives make followers receptive to charismatic leaders and their missions. Followers are willing to embrace radical missions and thus are more readily recruited when the social context includes widespread perceptions of crises. Cantril (1941) concluded:

> There is ample evidence that the German people during these critical years craved
> a strong leadership. . . . It is no wonder that the message of Hitler, his own obvious

belief in the righteousness of his program, his sincerity, and his faith in himself made an indelible impression on all who heard him. (p. 235)

He then described how

having found a leader, people rapidly identified with him. His goals became goals for them; his program gave them interpretations; his sincerity and conviction gave them *new* direction. (p. 233)

Like the people at a circus, potential Nazi followers were able to find, in the variety of appeals offered, some particular pattern which consciously or unconsciously attracted them. (p. 236)

Also, followers may hold beliefs that encourage their attributing exceptional gifts to the charismatic leader. Kanter (1972) reports that 78% (seven out of nine) of the successful utopian communities she studied had ideologies that promoted such attributions, and that only 20% of the unsuccessful ones had such ideologies for part or all of their histories. She also reports that some of the successful groups had ideologies that allowed members to partake in the charisma through their participation. "All members gained a measure of charisma just by being members." (pp. 114–115).

Conceptual advances have also moved beyond the limited view of charisma as grounded in abnormal persons and abnormal circumstances. In his systematic exploration of charisma, Shils (1965b) concluded that, rather than charisma being purely a phenomenon of abnormal situations and crises, it is quite possible for it to be a part of "some *very central* feature of man's existence and the cosmos in which he lives" (p. 201). When this centrality is coupled with intensity of expression, it becomes extraordinary and thus charismatic (p. 201).

Geertz (1977) further refined this view of charisma as a property of the dynamic center of social order. He points out that "there are multiple themes in Weber's concept of charisma" and that the

lost dimensions of charisma have been restored by stressing the connection between the symbolic value individuals possess and their relations to the active centers of the social order. . . . It is involvement with such arenas and with the momentous events that occur in them that confers charisma. . . . [It] does not appear only in extravagant forms and fleeting moments, but is an abiding, if combustible, aspect of social life that occasionally bursts into open flame. (p. 201)

It follows from these analyses and empirical results that followers of charismatics can come from many sources besides the neurotic and alienated. Moreover, charismatics themselves can emerge from a wide variety of contexts and centers of social life.

We see no reason why charismatics and their followers cannot emerge in any sector of social life. Bendix (1959) pointed out that "both very evil and very good men have exercised domination through their extraordinary gifts of mind and body" (p. 300). After reviewing Weber's work and various empirical data, Dow (1969) concluded that "charisma is neither old nor new, but an omnipresent possibility in all ages" (p. 316). Berger (1963) insisted that "charismatic innovation need not necessarily originate in social marginality. . . . It may also originate within traditionally established institutions" (p. 950). And Eisenstadt (1968, p. xxiv) cautioned against "the predisposition to the acceptance of the charismatic as rooted in some pathological state." For him, such a view cannot "explain the potentially continuous appeal of the charismatic in seemingly orderly and routine situations."

Indeed, the empirical literature on charisma reflects this universality. Table 1 (see p. 116–117) shows a wide diversity of types of settings in which charismatic leadership has been observed. Yet there are obviously many other collectivities, organizations, and social movements in which charismatic leadership has not emerged. The women's liberation movement and the U.S. antiwar movement of the 1960s and early 1970s are prominent examples.

The Pivotal Role of Success

For the charisma of leaders to achieve its full authority, "some victory must be registered that validates their charisma in the eyes of the followers" (Friedland, 1964, p. 24). Heberle (1951) argued that the charismatic can maintain authority only "by constantly proving to his followers his extraordinary ability" (p. 132). Without such repeated validation, the position of charismatics becomes unstable and the solidarity of their movements is jeopardized. Both of these authors are reiterating traditional interpretations of Weber's position: "If proof of his charismatic qualifications fails him for long. . . . above all if his leadership fails to benefit his followers, it is likely that his charismatic authority will disappear. This is the genuine charismatic meaning of the 'gift of grace' " (Eisenstadt, 1968, pp. 49–50). Weber illustrated his point by pointing to old Germanic kings who, if they failed in kingly expectations, were apt to be scorned. Gerth and Mills (1946) further summarized Weber on this point: "Heroic feats of valor and baffling success are characteristic marks of their stature. Failure is their ruin" (p. 52).

Friedland (1964, p. 25) described how charismatics in Tanganyika's labor movement gained success in the eyes of dockworkers in 1947 by means of a major strike that won substantial wage increases. Similarly, in 1936, John L. Lewis demonstrated his charisma by repeatedly packing the halls in cities in Ohio in the middle of severe winter blizzards. "Thousands stood in the streets outside in driving snow and numbing temperatures to listen to Lewis over a loudspeaker system" (Dubofsky & Van Tine, 1977, p. 228). Although Lewis had relatively few followers before this feat, it took only 6 weeks following it for the Congress of Industrial Organizations (CIO) to be officially established.

Charismatics apparently understand very well the pivotal role of success in maintaining their authority, for they go to unusual lengths to claim and redefine success. For example, the Reverent Sun Myung Moon "was able to redefine the movement's progress in such a way as to create 'spiritual progress' when 'physical victories' were conspicuously lacking" (Bromley & Shupe, 1979, p. 112). Friedland also described how successes in the Tanganyika unions could be "of a less material nature," until the simple act of writing a "demanding letter to an employer of a different race was defined as success" (1964, p. 25). In sum, as Bendix (1959) puts it, "[the charismatic] remains their master as long as he proves himself and his mission in their eyes" (p. 301).

Interrelating the Components of Charisma

Our use of an enumerative definition at the beginning of this section was meant to imply more than that charisma has multiple components. Our definition also was intended as a listing of conditions necessary for charisma to emerge and endure. However, we do not believe that all of the components of charisma must be present to a high degree in order for charisma to occur—only that they must be present to some minimal degree that has not yet been determined. Thus, we see charisma as a continuous variable with various levels of the five components we have delineated summing up to more or less charisma. We reject, moreover, the idea that any one or two of these components—even when present to an exceptional degree—are sufficient to constitute charisma. To settle for less than all of them is to do an injustice to the richness of Weber's original conception and to dilute the distinctive value of the concept. In particular, we feel it is a mistake to treat charisma as merely another style of leadership.

House (1977) seems to agree substantially with us on this point. He enumerated all but the success component in his theory. Another way of looking at the various components of charisma we have discussed is in terms of types of leadership theories. Looking at House's theory in this way, it can be seen as an amalgam of trait, style, and situational theories with a trace of the attribution approach: (1) trait theory because he clearly stated that charismatics have unusual personal qualities; (2) style because he specified leader behaviors—usually in terms of how followers experience them; (3) situational theory because like Weber, he posited that "charismatic leadership is born out of stressful situations" (p. 203); and (4) attribution theory because, by his definition, charisma is determined by the "charismatic effects" (p. 192) leaders have on followers, rather than by their objectively determined personal qualities or exceptional deeds. He suggested identifying charismatic leaders by eight effects on followers: follower trust in the correctness of leader's beliefs, and, similarly, in the corectness of followers' beliefs; unquestioning acceptance, affection, willing obedience, identification with and emulation of leader; emotional involvement in the mission; heightened goals; and feelings of being able to contribute to the accomplishment of the mission (House & Baetz, 1979, p. 399). The success component, which House did not mention, could be fit within a situational approach to leadership.

What is new and different in our enumerative definition of charisma and not easily subsumed under past approaches to leadership is the charismatic mission—the radical and novel visions and prescriptions of the charismatic leader. This component of charisma addresses the *content* of leadership—what the leader is trying to accomplish and is influencing the followers to do—an element not yet incorporated into general leadership theories. Although style theories of leadership verge on content, they really are focused more on how leaders behave than on what they are trying to accomplish.

We now will turn to the social processes that enable charisma to produce lasting change.

THE CONCEPT OF ROUTINIZATION

The routinization of charisma has received far less attention than has the concept of charisma itself. This neglect is puzzling because Weber and others go to considerable pains to point out the fundamental role it occupies in any consideration of charisma as an organizing force. Weber (1947) stated emphatically:

> If [charisma] is not to remain a purely transitory phenomenon, but to take on the character of a permanent relationship forming a stable community, it is necessary for the character of charismatic authority to become radically changed. . . . It cannot remain stable, but becomes either traditionalized or rationalized, or both. (p. 364)

As Gerth and Mills (1946) interpreted Weber on this point, "the genuine charismatic situation quickly gives way to incipient institutions, which emerge from the cooling off of extraordinary states of devotion and

fervor"[3] (p. 54). From time to time Weber and others provided some details
to flesh out this formulation, but the concept of routinization has received
little systematic examination or extension despite its pivotal position in
determining the effects of charisma on social change.

An Enumerative Definition Interpreting and Extending Weber

   According to our interpretation of Weber, charisma is routinized by (1)
the development of an administrative apparatus, that stands apart from
the charismatic, to cope with the ongoing operating needs generated by
putting the charismatic's program into practice; (2) the transformation and
transference of the charisma to others in the organization by means of
rites, ceremonials, and symbols; (3) the incorporation of the charismatic's
message and mission into the written and oral traditions of the organization;
and (4) the selection of a successor who resembles the charismatic sufficiently to be like a "reincarnation" (Eisenstadt, 1968, p. 55).
   In analyzing the two instances of routinization presented in this paper,
then, it seemed logical to assess the completeness and success of the routinization process by the presence and degree of each of these developments in each organization. We soon realized, however, that these four
developments only followed the routinization process through the selection
of a successor. For routinization to be truly successful and complete, the
organization should remain focused on the original message and mission
of the charismatic, following his or her succession as leader. The strictest
test of routinization would be a longitudinal one, assessing whether there
were discernible charismatic efforts long after succession had taken place.
These effects should involve more than ceremonial observances and the
continuance of an oral and written tradition, if they are going to reflect
the institutionalization of real social change. The most crucial test of the
routinization of charisma surely must be whether and to what degree the
charismatic mission is followed after the charismatic leader is no longer
present. We therefore added a fifth criterion by which we assessed routinization: (5) the degree to which the organization (or other collectivity)
continues to express, to work toward, and to cohere around the charismatic
message and mission of the founder (or reformer).

Past Empirical Results

   Only a few prior studies have directly addressed the issue of routinization; treatments tend to be quite brief and part of a larger effort to understand charisma. The exception is Clark's analysis of the histories of
three distinctive colleges, in which he referred to some of the components

of routinization as the "fulfillment" of their "organizational sagas" (Clark, 1972, p. 181). He observed five "essential carrying mechanisms" (1970, p. 246) by which fulfillment took place. The first of these was a key group of believers among powerful faculty who "routinize the charisma of the leader in collegial authority" (1972, p. 181). The second was program embodiment, which involved the "visible practices with which claims of distinctiveness can be supported; that is, unusual courses, noteworthy requirements, or special methods of teaching" (1972, p. 181). The third was a supporting social base among "outside believers devoted to the organization, usually the alumni" (1972, p. 182). The fourth was an allied student subculture, which "steadily and dependably transferred the ideology from one generation to the other" (1972, p. 182). The fifth was imagery of the saga "widely expressed as a generalized tradition in statues and ceremonies, written histories and current catalogs, even in the 'air about the place' felt by participants and some outsiders" (1972, p. 182). Although couched in different terms, Clark's analysis dealt extensively with three components of our definition of routinization, namely transformation and transference, incorporation, and continuity. His analysis also dealt partially with the development of an administrative apparatus, but only as confined to the academic program and not the general administration of these colleges. He did not deal explicitly with the issue of succession, perhaps because he saw the other carrying mechanisms as sufficient to achieve fulfillment of the charismatic mission. We suspect he preferred the term *organizational saga* over *routinization* because he wanted to emphasize the subjective, ideological components that were carried forward, and not the rational, administrative mechanisms (the first component of our definition) that are implied by the meaning of the word *routinization*.

Another empirical study that dealt with routinizaton, but called it something else, is Kanter's study of utopian communities. She used the term *institutionalized awe* (Kanter, 1972, p. 114; Shils, 1965b) to refer to the process by which charisma is "diffused throughout the corporate group" (Kanter, 1968, p. 514); we see her definition of this concept as similar to the second component of our enumerative definition—the transformation and tranference of charisma to others in the organization. In the communities she studied, awe was institutionalized through shared ideology, power, and leadership, and was an important mechanism promoting members' commitment to the community.

Constas (1961, p. 285) briefly discussed the routinization of Lenin's charisma via its transference and attachments to offices in the Communist Party. Unfortunately, she did not describe the process in any detail, but compared it with the charismatic bureaucracy of the Roman Catholic Church (1961, p. 286).

Madsen and Snow (1983) conducted a survey to assess the "dispersion" of the charisma of Juan Peron, the Argentine political leader. They collected their data in 1965, ten years after Peron's removal from power, from a probability sample of adult Argentines living in towns with populations of 2,000 or more. They then selected out the 100 cases that showed the greatest positive feelings of intensity toward Peron to analyze for factors explaining their continued following of his charisma. They assumed that routinization was most likely when these "secondary leaders have taken the initiative in advancing their interest" (p. 345) and when they were in a location that permitted close interaction with the Peronist organization centered in Buenos Aires. They found not only that there were followers concentrated in Buenos Aires in significantly larger numbers, but also that these followers had experienced greater material benefits from the success of Peron and his organization. Moreover, these secondary leaders did not exhibit as much normlessness, powerlessness, or anomie as some analysts of charisma (Apter, 1966; Galanter, 1982) would predict. Madsen and Snow's analysis touches upon the second and fifth components of our definition of routinization. Their analysis of the dispersion and diffusion of Peron's charisma is close to, but not the same as, our second component—the transformation and transference of charisma to others. Their analysis is closer to our fifth component—the continued adherence to the charismatic message—because it focuses upon the influence of Peron a considerable time after he left power.

All of the other empirical accounts of routinization focus upon the fourth component of our enumerative definition—the selection of an appropriate successor. In one study, the problem of succession was briefly mentioned, but no data were presented (Day, 1980, p. 57). Three others concluded that the routinization process had failed because the selection process or the successors chosen failed; one other predicted failure.

In Miller's (1966) field study of a Chippewa Indian tribe, he concluded that the charisma of the leader could not be transferred to his followers and that the leadership pattern was abandoned following numerous efforts to routinize it: "The chiefs were unwilling to grant potential successors the same degree of power that Barnett had exercised" (p. 183), largely because they all wanted to succeed him themselves. We cannot be sure because we did not observe the events involved, but we suspect that routinization was ineffective in this instance because the second and third components of our definition—transformation and transference through rites, ceremonials, and symbols, and incorporation of the charismatic message into written and oral traditions—had never occurred. At least, Miller does not describe any such occurrences.

Van de Ven et al. (1983) described a failed effort to plan for the succession of a charismatic-type founder. They concluded that the effort failed because the approach used was too rational; it involved changing the formal structure, and clarifying goals, procedures, job descriptions, and account-ability systems. "Had we been more concerned with Selznick's (1957) view of institutionalization, greater emphasis would have been placed on developing and measuring stories, scripts, symbolisms, and myths in the organization as the media by which the vision of the founder might be perpetuated into the folklore of the organization" (1983, p. 3). In sum, Van de Ven et al. saw the lack of the second component of our definition—transformation and transference via rites, ceremonials, and other symbolic means—as explaining the failure of the fourth component—the selection of the successor.

Much the same conclusion was reached by Drachkovitch (1954), who predicted that it was highly improbable that Tito's charisma would be successfully routinized. Despite extensive and careful plans for his succession, including the designation of a successor, Drachkovitch expected succession to fail because "the cult of personality is something too personal . . . for even the closest associate to be able to use it as an adequate cloak for his own authority" (1964, p. 64). In our terms, failure to transform and transmit Tito's charisma to other members meant there were no followers sufficiently imbued with it to provide a strong successor.

Although, as mentioned earlier, we are far from sure that Salaman's (1977) study involved a genuine charismatic leader, his analysis of what he considers a failure of routinization is interesting in that it emphasizes contextual features surrounding the routinization attempt—most promi-nently, the organizational structure—and their effects on followers. "The managers at Brown, as a result of their exposure to Mr. Brian's style of management and organizational features which supported his method of domination, experienced considerable role uncertainty and consequent role anxiety. Their experiences have caused them to be underconfident, to be uncertain about what they should do, and to have fears about their competence" (Salaman, 1977, p. 382). Also, it appears from this descrip-tion that the mission of the leader may not have been clearly transmitted to the followers.

Interrelating the Components of Routinization of Charisma

As with our enumerative definition of charisma, we believe that all of the components specified in our definition must be present to some minimal degree in order for routinization to occur. Thus, any instance that is missing one or more of these components we consider to be a failure of routini-zation. In instances where all of the components are present, the degree of success of a particular routinization could be compared to other in-stances by comparing the degree to which each component is present. Obviously, if all components are present to a high degree, routinization is more complete, and we would also expect a higher level of the final component—continuity of the charismatic mission within the social group or organization.

The empirical studies already summarized also suggest another interesting possibility: that some of these components may be necessary preconditions for others to occur. From the results of several studies, it appears that missing or perhaps inadequate levels of transformation and transference can make succession impossible. It seems likely that the lack or inadequate amounts of other components could have similar effects. For example, if no administrative mechanisms are put in place, perhaps succession becomes very difficult. Without a functioning formal structure that can keep the organization going during the disturbances entailed in a change in leaders, even if a suitable successor is chosen, perhaps by the charismatic, the successor may encounter difficulty in achieving practical control of the followers. Also, if successful succession does not occur, continuity of the charismatic mission may be impossible to achieve. In short, the limited existing data suggest that there may be a hierarchy or ordering of the five components of routinization we have identified such that some must precede others for routinization to go forward.

We will now turn to our own empirical data.

METHODS

Subjects and Settings

Both of the charismatic leaders we studied and the social movement organizations (Zald & McCarthy, 1980) they founded arose within the same general social movement. This movement consisted of efforts over the past 40 years by a variety of organizations to redefine alcoholism as an illness rather than a moral weakness. One social movement organization (SMO)—Alcoholics Anonymous (AA)—was founded in 1935 by a male charismatic who sought to revolutionize the treatment of the newly defined disease ("It is written that alcoholism is hopeless, but I say to you that it can be managed").[4] The other SMO—the National Council on Alcoholism (NCA)—was founded in 1946 by a female charismatic who sought drastic changes in public perceptions of the alcoholic ("Many think they are moral degenerates and skid-row bums, but I can personally tell you they are sick people who are like you and I and who respond to help and hope").[5] Both charismatics were successful in their missions during their lifetimes. Both are now dead.

There are certain similarities between these two charismatics. Both were alcoholics; both were in their early 40s when they founded their organi-

zations. Also, both had been reasonably successful in their chosen occupations before their alcoholism became acute. The founder of AA was
a stock broker; the founder of NCA was a magazine editor, photographer,
and freelance writer, and finally a fashion publicity director of a large
department store. She came from the higher status family, having attended
fashionable finishing schools, made her debut into Chicago society, and
been a member of the Junior League. He came from a middle-class, small-
town Vermont family, went to prep school, and failed to finish college
because of World War I. Both were married; neither had children. The
female charismatic was divorced at an early age (24) and never remarried.
She was also a member of AA (the organization founded by the male
charismatic), but her chosen mission was a distinct departure from the
mission of AA. In fact, her mission violated the strongly held norm of
anonymity symbolized in the very name Alcoholics Anonymous.[6]

Data Collection

The first author of this paper had many opportunities to observe AA
and its founder; he served as a nonalcoholic member of its Board of Trustees from 1956 to 1972, participated frequently in various meetings and
programs, and conducted several studies of AA and its members (e.g.,
Trice, 1958; Trice & Roman, 1970a). During these events, he consistently
took field notes, focused primarily on the behavior of AA's charismatic
founder and others' reactions to him.

Also, repeated opportunities to observe NCA and its founder arose in
connection with the first author's serving as a consultant from 1962 until
the present to one of NCA's chief funding sources; in that connection,
he conducted several studies of NCA, the last one in 1980 and 1981 in
collaboration with the second author. During this latter study, the founder
of NCA was interviewed at length, as were many of her early followers,
and all current administrators and officers. Over the years, the first author
participated frequently in numerous annual conferences and other meetings
of NCA. Finally, a variety of published sources, organizational documents,
and the personal papers of the NCA founder—located at the University
of Syracuse Archives—were consulted.

ASSESSING CHARISMA OF TWO LEADERS

Before we can analyze routinization, we must deal with the logically prior
question of whether both of the two leaders observed were indeed charismatic. According to our enumerative definition, charismatic persons must
meet five necessary conditions: (1) they must possess certain extraordinary

personal characteristics; (2) they must advance a radical message and mission; (3) that message and mission must be relevant to some widely perceived crisis or other source of social agitation; (4) their personal characteristics must attract followers, arouse in them excitement, awe, and reverence, and generate in them the willingness to break with traditional/rational norms to follow their radical mission; (5) their mission must meet with visible success in order to validate their charisma.

The Founder of Alcoholics Anonymous

The charismatic who founded AA met the preceding definition very well. He possessed to a high degree most of the personal characteristics that have been associated with charisma by various writers. In terms of the characteristics suggested by House (1977, p. 193)—high levels of confidence, dominance, and a strong conviction in the moral righteousness of beliefs—he lacked only dominance. Other characteristics observed in this leader that also explained his personal magnetism included eloquence, intelligence, tirelessness, exceptional commitment, and personal attractiveness.

His strong convictions and self-confidence were based in his own truly extraordinary recovery from alcoholism. After many personal losses arising from his uncontrolled drinking, he met another alcoholic—a physician—with whom he formed a mutual assistance bond; each helped the other to remain sober.[7] Their successful recovery using this technique formed the basis for the more elaborated set of self-help and group-support methods that became and have remained the hallmark of AA. To propose that alcoholism was a disease (an idea gaining some acceptance at that time among scientists concerned with alcoholism), and also that it could be treated successfully by the interventions of laypersons who were also alcoholics, was a truly radical combination of ideas that broke with traditional norms prescribing that the treatment of disease was performed by medical professionals.

The AA charismatic became a tireless and apparently irresistible promulgator of these ideas. Despite a few early failures of his methods, he persisted and was able to inspire other alcoholics to try them. As the successful cases of recovery accumulated and were publicized, he became a truly heroic figure—especially among the increasing numbers who followed him and were finally able to attain sobriety. These successes were so dramatic, when compared to the popular idea that alcoholism was a hopeless condition, that they generated much excitement in the press and popular imagination, and among his followers as well (Alexander, 1941). His success validated his charisma, which became more and more evident with the passage of time. He became an extremely facile, dynamic, and effective speaker and writer who expressed ideas with compelling and convincing simplicity. Although not handsome, his followers found him attractive enough to liken his appearance to the film star Gary Cooper. He worked with unremitting dedication to his mission: to create a better life for those who suffered from alcohol dependency.

His mission was relevant not only to those who suffered from alcoholism and wished to overcome their dependency, but also to general social concerns and turmoil about the use of alcohol. New prohibition drives were mounted in the U.S. during the 1930s and 1940s. They caused "waves of prohibitionist and antiprohibitionist agitation" (Lee, 1944, p. 65). The AA founder's message was that the worst consequences of the use of alcohol— chronic alcoholism and its dysfunctional behaviors—could be remedied by private and relatively informal interventions. His message meant that prohibition was not the only solution and thus made it seem less important as a topic of public agitation. Even today, the official AA doctrine is neutral on the subject of prohibition or measures designed to reduce general consumption of alcohol.

There is no doubt that at least some of his followers attributed to him a connection with transcendent powers. Legends and stories arose about his spiritual experiences and the events surrounding his first attempts to help other alcoholics. For example, according to one legend, he was in such despair one night that he stepped out of a third-story window intending to commit suicide. But supernatural forces intervened and held him up; he never fell to the ground, suddenly came to his senses, and stepped back into the room through the window. AA retains a spiritual flavor today; it has its own Serenity Prayer,[8] and most open meetings close with the Lord's Prayer.

The intelligence of this charismatic is evident from his writings on AA, which show keen insight into organizational dynamics and human behavior. He was able to incorporate sophisticated and complex ideas into his thinking and then somehow convey them to others in simple words. His intelligence was also evident in the unusual and highly successful organizational arrangements that he helped to bring about for AA, which has always been an extremely decentralized organization that has managed simultaneously to maintain remarkable cohesion.

Since its founding, AA has been so successful that it grew from 22 groups in 1944 to 26,000 groups in the U.S. and Canada by 1980, with an estimated membership of 800,000 (Maxwell, 1982). Because AA also has groups in many other countries, the total membership throughout the world must stand at well over a million. Every one of those members is a living testament to the vision of their founder—an overwhelming validation of his charisma. Other evidence of success is provided by the large numbers of other self-help groups imitating the basic AA approach: Narcotics Anonymous, Gamblers Anonymous, Recovery Incorporated, and the like.

In one respect, AA's founder did not fit House's description of charismatics. He was *not* very dominant in his behavior. Although he expressed his ideas with conviction, he tended to rely upon others to carry forward his arguments. After making his position known, he usually backed off, allowing others to express contrary views or raise questions. He usually did not insist on having his way; he did not need to, as he usually won over others by his persuasiveness. In this sense, he fit the general idea implicit in the analyses of Freidrich (1961), Berlew (1974), and Schwartz (1983) that charismatic leadership is something very different from and somehow antithetical to the use of coercion.

The Founder of the National Council on Alcoholism

The charismatic who founded NCA not only accomplished all that charismatics are supposed to accomplish but possessed *all* of the personal qualities associated with charisma. As mentioned earlier, although a member of AA, she broke with the AA tradition of anonymity to publicize her own personal story of addiction and recovery. Her mission was to educate the public that alcoholism was a treatable illness and thus to remove the stigma associated with this addiction, improve the treatment of alcoholics, and perhaps even prevent alcoholism.

She was an even more compelling and inspiring speaker than the founder of AA. A handsome woman who dressed very well, she told her story in dramatic and captivating detail. The combination of her refined appearance and speech with the sordid and tragic details of her drinking history invariably captured and riveted the attention of her audiences. She was eloquent and possessed unusual abilities to excite, to charm, and to convince others of her mission. During the first year of her efforts, 19 local committees formed and agreed to affiliate with her movement (*Quarterly Journal of Studies on Alcohol,* 1946). She was in great demand as a speaker, and continued to travel tirelessly—educating the public about alcoholism—for over 20 years. Clearly, her conviction in the rightness of her cause never wavered. Her personal papers include books of clippings illustrating the prominent and lengthy press coverage accorded to her talks by local newspapers throughout the country. She also carried on a voluminous correspondence, but did not write as extensively for publication as did the AA charismatic.

Like the founder of AA, her mission was highly relevant to the public agitation over alcohol during the 1930s and 1940s in the U.S. The climate of public opinion did not favor either the wets or the drys sufficiently to settle the issue. The two sides expended more energy on "promotion of pat propaganda theories than upon attempts to work out sensible and workable programs" (Lee, 1944, p. 77). Their dispute was irrelevant to the radical message and mission of the founder of NCA. She did not see her mission as preventing the immoral practice of drinking alcohol, but as preventing and ameliorating the disease of alcoholism. Those concerned about the effects of alcohol did not have to decide to line up behind either the wets or drys to do something about the problem. They could join her and work to educate the rest of the public that alcoholism was not hopeless—it was a *treatable* disease. Because alcoholism was not accepted by either the medical community or the general public as a disease, her message was genuinely radical at that time. She certainly met Etzioni's (1961, p. 203) description of charisma, exercising a diffuse but intense influence over normative orientations of others.

The success of her mission is evident in public attitudes today. As early as 1961, a study of public definitions of alcoholism showed that over 50% of the general public thought of alcoholics as sick rather than morally weak, as compared to 23% in 1941—shortly before NCA was founded (Mulford & Miller, 1961). Her efforts were accorded much more respect than were those of the usual zealot. Her personal communications of her mission reflected such intelligence that she was awarded several honorary degrees and was made an honorary member of the American Psychiatric Association. She became a genuine public figure, greeted everywhere with press coverage, widely quoted in the scientific and popular literatures, and consulted by Congress, U.S. presidents, and officials at all levels in government and private industry. Bolstered by her personal charisma, NCA—the organization she founded—became accepted by media as *the* authority on alcoholism, and its voice was spread by the establishment of local affiliates throughout the country. Currently, there are over 200 local affiliates of NCA, and the ideas that alcoholism is a disease that can be treated is now widely accepted.

It is not clear that the founder of NCA was seen by her followers as linked to transcendent powers. A story was told about her being held back from committing suicide by an invisible hand, but it was never widely circulated or an important aspect of her influence. If she was connected to any powerful influences, it was to the scientific/medical establishments, which came to accept her and applaud her efforts, and to the "higher power" of good public relations, in which she had an exceptional talent and considerable practical experience. Leaving aside the whole question of whether labeling alcoholism as a disease is accurate or not, her efforts were able to change public opinion to the point where this idea is a prominent perception of alcoholism today.

Finally, as will be discussed in more detail later, the NCA charismatic was a dominant individual in her personal interactions and especially in her organization. Apparently she tended to try to control virtually every detail of everything that concerned her. In this respect, she better fit House's (1977) conception and less well fit Friedrich's (1961), Berlew's (1974), and Schwartz's (1983) conception of the charismatic than did the founder of AA.

DIFFERENCES IN THE ROUTINIZATION OF CHARISMA

We will now compare the degree to which the charisma of each of these two leaders was routinized. Each of the five components of routinization will be assessed and compared across the two leaders and their organizations.

Development of Administration

Etzioni's (1961, p. 204) analysis of routinization focuses upon the creation of offices to implement the mission of the charismatic. Somehow the efforts of followers must be coordinated and financed. The process of routinization serves to relieve the charismatic of these mundane concerns, and also permits the expansion of the mission beyond the immediate purview of the charismatic. Furthermore, the separation of administrative concerns from the personal attention of the charismatic helps to preserve his or her aura of extraordinariness. As one translation of Weber put it, "The holders of charisma. . . must stand outside the ties of this world, outside of routine occupations, as well as outside the routine obligations of family life" (Gerth & Mills, 1946, p. 248).

In some respects, AA and NCA developed similar structures, which consisted of central offices located in New York City and a large number of decentralized units serving geographic regions throughout the country. They differ in their size, the number of subunits, and their degree of autonomy. AA may have over 100 groups in a large metropolitan community like New York City; NCA has a single New York City affiliate. AA groups have only a single office—that of secretary; the incumbents are unpaid volunteers who rotate frequently. There are no hired full-time staff at the local level. Little coordination is necessary beyond indoctrination of the members into the mission and methods of organization. Motivation tends to remain high, once a member succeeds in fully affiliating with AA, which involves both acceptance of the mission and methods and some degree of success in maintaining sobriety (Trice, 1958). Members not only maintain their sobriety through the peer support generated at meetings, but also by helping others to avoid "slips," and by winning new converts to the movement. Members pay no dues, but can make small donations (typically $2–4 today) at each meeting; large donations (over $200) are not accepted at the local or national levels. The national office, consisting of a staff of almost 150, is funded entirely through small donations and the sale of its literature, mostly to its members. The governing structure is simple: there is a 15-person Board of Trustees, and an annual General Service Conference, which consists of elected delegates from 91 geographic areas. Neither of these groups attempts to exercise formal authority over the membership, but instead promulgates advice and guidelines on a variety of issues to the chapters via their secretaries. With this relatively simple structure, AA carries out its mission of helping alcoholics to help themselves.

Local NCA affiliates are relatively autonomous also, but consist of a paid staff, as well as volunteers. Affiliates usually have a full-time, paid executive director, and, depending on the size of the community and the affiliate's success, a number of paid, full-time staff. Most of the day-to-day activities of NCA affiliates are carried out by the paid staff. Very few volunteers work regularly on a part-time basis; most are engaged only sporadically in AA activities. NCA affiliates tend to operate like many other community social service agencies; they are funded by United Way, local governments, state governments, individual and firm contributions, grants and contracts, bequests, and various fund-raising activities, including fees for services. Not all affiliates obtain funding from all of these sources. The central office is supported by contributions from individual donors, private foundations, and private industry; federal grants and contracts; the sale of literature on alcoholism; a membership fee levied against each affiliate; and various fund raisers (banquets, golf tournaments, etc.). Coordination of affiliates' activities is provided by training, an annual meeting, a board of directors, and most importantly, by a paid executive director and a staff of functionally differentiated division heads at the central office.

As is evident from even this brief description, NCA has developed a more elaborate structure than AA, probably because its central mission—to educate the public—is more diffuse and tends to lead to a greater proliferation of specialized activities. There is no question, however, that each organization has created a system of offices to implement its mission, and, in that sense, has routinized the charisma of its founder.

Marked differences in routinization are evident, however, in the degree to which the charismatic founder was freed from the "ties of the world" by the creation of these offices and administrative structures. In the case of NCA, the charismatic was heavily involved in the day-to-day administration of the organization. She assumed a bureaucratic role—that of executive director—from the very beginning and remained in that top office for a quarter of a century. During that time her personal charisma, combined with her bureaucratic position, dominated practically all of the developments that occurred within NCA. Over and over, followers and others observed that "she was NCA" for all those years.

A memo from her to three of her staff, apparently written before departing on a trip and dated June 20, 1947, illustrates the closeness of the administrative oversight she attempted. In explaining why she wrote the memo, she tells them: "I want no doubts about the allocation of responsibilities—and no changes in my planning, since there is good reason behind it." She then goes on to give each of the three staff members detailed instructions on what to do while she is gone. For example, one is told to carefully read and answer any letters. Another is told "every minute is to be given to the clipping books." The third is instructed: "All mailing, entering in the stock book, etc. must be done by you." They are then all told to "pitch in," and help one another when their own work is done, work overtime if necessary, and, "If any one takes time off for hairdresser, shopping or any other reason, I want that reason put on the time sheet. I have no objection to such things within reason, but I want to know about it."

In sharp contrast, the AA charismatic consistently remained rather aloof from the administrative mechanisms and routines that grew up in AA. His early followers included some experienced executives, and he was willing to share the administrative reins of his new organization with them. He was probably right when he insisted that he had little managerial experience compared with many of his followers. Under his benign and relaxed oversight, the organization of AA evolved gradually. With his advice and counsel, the New York City AA group—one of the earliest to develop—set up a charitable trust with a board of trustees comprised of both alcoholics and nonalcoholics. In an effort to raise money, this board established a headquarters in New York City to answer inquiries and generally to stimulate growth of the movement. As a part of this drive, early members wrote and published their personal stories about the AA program in a book entitled *Alcoholics Anonymous* (Anonymous, 1939), which was soon dubbed "The Big Book" and functions as the bible of this movement to this day. During the period 1942 to 1946, a headquarters staff evolved to manage the rapidly growing organization. The charismatic worked closely with them to formulate *The Twelve Steps and Traditions* (Alcoholics Anonymous World Services, 1953) to guide the formation of local groups. As expansion continued, the headquarters staff, with the charismatic much involved, became concerned about coordination of the far-flung developments. In 1951, the Board of Trustees authorized an experimental plan for elected representatives to attend a General Services Conference each year. This yearly conference was intended to communicate the "group experience" of the local groups to the trustees and to permit them, in turn, to influence local groups. After a 5-year trial, the 20th anniversary convention of Alcoholics Anonymous, held in 1955, recognized the General Service Conference as "the voice of the group conscience of our entire fellowship, and the *sole successor* of its cofounders, _____ and _____ " (Trice, 1958, p. 111).[9]

A comment from a devoted follower of this period to the senior author of this paper summarized rather nicely the way the AA charismatic made inputs into the formulation of these routinizing mechanisms. "_____ pushed it off on others and stayed somewhat in the background; but he was always around when we needed him for important stuff." Kurtz (1979) described his role in these events as follows: "[He] realized that his own role would always be special. Therefore he attempted to delimit it precisely. He would 'help out in a pinch' but would no longer act for, or try to protect the movement from itself" (p. 134). Maxwell (1982) reports that after 1957, he "continued to play a useful senior statesman role" (p. 303). Field notes from observations of trustee meetings in the mid- and late-1950s confirm his quasi-withdrawal from the day-to-day decision-making and administrative processes of AA. He spoke and argued along with the trustees, but consistently refrained from attempting to control the administrative process. On some occasions he was not present, and on others, he only attended part of the meeting. He did, however, press very hard for certain changes he felt were important, and argued particularly against a majority of nonalcoholics on the board of trustees. Otherwise he manifested a noticeable degree of aloofness.

Transformation and Transference via Rites, Ceremonials, and Symbols

Weber (1947, p. 366) wrote at some length about the transference of charisma "by ritual means." For example, he emphasized the transmission of priestly charisma "by annointing, consecration and the laying on of hands." Through such rites, charisma became disassociated from its original possessor, and was turned into a property that could be transferred to others (Dow, 1969). Such rites obviously also transform the charisma from a set of personal attributes to a set of mechanisms and offices in the organization. In her research on successful utopian communities, Kanter (1972, p. 113) concluded that dispersion of charisma "throughout the corporate group" was necessary for members to become committed to the organization. She described this dispersion as "an extension of charisma from its original source into the organization of authority and the operation of the group, but not necessarily attached to a particular office or heredity line," but she fails to describe in concrete terms exactly how the dispersion was accomplished. If, as she argues, dispersion is essential to routinization, then the transformation and transference that Weber describes must be reenacted on numerous occasions with many different members. Instead of a few all-encompassing rites, dispersion seems to require many numerous, more specific rites that can serve to transfer charisma to many participants throughout the organization. Clark (1972, p. 181) describes in detail how an extensive pattern of rites helped to routinize the charisma of three college presidents. The unusual courses, noteworthy requirements, or special methods of teaching, already mentioned, became "a set of communal symbols and rituals, invested with meaning." At Reed, not reporting grades became heavily symbolic; at Swarthmore, it was the special practices and exams of the honors program; at Antioch, it was the work-study cycle.[10]

AA has many rites that have helped to transform and transfer the charisma of its founder throughout its membership. Trice and Roman (1970b, p. 539) described the "highly visible and explicit 'delabeling' or 'status return' ceremonies" that characterize every open meeting of AA. Members tell their stories, repeat legends about their charismatic founder, and refer to their sacred literature. A ritualistic introduction of "My name is _____ and I'm an alcoholic" has become part of tradition, as has the general format for the story: the pleasures realized in early drinking, the slow but certain segregation into heavy drinking groups, the accumulation of failure and tragedy produced by later drinking, learning about AA, rejecting the idea, hitting bottom, and finally accepting AA. Both in informal groupings before the more formal talks and stories, and in the talks themselves, members use a gutsy argot that is part of the rite and helps to mold them into a group (Pondy, 1977). Other potent rites also diffused the founder's charisma within AA. Most notably, large anniversary conventions held every 5 years serve as massive rites of integration (Trice & Beyer, 1984), carrying his message and mission into new generations of members. Throughout these ceremonies, his name and memory are invoked and revered. Clearly, his persona became and remains a potent symbol to members of what AA stands for.

By contrast, relatively few rites and ceremonials grew up in NCA through which its founder's charisma could be transformed and transferred to others. Local meetings had none of the ritual and ceremony found in AA meetings, although the basic themes of her message typically were reiterated. If she happened to be present, however, a somewhat ceremonial atmosphere was produced by her presence, animated speech, and persuasive powers. There were no often-told organizational stories, no sacred literature, and no specialized group argot. But there were some legends about her: how she tried to outdo her own average of over 200 lectures during the year, and one year got up to 237; her inner struggles about breaking the "anonymity" tradition to found and direct NCA. In the absence of appropriate occasions to celebrate them, these legends were not widely diffused, and they therefore receded into a rather dim past, ritually mentioned at large formal gatherings, but not as the central focus of what the organization is about. Annual meetings and affiliate dinners could have served to enhance and diffuse her charisma, but they usually focused instead on prominent community activists and donors. The annual meetings served to somewhat integrate the affiliates, which became more divergent as time passed, but the diversity of their interpretations of NCA missions and tasks seemed to lead to a greater emphasis on political maneuvering on these occasions than on transferring a shared ideology derived from the founder. Furthermore, because the mission of NCA was to influence public attitudes about alcoholism and its treatment, various elements of NCA's task environment were highly motivated to penetrate the organization (Miles, 1982). Until recently, the board of directors included representatives of the distilled spirits, beer, and wine industries, executives from profit-making firms providing treatment for alcoholism, and various others with clear monetary interests in the policies pursued by NCA.

Incorporation into Tradition

In his analysis of routinization, Bendix (1959) stated:

> The charismatic message becomes variously a dogma, theory, legal regulation, or the content of an oral or written tradition. The relation between the leader and his followers—or between the successors to that relationship—loses the belief in an extraordinary power and mission and becomes founded instead upon a belief in authority sanctified by tradition.

In addition, Weber, in his analysis of organizational changes among the Chinese literati, declared emphatically that "tradition displaced charisma" (Gerth & Mills, 1946, p. 420). Consequently, another way to judge whether or not charisma has been routinized is to trace the appearance or disappearance of the charismatic's mission and program in organizational tradition.

In his analysis of distinctive colleges, Clark (1972) pointed out that important historical events connected with the founding and any subsequent large changes in these organizations had become incorporated into sagas that helped to establish traditions guiding subsequent organizational developments. The saga of the AA charismatic was built and elaborated during his lifetime. The early events surrounding the founding of AA were soon legendary; their continuing historical import for the organization is evidenced by the repeated published accounts of these events—for example, numerous accounts in the *Grapevine*, the official AA magazine; a lengthy description and justification of AA's administrative arrangements (Alcoholics Anonymous World Services, 1957); and a biography of the founder (Kurtz, 1979). The lessons to be learned from these events soon became part of the written traditions of AA incorporated in the movement's bible—first published in 1939 (Anonymous, 1939)—in which the founder and his early followers tell their stories. Further written codification of the traditions followed with the publication of *Twelve Steps and Twelve Traditions* (Alcoholics Anonymous World Services, 1953). Although others participated in writing down AA's traditions, the charismatic founder was always the catalyst and an active participant. There is no question but that these writings form the core of his personal testament to his followers. This extensive written testament provides AA with a well-articulated set of norms and behaviors to guide its members. His testament also provides members with reference points and comparisons to use in telling their own stories to one another. The activities of AA center around talk—and this talk frequently makes reference to the founder and his testament. At formal meetings, especially the anniversary conventions, special sessions are devoted to oral discussions of the written traditions; for example, to discussing the relevance of *The Twelve Traditions* within local groups.

By comparison, NCA lacks important oral or written traditions that carry forward the ideas or history of its charismatic founder. The written history of NCA is available only in brief, unpublished form. No extensive biographies of the founder have yet appeared. Her views were never codified into a testament or bible to guide her followers. Evidently, NCA's founder and her early followers were not concerned with establishing a written tradition, perhaps because they were so intent on reaching the public and changing its views. Because the organization has had considerable turnover among its officers, and especially among its paid staff, any oral traditions that may have grown up have been interrupted. In the talk that goes on in NCA, little explicit mention is made of the founder or her ideas. The tradition she left behind seems to be a very general one of emphasis on and skill in public relations on behalf of the redefinition of alcoholism as a treatable illness.

Selection of a Successor

A crucial phase of routinization takes place with the retirement, or the inevitable death, of the charismatic. The organization must either abandon charisma as an organizing force, allowing any routinization present to wither away, or find a new leader who will carry forward the charisma and its routinization. Weber (1947; Gerth and Mills, 1946) set forth five ways in which the selection of a successor could reflect routinization: (1)

reincarnation, or selection on the basis of personal qualities that resemble the charismatic as closely as possible; (2) revelation, or selection by oracles, the casting of lots, or divine judgment; (3) designation by the original charismatic; (4) selection by close disciples of the charismatic, usually unanimously; (5) selection by heredity, in which charisma is expected to be transmitted by the charismatic to his or her descendants.

In our two cases, succession did not conform to any of the ways Weber suggested for routinizing charisma. In NCA, the founding charismatic retired, ostensibly because of her age, and was succeeded by an executive director who was chosen, not unanimously, by the Board of Directors, on the basis of his administrative experience in voluntary health movements in general. He had little knowledge of alcoholism or proven commitment to NCA missions. He had had virtually no contact with NCA, its founder, or its members before being recruited for the post. Rather, he saw himself as a professional administrator, who would use his post at NCA as a career stepping-stone to a better position, which is what he did; he stayed at NCA about four years and then went back to his old employing organization as its director.

Because this successor represented such a radical shift in administrative style and organizational values, the founding charismatic's followers were split in their support for the successor. There was general consensus, however, that his appointment meant increased emphasis on treating alcoholism as a disease similar to other medical disorders. Such an emphasis tended to pull the organization toward a scientific–medical rationale for alcoholism and its treatment and away from the self-help, group-support ideology of AA—creating some ideological conflict for AA members active in NCA. The initial successor was soon considered "a disaster" by the founder and her followers. The successor and the charismatic came to be bitterly antagonistic. He was staunchly opposed to her remaining on the premises with her secretary. He insisted he could not work with her and forced her to withdraw more and more. In her eyes he threatened the entire structure of the organization, especially the relationship between the outlying affiliates across the country and the national office. Other factions tried to resolve the conflict by taking control of the organization. The board of directors established a Delegate Assembly, probably to help to mitigate growing tensions between the New York office and the numerous affiliates.

It was evident from these events that, rather than routinizing the NCA founder's charisma, the selection of her successor diluted and confused it. Moreover, a third bureaucratic title—that of consultant—was assumed by her at the time of her retirement. When added to her earlier title of executive director, and to her status of retired, this label pushed her role even further into a bureaucratic frame of reference incompatible with the exceptional status of charisma.

Her next successor was also a professional administrator, but with considerable experience in the field of alcoholism. He was especially active in establishing a political movement to push causes related to alcoholism. He attempted to reestablish a better relationship with the founder and encouraged her greater participation, but was unable to win her enthusiastic support. The membership of NCA remained ideologically split; the early traditions became more and more hazy, and the charisma of its founder was no longer a potent organizing force. A subsequent successor may have represented a late attempt to recapture some of the founder's charisma; he was one of her followers, and his expertise was in public relations—clearly the area of her strength and the one area in which the organization can be said to have a tradition based in her charisma. But NCA is still a fragmented organization.

In the case of AA, the death of its founder seemed to have only scant effects on the ongoing activities of that organization. A few rather feeble efforts were mounted to find a "spiritual" successor, but none gathered much support. Rather, long-standing routinization mechanisms, already in place, acted as a sort of "designated" successor. These mechanisms had emerged and been put in motion over a period of almost 20 years, allowing for a regular, constant interaction between the personalized charisma of the founder and the emergence and perfection of the routinizing mechanisms. The Board of Trustees, the General Services Offices, the annual General Services Conference, and the anniversary conventions held every 5 years acted as a series of interlocked offices in which charisma had become invested and transformed into action. And it worked. Somehow, within this system of offices, the personal charisma of the founder continued to be evident; not much depersonalization of his charisma (Bendix, 1962) occurred, probably because the organization relied heavily on written and oral traditions in which he had played a central role. This is especially surprising because AA lacks any figurehead office to which this transformed charisma could be attached as office charisma (Etzioni, 1961). Apparently, as Kanter (1972) and Shils (1965b) suggested, the charisma of the AA founder has been diffused so that all members share it.

Continuity and Cohesion

The final test of the completeness of the routinization of charisma is whether the organization continues to cohere around and try to achieve the charismatic mission. An especially cogent test is what happens after the charismatic has been succeeded by another leader. Presumably, when relatively complete routinization of charisma has occurred, the organization will be unlikely to change following succession: it will be likely to continue activities consonant with the message and mission of its charismatic leader, and its membership will be able to maintain its cohesion and avoid ideological conflict. Zald and Ash (1966, p. 338), in their analysis of growth, decay, and change in SMOs, predicted less transformation following succession in more bureaucratized SMOs. They also identified three possible kinds of change that are likely to occur in less bureaucratized SMOs following the replacement of the charismatic: (1) decline in membership and audience; (2) factionalization, and (3) increased attempts to rationalize the administrative structure. Another likely possibility when routinization is weak is goal displacement or dilution.

None of the changes predicted for less routinized SMOs have occurred in AA since the death of its founder in 1971. The membership and audience have grown enormously. The only attempt at factionalization—an internal women's movement started in the early 1970s called Women for Sobriety—has survived on a small scale but has not prospered; between 1968 and 1977, the proportion of female members in AA rose from 22% to 32% (Maxwell, 1982, p. 296). Nor has the administrative structure of AA changed, been professionalized, or grown markedly. Finally, the goals of AA remain the same as they were at the time of its charismatic founder's death. In sum, AA has maintained remarkable continuity and cohesion and has prospered.

By comparison, NCA has had mixed developments. Despite its lesser prior routinization, since 1967 when its charismatic founder retired, the organization has not declined in membership, but instead has grown substantially. In 1967, there were 81 local affiliates and group members in the U.S. and 7 affiliates and group members in other countries; by 1982, NCA had 192 local and state affiliates in the U.S. and 3 international affiliates. However, during this same period, the financial status of the organization waxed and waned. In the early 1970s, NCA temporarily prospered from government support via grants and contracts; when this support ran out, the organization found itself in a precarious financial position. Bequests and large donations, needed to fund the increasing scope of the organization's activities, have not grown at the same rate as the number of affiliates, Recently, the central office staff and the services it provides were cut back severely.

In support of the second prediction of Zald and Ash (1966), NCA has also experienced considerable factionalization. Individual affiliates come and go, whole states and regions threaten to break off, numerous special constituencies (blacks, native Americans, gays, etc.) generate specialized activities and special interests, ideological conflicts over policies are common, and the activities and operating rationales of the various affiliates have become increasingly diverse over time. In sum, NCA had disintegrated by 1980 into a large number of relatively autonomous subunits, each going its own way, without benefit of a unifying leadership. To the degree that NCA had maintained any coherence, the original concern of its founder—to educate the public—seemed to provide the unifying principle.

NCA also fits Zald and Ash's third prediction for less-routinized SMOs in the fitful growth and professionalization of its administrative structure. As already mentioned, subsequent executive directors all have been professional types. Under their leadership, a cadré of other professionals were hired to provide services and to staff the central office, including an accountant, a labor relations expert, medical research administrators, fund raisers, public relations specialists, editors, and community development organizers. Also, as time passed, local affiliates were increasingly headed by career-oriented professionals. The reason these developments probably have not been more steady is that NCA has experienced ups and downs in its financial support. Generally, in prosperous times the number of professional administrators has grown, and in times of financial cutbacks their numbers have declined.

Finally, although NCA has never abandoned educating the public as its central goal, it has added a variety of other goals over time, with the result that emphasis on its educational mission has been diluted at various times. Particularly tempting other goals have included oversight over government agencies dealing with alcoholism, political lobbying, and coalition building. Concomitant with the accession of its most recent executive director and some other organizational changes, NCA deliberately cut back its goals and activities; the organization appeared to be returning to a position much closer to its founder's original mission.

DISCUSSION

On four of the five indicators of routinization we have considered, the two social movement organizations studied differed markedly. The charismatic founder of AA and his early followers set that organization on a path that led to a high degree of routinization. They not only established an appropriate administrative structure, but also developed rites that diffused charisma throughout the membership and began a strong oral and written tradition to keep the charismatic message alive. They avoided the thorny problems of succession by devising a structure that could function well without a strong leader. In keeping with the emphasis on group process present in their radical methods for helping alcoholics, the function of leading the organization was instead vested in various groups, most importantly and symbolically, in yearly conferences of elected representatives. In these ways AA routinized its founder's charisma so well that his message and mission continue to provide the central focus for that organization more than a decade after his death. The organization has been so successful in realizing the mission of its founder that it has spawned a large number of imitations.

By contrast, the routinization of charisma that occurred in NCA was very incomplete. The charismatic founder was preoccupied not only with establishing the administrative structure, but also with running it. One likely result is that her charisma itself was tarnished by her involvement in the mundane details and petty disputes of being an administrator. But NCA did succeed in establishing an adminstrative structure that functioned reasonably well relative to its mission. On the other indicators of routinization the organization is much more deficient. NCA has few rites and traditions, and those that exist do not reflect its founder's charisma. Thus, the organization has lacked means by which her charisma could be transferred, transformed, and diffused. Furthermore, when the time came to choose her successor, NCA chose a person who bore little resemblance to its founder. By this act, decision makers in NCA further diluted her charisma and its already weak routinization. Thus, it is not surprising that NCA subsequently experienced factionalization and difficulties in maintaining the support of its members and donors. Despite these handicaps, NCA has been reasonably successful in realizing its founder's mission of changing public attitudes toward alcoholics and alcoholism.

Our observations are consistent with earlier cited cases of failed routinization (Drachkovitch, 1964; Miller, 1966; Van de Ven, et al., 1983). Probably the single most damaging factor in the failure of NCA to routinize the charisma of its founder more successfully was the selection of a inappropriate successor. However, two other components in the routinization process—transference and incorporation—also lacking were: given the absence of these two routinizing components, it was highly unlikely that NCA would choose a successor in the mold of its founder. It is impossible to be certain from a qualitative, historical analysis whether events that precede others are the causes of later events. However, we can say that the data from NCA are not inconsistent with the general idea advanced earlier that some components of routinization may be preconditions for others.

What accounts for these pronounced differences in routinization? Why did the founders of AA and NCA and their followers behave so differently? Friedland (1964) suggested that "If genuine charisma is to be understood, analysis must be directed toward the social situation within which the charismatic figure operates, and the character of his message" (p. 21).

Differences in Missions

Although both were concerned with helping alcoholics, the messages and missions of the two charismatics differed in their simplicity and in their basic orientations. The message and mission of AA's founder were direct and plain, and AA refrained from embellishing or complicating them. Instead, their simplicity became part of the AA message; perhaps the two most frequently repeated mottoes of that organization are "One day at a time" and "Keep it simple." The message and especially the mission of the NCA founder were inherently more complicated. Changing public opinion and mobilizing divergent sources of support are not simple activities. Also, AA's mission was oriented toward helping individuals, and NCA's mission was oriented toward changing society. Thus, AA could rely on the ever-present selfish motives of its members to try to rehabilitate themselves, whereas NCA had to depend more upon mobilizing in its members altruistic motives to work for the benefit of others.

These differences in orientation also had implications for societal reactions to these two organizations. As Zald and Ash (1966, p. 331) pointed out, organizations that aim to change individuals are less threatening to the dominant values and other institutions of a society than are organizations that aim to change society itself, and thus are less likely to provoke resistance and counter pressures from the wider society.

Furthermore, AA's mission was oriented around radical new means, whereas NCA's mission was oriented around radical new goals. Maintaining sobriety was hardly a radical new goal—what was new in the AA charismatic's message was the means to that goal. Thus, AA did not need to sell its goal—only its radically new means to the goal. Because the success of those means was soon demonstrated, selling the mission became relatively easy and straightforward. But NCA's message involved genuinely new goals, and the means to these goals were not specified by the charismatic in her message. If the organization had simply followed her example, it would have sent recovered alcoholics around the country to tell their stories and thereby convince the public that alcoholism was *not* just a moral weakness, but a painful and costly disease. But no such tradition grew up, and no real uniformity of means was prescribed. Consequently, a wide variety of means and subgoals arose that greatly embellished, complicated, and almost overwhelmed the original message and mission. The multiplicity, complexity, and difficulty of the goals and means in NCA made success very hard to realize or to demonstrate.

Differences in Reasons for Belonging

Another factor likely to affect the ease of routinization was the basis of membership for each organization. Members were attracted to AA by the promise that its revolutionary means would help them conquer an addiction that was doing them a great deal of harm. They were then highly motivated to follow closely the prescribed means, and when the means proved successful in helping them, to maintain an almost slavish devotion to continued compliance with them. This ritual devotion to the means has been further refined and institutionalized in the 12th step of the AA recovery program, which states that helping others to achieve and maintain sobriety is a good way to maintain one's own sobriety. Although AA has not been equally successful in attracting and holding members from all segments of society (Trice & Roman, 1970a), its membership is quite diverse. Obviously, what gives this membership some homogeneity is their common concern with maintaining sobriety. Like soldiers in the trenches, members are drawn together by a common threat—the threat posed by the addictive properties of alcohol in a society where the drinking of alcohol is so accepted and pervasive that it is almost prescribed in some situations.

There were no comparable motives or threats to help to unite the members of NCA. The most valuable early followers were likely to be busy clergy, doctors, social workers, businessmen, and social leaders—most of whom were nonalcoholics who had little personal involvement with alcoholism, but were impressed and convinced by the gifts of persuasion of the charismatic. They were valuable to NCA for the social networks to which they gave access, but their ability and willingness to participate in NCA affairs were limited. They lacked the intense zeal of AA converts. Other followers included various professionals whose commitment to the cause was responsive to the opportunities and prestige that membership and activities conferred. Their subsequent commitment was largely determined by their ability to realize their personal ambitions, which often involved trying to fit NCA activities to their preferred skills. Thus, there was little homogeneity or commonality among NCA members and the agendas they brought to that organization.

Differences in Resource Requirements

Another factor that was found to affect routinization was the relative adequacy of the resources available to the two organizations. In the absence of adequate resources, routinizing activities must be curtailed. AA had the great advantage of employing a technology that required very modest financial resources. AA members needed only a meeting place with minimal furnishings—usually made available at no charge by local churches—to achieve their mission. Thus, AA could manage quite well on the basis of small voluntary contributions from its many highly committed members and their purchases of large quantities of AA literature and materials. These became quite reliable and growing sources of income.

By contrast, NCA's mission required much more extensive financial resources to cover travel expenses, to print materials, to advertise in the media, and to hire the professionals needed to carry out and coordinate a variety of activities. Although NCA needed larger sums, its membership was not as large or committed as was AA's, and therefore it became dependent on large donors, bequests, and government grants for operating revenues. Because few of these sources of funding were dependable in the long term, NCA's financial position frequently was shaky. Such a pervasive source of instability was damaging to member and staff commitment, and tended to dampen efforts toward continuity of program.

Differences in Sex of Founders

Another obvious difference between these two instances of routinization is the sex of the charismatic. It is possible that sex-role stereotypes or other sex-linked factors operated to help routinization of the male founder's charisma and to hinder routinization of the female founder's charisma. The AA charismatic fit the male stereotype for leaders: he was a commanding figure—tall, well-built, and quietly confident. His participative leadership style made him easy to follow and elicited minimal resentments. It also fit the ethos of the times.

In appearance, the NCA charismatic was very feminine. But her rather authoritarian style of leadership apparently created some resentments and also conflicted with her femininity for some of her followers and other observers. That they perceived such conflict is evident from expressions they used to refer to her that implied (1) that she was more male than female; or (2) that she was male in every respect save for the appropriate genitalia. Both attributions implied she should be male, was almost male, but still fell short of maleness. Other followers accepted her femininity and then responded in sex-stereotypical ways. Some had chivalrous reactions and wanted to take care of her. Male followers and subordinates spoke about her lack of experience in coping with the "tough, real world" and of her need for male guidance and counseling. In general, the ethos of her times helped to suggest that any imperfections—real or imagined—could be attributed to her sex, which meant she lacked something compared to males. Under such circumstances, it is clear that her charisma was also suspect as somehow imperfect. It is impossible to assess with any confidence how important the sexual difference was for routinization, but, if it had any effects at all, it was probably detrimental to the routinization of this female leader's charisma.

There is no evidence that being female is an insurmountable barrier to being a successful charismatic leader, but relatively few female charismatics come to mind. Mary Baker Eddy, the founder of the Christian Science Church, is one well-known and successful example (Dakin, 1929).

Joan of Arc may have been another. In the empirical literature we reviewed, only Roberts (1984) studied a woman she considered charismatic. All of the other empirical studies focused on male leaders. Perhaps women with charismatic personal qualities are less likely to be accepted by followers. These speculations, however, go beyond our data. The founder of NCA was accepted and was a successful charismatic leader; her charisma, however, was not successfully routinized. Whether gender affects the emergence as well as the routinization of charisma is a question for further research.

CONCLUSIONS

Factors affecting routinization of charisma can be divided into those internal to the routinization process and those present in the social context within which it unfolds. Our comparison of two cases strongly suggests some lessons that may be applicable to other cases: First, as Weber suggested, routinization is hampered by the direct involvement of the charismatic in the mundane features of administration. Because charisma requires its possessor to have exceptional qualities, anything that tends to compromise that exceptionality dilutes the charisma. Followers probably will accept some foibles (for example, some degree of sexual misconduct may be tolerated), but a continuous, active role in the mundane side of the movement or organization creates frequent and pervasive occasions in which exceptionality is clearly *not* preserved.

Second, when organizations fail to develop a strong, reinforcing culture—including ritual and ceremonies to transfer and diffuse charisma, together with a written testament and oral tradition to guide behavior—the organizing force behind the charisma tends to fade away over time. Because the appeal of charisma is based more on emotional than on rational responses, it is extremely important that the emotional content of the charismatic's message continue to find expression within the organization. Such expression can be assured only by the creation of a viable culture around the charismatic message and mission.

Third, if the question of succession is not managed so that the successor chosen is tied firmly into the charisma, the organization is unlikely to retain a clear direction consonant with the charismatic mission. Successors who lack prior commitment to the mission are likely to try to implement their own visions and mission, which are unlikely to coincide with or reinforce those of the charismatic.

Fourth, the creation of an administrative structure is not sufficient to hold together the followers of a charismatic and to insure continuity of the charismatic mission. In the absence of other forms of routinization, the administrative task may become dominant, leading to increased specialization and professionalization of the staff, and to ideological divisiveness and political splintering within the membership.

Finally, factors in the social situation can help or hinder the routinization of charisma. As has also been observed for successful business organizations (Peters & Waterman, 1982), the successful male charismatic in our study made a point of "keeping it simple." There was little chance for confusion or ambiguity about his message, his mission, or his success. Also, he was able to recruit followers who already subscribed to his goals and only needed to be convinced of the efficacy of his means, and he had the further advantage that his followers were affected by the same potent and real threat. Financial resources were not problematic because the technology of AA was not expensive, which made it easy to expand the membership and thus broaden the organization's financial base. Finally, belonging to the dominant sex could not have hurt his effort. The combination of such favorable circumstances facilitated routinization and produced a remarkably effective SMO.

The female charismatic operated in a much less favorable situation. Her mission was complex and involved relatively expensive activities. Its outcomes were harder to demonstrate, especially over the short term. Her followers were motivated largely by altruism, and had other, more important, motivations and interests in their lives. Also, those members motivated by more powerful self-interests were usually motivated to deflect her mission for their own ends. Although the complexity of her mission enabled her organization to seek funding from various sources, these sources also tended to encourage further elaborations of the mission and were not dependable over the long term. Finally, being a female during a period in which sex stereotyping was prevalent may have created a disturbing, distracting element in her charisma. Despite these relatively unfavorable circumstances and incomplete routinization, her charisma still had powerful effects. Her mission has been partially realized, and the SMO she founded continues to exist and recently shows signs of reemphasizing that mission.

Clearly, charisma is a potent force for change—a force so potent that even when it is only partially routinized, it can bring about important change. By better understanding its manifestations and its routinization in formal organizations, organizational scholars eventually may be able to guide the nurturance of charisma and thus provide another way for organizations to produce desired change.

ACKNOWLEDGMENTS

We wish to acknowledge with sincere thanks the helpful comments of Lou Pondy and Robin Williams on an earlier draft, the assistance of Robert House in locating empirical studies relevant to his theory, and the cheerful and persistent talents of Shirley Foster in locating relevant materials in the Cornell University library.

NOTES

1.   Weber (1947, p. 364) states that charisma "becomes either traditionalized or rationalized, or a combination of both;" Gerth and Mills (1946, p. 420) provide an example of the traditionalized outcome among the Chinese literati of the Middle Ages. Other examples are Geertz's analyses (1977) of the routinization of royal charisma into traditionalized authority in Java and Morocco. Blau and Scott (1962, p. 31), however, interpret Weber as viewing the crystallization of charisma as "more often" becoming "bureaucratized into the legal authority of a formal organization."

2.   Weber (1949) provided specific guidelines for constructing "ideal types;" they have been examined in detail by McKinney (1966, p. 5). He defined a constructed type as "a pragmatically devised system of characteristics, made up of abstracted elements and formed into a unified conceptual pattern wherein there may be an intensification of one or more attributes for purposes of utility." Moreover, these types focus on uniformity, the deviations from which provide the basis for hypothesis construction. Consequently, "although examinations of empirical cases may never reveal anything more than approximations or deviations from the constructed type, it is essential. . . that the type should be formulated as being objectively probable" (McKinney, 1966, p. 5). In essence, the constructed type, for Weber, isolated and emphasized the most distinctive and salient aspects of an empirical phenomenon.

3.   Gerth and Mills are taking the long view, so by "quickly" they probably mean within the lifetime of the charismatic.

4.   The founder of AA so quoted his own earlier pronouncements during a discussion at a meeting of the Board of Trustees in 1957; the quotation is taken from notes of that meeting.

5.   The founder of NCA was restating what she had been saying "all along." The quotation is from notes taken at a public address in Syracuse, NY, during 1957 or 1958.

6.   In respect for this norm, we will not name these two leaders.

7.   AA says officially it was founded by both men, but the doctor died in 1950—more than 20 years before the other founder, and his leadership was much less influential than that of the charismatic. He had none of the personal characteristics of a charismatic leader. We doubt AA would be the successful organization it is today if the doctor had been the sole founder. Thus, we consider the charismatic to be the pivotal founder of AA.

8.   "God grant me the serenity to accept the things I cannot change, courage to change the things I can, and wisdom to know the difference."

9.   See note 7.

10.   A fuller treatment of rites and ceremonials is available in Trice (1985) and Trice and Beyer (1984).

REFERENCES

Alcoholics Anonymous World Services. (1953). *Twelve steps and twelve traditions.* New York: Alcoholics Anonymous Publishing.

Alcoholics Anonymous World Services. (1957). *Alcoholics Anonymous comes of age.* New York: Alcoholics Anonymous Publishing. (Original work published 1939).

Alexander, J. (1941, March). Alcoholics Anonymous. *Saturday Evening Post, 213,* 9–11, 89–90.

Anonymous. (1939). *Alcoholics Anonymous.* New York: Works Publishing Co.

Apter, D. (1966). *The politics of modernization.* Chicago: University of Chicago Press.

Bacharach, S. B., & Lawler, E. J. (1980). *Power and politics in organizations.* San Francisco: Jossey-Bass.

Bendix, R. (1959). *Max Weber: An intellectual portrait.* London: Methuen.

Berger, P. L. (1963). Charisma and religious innovation: The social location of Israelite prophecy. *American Sociological Review, 28,* 940–949.

Berlew, D. E. (1979). Leadership and organizational excitement. In D. A. Kolb, I. M. Rubin, & J. M. McIntyre (Eds.), *Organizational psychology: A book of readings* (3rd ed.) (pp. 343–356). Englewoods Cliffs, NJ: Prentice-Hall.

Blau, P. M. & Scott, W. R. (1962). *Formal organizations.* San Francisco: Chandler.

Bradley, R. T. (1984). *Charisma and social structure: A relational analysis of power and communion in communes.* Unpublished working manuscript, University of Minnesota, Minneapolis.

Bromley, D. G., & Shupe, A. D. (1979). *Moonies in America: Cult, church, and crusade.* Beverly Hills, CA: Sage.

Burns, J. M. (1978). *Leadership.* New York: Harper & Row.

Cantril, H. (1941). *The psychology of social movements.* New York: Wiley.

Clark, B. R. (1970). *The distinctive college: Antioch, Reed, and Swarthmore.* Chicago: Aldine.

Clark, B. R. (1972). The organizational saga in higher education. *Administrative Science Quarterly, 17,* 178–184.

Constas, H. (1961). The USSR—From charismatic sect to bureaucratic society. *Administrative Science Quarterly, 6,* 282–298.

Dakin, E. F. (1929). *Mrs. Eddy: Founder of Christian Science.* New York: Grosset & Dunlop.

Day, P. J. (1980). Charismatic leadership in the small organization. *Human Organization, 19* (1), 50–58.

Dornbusch, S. M. (1955). The military academy as an assimilating institution. *Social Forces, 33,* 316–321.

Dow, T. E. (1969). The theory of charisma. *Social Quarterly, 10,* 306–318.

Drachkovitch, M. M. (1964). Succession and the charismatic leader in Yugoslavia. *Journal of International Affairs, 18* (1), 54–66.

Dubofsky, M., & Van Tine, W. (1977). *John L. Lewis: A biography.* New York: Quadrangle/The New York Times Book Company.

Eisenstadt, S. N. (1968). *Max Weber: On charisma and institution building—Selected papers.* Chicago: University of Chicago Press.

Etemand, B. (1978). Extrication from cultism. *Current Psychiatric Therapy, 18,* 217–223.

Etzioni, A. (1961). *A comparative analysis of complex organizations.* Glencoe, IL: The Free Press.

Fine, G. A. (1982). The Manson family: The folklore traditions of a small group. *Journal of the Folklore Institute, 19,* 47–60.

Friedland, W. H. (1964). For a sociological concept of charisma. *Social Forces, 43*(1), 18–26.

Friedrich, C. J. (1961, February). Political leadership and the problem of the charismatic power. *Journal of Politics, 23,* 3–24.

Galanter, M. (1981). Sociobiography and informal social controls of drinking: Findings from two charismatic sects. *Journal of Studies on Alcohol, 42* (1), 64–79.

Galanter, M. (1982). Charismatic religious sects and psychiatry: An overview. *American Journal of Psychiatry, 139* (12), 1539–1548.

Geertz, C. (1977). Centers, kings and charisma: Reflections on the symbolics of power. In J. Ben-David & T. N. Clark (Eds.), *Culture and its creators: Essays in honor of Edward Shils* (pp. 150–171). Chicago: University of Chicago Press.

Gerth, H., & Mills, C. W. (Eds.) (1946). *From Max Weber.* New York: Oxford University Press.

Heberle, R. (1951). *Social movements: An introduction to political sociology.* New York: Appleton-Century-Crofts.

Holusha, J. (1983, July 15). Cuts, U.S. Aids, and Iacocca were factors in Chrysler turn around. *The New York Times,* D1, D6.

House, R. (1977). A 1976 theory of charismatic leadership. In J. G. Hunt & L. L. Larson (Eds.), *Leadership: The cutting edge* (pp. 189–273). Carbondale, IL: Southern Illinois University Press.

House, R. J., & Baetz, M. L. (1979). Leadership: Some empirical generalizations and new research directions. In B. M. Staw (Ed.), *Research in organizational behavior* (Vol. 1) (pp. 341–423). Greenwich, CT: JAI Press.

Kanter, R. M. (1968). Commitment and social organizations: A study of commitment mechanisms in utopian communities. *American Sociological Review, 33*(4), 499–518.

Kanter, R. M. (1972). *Commitment and community.* Cambridge, MA: Harvard University Press.

Kenniston, K. (1965). *The uncommitted: Alienated youth in American society.* New York: Harcourt Brace and World.

Kurtz, E. (1979). *Not-God: A history of Alcoholics Anonymous.* Center City, MN: Hazeldon Education Services.

Lee, Alfred L. (1944). Techniques of social reform: An analysis of the new prohibition drive. *American Sociological Review, 9,* 65–77.

Levine, S. V., & Salter, N. E. (1976). Youth and contemporary religious movements: Psychological findings. *Canadian Psychiatric Association Journal, 21,* 411–420.

Lodahl, A. (1982). *Crisis in values and the success of the Unification Church.* Unpublished thesis, Department of Sociology, Cornell University, Ithaca, NY.

Madsen, D., & Snow, P. G. (1983). The dispersion of charisma. *Comparative Political Studies, 16*(3), 337–362.

Maxwell, M. A. (1982). Alcoholics Anonymous. In E. L. Gomberg & H. R. White (Eds.), *Alcohol, science and society revisited* (pp. 295–305). Ann Arbor, MI: University of Michigan and Rutgers University Center of Alcohol Studies.

McIntosh, D. (1970). Weber and Freud: On the nature and source of authority. *American Sociological Review, 35,* 901–912.

McKinney, J. C. (1966). *Constructive typology and social theory.* New York: Appleton-Century-Crofts.

Miller, F. C. (1966). Problems of succession in a Chippewa council. In M. J. Swartz & V. W. Turner (Eds.), *Political anthropology* (pp. 173–185). Chicago: Aldine.

Miles, R. H. (1982). *Coffin nails and corporate strategies.* Englewood Cliffs, NJ: Prentice-Hall.

Mitroff, I. O., Kilman, R. H., & Saxton, M. J. (1983). *Organizational culture: Collective order-making of an ambiguous world.* Unpublished manuscript, School of Management, University of Southern California, Los Angeles, CA.

Mulford, H. A., & Miller, D. E. (1961). Public definitions of the alcoholic. *Quarterly Journal of Studies on Alcohol, 22,* 312–320.

Padover, S. K. (1955). George Washington: Portrait of a true conservative. *Social Research, 22,* 199–222.

Parsons, T. (1947). Introduction. In M. Weber, *The theory of social and economic organization* (A. M. Henderson & T. Parsons, Eds. & Trans.) (pp. 3–86). Glencoe, IL: The Free Press.

Peters, T. J., & Waterman, R. H., Jr. (1982). *In search of excellence: Lessons from America's best-run companies.* New York: Harper & Row.

Pettigrew, A. M. (1979). On studying organizational cultures. *Administrative Science Quarterly, 24,* 570–581.

Pondy, L. R. (1977). The other hand clapping: An information processing approach to organizational power. In T. H. Hammer & S. B. Bacharach (Eds.), *Reward systems and power distribution* (pp. 56–91). Ithaca, NY: School of Industrial and Labor Relations, Cornell University.

Quarterly Journal of Studies on Alcohol. (1946). Report on activities of the National Committee for Education on Alcoholism. *Quarterly Journal of Studies on Alcohol, 7,* 471–490.

Roberts, N. C. (1984, August). *Transforming leadership: Sources, process, consequences.* Paper presented to the annual meeting of the Academy of Management, Boston, MA.

Salaman, G. (1977). A historical discontinuity: From charisma to routinization. *Human Relations, 30*(4), 373–388.

Schwartz, B. (1983). George Washington and the Whig conception of heroic leadership. *American Sociological Review, 48*(1), 18–33.

Schweiter, A. (1984). *The age of charisma.* Chicago: Nelson-Hall.

Scott, W. R. (1981). *Organizations: Rational, natural, and open systems.* Englewood Cliffs, NJ: Prentice-Hall.

Selznick, P. (1957). *Leadership in administration: A sociological interpretation.* New York: Harper & Row.

Shils, E. (1965a). Charisma. In D. Sills (Ed.), *International encyclopedia of the social sciences* (Vol. 2) (pp. 386–390). New York: The Macmillan Company and The Free Press.

Shils, E. (1965b). Charisma, order, and status. *American Sociological Review, 30,* 199–213.

Smith, B. J. (1982). *An initial test of a theory of charismatic leadership based on the responses of subordinates.* Unpublished doctoral dissertation, University of Toronto.

Trice, H. M. (1958). Alcoholics Anonymous. *The Annals of the American Academy of Political and Social Science, 315,* 108–116.

Trice, H. M. (1985). Rites and ceremonials in organizational cultures. In S. B. Bacharach (Ed.), *Perspectives in organizational sociology: Theory and research* (Vol. 4). Greenwich, CT: JAI Press.

Trice, H. M., & Beyer, J. M. (1984). Studying organizational cultures through rites and ceremonials. *Academy of Management Review, 9*(4), 653–669.

Trice, H. M., & Roman, P. M. (1970a). Sociopsychological predictors of affiliation with Alcoholics Anonymous: A longitudinal study of 'treatment' success. *Social Psychiatry, 5,* 51–59.

Trice, H. M., & Roman, P. M. (1970b). Delabeling, relabeling, and Alcoholics Anonymous. *Social Problems, 17,* 538–546.

Van de Ven, A., Ludwig, D., Oppenheim, L., & Davis, P. (1983). *An attempt to institutionalize an organization's culture.* Paper presented at Symposium on Organizational Culture, Academy of Management Annual Meeting, Dallas.

Weber, M. (1947). *The theory of social and economic organization* (A. M. Henderson & T. Parsons, Eds. & Trans.). Glencoe, IL: The Free Press.

Weber, M. (1949). *The methodology of the social sciences* (E. A. Shils & H. A. Finch, Eds. & Trans.). Glencoe, IL: The Free Press.

Yulk, G. A., & Van Fleet, D. D. (1982). Cross-situational, multi-method research on military leader effectiveness. *Organizational Behavior and Human Performance, 30,* 87–108.

Zald, M. N., & Ash, R. (1966). Social movement organizations: Growth, decay, and change. *Social Forces, 44,* 327–341.

Zaleznik, A., & Kets de Vries, M. F. R. (1975). *Power and the corporate mind.* Boston: Houghton Mifflin.

PARTICIPATION IN DECISION-MAKING: ONE MORE LOOK[1]

Edwin A. Locke and David M. Schweiger

ABSTRACT

The issue of worker participation in decision-making involves more ideological connotations than any issue in organizational behavior. This has led to biased research in the U.S. and to extensive legislation in Europe. It is argued that the ideological arguments for PDM are not logically defensible and that it is properly treated as a practical issue. Participation is best defined as "joint decision-making" and therefore excludes delegation (job enrichment). Various types and degrees of PDM are identified. Theoretically it has been argued that PDM increases morale because it helps the worker to get what he wants from the job. It also has been asserted that PDM increases productive efficiency through both cognitive and motivational mechanisms. An extensive review of research on PDM leads to the conclusion that: (a) a number of experimental field studies involved so many variables that no conclusions can be drawn from them regarding the effects of PDM: (b) three other categories of studies (experimental laboratory, correlational field, and univariate experimental field studies) found that: PDM usually leads to higher satisfaction but not to higher productivity than more authoritative management styles. Numerous contextual factors which determine the conditions under which PDM will lead to increased satisfaction and productivity are identified. The relationship of PDM to three other motivational techniques (money, goal setting and job enrichment) are discussed. It is concluded that subordinate knowledge is the single most important contextual factor determining the usefulness of PDM, assuming that productivity is the major goal of an organization. It is shown why productivity and not satisfaction is the proper goal of a profit making organization.

I. INTRODUCTION: PARTICIPATION AND IDEOLOGY

No issue in the field of organizational behavior and industrial relations is more loaded with ideological and moral connotations than that of worker participation in decision making (PDM). As is characteristic of ideological movements, the impetus for PDM has come from intellectuals rather than from workers (Strauss and Rosenstein, 1970). The attitude of many contemporary intellectuals with respect to PDM is illustrated by the following two incidents (witnessed by the senior author).

A college professor was lecturing a group of executives on "humanistic management" and told them the following anecdote: "I once asked one of my graduate students what he would recommend, as a management consultant, if 95 percent of the studies of participation in decision making had found that it worked no better or worked worse than nonparticipative methods. The student answered: 'I guess I would tell managers not to use it.' At that point [said the professor] I realized that we had failed in our graduate training."

The professor's point was that the student should recommend the use of participation regardless of its practical consequences.

The second incident involved a young assistant professor being interviewed for a job at a large eastern university. He was explaining, to the senior professors interviewing him, a method he had devised for organizational change which always involved the use of participation. One of the senior professors asked him how he reconciled the use of PDM with the somewhat contradictory research findings on the subject. "I don't care what the research shows," he replied curtly, "it's a moral issue."

Views similar to these have been advocated or are cited in numerous published books and articles (Blumberg, 1968; Davies, 1967; Foy and Gadon, 1976; Hespe and Wall, undated; Lischeron and Wall, 1975; Schregle, 1970; see Dachler and Wilpert, 1978, for further documentation). Systems of management which do not stress PDM have been accused of being "exploitative," "dictatorial," "ahuman," and even "neo-Nazi" (Macrae, 1977; Davies, 1967; Leavitt, 1965; Nicol, 1948) at worst, and hopelessly anachronistic and inefficient at best. As Tannenbaum (1974) puts it, "The question for many . . . is not whether participation works but rather how to *make* it work" (p. 105).

This antagonism toward nonparticipative management and the "authoritarian-materialistic" culture with which it is often associated is revealed in the following poem which was quoted in one pro-PDM article:

> Sweet Mary your production's poor,
> Just dry your tears and go,
> For speed and greed are rated high,
> But love-for-others, no.
> (Gillespie, 1971, p. 74)

Despite the moralistic tone in which PDM is often discussed, most supporters of PDM in the United States, in contrast to those in Europe, have thus far advocated the *voluntary* adoption of participative practices in industry. There are two major reasons for this. First, most Americans still value freedom, at least to some extent. Second, many American intellectuals in the social sciences are reluctant to advocate public policy on moral grounds alone. They are skeptical of systematic ideologies and demand "practical" evidence that ideas will work before applying them.[2] Thus many articles advocating PDM have taken a pragmatic approach (e.g., Bennis, 1966; Likert, 1961, 1967; McCormick, 1938; White and Lippitt, 1960). However, since the research evidence is somewhat equivocal, this approach provides little impetus for immediate legislation.

While there are groups such as the New Left who advocate the imposition of "participatory democracy" onto society as a whole by revolutionary means, their views have not gained wide acceptance in the United States—mainly because their real motive, the establishment of dictatorship, has been effectively exposed (Hessen, 1968; Rand, 1971b).

More recently, some respected social scientists have advocated government legislation to force organizations to improve the "quality of work life" (e.g., Lawler, 1976; see Locke, 1976b, for a rebuttal), but these suggestions have not yet attracted the serious attention of Congress. This may seem surprising in view of the present Welfare State climate. However, the "quality of work life" is a vague concept and therefore difficult to use as a basis for specific legislative proposals. Furthermore, the labor movement has been effectively stressing their particular brand of "participation" (i.e., collective bargaining to determine wages, seniority rights, working conditions, fringe benefits, etc.) with legislative help for decades, and have shown a strong reluctance to being "co-opted" by management-sponsored participation schemes (e.g., Gomberg, 1966).

While the advocates of PDM in the United States have not seen their pragmatic arguments translated into legislation, their ideological pre-, commitment to PDM is clearly evident even in research articles. This pro-PDM bias can be seen at every stage of the research process: in the design of experiments, in the interpretation of results, and in the reporting of findings.

Consider first experimental design. Typically those assigned the role of participative leaders in PDM experiments are considerate, polite, friendly, and rational. Such leaders are often compared with "authoritarian" leaders, who are cold, punitive, tactless, arbitrary, and often not very knowledgeable about the task being performed (Anderson, 1959). Not surprisingly, experimental subjects typically like the participative leaders better. Such package dealing diverts the reader from consideration of other possible combinations of traits, e.g., an authoritative leader who is considerate and highly knowledgeable, or a participative leader who is ignorant and unassertive.

Interpretations of research are also frequently biased. For example, one can find many reports of research projects in organizations in which anywhere from two or three to nine new policies or procedures were introduced (e.g., changes in incentives, technology, hours of work, participation, etc.), but in which PDM is arbitrarily singled out as *the* variable responsible for the positive results obtained. Or, in cases where the PDM group performed less well than the non-PDM group, it is baldly asserted that the effectiveness of the latter group *would* have deteriorated if the experiment had lasted longer. Or, in studies where only correlational analyses were performed, the results are interpreted as demonstrating the causal efficacy of PDM. (PDM advocates, however, are by no means the only group guilty of interpreting correlations as proving causality; Locke, 1969.) Another tactic is "criterion switching" in which certain experimental outcomes such as productivity are downplayed, while other outcomes more favorable to PDM, such as satisfaction, are arbitarily stressed as being more significant.

Even more blatant bias can be found in the reporting of results of PDM research. For example, borderline results may be exaggerated; particular findings from a given study which would change the overall interpretation may be omitted; and negative studies may not be mentioned at all.

Thus it is not surprising to encounter such incredible statements as:

There is hardly a study in the entire literature which fails to demonstrate the satisfaction in work is enhanced or that other generally acknowledged beneficial consequences accrue from a genuine increase in workers' decision-making power (Blumber, 1968, p. 123, italics omitted)

For a similarly sanguine view, see Kahn, 1974. The design, interpretation, and reporting of PDM research is not without its critics, however, as we shall see later in this essay (e.g., Leavitt, 1965; Lowin, 1968; Mansbridge, 1973; Strauss, 1963).

The pro-PDM bias in other countries, especially Europe, is even more extreme that that in the United States (Dachler and Wilpert, 1978; Strauss & Rosenstein, 1970). The ideological preference for PDM is more explicit, more universal, and more openly political in tone. Consequently, there has been less interest in small-scale research projects involving direct participation on the shop floor and more emphasis on establishing PDM, often called "industrial democracy," by force of law or government decree (McInnes, 1976).

These laws often require the formation of "works (or worker) councils" which assure representation of the rank and file on committees or boards which make or are consulted on decisions regarding the firm as a whole (Sturmthal, 1964). Germany is the most well-known advocate of "codetermination" through works councils (Raskin, 1976). Similar or related mechanisms exist in France, Israel, Sweden, Yugoslavia, and many other countries (Derber, 1970; Lammers, 1967; Schregle, 1970; Strauss and Rosenstein, 1970; Tannenbaum, 1974; Teague, 1971; Van de Vall and King, 1973). Radical legislative proposals along the same lines are now being considered in England (McInnes, 1977).

Since it is asserted (in differing degrees) by both American and European advocates of PDM that it is a moral issue, it is worth discussing the arguments on which this assertion is based. Again we must distinguish between the United States and Europe, since the arguments are somewhat different in each case, although at root (as we shall see) they stem from a common premise.

As noted above, the arguments offered in favor of PDM in the United States are less openly ideological than in Europe. The moral argument, when used, is often implicit and goes approximately as follows: The United States is a democracy; democracy is good; PDM is democratic; therefore PDM in business organizations is good (or good for the United States).

This argument has two major fallacies. First, the United States is not a democracy. It is a constitutional republic. A pure democracy, in the original Greek sense, is a system of government based on unlimited majority rule.[3] In contrast, our form of government protects the rights of the minority (i.e., of the individual) through constitutional guarantees.

Second, it does not follow logically that the form of organization appropriate to the government of a country is equally appropriate to the management of institutions within that country. For example, a government has a monopoly over the use of physical force, but no one would suggest that business organizations be given the power to use force, since the result would be anarchy and the destruction of all rights. Similarly, republics give their citizens the right to elect government representatives as a means of insuring that their rights will continue to be protected. This is necessary precisely because a government has the power to use physical force and therefore the potential to violate rights. In contrast, a legally mandated majority vote of the employees of a business organization as a means of electing directors and making decisions would not protect rights. Rather, it would abrogate the rights of the owners of the business to use their property as they see fit.

The rights of employees do not go unprotected in a free economy. Employees who are defrauded by owners can seek redress in the courts. Those who disagree with their employer's policies are also free to attempt to change them through persuasion, to organize unions, to quit the company, to seek employment elsewhere, or to start their own companies. Employees are also protected by competition among companies for reputation. Those which become known as "good companies to work for" are able to attract the best employees and gain a competitive advantage, thereby forcing other companies to improve their policies.

The degree of respect for property rights is precisely the issue that most fundamentally separates the United States and Europe. In the United States there is still a degree of respect for such rights, and therefore PDM has not been legislated within business organizations to the degree that it has in Europe.

Advocates of compulsory PDM in Europe are often socialists (Strauss and Rosenstein, 1970), who see PDM as a useful method of helping to abolish private property. (Some leftists, however, oppose participation schemes, fearing that they will reduce the revolutionary fervor of the masses or will prevent workers from opposing management).

Pursuing the issue a step further, let us consider the grounds on which the socialists advocate socialism. The pragmatic answer would be that socialism promotes economic prosperity and the general welfare. However, this cannot be accepted as the real motive, since there is overwhelming evidence that socialism cannot achieve prosperity in theory (Von

Mises, 1951/1962) and does not achieve it in practice (Kaiser, 1976; Smith, 1976).

Furthermore, under socialism the individual citizen does not even achieve influence. Since all property is owned by the state, if a consumer or employee is dissatisfied with products, wages, or working conditions, there is nothing he can do about it except to become head of state. Contrast this with capitalism, where businesses must adjust their products, prices, and working conditions to what the market demands (i.e., the individual monetary vote of the citizens) or go out of business.

If socialism cannot and does not achieve material prosperity, then why is it so widely advocated in preference to capitalism?

Rand (1964, 1966) has identified the basic conflict between capitalism and socialism as a *moral* one. Capitalism rests on the morality of egoism, the doctrine that man is an end in himself and not a means to the end of others. Socialism is advocated in the name of altruism, the doctrine that man is a means to the ends of others, an object of sacrifice, e.g., to the State, the Party, the Race, God, society, etc. Socialists, in short, consider socialism to be morally superior to capitalism whether it works (economically) or not.

However, the issue is not consciously expressed in this form in the PDM or industrial democracy literature, but rather in a form which derives from this basic moral conflict. Egoism implies individualism and rights (including property rights), i.e., the freedom to act on and reap the consequences of one's individual choices. Altruism implies the sacrifice of individuality and freedom. One way to sacrifice individuality is to make everyone equal.

Socialism, (pure) democracy, and participation are all ultimately advocated in the name of *egalitarianism* as a moral ideal. One article (written in the United States!) actually likened the perfect participative organization to an *amoeba* in which there are no separate parts or elements and all actions are totally integrated (Preston and Post, 1974).

Thus, contrary to a commonly held view (e.g., Strauss and Rosenstein, 1970), PDM in the last analysis is not advocated from two entirely different viewpoints; i.e., human relations theory in the United States and socialist ideology abroad, but in the name of the *same* moral ideal of equality in each case. The only difference is that the implications of egalitarianism have not been carried as far in the United States due to the strength of the conflicting ideal of individualism.

Let us now consider briefly the issue of equality. (We are indebted to Rand, 1971a, for the arguments to follow.) As the Founding Fathers viewed it, the principle that "all men are created equal" referred to equality before the law. It meant that all men, by virtue of being human, possessed the same "natural rights" (to life, liberty, and the pursuit of happiness. Rand, 1964, has defined a right as "a moral principle defining and sanctioning a man's freedom of action in a social context. . . . It means freedom from physical compulsion, coercion or interference by other men" pp. 93–94). Equality in this context has a strictly *political* meaning. It was *not* meant to imply that all men had the same degree of intelligence, knowledge, character, or ambition, since they obviously do not.

Nor would *voluntary* participation in decision making among men of differing ability make them equal in their performance, since, given that all share the same rational goal, the more able men will exert the most influence on the decision (e.g., see Mulder and Wilke, 1970). In a free economy the more competent and ambitious men will ordinarily reach positions of higher responsibility and receive higher wages than those with less ability and motivation.

One could only insure equality among men with respect to actions and results by *force,* i.e., by *abrogating,* through political means, the freedom of men to act (e.g., such as throttling the potential entrepreneur under socialism) or the freedom to keep or use the fruits of their actions (e.g., through taxation, wage price controls, and the progressive abrogation of property rights in a welfare state).

Note that this form of forced equality of actions or results is diametrically *opposed to* and incompatible with the view of political equality held by the Founding Fathers. Forced equality makes men either equal in having *no* rights, or *unequal* before the law since the less competent receive special, unearned favors at the expense of the more competent.[4]

What conclusions, then, can be drawn about the status of PDM as a moral issue?

While it is not the purpose of this essay to prove any particular theory of morality or of rights (but see Rand, 1964), *if* one accepts the premise that man has rights (including property rights, since these are inseparable from the right to life), then equality achieved through forced participation (including pure democracy) must be rejected as *immoral* on the grounds that it negates rights.

Alternatively, if one holds that PDM should be established voluntarily on the grounds that it promotes the U.S. form of government, this must be rejected as false, since PDM is not analogous to republican forms of government and since it does not follow logically that all methods appropriate to governing countries are appropriate to running private organizations.

Finally, even if equality of actions and results as such were held to be a morally desirable goal, voluntary participation does not attain it, since, with respect to knowledge and motivation, men are not equal.

Thus, we must conclude that, unless one denies the existence of rights, the arguments offered in support of the view that participation is desirable on moral grounds alone are not logically defensible.

This leaves only one other basis on which to advocate participation. It could be promoted on practical grounds, i.e., on the premise that the use of PDM will make organizations function more efficiently. As noted earlier, this argument has been widely promulgated by social scientists, especially those from the United States; however, since there has been considerable bias in the analysis and reporting of the results, it is time for one more look. The remainder of this essay will be devoted to exploring the evidence offered in support of the view that PDM fosters greater organizational effectiveness than other methods of managing and decision making.

Before we can discuss the research findings, however, we must clearly identify what the concept of participation means in an organizational context and the reasons it is alleged to be effective.

II. DEFINING PARTICIPATION

Despite the intellectuals' ideological attachment to PDM, there is surprisingly little consensus as to its exact meaning. As one writer observed, "Workers' participation has become a magic word in many countries. Yet almost everyone who employs the term thinks of something different" (Schregle, 1970, p. 117). One writer, for example, identifies PDM as active (ego) involvement (Allport, 1945); another argues that it entails a feeling of obligation to work for the best interests of the group (Schultz, 1951). American social scientists define PDM as a specific managerial style while European writers see it as a legally mandated mechanism for employees to influence organizational decisions (Strauss and Rosenstein, 1970). Some writers see PDM as including delegation (Lowin, 1968; Sashkin, 1976; Sorcher, 1971; Strauss, 1963; Tannenbaum, 1962), while others view them as separate phenomena (Davis, 1963). Several approaches identify PDM with group involvement or group decision making (Davis, 1957, 1963, 1967). A common element in many definitions is the concept of equalization of influence or power sharing (Heller and Yukl, 1969; Lammers, 1967; French, Israel, and As, 1960; Leavitt, 1965; Tannenbaum, 1974).

To resolve this confusion, let us begin by consulting the dictionary. The 1961 *Oxford English Dictionary* defines participation as:

1. The action or fact of partaking, having or forming a part of; the partaking of the substance, quality, or nature of some thing or person. 2. The fact or condition of

sharing in common (with others or with each other); association as partners, partnership, fellowship; profit-sharing. b. A taking part, association, or sharing (with others) in some action or matter.

The first definition would not be particularly useful in an organizational context, since it would make participation virtually synonymous with organizational membership as such. The second definition is more pertinent. It implies, first, that there must be at least two persons involved, and second, that something must be shared in common among these persons. Thus PDM may be defined in essence as "joint decision making," in agreement with Tannenbaum and Massarick (1950) and Vroom (1960).

Note that this definition does not logically necessitate decision making by groups of subordinates; it could involve just one supervisor and one subordinate. Furthermore, this definition does not necessitate that the sharing be equal, but only that there be *some* degree of sharing. Finally, the definition does not specify the content of what is shared. The example given in the dictionary is profit sharing, which refers to the *results* of the common effort. The concept of PDM itself refers specifically to participation in the process of reaching decisions.

PDM vs. Delegation

In the opinion of the present writers, the above definition of participation *excludes* delegation. The process of delegation, in an organizational context, involves *assigning* specific responsibilities to subordinates. The result is not a "sharing in common" with others, but rather an explicit division of labor which is determined hierarchically. The subordinate does not participate in the decision to delegate, nor does the supervisor participate in the decisions which are delegated. PDM would be involved (in addition to delegation) if the supervisor and subordinate decided together how much responsibility the subordinate would be given. While delegation could, then, be achieved participatively, it need not be. Thus participation does not logically imply delegation, nor vice versa.

The failure to separate these two concepts, in our opinion, has led to serious confusion in the PDM literature. The merging of PDM with delegation has led to a merging of the human relations school with the cognitive growth school (for example, see Susman, 1976). While there is nothing wrong with combining elements of these two schools of thought in practice, they are conceptually distinct. The human relations school stresses the importance of developing good supervisor-subordinate relationships (through PDM) and cohesive work groups in order to satisfy man's social needs. The cognifive growth school advocates job enrichment through delegating individual responsibility in order to satisfy man's need to grow in his knowledge, efficacy, and individuality (Herzberg, 1966).

Furthermore, PDM as a technique implies no specific content; it is simply a *method* of reaching decisions. Job enrichment, in contrast, explicitly involves the restructuring of the work task so as to provide additional mental challenge (although in practice other elements may be involved, e.g., see Locke, 1975).

As noted above, participation could be used (and has been used, e.g., see Locke, Sirota, and Wolfson, 1976) as a method of introducing job enrichment, but it could also involve joint decision making regarding many other issues, such as pay. (When PDM is used to introduce job enrichment, the kinds of job changes made may deviate considerably from what job enrichment theory specifies, e.g., see Seeborg, 1978). Job enrichment sometimes involves the development of work groups, but it need not do so. Similarly, jobs may be enriched successfully without using participation (Ford, 1969).

Let us now consider some dimensions on which PDM can vary.

Types of PDM

First, PDM can be *forced* or *voluntary*. The force, when it exists, is applied by law or government decree (e.g., codetermination); partially forced PDM would occur in cases where it results from a contract between management and labor but where management legally is compelled to bargain (e.g., American labor unions); voluntary PDM would occur where management initiates the idea of PDM and the employees agree to it (e.g., most Scanlon Plans), or vice versa.

Second, PDM can be *formal* or *informal*. Formal PDM involves the creation of officially recognized decision making or bargaining bodies, e.g., unions, committees, councils, boards, whereas informal PDM is based on the personal relationship between each supervisor or manager and his subordinates.

Third, participation may be *direct* or *indirect* (Lammers, 1967). Direct PDM is usually of the shop floor variety where each employee has the opportunity to assert his views, whereas indirect PDM involves the election of representatives who speak for the employees as members of higher-level committees and decision-making bodies.

Typically, these three dimensions form a pattern. Forced PDM tends to be formal and indirect and is most common in Europe, whereas voluntary PDM tends to be informal (except for unions) and direct and is more common in the United States (Dachler and Wilpert, 1978; Lammers, 1967; Tannenbaum, 1974; Van de Vall and King, 1973).

Participation may also involve parties outside the organization, e.g., stockholders, government bodies, and national and international unions.

Degree, Content, and Scope of PDM

Participation can vary in *degree* (Sadler, 1970; Tannenbaum and Schmidt, 1958; Vroom and Yetton, 1973). The standard continuum goes from *no participation* (supervisors tell the employees what to do, although they may or may not explain the reasons); to various degrees of *consultation* (the supervisors or managers consult the employees either before or after making a tentative decision, and then make the final decision themselves); to *full participation* (in which supervisors become group members and vote with their subordinates as equals).

PDM can also vary in *content,* according to the type of issue involved. The types of decisions which might be included in PDM schemes generally fall into four broad categories:

1. *Routine personnel functions:* hiring, training, payment method, discipline, performance evaluation.
2. *Work itself:* task assignments, work methods, job design, goal setting (including production level), speed of work.
3. *Working conditions:* rest pauses, hours of work, placement of equipment, lighting.
4. *Company policies:* layoffs, profit (or productivity)- sharing, general wage level, fringe benefits, executive hiring, capital investments, dividends, general policy making.

In many studies the specific content of the decisions made under participative management are not specified in much detail, but it is our impression that in studies involving voluntary, informal, direct PDM, the participation is typically restricted to issues in the first three categories (especially the second). In contrast, where forced, formal, indirect PDM is involved, the decisions may also include issues in the fourth category. Higher-level committees focus mainly on organizational policies while the lower-level committees are more concerned with the work itself and working conditions.

One writer has estimated that codetermination, as practiced in Germany, entails the greatest degree and scope of participation, followed by workers' management in Yugoslavia,[5] and joint consultation as practiced in Britain (Van de Vall and King, 1973).

Another aspect of scope, which has been given little attention in the literature, is the *stage* of problem solving at which PDM occurs, e.g., the discovery of problems, the generation of proposed solutions, the evaluation of proposed solutions, and the choice of solution. Vroom (1969) and Wood (1973) have observed that PDM may be more effective at some stages than at others.

III. THE PSYCHOLOGICAL BASIS
OF PARTICIPATION EFFECTS

The benefits alleged to result from PDM by workers fall into two major categories. The first includes increased *morale and job satisfaction* and their frequent concomitants, reduced turnover, absenteeism, and conflict. The second category includes outcomes pertaining directly to *productive efficiency*, e.g., higher production, better decision quality, better production quality, and reduced conflict (again) and costs (Argyris, 1955; Davies, 1967; Davis, 1957; French, Israel, and As, 1960; Lammers, 1967; Likert, 1961, 1967; Lowin, 1968; Maier, 1973; Rosenfeld and Smith, 1967; Sadler, 1970; Schultz, 1951; Strauss, 1963; Strauss and Rosenstein, 1970; Tannenbaum, 1966, 1974; Tannenbaum and Massarik, 1950; Vroom, 1969).

Less frequently discussed are the *mechanisms* by which PDM will bring about these alleged benefits. With respect to morale, the simplest explanation is that allowing participation will increase the likelihood that the employee will get what he wants (Mitchell, 1973), or satisfy his motives (French, Israel, and As, 1960; Lowin, 1968; Strauss, 1963), i.e., that he will attain his values—value attainment being the direct cause of job satisfaction (Locke, 1976a).

If value attainment is, in fact, the mechanism involved, it becomes problematic as to the conditions under which PDM will achieve it. It depends, first, upon what it is that the employee wants, and, second, upon whether PDM actually brings it about.

If the employee wants simply to *express* his views (Argyris, 1955), then PDM will, if practiced, virtually always bring it about. If the employee wants respect or dignity (Davis, 1957), PDM may attain it, providing the participative method used corresponds to his concept of dignity. If actual influence in the decision process is what the employee desires, then satisfaction will depend upon *how much* influence is actually exerted (or perceived as being exerted) in relation to the amount desired. In many cases an employee may participate in discussions but have little influence over the final decision (Hoffman, Burke, and Maier, 1965; Mulder, 1959).

If full equality with supervisors or managers is what the employee wants, then it is unlikely that he will be satisfied by PDM. We have not found a single case (even in the Israeli kibbutzim; Tannenbaum, 1974) in which a managerial hierarchy was totally dissolved in practice through PDM. In many cases the employee may want tangible benefits from PDM such as more pay. This desire is recognized explicitly in the Scanlon Plan (to be discussed in the next section), which combines PDM with monthly bonuses for increased efficiency.

With respect to the mechanisms causing increases in productive efficiency, the probable factors are more varied. They can be divided into two subcategories—*cognitive* and *motivational.*

A major cognitive factor is the increase in information, knowledge, and creativity that will allegedly be brought to bear on organizational problems as the result of PDM (Davis, 1963; Lammers, 1967; Lowin, 1968; McGregor, 1944; Miles, 1965; Rosenfeld and Smith, 1967; Schultz, 1951; Strauss, 1963). This, in turn, has been attributed to improved upward communication (Nicol, 1948; Rosenfeld and Smith, 1967; Sashkin, 1976; Schultz, 1951; Strauss, 1963). This argument assumes, of course, that the subordinates actually have knowledge which the supervisor lacks and which is relevant to the problem. (We shall return to this very important issue later in this essay.) It is also assumed that the process of group decision making, when it is involved, will lead to better utilization and integration of knowledge than individual or consultative decision making, but again the evidence on this issue is equivocal (Vroom, 1969).

A second cognitive factor involves the greater understanding on the part of the employees who are to execute the decisions which will allegedly result from PDM (Lawler and Hackman, 1969; Maier, 1967; Rosenfeld and Smith, 1967; Vroom, 1969). This may involve such factors as greater goal clarity, a fuller grasp of the methods to be used in accomplishing the work, or a more thorough understanding of the reasons for organizational changes, decisions, and policies. Again, the validity of this premise depends upon whether greater understanding *is* actually achieved by PDM and the degree to which full understanding is crucial to job performance.

The most widely discussed motivational mechanism of PDM is reduced resistance to change (Coch and French, 1948; Davis, 1957; French, Israel, and As, 1960; French, Ross, Kirby, Nelson, and Smyth, 1958; Kahn, 1974; Lawrence, 1971; Marrow and French, 1945; Rosenfeld and Smith, 1967; Schultz, 1951). This, in turn, has been attributed to greater trust on the part of employees (Davis, 1963; Lawler, 1975; Lammers, 1967), which results from being consulted about proposed changes.

Another possible cause of reduced resistance which has rarely been mentioned is the greater feeling of control (and reduced anxiety) which may result from PDM. For example, an employee who thought a particular change would not be beneficial to his welfare or would not promote efficiency would have the opportunity to protest and perhaps modify the proposed policy.

The positive side of the coin of reduced resistance is increased acceptance of and commitment to changes or decisions, including goals (Davis, 1963; Lawler and Hackman, 1969; Meyer, Kay, and French, 1965; Rosenfeld and Smith, 1967; Sashkin, 1976; Sorcher, 1971; Strauss, 1963; Vroom, 1969). This, in turn, has been attributed to a greater degree of ego

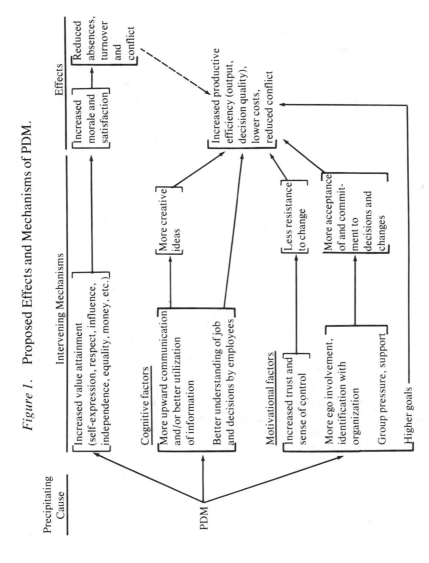

Figure 1. Proposed Effects and Mechanisms of PDM.

151

involvement or identification with the organization induced by PDM (Allport, 1945; Lewin, 1952; Patchen, 1964; Tannenbaum and Massarik, 1950; Vroom, 1964) and to the effects of group pressure or "support" in cases where group decision making was involved (Lewin, 1947, 1952; Mitchell, 1973; Patchen, 1964; Rubenowitz, 1962; Sashkin, 1976; Strauss, 1963; Vroom, 1969). Again these arguments involve a number of problematic assumptions, e.g., that PDM will necessarily lead to greater ego involvement than other methods of managing (e.g., incentives, delegation); that ego involvement is necessary for effective performance; that group pressures will always be in the direction of goal acceptance; and that group members will always give in to group pressures.

A final motivational mechanism, which was not originally predicted by PDM theorists but which has been found in a number of cases, is goal level. It has been argued that PDM groups may set goals which are higher than those which would have been assigned by management (Dowling, 1975; Latham and Yukl, 1975b).

The mechanisms discussed above and their hypothesized interrelationships are shown in Figure 1.

IV. RESEARCH ON PARTICIPATION

The PDM literature is so enormous that to achieve a "complete" review is virtually impossible. We have not made any special attempt to include unpublished material in this review, nor have we included many foreign articles or any not written in English. We have also excluded studies which involve more general dimensions of supervisory style (e.g., consideration), studies involving mainly delegation, and PDM studies in educational settings which have been summarized elsewhere (Anderson, 1959). Within these limits we believe that our literature research was thorough. While we cannot claim to have included every PDM study ever done in the United States, we have not knowingly omitted any significant study. Thus we believe that our review gives an accurate indication of what is known about the effectiveness of PDM.

As noted in the previous section, two broad classes of criteria have been used to evaluate PDM effectiveness—satisfaction or morale, and productive efficiency, including decision quality. Each of these criteria are discussed separately within each of the four subsections to follow.

The four subsections are: laboratory studies, correlational field studies, multivariate experimental field studies, and univariate (controlled) experimental field studies. This classification was based on what we judged to be the two most fundamental differentiating characteristics among the studies—those pertaining to external validity and to the inference of causality. The specific strengths and/or weaknesses of each type of study will be discussed in each subsection.

Laboratory Experiments

While a laboratory environment enhances the experimental control of variables and therefore allows causal inferences to be made, the artificiality of the situation may limit generalizability to real organizational settings. For example, lab studies are short term rather than long term. The subjects usually consist of college students who may have different attitudes and values from workers (cf. Litwin and Stringer, 1968). Furthermore, volunteer subjects may be more prone than employees to do what they think the experimenter wants (although these two situations may not be as different as is typically assumed; Locke, 1978). Finally, less is "at stake" in an artificial lab situation as compared to the real world with respect to such issues as self-esteem and success in one's career.

Despite these potential drawbacks, the results of some laboratory studies have been found to generalize to field settings (e.g., Latham and Yukl, 1975a). Thus findings of such experiments may be valuable in identifying causal relationships which could apply to genuine organizations.

Productive Efficiency

Several studies by Maier and his associates have investigated the effects of training group leaders in democratic leadership techniques on group problem-solving quality and decision acceptance. With subjects role playing an assembly-line situation, Maier (1950) found that decision quality[6] and decision acceptance were greater under leaders trained to use democratic techniques than under untrained leaders. Untrained leaders obtained full agreement to their solution in 62.1 percent of their attempts as compared to 100 percent for the most highly trained leaders.

In a later study, Maier (1953) found results similar to those cited above. All groups role-played a problem involving the introduction of more efficient methods of doing assembly work. Half the groups with untrained leaders accepted the change in work methods implied by the foremen while half rejected his recommendation. Of the groups with trained leaders, 59.1 percent accepted the change and 4.5 percent refused to make any changes. The remaining 36.4 percent of the groups compromised and accepted other changes. Maier and Sashkin (1971), using the same technique, found that democratic leadership led to better decision quality.

Decision quality, according to Maier, is better in democratically led groups because this leadership style encourages group members to express and consider conflicting points of view. These differences in opinion can promote, through discussion and integration, creative problem solving. A study by Hoffman, Harburg, and Maier (1962) tested this claim. Role playing a work method change situation, it was found that conflict of opinion increased the frequency of high-quality decisions. Such decisions, however, were obtained more often in groups intent on change than in those indifferent to it.

Two other studies, however, failed to replicate the findings of Maier and his associates. McCurdy and Eber (1953) studied groups composed of authoritarian and democratic subjects. Their leaders were coached in either democratic or authoritarian patterns of behavior. Authoritarian groups were somewhat more effective than the democratic groups in speed of problem solving on a group maze, although the differences were not significant. Similar results were reported in an earlier study by McCurdy and Lambert (1952).

Torrance (1953) reported that bomber crew members who were critiqued in a performance evaluation by structured methods exhibited greater performance improvement than those crew members who were critiqued by a less authoritarian method.

An experiment by Shaw (1955) investigated the problem-solving performance by four-man groups in different communciation nets under authoritarian and democratic leadership. Problems were solved faster and with fewer errors under authoritarian leaders. This was attributed mainly to the reduction in "saturation" (input and output communication requirements) which resulted from the more directive style.

A series of three group problem-solving ("Twenty Question") experiments by Calvin, Hoffman, and Harden (1957) compared democratic and authoritarian leadership styles. There was no consistent trend in favor of either style; however, the less intelligent subjects performed better under authoritarian leaders while the more intelligent ones performed slightly better under democratic leadership.

Lanzetta and Roby (1960) found that both time and error scores for problem-solving groups were better under participative than directive styles of leadership. They noted, however, that the best-performing groups were those in which leadership and influence in decision making were congruent with ability differentials of the group's members. Thus, participation was effective when the most able members of the group exerted the most influence in decision making.

Using an air controller simulator, Kidd and Christy (1961) studied three patterns of leader behavior—laissez-faire, active monitoring (autocratic), and direct participant (participative)—on several measures of air-controller effectiveness. It was found that leadership style led to a distinct trade-off effect between performance criteria. The laissez-faire pattern allowed the controller to concentrate on maintaining a rapid flow through the system but produced high error scores. The active monitoring pattern, on the other hand, reduced error scores but inhibited the rapidity of flow. The participative style led to intermediate results.

Using a complex management game, Dill, Hoffman, Leavitt, and O'Mara (1961) studied the effects of an egalitarian distribution of influence in a laboratory simulation of organizations on the quality of problem solving and profit. Using six simulated organizations, they found that the two firms with the highest profit showed the highest dispersion of influence and were the least egalitarian. They noted that profitability was also affected by the "perceptual consonance" of the members of the work group, that is, the expectations of group members as to who should exert the greatest influence in decision making.

The effects of task structure on leadership style and group performance in problem solving were studied by Shaw and Blum (1966). Eighteen groups were assigned to either a directive or nondirective leader where they were given three tasks to solve which differed in structure. Using time scores as the measure of performance, it was found that directive leadership was more effective than nondirective leadership when the task was highly structured. Tasks that were unstructured and required varied information were more effectively solved when a nondirective leadership style was used.

The "Twenty Questions" parlor game was used by Katzell, Miller, Rotter, and Venet (1970) to examine the effects of leadership and other variables on group problem solving. They found that directive leadership was somewhat more effective than nondirective leadership in attaining solution quality. The authors attribute its effectiveness to a higher member interaction rate among the groups with directive leaders.

Finally, a study by Hannan (in press) compared the effects of participatively set and assigned goals on performance. The task was evaluating credit card applications using a formula. Hannan found that participative goal setting was marginally related to increased goal acceptance, especially for difficult goals. However, PDM was not related to performance, which was determined instead by ability and the subjects' personal goals.

The findings of the laboratory experiments discussed above are summarized in Table 1.

Satisfaction

In a study of democratic and autocratic leadership, Gibb (1951) found that subjects were more satisfied with leader behavior when it was more autocratic and when the group was more structured and unified. Satisfaction with the leader was correlated .76 with autocratic leadership and − .60 with group freedom.

Shaw (1955) found that morale was significantly higher under democratic leaders than under autocratic leaders. He noted that morale was heavily influenced by independence, which is reduced by authoritarian leadership. Democratic leadership, on the other hand, increases independence and thus morale.

Table 1. Summary of Results of Laboratory Experiments on PDM

Study	Task	Manipulation or Comparison	Results Prod.	Sat.
Maier (1950)	Role play of an assembly-line situation	Trained in PDM vs. untrained	+	−
Gibb (1951)	Various activities	Democratic vs. autocratic		
McCurdy & Lambert (1952)	Group maze	Democratic vs. autocratic	0	
McCurdy & Eber (1953)	Group maze	Democratic vs. autocratic	0	
Torrance (1953)	Performance appraisal	PDM vs. autocratic	−	
Maier (1953)	Role play in work change	Trained in PDM vs. untrained	+	+
Shaw (1955)	Arithmetic problems	Democratic vs. autocratic	−	
Calvin, Hoffman & Harden (1957)	"Twenty Questions"	Democratic vs. autocratic	0	
Fox (1957)	Decision making in a conference situation			
Mulder (1959)	15 problem-solving tasks	Positive vs. negative		++
Lanzetta & Roby (1960)	Mechanical task	High vs. low power	+	+
Kidd & Christy (1961)	Air controller simulator	Laissez-faire, vs. direct participant vs. active monitoring	0	
Dill, Hoffman, Leavitt & O'Mara (1961)	Management simulation game	Dispersion of influence	−	−
Shaw & Blum (1966)	Problem solving	Directive vs. nondirective	0	
Katzell, Miller, Rotter, & Venet (1970)	"Twenty Questions"	Directive vs. nondirective	−	+
Maier & Sashkin (1971)	Role play in work change	Trained in PDM vs. untrained	+	
Wexley, Singh, & Yukl (1973)	Appraisal interviews	Tells vs. problem solving (PDM)	[a]	
Hannan (in press)	Goal setting	Participative vs. assigned	0	+
		PDM Superior	(+) 4	5
		No difference or contextual	(0) 6	0
		PDM Inferior	(−) 4	2

[a]This study used an attitude rather than a performance measure of motivation; since we considered this weak evidence for a laboratory study, the performance results were not included in the analysis.

The effects of "positive" and "negative" leadership styles on member satisfaction in conference groups were explored by Fox (1957). What he called positive and negative styles can be classified as participative and autocratic, respectively. The positive style of leadership induced a more permissive and friendlier group atmosphere, greater member satisfaction with the leader, and greater member satisfaction with and acceptance of group decisions than the negative leadership style.

Mulder (1959) investigated the relationships between power-exertion, self-realization, and satisfaction of members of problem-solving groups. In this experiment two degrees of power-exertion (defined as the passing on of essential information in a group, i.e., expert power) and two degrees of self-realization (defined as the responsibility for the completion of one's own task) were compared. The power variable is related to PDM in that it pertains to the amount of influence a person has. In each condition, fifteen problem-solving tasks were completed. It was found that only the power variable had any effect on satisfaction. Those subjects in the "more power" condition showed significantly greater satisfaction than those in the "less power" condition.

Dill, Hoffman, Leavitt, and O'Mara (1961) found in their simulation that the two organizations with the highest morale had the greatest dispersion of influence and were the least egalitarian. These companies had also the highest degrees of "perceptual consonance" as to the roles of each member.

Katzell, Miller, Rotter, and Venet (1970) in a study of groups solving the "Twenty Questions" parlor game found that satisfaction with the task was significantly less for those subjects under highly directive leaders than under less directive leaders.

In an experiment using simulated appraisal interviews, Wexley, Singh, and Yukl (1973) found a positive association between degree of PDM and satisfaction with the interview.

The findings from the laboratory experiments discussed above are also summarized in Table 1. It can be seen in the lower right corner of the table that with respect to performance, there is no overall difference between PDM and more directive methods. With respect to satisfaction, the results favor PDM, although in two cases, satisfaction was higher in the groups with more directive leaders.

Correlational Field Studies

The studies in this subsection were all conducted in field settings, but this advantage was more than offset by the limitations involved in the use of the correlational method. (We define the term "correlational" broadly in this context to mean any method which correlates observed differences on one attribute or behavior with observed differences in another without having manipulated the hypothesized cause.) Such studies may suggest causal relationships but cannot prove them.

Productive Efficiency

A classic study by Katz, Maccoby, and Morse (1950) investigated the relationship between the productivity of clerks in an insurance company and various leadership characteristics. Twelve pairs of work groups which performed the same type of work but which differed in their productivity were studied. The supervisors of the high-producing groups employed less "close" and more "general" supervision, were rated as less "production centered" and more "employee centered"; exercised better judgment; were more rational and less arbitrary; and were more democratic and less authoritarian than supervisors of low-producing sections. In addition, the high-producing supervisors reported that they were supervised less closely by their own superiors and were more satisfied with the degree of their authority and responsibility than the low-producing supervisors.

An obvious problem with this study is the failure to separate the effect of PDM from those of the other factors correlated with high work group productivity.

Katz, Maccoby, Gurin, and Floor (1951) attempted to replicate the insurance company study in three divisions of a railroad company. Thirty-six pairs of sections of maintenance workers who were similar with respect to working conditions but different in their level of productivity were compared.

As in the insurance study, high-producing foremen were described by their subordinates as more "employee centered" and less "production centered" than the low-producing foremen. In addition, high-producing foremen spent more time in supervising; planned more often and were better at it; spent more time teaching their men new techniques; and gave more constructive and less punitive comments to subordinates than supervisors of low-producing sections. However, unlike the insurance study, there was no relationship between productivity and PDM.

Two divisions of a naval research laboratory were surveyed by Weschler, Kahane, and Tannenbaum (1952). One division was headed by a permissive leader, the second by a restrictive leader. The productivity of the permissively led division was rated considerably higher than that of the restrictively led division by the division members. However, according to a more objective evaluation of performance by five superiors and two staff people who were more familiar with the *actual* performance of the two divisions, the performance of the restrictively led division was rated slightly higher. (No statistical tests were employed to test this difference.)

Adams (1952) reported that members of bomber crews performed better under medium than either high or low degrees of equalitarian leadership.

Berkowitz (1953) observed seventy-two small decision-making (conference) groups in business and government organizations. Unlike most PDM studies, the leaders of these groups were not assigned but were chosen by the group's members. It was found that PDM was negatively but not significantly correlated with performance. Berkowitz explains though that those members who chose the leader perceived his role as the *sole* leader and not as a member of a participating group. Since there was an expectation of role differentiation between the designated leader and the group members, participation was not viewed by the members as being legitimate and did not facilitate performance.

In a medical laboratory study by Pelz (1952), participative leaders who interacted daily with their subordinates were rated as being more effective than directive leaders but less effective than leaders who delegated responsibility. No substantial differences between styles emerged when there was less than daily contact, however.

In a study of assembly departments in a manufacturing firm, Argyle, Gardner, and Cioffi (1958) found democratic leadership style to be positively correlated with productivity only in those departments where direct incentive pay was not in force. In incentive departments, no relationship was found.

Mullen (1965) compared the leadership styles of three division managers in a large automobile insurance company and its relationship to each division's efficiency and effectiveness. Each manager exhibited a distinct leadership style: one was democratic, another laissez-faire, and the third was authoritarian. Using several measures of efficiency (e.g., policy issuance rate), it was found that all three divisions were operating at an equally high rate of efficiency. (No statistical tests were employed.)

The measures of effectiveness (cost and profitability) indicated that all three divisions had experienced a decline during the study, in line with the trend of the entire automobile insurance industry during this period. Although the trend was in the same direction for all the divisions, the absolute dollar figures indicated, surprisingly, that the division with the laissez-faire manager was the only one which made a profit in this interval. However, a more accurate measure of effectiveness (average closing cost of bodily injury claims) did not show any differences between divisions.

Vroom (1960), using a sample of 108 supervisory personnel, found that participation was significantly correlated with performance for the total sample, but the correlations were significantly higher for supervisors high in independence than for supervisors low in independence, and for those low in authoritarianism than high in authoritarianism. When need for independence and authoritarianism were combined, the relationship between participation and performance was significant only for those high in need for independence and low in authoritarianism.

In an attempted replication of Vroom's study with consumer finance office managers, Tosi (1970) found no relationship between perceived PDM and performance for any group.

Mahoney (1967) surveyed the judgments of eighty-four managers in thirteen organizations as to the factors that they perceived to be related to organizational effectiveness. Democratic leadership was not related to perceived effectiveness whereas supervisory control, defined as the supervisor being "on top of things," was perceived as being positively related to effectiveness. These findings, of course, were not validated by reference to any objective measures of performance for any of the organizations studied.

A similar study by Stagner (1969) found results in agreement with those of Mahoney. Using a questionnaire mailed to 500 vice presidents of 125 large firms, Stagner found that corporate profits were perceived as being associated with more formality (bureaucratic routines), centralization of decision making, and less personalized management.

Patchen (1970) administered questionnaires to 834 employees in two Engineering Divisions and three Steam Power Plants of the Tennessee Valley Authority (TVA) in order to investigate the effects of involvement in the work environment. To help create a sense of involvement, top TVA management encouraged employees to participate in decisions affecting their work. The major mechanism for such participation was direct work group participation and the TVA'a cooperative conferences and committees where representative (indirect) participation in a wide range of work problems was encouraged. At the time of this study the cooperative program had been in operation almost two decades.

Control over work methods emerged as the one factor which had sizeable associations with all attitudinal indicators of job motivation (no "hard" criteria were obtained). Influence in goal setting was also positively related to job motivation. However, the strength of this relationship was moderated by the opportunity that an employee had for achievement. Patchen comments ". . . that people will value more highly goals which they help to set for themselves . . . and . . . this is likely to be so particularly when attainment of the goal has significance as a personal achievement" (Patchen, 1970, p. 239). Clearly there is some confounding of PDM with job enrichment (delegation) in this study.

The effects of participation in a Management by Objectives program were examined by Carroll and Tosi (1973) in a questionnaire study. They found no overall correlation between degree of influence in the goal setting process and employee effectiveness (as rated by managers). However, a supplementary analysis found a marginal correlation between PDM and performance for those employees who were accustomed to PDM (a finding which replicates that of French, Kay, and Meyer, 1966).

Schuler (1977) found no overall correlation between PDM and performance among a sample of manufacturing employees.

The findings from the correlation field studies discussed above are summarized in Table 2.

Satisfaction

Weschler, Kahane, and Tannenbaum's (1952) naval research laboratory study reported that 63.3 percent of the members of the division headed by the permissive leader were "well satisfied" with their job, whereas 39.3 percent of the members of the division headed by the restrictive leader were "well satisfied" with their job. In addition, the employees' perceptions of morale in their immediate work group, the division, and the laboratory were considerably higher in the permissively run division than in the restrictively run division.

A research laboratory setting was also used by Baumgartel (1956, 1957) to study three leadership styles (participative, directive, and laissez-faire). It was found that job satisfaction was higher under participative leaders than either the directive or laissez-faire leaders.

Foa (1957) studied crews and officers of eighteen ships of an Israeli shipping company under permissive and authoritarian supervision. It was found that the group members' expectations toward discipline moderated the relationship between satisfaction and leadership style. Groups with authoritarian expectations were equally satisfied with either leadership style, whereas groups with permissive expectations were more satisfied with permissive leaders. Authoritarian leaders satisfied authoritarian crews more than permissive crews and the trend was in the same direction for permissive leaders. The term "permissive," of course, which was based on attitude toward strict discipline, is not identical in meaning to participative.

In the study of small decision-making (conference) groups by Berkowitz (1953), satisfaction with the conference was negatively and significantly correlated with PDM.

Argyle, Gardner, and Cioffi (1958) did not directly measure satisfaction in their study of assembly departments, but reported two measures usually associated with it, absenteeism and turnover. There was no relationship between turnover and leadership style, but democratic supervision was positively related to low absenteeism. This relationship was significant for the combined departments but not within the incentive departments.

Vroom (1960), in his delivery company study, found that participation

Table 2. Summary of Results of Correlational Field Studies of PDM

Study	Task	Manipulation or Comparison	Results Prod.	Results Sat.
Katz, Maccoby & Morse (1950)	Clerical work	Democratic vs. authoritarian	+	
Katz, Maccoby, Gurin & Floor (1951)	Railroad maintenance	Democratic vs. authoritarian	0	
Weschler, Kahane & Tannenbaum (1952)	Scientific research	Permissive vs. restrictive	–	+
Adams (1952)	Bomber crews	Degrees of equalitarianism	0	–
Berkowitz (1953)	Conference groups	Degrees of PDM	0	
Pelz (1956)	Scientific research	Participative, laissez-faire, & directive styles	0	0
Foa (1957)	Shipping crews	Authoritarian vs. permissive		+
Baumgartel (1956, 1957)	Scientific research	PDM, directive, and laissez-faire		+
Argyle, Gardner & Cioffi (1958)	Assembly	Democratic style	0	+,0[a]
Vroom (1960)	Delivery work	Degree of authoritarianism	+,0	+,0
Vroom & Mann (1960)	Delivery work	Degree of authoritarianism		0
Mullen (1965)	Insurance	Democratic, laissez-faire, and authoritarian styles	0	+
Ley (1966)	Production work	Degree of authoritarianism		+
Mahoney (1967)	Managing	Democratic vs. controlling	–	
Stagner (1969)	Managing	Degree of formality, centrality, and personalization	–	
Patchen (1970)	Engineering and maintenance work	Degree of control of job by employee	+	0
Sadler (1970)	All job levels and functions	Tells, sells, consults, joins		0

162

Study	Context	Measure		
Tosi (1970)	Office management	Degree of PDM	0	+
Miles & Ritchie (1971)	Managing	Degree of consultation		+
Carroll & Tosi (1973)	MBO program	Degree of influence in goal setting	0	
Ruynon (1973)	Chemical work	Degree of PDM		+,0
Alutto & Acito (1974)	All job functions	Degree of PDM deprivation		+
Falcione (1974)	Industrial work	Degrees of PDM		+
Lischeron & Wall (1974)	Local governments	PDM at various levels		+
Schuler (1977)	Manufacturing	Degree of PDM	0	+,0
			(+) 3	PDM Superior 13
			(0) 10	No difference or contextual 8
			(−) 3	PDM Inferior 1

[a] +,0 indicates a significant main effect which only applied to one sub-group when the sample was subdivided.

163

was positively related to supervisors' attitudes toward their jobs. However, when subjects were grouped simultaneously, on the basis of independence and authoritarianism, there was a significant positive correlation between PDM and satisfaction only in the high need for independence, low authoritarian subgroup. Tosi's (1970) replication study, however, found an overall correlation between PDM and job satisfaction, but no moderating effects for either variable.

In another study, Vroom and Mann (1960) investigated the effects of leader authoritarianism on employee attitudes. Using two samples of employees, the authors found that employees in small work groups which were characterized by a great deal of interaction among workers and between workers and their supervisors, and by a high degree of interdependence, had more positive atittudes toward equalitarian leaders. Employees had more positive attitudes toward authoritarian leaders, however, in large work groups whose members worked independently and where interaction between them and their supervisor was infrequent.

Mullen's (1965) insurance company study used measures of job satisfaction, absenteeism and turnover. The results indicated that democratic leadership was associated with employee satisfaction, but not with turnover or absenteeism. The author speculates that although there was less satisfaction in the divisions run by the laissez-faire and authoritarian leaders, other factors in the job situation (e.g., good wages, pleasant working conditions, job security, etc.) were far more important than the leadership style in determining turnover and absenteeism.

Using a sample of production employees, Ley (1966) found that turnover was positively correlated ($r = .76$) with the related authoritarianism of foremen.

Miles and Ritchie (1971) found that managers who felt that they were more frequently consulted by their bosses were more satisfied with them than were managers who were less frequently consulted.

Using a sample of hourly employees in a chemical company, Runyon (1973) found a positive correlation between perceived degree of PDM and satisfaction with supervision. However, when the sample was subdivided on the basis of "locus of control" (Rotter's I-E scale), the correlation was positive for those high in Internal locus but negative for those high in External locus.

Degree of PDM deprivation was found to be negatively correlated with a number of dimensions of job satisfaction by Alutto and Acito (1974), although the results may have been confounded somewhat by age.

In a study of a large industrial organization, Falcione (1974) found a significant positive correlation between participation and satisfaction with the immediate supervisor. The author points out though that the participation utilized in this study was consultative and rarely did the employees have a final say in the decisions. Nor surprisingly, participation explained a very small amount of the variance in satisfaction. A second factor which explained a considerably greater variance was the perceived credibility of the supervisor. Falcione speculates that ". . . a supervisor who allows for subordinate participation but has low credibility in the eyes of his subordinates may be viewed as a 'weak' supervisor. A supervisor who allows for subordinate participation and is viewed as a high credible source may have a much more satisfied group of subordinates" (Falcione, 1974, pp. 51–52).

Lischeron and Wall (1974) examined the effect of participation at various organizational levels on several dimensions of satisfaction (organization, pay, promotion, work itself, superior, coworkers). A survey was administered to 127 blue-collar workers in four divisions of a local government department in England. Satisfaction measures were taken for perceived participation in decisions at medium and distant levels in the organization. Degree of perceived participation was significantly and positively correlated to overall job satisfaction. It was also found that those workers who were least satisfied expressed the strongest desire to participate.

In his study of the TVA, Patchen (1970) measured specific aspects of satisfaction (pay, promotion, immediate supervisor, and coworkers) as well as overall job satisfaction. Neither the overall index of satisfaction nor specific aspects of satisfaction were associated with participation for the organization-wide cooperative program. In fact, the associations tended to be negative. The effects of participation in immediate work-group decisions on satisfaction were not reported.

In a comparison of different types of employees in two British companies, Sadler (1970) found that most preferred a "consults" leadership style (i.e., moderate participation) to other styles (tells, sells, joins); however, the highest degree of satisfaction was associated with getting the style of leadership that the employee wanted, regardless of the actual style.

Schuler's (1977) results seem to indicate an overall relation between work satisfaction and PDM, but after subgrouping, the relationship held only where high levels of role conflict and/or role ambiguity existed. Possibly PDM was experienced as a means of coping with these sources of frustration.

The findings from the corrrelational field studies discussed above are summarized in Table 2. The results compiled at the bottom of the table show that with respect to performance there is no overall difference between PDM and non-PDM leadership styles. With respect to satisfaction, the results are more favorable to PDM, even though over 40 percent of the studies did not show any positive effect.

Multivariate Experimental Field Studies

Many of the studies to be discussed in this subsection are considered to be "classics" in the PDM literature. All were conducted in field settings and together encompass a time span of more than 50 years. Since they are all experimental studies, cause-and-effect inferences can be made. However, since all of the studies in this group involved the manipulation of at least one major variable in addition to PDM, conclusions about the efficacy of PDM as such are impossible to draw.

Except where logical continuity dictates otherwise, the studies will be examined in approximate chronological sequence; in cases where groups of studies are involved, the date of the earliest study in the group will be used to determine the sequence. Since most of these studies claim to have achieved improvements in both productivity and morale, these criteria will not be specifically separated as in the other subsections.

Mayo's "first inquiry"   While Elton Mayo is most well known as the director of the Hawthorne studies, his first field experiment was conducted in the mule spinning department of a textile mill near Philadelphia in 1924 (Mayo, 1924, 1945/1970). The department suffered from a 250 percent annual turnover rate, low morale, and productivity which was too low to allow the workers to benefit from an incentive bonus which was contingent upon attaining a minimum level of efficiency. The work week consisted of five 10-hour days with a 45-minute break each day for lunch. Interviews with the employees of the mule spinning department revealed that they suffered from severe fatigue.

As a result of these consultations with the workmen, Mayo suggested allowing four 10-minute rest periods spaced throughout the working day. A proposal to try out this idea on one-third of the workmen in the department was accepted by management. As a result, turnover dropped and morale improved. When the rest periods were given to the remaining department members (with cots being provided for them to lie on) overall production increased and the workers made the bonus for the first time. Later the rest periods were taken away, whereupon morale and production dropped. Subsequently they were reinstated with the added benefit that groups of employees could decide among themselves who would rest and when, providing they all received their four breaks. Again morale and efficiency increased. Turnover eventually dropped to between 5 and 6 percent.

Mayo's original (1924) report of this study attributed the results to the rest pauses, which appeared to reduce fatigue and "pessimistic revery." However, in his later (1945/1970) post-Hawthorne interpretation, he stressed the role of social factors such as participation, but admitted that too many factors were changed to make any definitive conclusion possible. While consultative participation was involved in the study, this only entailed asking the employees how they felt. Later the employees were delegated the authority to schedule the rest pauses themselves, group formation being encouraged for this purpose. There were also some technological improvements made in the department. But the central factor seems clearly to have been the introduction of the rest pauses as such. If the workmen had been consulted and the rest pauses *not* introduced, it seems very doubtful whether the increase in morale and productivity would have occurred.

The Hawthorne studies   These studies conducted in the late 1920s and early 1930s under Mayo's direction (Roethlisberger and Dickson, 1939/1956) are probably the most famous experiments ever conducted in the social sciences. They have been widely interpreted as demonstrating the value of PDM in industrial settings (Blumberg, 1968; Davis, 1967; French, 1950; Kahn, 1975; White and Lippitt, 1960), although contrary interpretations have been offered (Carey, 1967; Lawler, 1975; Parsons, 1974). The former interpretation was based primarily on the results of the Relay Assembly Test Room and Mica Splitting Test Room experiments. Let us examine what actually occurred in these experiments, following the incisive critique of Carey (1967).

Stage I of the Relay Assembly Test Room study included the introduction of a simpler, less-varied task, a new incentive system (more closely geared to individual effort), improved feedback, looser, more considerate supervision (which later became more harsh when productivity did not rise as expected), rest pauses, reduced hours of work, and the replacement of two of the five girls in the original group. No substantial increases in productivity occurred in this group until the two lowest producers were removed and replaced by two other, highly motivated women (whereupon supervision again became considerate). Thus the most plausible conclusion to be drawn from this study is that selection (or transfer) is an effective method of raising productivity! Carey implies that about 25 percent of the overall 30 percent increase in productivity obtained in Stage I was caused by this factor.

In Stage II of the Relay Assembly study, the only change made from the original conditions of work was the introduction of an incentive system. This led to an immediate increase of nearly 13 percent in productivity and a decrease of 16 percent when it was later withdrawn.

In the Mica Splitting Test Room study, there was, of course, a different task, and the hours of work were reduced. There was also more considerate, participative supervision. The Hawthorne investigators claimed that a 15 percent increase in productivity resulted from the introduction of the new supervisory style. Carey (1967), however, demonstrates that this result is purely fictional, since the investigators had changed their implicit definition of the term "productivity" between this and the previous studies. In the Mica Splitting Test Room there was an increase in *rate* of production, but no increase in *total* production due to the decrease in hours of work. Even the finding of an increase in rate is suspect, because the investigators included different time intervals in calculating the production of each worker, a fundamental breach of proper experimental design.

The most legitimate conclusion to be drawn from the Hawthorne studies is that there is some evidence for the beneficial effects of selection and for the effects of incentives (Lawler, 1975) on productivity. Even these findings are not conclusive because of the absence of control groups.

McCormick's multiple management (McCormick, 1938, 1949) In 1932, Charles P. McCormick inherited his uncle's position as president of a well-known spice company. Since the company was in some financial trouble, he immediately initiated a number of changes, including an increase in pay for the workmen of $2.00 a week, a reduced work week, and possibly (this is not clear in his writings) a profit-sharing plan, and a promise of no layoffs. Later new equipment was introduced and tea was served during rest breaks.

However, McCormick is known mainly for his idea of the introduction of a Junior Board of Directors (later supplemented by a Sales Board and a Factory Board). These boards consisted of junior executives who were elected by other members of the board. Their function was to develop ideas to improve the management of the company and to propose these changes to upper management (e.g., the senior Board of Directors). The development of these boards, according to McCormick, led not only to better training for the junior executives, but to a more objective merit system, increased competition, and a clearer promotion ladder.

McCormick claimed that the long-term benefits of these changes included the development of higher employee motivation and morale (including labor peace), the deradicalization of young executives with Marxist ideas, and the development of many good ideas which, when put into practice, produced greater profitability for the company.

While McCormick presents a convincing case for the value of the Junior Board (and other boards) which were a form of consultative management, the effects of the boards as such cannot be isolated from the effects of the other changes which he introduced. Certainly the changes in pay, hours of work, and job security (made in the midst of the Depression) must have had a major effect on the motivation and morale of the rank-and-file employees.

The Scanlon plan   Devised by steelworker and union officer Joseph Scanlon in the late 1930s, this plan is used by many companies today (Frost, Wakeley, and Ruh, 1974). It consists of two main elements, a participation system which involves the formation of committees composed of workers and managers to develop and evaluate ideas to improve efficiency and lower costs, and an equity system which provides the employees with monthly bonuses based on the degree of labor efficiency attained in relation to a previously-agreed-upon standard.

The results of a number of studies indicate that this plan has often been effective in increasing both employee income and company productivity. Some of the failures have been attributed to higher-level managers not allowing the employees sufficient opportunities for PDM (Frost, Wakeley, and Ruh, 1974). However, since the restrictions on PDM are often associated with a decrease in or lack of bonus payments (Geare, 1976), it is impossible to say which is cause and which is effect, or whether they are mutually reinforcing.

It should be mentioned in this context that another company-wide incentive plan, Fein's Improshare (Fein, 1976a, 1976b, 1977), has claimed results which certainly match those obtained by the Scanlon Plan, and yet Improshare makes no *formal* provision for PDM. Fein argues that his incentive plan results in greater employee effort and cooperation.

One well-known application of the Scanlon Plan at Donnelly Mirrors (Donnelly, 1977) involved even more complexities than does a normal Scanlon Plan. One modification was to include savings in the materials and operating supplies in the same pool as the savings in labor. Another was a guarantee against layoffs which resulted from changes in technology or work organization. Third, interlocking work teams, based on Likert's ideas, were introduced to encourage communication and cooperation. Fourth, all employees were represented at higher levels through a company-wide committee. And fifth, the machinery was improved. As with many Scanlon Plans, the results have been impressive, but the changes made were so numerous that the effect of PDM, per se, cannot be determined.

Lewin's group-decision experiments   These well-known experiments conducted by Lewin and his colleagues in the mid-1940s involved comparisons of the effectiveness of different methods of changing food habits (Lewin, 1947, 1952). The experiments compared the lecture method with that of group discussion and decision (a form of PDM); both methods were used to attempt to get housewives to serve more of such foods as beef hearts, kidneys, milk, cod liver oil, orange juice, etc. It was concluded from the experiments that the group discussion method was considerably more effective than the lecture method. Levine and Butler (1952) replicated these results in a factory situation where the problem involved reducing rating bias.

Numerous flaws in the design of Lewin's studies are evident. For example, no independent assessment of behavioral changes was obtained. Apparently the housewives' reports were taken at face value despite the existence of obvious pressures toward false reporting. Bennett (1955) observed that the discussion groups differed in at least six respects from the lecture groups: (1) group discussion vs. lecture, (2) decision made vs. none required, (3) 100 percent consensus vs. unknown consensus, (4) public vs. private decision, (5) specification of the time period during which action was to be taken vs. no specification, and (6) announcement that a follow-up would be made regarding any behavior taken vs. no announcement.

Bennett designed an experiment to separately determine the effects of the first four factors while holding the last two constant, and using an objective action criterion (volunteering to participate in a psychological experiment). Only one major effect was found—that of coming to a decision, a procedure which could occur either in the presence or in the absence of group discussion. Perceived degree of group consensus (but not objective degree of consensus) showed a weak relationship to action.

Sociotechnical systems   This approach, developed by Trist, Bamforth, and Rice, argues that production systems cannot be efficient unless the employees' social needs (e.g., the needs to belong, to participate) are met and thus aims to integrate the technical and social components of organizations (Emery and Trist, 1960; Miller, 1975; Rice, 1953; Trist and Bamforth, 1951). A more philosophical description is given by Susman (1976), who argues that the technical world is grasped through reason while the phenomenal world, which may be unrelated to the technical world, is organized around fantasies, beliefs, and emotions. He argues that the sociotechnical systems approach tries to develop a best match between the two. (Just how one overcomes this fundamental schism between reason and reality on the one hand and whim and fantasy on the other is never made clear.)

Let us consider what sociotechnical systems analysts actually do. The most famous of these studies is that of Trist and Bamforth (1951), who argued that the introduction of the longwall method of coal mining in England failed to raise productivity as predicted because it disrupted the accustomed social relationships among and frustrated the social needs of the miners (see also Albrook, 1967). Before the changeover, the miners worked in small groups, did a variety of different jobs depending upon what was needed at the time, and were able to adjust their pace to the particular working conditions encountered.

After the changeover to the longwall method, the miners worked in crews of forty to fifty men, had more specialized tasks, had different rates of pay, and were assigned a fixed pace. The result was an inflexible, rigid, and poorly integrated work arrangement. The problem was largely solved[7] by dividing the men into work groups with each member getting the same pay, and letting them work on several different tasks as needed rather than being confined to only one specialty (Bucklow, 1966; Trist, Higgins, Murray, and Pollock, 1963). It should be noted that the friendships that developed under this system were confined to the technical requirements of job accomplishment (Emery and Trist, 1960).

The only conclusion one can draw about this study is that flexibility is superior to rigidity when the working conditions are not totally predictable. One means to achieve this, often entailed in job-enrichment studies (e.g., see Locke, Sirota, and Wolfson, 1976), is job enlargement combined with a modular working arrangement. Thus a group of employees, cross-trained in each specialty, work together on one meaningful part of a task, each person working where they are needed (and, within limits, where they prefer). There is no evidence that social factors as such have any role in determining the success of such arrangements.

The Trist and Bamforth monograph was followed two years later by Rice's (1953) studies of Indian Weaving Sheds. Before the changes which he introduced, there was extensive individual specialization, confused lines of authority, different employees working different numbers of looms ("twelve tasks performed by twenty-nine workers were performed in a total of nineteen overlapping loom groups of five kinds" Rice, 1953, p. 304). In addition, there was low mobility among pay grades, and some employees were on piece rates while others were not.

The "sociotechnical" reorganization involved cross-training the workers on several jobs (and decreasing the number of looms), clarifying authority relationships (and increasing the autonomy of the group leader), increasing the pay of some workers, putting all group members on piece rate, and increasing the running time of the looms. The eventual result was reduced damage and increased efficiency of production. Participation was used only to allow the employees to determine the composition of the work groups.

Again, so many changes were made that it is impossible to separate the effects of each. There is very little evidence that social factors as such (including PDM) played any role in the improvements obtained. Dubin

(1965) argues that the improved organization or structuring of the work was the main factor responsible for the improved performance.

A follow-up of Rice's study through 1970 (Miller, 1975) found that some of the groups had retained their efficiency during this period while others had deteriorated somewhat. A number of factors seemed to have caused the deterioration, including upper management pressure for higher production, which led to a partial breakdown of group autonomy, resentment of group members against other members who were loafing, some unfairness in the application of the pay system, decreased group cooperation (due probably to the above factors), and inadequate training.

A final example of a sociotechnical approach to job design is a more recent coal mining study conducted in the United States by Susman (1976).[8] Unlike the English study, no major problem with technological changes precipitated the experiment. The main concern in this case was with improving safety.

The changes introduced in the experimental group (three shifts of nine men each) included training each miner in several different jobs, followed by job rotation and flexible work assignments, uniform pay for all group members with the lower-paid workers being raised to the level of the higher-paid ones, increased autonomy (delegation), a new work measurement system that made it easier to keep track of performance, confining the foreman's role mainly to safety matters, and minor improvements in technical efficiency (through reducing transport delays).

The result of these changes was a noticeable decrease in safety violations and accidents for the experimental groups as compared with two control groups. This is most easily attributed to the more explicit role played by the foreman in the safety realm. The results for absenteeism and costs were less clear, the experimental groups showed improvements on both measures but so did some of the control groups.

A more recent series of sociotechnical systems experiments conducted in Norway (which will not be described in detail here, but see Emery and Thorsrud, 1976; Thorsrud, Sorensen, and Gustavsen, 1976) were just as complex as the studies described above. Key elements in most of the Norwegian experiments were job enrichment (delegation and modules), group work, and new incentive schemes in addition to PDM. Nevertheless, both of the above references classified all of the studies under the general heading of "industrial democracy" experiments. (A few experiments reported by Thorsrud, Sorensen, and Gustavsen, 1976, which did involve only PDM—attained through employee representation on the governing boards of companies—were found not to be successful).

The Harwood-Weldon studies   This classic in the field of organizational development (Marrow, Bowers, and Seashore, 1967) describes what occurred after the Harwood Manufacturing Company purchased the Weldon Company in 1962. Weldon, founded by two dynamic entrepreneurs, had prospered until their highly centralized decision-making style began to break down in the face of growth.

Between 1962 and 1964, an enormous number of changes were initiated at Weldon by the Harwood management. In the technical realm, the modifications included changing to a system of unit production with each semi-autonomous department responsible for a single product line, a reorganization of the shipping department, replacement of equipment, and the introduction of work aids for the operators.

The selection process was also changed, with new employees being chosen by the use of previously validated tests. A more effective (vestibule) training program was introduced for new operators. Trained operators whose production was substandard were put through an earnings development program which involved individual coaching. Operators who could not meet assigned production standards after training and coaching were fired, as were workers who showed excessive absenteeism.

Work standards and incentive pay were introduced in certain departments. The minimum pay level in the plant was raised to conform with the federal minimum wage standards. Improved feedback systems were developed so that supervisors could keep better track of the progress of the work. Authority was delegated downwards at all levels. Finally, supervisors and managers were trained in the procedures of PDM. This included sensitivity training, group discussion, and the use of joint problem-solving techniques.

The result of the sum total of these changes was that by the end of 1964, the Weldon Company showed a positive return on capital investment, increased productive efficiency, higher employee earnings, and lower turnover and absenteeism. Before-after attitude measures showed only modest improvements.

While the bottom-line results are impressive, the problem is to determine precisely what caused them. After an extensive discussion, the authors attributed 11 percent of the 30 percent gain in productivity to the earnings development program, 5 percent to the dismissal of low producers, 8 percent to the improvement in interpersonal relations and use of group problem-solving methods, and 6 percent to miscellaneous factors.

The authors must be commended for trying to sort out the contribution of the various factors, but their estimates cannot be taken at face value, since their method of determining the various effect ignores such possibilities as delayed effects and interactions among the changes.

While it seems almost certain that the sum total of the organizational changes made were responsible for the effects observed, isolating the precise degree of effect produced by each change is virtually impossible from the methodology employed in this study. Thus the title used for the book which summarized this project, *Management by Participation*, must be viewed as somewhat misleading at best.

An earlier study at Harwood reported by French, Ross, Kirby, Nelson, and Smyth (1958) was also guilty of confounding variables, although not to the same degree as in the Weldon study. In the 1958 study, extensive technological changes were introduced in three plants using consultative participation. A year later production was 10 percent higher on one of the items involved in the change, but there was no improvement for the other item. Since there was no control group in which the same changes were introduced without the use of PDM, no conclusions can be drawn about its effectiveness.

Goal setting and participation studies   Bavelas conducted a separate study at the Harwood plant in which a group of employees participated in a discussion of production goals (reported in Viteles, 1953, p. 167). It was "suggested" that the group might wish to set a team goal for higher production. While the output of this group did improve as compared to a control group, the design confounded the effects of goal setting (i.e., goal level) with those of PDM, thus making it impossible to determine which factor caused the change. A similar confounding of PDM and goal setting occurred in two other successful field studies conducted by Lawrence and Smith (1955)[9] and Sorcher (1967). A larger-scale project involving the same confounding of variables was conducted at a division of North America Rockwell (Chaney and Teel, 1972). Group goal setting (with feedback) under participative leadership was introduced in forty different groups, twenty-seven of which subsequently showed performance gains. The authors acknowledge, however, that in some cases high performance was achieved when the supervisor set the new production goal unilaterally (accompanied by an explanation of his reasons for choosing it) and allowed PDM only with respect to methods and procedures.

More recent field studies using improved experimental designs which separated the effects of goal setting from those of participation have resulted in more negative conclusions regarding the efficacy of PDM than the three studies described above. The newer studies will be discussed in the next subsection. (A relevant laboratory study by Hannan, in press, was discussed earlier.)

Likert's System 4   The essence of Likert's philosophy of management is participation and group decision making (Likert, 1961, 1967). However, it is difficult to get enough information from Likert's books to determine what actually happens when System 4 is introduced. Fortunately, a report by Dowling (1975) provides considerable detail on the application of Likert's system to the Lakewood Plant at General Motors.

In addition to introducing PDM and group decision making, Likert and his colleagues introduced increased training at all levels, increased feedback especially for hourly employees, the provision of assistants for the foremen, group goal setting, the use of cross-functional business teams, and increased delegation of authority.

Dowling (1975) emphasized the importance of feedback in causing the increases in efficiency which resulted from the intervention. On the other hand, the dramatic decrease in grievances which occurred were probably due to the greater use of PDM. As with previous studies, however, so many factors were changed that the particular causes of each effect cannot be isolated.

Conclusion

The types of changes made in each of the major multivariate studies or groups of studies (omitting the Lewin group-decision experiments, which were not done in an organizational setting) are summarized in Table 3. The total number of changes made in each study is shown in the far right column. These numbers must be considered a minimum, since some changes, which seemed trivial, were not included in the table (e.g., the serving of tea by McCormick—although since tea may serve as a stimulant, it may not be so trivial!)

The frequency with which each type of change was made is shown in the bottom row of the table. While PDM was involved, of course, in all of the studies, changes in the pay system were involved in eight cases, while technological changes, delegation, and the use of work teams were introduced about half the time. On the average, there were about five changes per study or group of studies.

While one cannot deny that most of these studies demonstrated beneficial results of the interventions, it is equally undeniable that the complex nature of the changes made precludes any clear attribution of the results to PDM as such.

In this context, it is worth discussing briefly the studies of PDM conducted in Israel and Yugoslavia, where government-sponsored participation plans have been in effect for more than two decades.

Israel The Israeli plans have been sponsored by the Histadrut, the General Federation of Labor and owner/manager of many industrial enterprises. Its leaders have been ideologically motivated socialists, although this influence is alleged to be declining (Derber, 1970). The various participation schemes, organized mainly at the plant-wide level, have evolved through a series of stages (e.g., workers' committees, joint pro-

Table 3. Summary of Types of Changes Introduced in Multivariate Field Experiments on PDM

Study	Selection and/or Firing and/or Added Help	Training, Coaching	Job Security (Increased)	Pay Changes	Work Simplification	Job Enlargement/ Rotation	Work Standards, Goal Setting	Feedback (Improved)	Rest Pauses	Reduced Hours	Work Teams	Delegation	PDM	Technology	Total Number of Categories Changed
Mayo's First Inquiry (Mayo, 1924, 1945/1970)	X								X				X	X	4
Hawthorne Studies (Roethlisberger & Dickson, 1939/1956) Relay Assembly I			X	X				X	X	X			X	X	7
Multiple Management (McCormick, 1938, 1949)				X	X			X		X			X	X	5
Scanlon Plans															
1. General (Frost, Wakeley & Ruh, 1974)				X									X		2
2. Donnelly Mirrors (Donnelly, 1977)			X	X							X	X	X		5
Socio-Technical Systems Studies															
1. Trist & Bamforth (1951)				X		X					X	X	X		5
2. Rice (1953)		X		X		X					X	X	X	X	7
3. Susman (1976)		X		X		X		X			X	X	X	X	8
Harwood-Weldon Studies															
1. Marrow, Bowers & Seashore (1967)	X	X		X	X		X	X				X	X	X	9
2. French, et al. (1958)													X	X	2
Goal Setting & PDM Studies (Bavelas, in Viteles, 1953; Lawrence & Smith, 1955; Sorcher, 1967; Chaney & Teel, 1972)							X						X		2
Likert's System 4 (Dowling, 1975)	X	X					X	X			X	X	X		7
TOTAL	3	4	2	8	2	3	3	4	2	2	5	6	12	7	63

duction committees, plant councils, etc.), each new stage typically following the failure of the previous stage (Rosenstein, 1970).

The goals of the PDM schemes were to increase worker identification
with the enterprise, to equalize influence between managers and workers,
and to increase productivity. With respect to the first two goals, the
consensus is that the plans have failed (Derber, 1963, 1970; Rosenstein,
1970). The Histadrut intellectuals were unable to integrate the goal of
economic efficiency with the goal of total satisfaction of the work force
(Rosenstein, 1970). Furthermore, plant managers have effectively resisted
attempts to encroach upon their authority, arguing that they are professionals and therefore the most qualified to make higher-level decisions
(Derber, 1963, 1970). The goal of increasing productivity has, in some
cases, been fulfilled, but only when the workers have been offered monetary rewards in return for their participative efforts (Rosenstein, 1970). (In
many cases Histadrut intellectuals have opposed rewarding individual
effort or plant-wide profit-sharing on ideological grounds.)

Yugoslavia Studies of the effects of worker participation in workers'
councils in Yugoslavia have shown similarly modest outcomes. Workers
who are members of the councils are only slightly more satisfied with their
jobs (and *more* alienated from their work) than workers who are not
council members (Obradovic, 1970). Council members with a strong desire to participate in decision making are actually no more satisfied than
those who are not on the council (Obradovic, French, and Rodgers, 1970).
The reason for these findings is that the council members have relatively
little influence compared to the enterprise managers.

Despite these modest findings, the workers' councils have been credited with causing a dramatic increase in Yugoslavia'a rate of economic
growth since the mid-1950s (Glueck and Kavran, 1971). Even if these
figures (published by a communist dictatorship!) can be believed, the
degree of growth attained cannot necessarily be attributed to the workers'
councils. More likely it was due to the greater degree of "economic freedom" (if this concept makes sense in a socialist country—see note 5)
which accompanied the establishment of the workers' councils, especially
the increased authority delegated to the managers of the enterprises.

In summary, the results of PDM in both Israel and Yugoslavia have
been modest, and the benefits that have followed the introduction of PDM
cannot clearly be attributed to this factor, since it was confounded with
economic factors in both cases.

Controlled Experimental Field Studies

The studies in this group have largely avoided the drawbacks of those in
the three previous subsections. Because they are field or at least quasi-

field studies, they have a high degree of external validity. Because they are experimental studies, causal inferences can be drawn from the results. And because these experiments were fairly well controlled, the effects of PDM as such can be determined. In this section the experiments done with children or in quasi-field settings are discussed first.

Productive Efficiency

The Lewin, Lippitt, and White (1939) studies (reported in Lippitt and White, 1958; White and Lippitt, 1953, 1960) carried out in the late 1930s have been among the most widely reported experiments in the PDM literature. While these studies were conducted in a field setting, they did not involve adults in a work organization, but rather 11-year-olds participating in after-school clubs. The first study included two groups of five boys and girls. Each group met eleven times under either autocratic or democratic leadership. The second, more carefully controlled and more extensive study, involved four different groups of five boys, each of whom met six times under each of three different leaders. The groups alternated between autocratic and democratic leaders, although two of the groups had one session with laissez-faire leadership.

The autocratic leaders were instructed to stress giving orders, limiting freedom, and minimizing friendliness. Observers found that as compared to the democratic leaders, the autocratic leaders did give more orders, disrupting commands, praise, approval, and nonconstructive criticism. The democratic leaders were instructed not to neglect giving guidance but to allow the members freedom to do whatever they wanted and to be friendly. Observers rated the democratic leaders as giving more: guiding suggestions, stimulation of self-guidance, information, emphasis on group decision making, and as being more friendly than the autocratic leaders.

With respect to performance, the autocratically led clubs accomplished more work than those with democratic leadership while the leader was present, but the results were reversed when the leader was absent.

While these studies were well controlled by most standards (e.g., as compared to the multivariate studies described earlier), the differences in leadership style seemed to involve more than PDM as such. Democratic leadership was used as an umbrella term to include not only PDM, but knowledge, friendliness, suggestion-giving, etc. It would be instructive to isolate the effects of these difficult elements.

Another problem which limits the generalizability of these results to organizational settings is the substantial difference in age between the boys and adults. Furthermore, the goal of the boys' clubs was to have fun, whereas that of most organizations is to get work done.

In another nonorganizational field experiment, Veen (1972) studied the effects of participation on the performance of forty boys, 10 to 14 years old, participating in an 8-week (one session per week) field hockey training course. The boys were randomly assigned to one of ten groups. Five of the groups were in the participation condition and the other five in a nonparticipation condition. The participation condition was characterized by a 5-to-10-minute conference before each training session in which the boys conferred about the program. In the first three training sessions, these boys had limited involvement in the program while being given relevant knowledge. Thereafter they were allowed to decide on the content of the training. In the nonparticipation condition, the trainer made all the decisions as to program content. In contrast to Lippitt and White, Veen was careful to control for degree of leader friendliness when manipulating PDM. Performance was measured by having the subjects run through an obstacle course. Both time and error scores were used as the criterion.

It was found that scores on performance tests, given during the fourth and sixth week of the program, were significantly better for the participation group than for the nonparticipation group. (In a follow-up performance test one year later, there was no significant difference between the scores of the two groups; however, this is probably an unfair standard in view of the limited amount of PDM involved in the experimental program.)

Another study (Litwin and Stringer, 1968) used an experimental quasi-field study to test the effects of various leadership styles on organizational climate and organizational effectiveness. Using a simulated business environment, three "organizations" were formed. Fifteen subjects (college students) who were matched on various criteria were assigned to each of three organizations. All three organizations started the experiment with an equal amount of physical resources and the same position in the same market environment. The experiment was conducted over a 2-week period comprising 8 actual days of organizational life.

The leadership manipulations resulted in the formation of three climates that were significantly different. The climate of organization A (British) was autocratic. Management exercised firm control and made all decisions. Organization B (Balance), on the other hand, exhibited a democratic climate where there was a heavy emphasis on participative decision making throughout the entire organization. The third organization C (Blazer) exhibited a high degree of achievement orientation; goal setting and delegation prevailed throughout the organization.

The results of this study indicate that the leadership styles had different effects on productive efficiency. The achievement-oriented company (Blazer) significantly outperformed both the democratic (Balance) and autocratic (British) organizations. It introduced the most new products, had the highest profits, and reduced material costs the most. The autocratic organization outperformed the democratic organization with respect to profit and had the best product quality. While the democratic organization had the poorest profit showing, it had intermediate product quality.

The major limitation of this study was that it did not take place in a bona fide organizational setting. Thus, generalizability is difficult. The authors note that the simulation might have failed to include certain boundary variables which prevented practices that are common to real businesses from occurring (e.g., building-up of inventories, concrete monetary feedback, etc.).

In another quasi-field study, Seeborg (1978) measured the effects of participation in job enrichment. A 2½ day simulation of an organization was utilized with a three-level hierarchy (plant level manager, first-level supervisors, and workers). The "organization's" goal was to manufacture decision boxes, a small electronic device that could be made by either one person or manufactured on a small assembly line.

Subjects with varying work experience were recruited from business organizations. All twenty-five subjects, with the exception of five who had experience in the technology involved in the job were randomly assigned to five work groups. The remaining five were selected for supervisory roles. During the first day of the experiment, all groups worked on an assembly line. On the second day, jobs were changed for each group in one of three ways: supervisory condition—the supervisor discussed job changes with a consultant and redesigned the jobs for his work group; participative condition—the work group was given the information that the supervisor was given in the supervisory condition and the group redesigned the job; and plant manager condition—the plant manager instructed the supervisor to implement certain changes based on the changes developed by one of the participation groups.

It was found that the content of the job changes differed between the supervisory and participative conditions. The focus of change in the supervisory condition was to load the job vertically. Workers in the participative condition "never mentioned vertical loading" (e.g., increased responsibility; Seeborg, 1978, p. 91) and were concerned mainly with the social impact of the changes.

Quality of performance was the only measure of productive efficiency used. It was concluded that the supervisory condition had better quality than the participative group (no statistical tests were employed). However, it was apparently not the method of implementation per se that led to increased quality but the nature of the job changes made as a result. In the supervisory condition, vertical loading was emphasized, resulting in increased task identity and concern for the item being produced.

There have been several controlled experimental studies of PDM in bona fide work organizations. A classic study, and still one of the best designed field experiments on PDM, was reported by Coch and French

(1948). It was conducted in a pajama manufacturing plant (Harwood) experiencing high turnover and absenteeism, resistance to methods and job changes, a high grievance rate, low efficiency, restriction of output, and aggression against management. In the experiment, small groups of employees participated in evaluating and redesigning their jobs. Three experimental groups and one control group were used to implement these changes. The first experimental group was allowed indirect participation through representation, whereas the second and third experimental groups were allowed total participation by all members of the group. Following the job changes, the PDM groups learned the job changes faster than the control group and quickly surpassed prechange productivity levels. In addition, the total PDM group learned the changes faster than the representative group. The authors noted that the rate of recovery was directly proportional to the amount of participation. In a second experiment, the control group from the previous experiment used the direct participation condition in transferring to a new job. The employees' productivity recovered rapidly and to a final level of production well above the prechange level before the transfer.

The results of this study show impressive evidence for the effectiveness of PDM in decreasing resistance to job and methods changes.

Fleishman (1965) attempted to replicate the Coch and French study in a dress factory. Using one experimental and two control groups, he found results similar to that of Coch and French with one important difference—*both* the control group and the experimental PDM groups increased their productivity. However, the research methodology was problematic and might explain the results. The experimental and the control groups were not separated from one another but were intermingled back on the job. Thus it was difficult to isolate the effect of the participation manipulation because of a possible transfer effect to the control group.

In a Norwegian replication of the Coch and French study, five experimental groups with varying degrees of participation and one control group were compared (French, Israel, and As, 1960). There were no significant differences among the groups in productivity. This may be traced in part to the unilateral exclusion by management of the central issues of rate setting and production level from PDM. Thus, only matters peripheral to productivity were discussed by the employees in the PDM conditions.

Morse and Reimer (1956) conducted a study in one department of a nonunionized industrial organization which had four parallel divisions engaged in relatively routine clerical work. This study was impressive in that PDM was manipulated not in small subgroups as in other studies but by changing the structure of four divisions of a company. In two of the divisions, PDM was increased by increasing the involvement of the rank and file in decision making. In the other two divisions, unilateral decision making was increased by centralizing all decision making (HIER).

The results of the study show that productive efficiency in all four divisions increased. However, the productivity of the HIER divisions improved significantly more than that of the PDM divisions.

It is important that the measures of productivity be considered when interpreting the results. Productive efficiency was measured by total clerical costs as compared to a prechange baseline period. The increase in productive efficiency is a result of the elimination of inefficiences prior to the change. It appears that the HIER divisions had reduced clerical costs by cutting the number of employees. The PDM divisions, however, were reluctant to eliminate their own members.

An experimental study at General Electric by French, Kay, and Meyer (1966) varied the degree of participation in the goal-setting process during performance appraisal sessions on lower-level managers. The major factor affecting subsequent performance was whether performance goals were set during the interviews. There was increased acceptance of goals in both the high and low PDM conditions, although the increase was slightly higher in the former case. The effect of PDM on performance depended on several contextual factors. When the manager was used to participation based on prior experience, the high PDM manipulation led to improved performance. But when the manager was not accustomed to PDM, the high PDM manipulation led to poorer performance than low PDM for those managers who had found the preceding appraisal (given two weeks before the experiment started) threatening. Degree of experimental PDM had no differential effect on those not used to PDM who had not been threatened by the first interview.

The authors concluded that PDM works best in a context of supportiveness caused by high usual PDM. Some support was found for Vroom's (1960) finding that those high in need for independence responded more favorably to PDM.

Six skilled construction and electrical crews were given varying degrees of participation in work scheduling in a field study conducted by Powell and Schlacter (1971). They found that PDM had no effect on productivity.

Latham and Yukl (1975b) compared three methods of goal setting among independent logging crews with different levels of education. Loggers in the participative and assigned goal-setting conditions outperformed those in the "do your best" condition. However, for the uneducated sample, workers in the participative goal-setting condition also showed higher output than those in the assigned condition. In the participative condition, goal difficulty was higher, but not significantly so. The authors concluded that the superiority of participation for this sample was due to greater goal acceptance.

For the educated sample, however, there was no significant difference in performance between the participative and assigned goal-setting methods. Nor was there a significant difference in either goal difficulty or goal acceptance between the two conditions. The authors suggest that the difference in results of the two studies might be caused by education, confounding of demographic variables, or by lack of support by local management in implementing the research.

In another study by the same authors (Latham and Yukl, 1976), female typists in a large corporation were randomly assigned to participative and assigned goal-setting conditions. They found no significant differences in goal difficulty or performance between the two treatments. The authors concluded that "subordinates with the assigned goals eventually accepted them as much as subordinates who participated in goal setting" (Latham and Yukl, 1976, p. 170).

Using a sample of sales personnel, Ivancevich (1976) compared participative, assigned, and "do your best" goal-setting groups. Four quantitative measures of performance (called frequency index, order/call ratio, direct-selling cost, and market potential) were taken for each group at four periods of time (baseline, 6 months, 9 months, and 12 months). It was found that over the 12-month period, significant positive changes in the four performance measures occurred for both the participative and assigned groups. No significant changes, however, were found for the "do your best" group. In comparing participative and assigned groups at the four periods of time, only three significant differences occurred. The performance of the participation group on the call frequency variable was significantly better at 6 months. However, at 12 months, there were no significant differences between the two groups, indicating that over time both methods were equally successful in increasing performance.

In a second study, Ivancevich (1977) investigated the effects of participative goal setting on the performance of skilled technicians and supervisors in three plants of a medium-size equipment and parts manufacturing organization. The employees in each plant were assigned to a different goal-setting condition (participative, assigned, and "do your best"). Four quantitative measures of performance (unexcused absenteeism, service complaints, cost of performance, and safety) were taken for each plant at four periods of time (baseline, 6 months, 9 months, and 12 months). An analysis of the data at 6 months revealed that both assigned and participative goal-setting conditions were significantly better on three of the performance criteria than the "do your best" condition.

The assigned goal employees showed significantly few complaints and had lower performance costs than the participative employees. On the other hand, the participative condition showed a significantly better safety record. There was no significant difference between the three groups with respect to unexcused absenteeism. (Performance scores for every criterion decreased between the ninth and twelfth month for both groups.)

Latham, Mitchell, and Dossett (1978), using a sample of engineers and scientists, studied the effects of participative versus assigned goal setting on both goal difficulty and goal acceptance. Specific goals were either participatively set or assigned by a supervisor. To measure goal difficulty, both an objective and a subjective measure were taken. The results indicate that some participative subjects set objectively higher goals than those with assigned goals. However, subjective goal difficulty was equal in the participative and assigned conditions. Rated goal acceptance was also the same.

Six months after the first study, performance measures were obtained on these subjects plus two control groups. An analysis of the data indicated no significant difference in performance between the participative and assigned goal-setting conditions, although both combined outperformed the control groups.

The findings from the experimental field studies discussed above are summarized in Table 4.

Satisfaction

In the Lewin, Lippitt, and White studies described earlier (White and Lippitt, 1960), the satisfaction of the democratically led groups appeared to be higher than that of the autocratically led groups. However, there is a potential problem with this conclusion. As noted earlier in this section, other traits (e.g., arbitrariness, tactlessness, coldness, etc.) besides participation were included in the manipulations. If this is the case, the subjects could have been satisfied with a "polite, considerate, or rational" person rather than a democratic leader. On the other hand, other subjects could have been dissatisfied with a "cold, insulting, tactless, or arbitrary person" rather than an autocratic leader.

Veen (1972), in his study of boys participating in field hockey training, obtained two questionnaire measures of satisfaction: general satisfaction and satisfaction with the training program. It was found using measures at 4 and 8 weeks that there was no significant difference between the participative and nonparticipative conditions as to general satisfaction. The participatively led boys, however, were significantly more satisfied with the training program than the nonparticipatively led boys.

Litwin and Stringer (1968) obtained pre- and post-manipulation measures of satisfaction of the employees of their simulated companies. Employees in the achievement oriented and participative companies were more satisfied than those in the authoritarian company but did not differ from each other.

Seeborg (1978) used the Job Diagnostic Survey (JDS) to assess various

Table 4. Summary of Results of Univariate Field Experiments on PDM

Study	Task	Manipulation or Comparison	Results Prod.	Sat.
Lewin, Lippitt & White (1939), etc.	Children working on arts and crafts	Autocratic vs. democratic	0	+
Coch and French (1948)	Pajama manufacturing	Indirect PDM, Direct PDM, control	+	+
Morse and Reimer (1956)	Clerical work	PDM vs. HIER	–	+
French, Israel and As (1960)	Manufacturing	PDM vs. control	0	+
Fleishman (1965)	Dress manufacturing	PDM vs. control	0	
French, Kay & Meyer (1966)	Engineering and manufacturing	PDM vs. assigned	0	
Litwin and Stringer (1968)	Simulated business	Democratic, autocratic, achievement	–	+
Lawler and Hackman (1969)	Janitorial work	PDM vs. assigned		+
Powell and Schlacter (1971)	Construction and electrical	Degree of PDM	0	0
Veen (1972)	Children training in field hockey	PDM vs. control	+	+
Latham & Yukl (1975b)	Goal setting (logging)	PDM vs. assigned	$+,0^a$	
Lischeron and Wall (1975)	Organizational PDM	PDM vs. control	0	0
Latham and Yukl (1976)	Goal setting (typing)	PDM vs. assigned	0	0
Ivancevich (1976)	Goal setting (sales)	PDM vs. assigned	0	0
Ivancevich (1977)	Goal setting (technicians)	PDM vs. assigned	0	–
Latham, Mitchell, and Dossett (1978)	Goal setting (engineering)	PDM vs. assigned	0	0
Seeborg (1978)	Job enrichment simulation (assembly)	PDM vs. assigned	–	+
		PDM Superior	(+) 3	8
		No difference or Contextual	(0) 10	5
		PDM Inferior	(–) 3	1

[a] See Table 2, note a.

aspects of job satisfaction and motivation in his simulation of a job enrichment program. The subjects in the groups enriched by participatory methods were more satisfied than those whose jobs were enriched unilaterally by the supervisor or plant manager.

In the Coch and French (1948) study, turnover and grievance rates, which are concomitants of job satisfaction, were reported to be lower for employees in the PDM conditions than for those in the control group. This conclusion was based on limited turnover data and the investigators' impression of the number of positive work attitudes exhibited by the subjects. The authors argued that PDM is beneficial because it reduces frustration.

In the Norwegian replication by French, Israel, and As (1960), attitudes were measured with a fourteen-item postexperimental questionnaire. The experimental groups had more positive attitudes than the control group on ten of the fourteen items, but only three of the differences were significant. Two of these three items referred specifically to training. Two of the items which failed to reveal any difference were those which most closely represented the concept of job satisfaction—"How do you in general like to work here?" and "Do you feel that you have found the kind of job you would like to keep in the future?" One reason for these marginal results may have been the limited degree of participation experienced by the employees in the PDM conditions.

Morse and Reimer (1956) used pre- and postchange measures of satisfaction, employees' attitudes toward their supervisor and with the company and their jobs in both the PDM and HIER conditions. All fourteen measures were taken prior to the change program and then again 1 year after the program had been operating successfully.

Changes in satisfaction toward the company increased significantly in most cases in the PDM divisions whereas they decreased significantly in the HIER divisions. Overall, in the PDM divisions, nine of the fourteen prechange and postchange measures showed statistically significant differences indicating that attitudes were more positive after participation was introduced. In the HIER divisions, ten of the fourteen measures changed significantly in the opposite direction.

With respect to the measures of overall job satisfaction, no changes were observed in the scores of PDM divisions, whereas one of the two HIER divisions demonstrated a significant decrease in job satisfaction.

A field experiment by Lawler and Hackman (1969) and a follow-up by Scheflen, Lawler, and Hackman (1971) studied the effects of participation by janitorial workers in the development of a pay incentive plan to reduce absenteeism. Two experimental conditions and two control groups were used. In the first experimental condition, three autonomous work groups developed their own incentive plan viz. PDM. These plans were then imposed by the company upon the two work groups that made up the second experimental condition.

The results show, based on pre- and postmanipulation measures, that there was a significant increase in attendance only in the participative condition 16 weeks after the plan started, but there was a significant increase in the attendance of the imposed groups after a year. The authors cite three possible reasons for the claimed success of the participation condition: (1) participation caused greater commitment by the subjects to the plan; (2) subjects who participated in the plan were more knowledgeable about it; and (3) participation increased the employees' trust of the good intentions of management with respect to the plan. However, severe criticisms of the methodology of this study by Cook and Campbell (1976) make any firm conclusions suspect.

In the Powell and Schlacter (1971) study, the two groups which had the highest degree of PDM showed improved morale, but this was neutralized by a surprising increase in absenteeism.

Lischeron and Wall (1975) darried out a field experiment in Great Britain to examine the effects of employee decision making at higher levels of an organization. An experimental group of 150 subjects was formed from a prechange control group of 350 subjects on the basis of responses to a questionnaire measuring attitudes toward participation. The remaining 200 subjects were assigned to the control group. The Worker Opinion Survey, a version of the Job Description Index, modified for use with British blue-collar populations, was used to measure job satisfaction. No significant effect of participation on satisfaction was found. The authors conclude that participation may improve relationships between the worker and management, but will not necessarily increase job satisfaction.

Latham and Yukl (1976), in their study of typists, found no significant difference in job satisfaction between those subjects in participative and assigned goal-setting conditions. As compared to prechange measures, employees in both conditions experienced a significant decline in job satisfaction after the manipulations.

Ivancevich (1976), in his study of sales personnel, found opposite results. Using the Job Description Index, he found that both the assigned and participative goal-setting treatments led to increased work satisfaction over a 9-month period, although this washed out after 12 months. With respect to satisfaction with the supervisor, the assigned group showed a greater increase than the PDM group after 9 months but the difference again washed out after 12 months.

In his later study of skilled technicians, Ivancevich (1977) found that both assigned and participative goal-setting conditions led to increased satisfaction with work and with supervision. There was no significant difference in work satisfaction between the conditions. The assigned goal-setting group, however, reported significantly *higher* satisfaction with the supervision. (In both studies the satisfaction increases diminished over time.)

Finally, Latham, Mitchell, and Dossett (1978) found no significant difference in intrinsic satisfaction with goal accomplishment between the participative and assigned goal-setting groups.

The results of the studies of satisfaction are shown in Table 4. It is evident from the summary in the bottom right corner that there is no evidence that PDM is superior to more directive methods in increasing productivity. The results are more favorable to PDM with respect to the satisfaction criterion, but again over 40 percent of the studies showed no general superiority of PDM.

Conclusions

Omitting the multivariate studies, the results of all the studies discussed in this chapter are summarized in Table 5. An examination of the totals in the right-hand columns show that: (1) with respect to the productivity criterion there is no trend in favor of participative leadership as compared to more directive styles; and (2) with respect to satisfaction, the results generally favor participative over directive methods, although nearly 40 percent of the studies did not find PDM to be superior.

A striking aspect of these results is that each of the three types of study yields the same conclusion regarding the efficacy of PDM as a motivator and a satisfier.

Another remarkable aspect of these results is that they agree perfectly with the conclusions drawn from two other extensive literature reviews of PDM.[10]

In 1959, Anderson summarized the studies comparing authoritarian and democratic approaches to teaching. He found no trend with respect to a learning criterion (eleven studies favored democratic methods, thirteen showed no difference, and eight favored directive methods), but democratic approaches were generally superior with respect to a morale criterion.

Similarly, an earlier review of the general PDM literature by Stogdill (1974), which overlapped but was not identical with the literature reviewed here, concluded that participative leadership did not necessarily lead to higher performance but usually led to higher morale than directive leadership.

The consistency with which the results of PDM studies fail to show any clear trend with respect to effect on productivity (and to a lesser extent with respect to effects on morale) leads to only one possible conclusion—there is a great deal we do not yet know about the conditions under which PDM will "work." What we do know is the subject of the next section.

Table 5. Combined Results of PDM Studies[a]

	Type of Study							
	Laboratory		Correlational		Field		Combined	
Result	Prod.	Sat.	Prod.	Sat.	Prod.	Sat.	Prod.	Sat.
PDM superior	4	5	3	13	3	8	10 (22%)	26 (60%)
No difference or contextual	6	0	10	8	10	5	26 (56%)	13 (30%)
PDM inferior	4	2	3	1	3	1	10 (22%)	4 (9%)
TOTALS	14	7	16	22	16	14	46	43

[a]Based on Tables 1, 2, and 4.

189

V. CONTEXTUAL FACTORS DETERMINING THE EFFECTIVENESS OF PARTICIPATION

Both logic and the results of research on PDM make it unmistakably clear that its effectiveness depends on a number of contextual factors. In this respect, we are in agreement with the position of Vroom and Yetton (1973), although we will make no attempt to develop a sequential model here or to modify theirs. We will simply summarize the contextual factors that have been found or asserted to determine the effectiveness of PDM. (For other contextual approaches, see Lowin, 1968; Strauss, 1963; and Tannenbaum and Massarik, 1950.)

Individual Factors

Knowledge   As noted earlier in this chapter, people are not equal in the extent of their knowledge or intelligence. Thus we cannot accept unqualified statements to the effect that "the information in a group exceeds that of any individual in the group" (Maier, 1970, p. 595). It depends upon the individuals and the nature of the task. PDM should be most helpful in generating high-quality decisions when the participants have relevant knowledge to contribute (Davis, 1963; Derber, 1963; Strauss and Rosenstein, 1970; Vroom, 1969). In cases where one member (e.g., the leader) has significantly more knowledge than the others, PDM would be wasteful of time and effort at best, and harmful to decision quality (if those with less knowledge outvoted the most knowledgeable member) or to efficiency (caused by delays) at worst.

Lanzetta and Roby (1960) found that "where the relative contribution of individuals to decision making was congruent with their relative differences in ability, performance of the group was better" (p. 147).

Furthermore, Mulder and Wilke (1970) observed that in cases where there are substantial differences in knowledge among group members, PDM leads to a progressive *decrease* in equality of influence over time. Similarly, Mansbridge (1973) has observed that group members who have the most critical and irreplaceable skills have the most power to influence decisions. The discovery that knowledge is power is not new, of course. It was identified by Francis Bacon over three centuries ago.

F. W. Taylor's system of Scientific Management was based on the principle of authority based on knowledge. Taylor did not advocate PDM, because he believed that the average untrained workman of his time did not know as much about the best way to do his job as a trained expert. Taylor did argue, however, that: "Every encouragement . . . should be given [the workman] to suggest improvements, both in methods and implements. And whenever a workman proposes an improvement, it should be the policy of the management to make a careful analysis of the new method, and if necessary conduct a series of experiments to determine accurately the relative merit of the new suggestion and of the old standard" (Taylor, 1911/1967, p. 128). While Taylor has been criticized for decades for advocating authoritarian practices, he did not advocate obedience to authority as such, but rather obedience to facts.

The significance of individual differences in knowledge has also been recognized, albeit reluctantly, by human relations advocates. Marrow, for example, writes, "Nor does participation mean that everyone decides on everything . . . its effectiveness is tied closely to how much the participants know and contribute" (1972, p. 88). Maier (1970) admits that in some cases the leaders' expertise is so great in relation to that of his followers that PDM would not be useful. Advocates of group decision-making acknowledge that the group's judgment is often inferior to that of the best individual member (Hall, 1971). Likert, too, recognizes that supervisors must be technically skilled (1961, 1967).

Vroom has aptly observed that "in no sense can the manager of a group be considered to be an average group member. He has been selected by different criteria, exposed to different training, and has access to different information than other group members" (1969, p. 230).

More recently, Maslow, a leading exponent of "humanism," expressed grave reservations about PDM on grounds identical to Taylor's: "More stress needs to be placed on the leader's ability to perceive the truth, to be correct, to be tough and stubborn and decisive in terms of the facts." Rather than stressing, "democracy, human relations and good feelings [t]here ought to be a bowing to the authority of the facts" (Maslow, 1970, p. 36).

In implicit agreement with Maslow's position, most nonsupervisory employees show no desire to make top management decisions;[11] those who want increased participation want to be involved in decisions regarding their own job and immediate work surroundings, i.e., issues about which they are likely to have pertinent knowledge (Holter, 1965).

Human relations advocates have stressed repeatedly that the importance of knowledge has been overemphasized and have urged that more emphasis be placed on gaining commitment to the decision reached, i.e., through PDM. Their assumption is that there will necessarily be resistance to decisions which are not made by the employees themselves.

While resistance to change obviously does occur, it has never been proven that such resistance is inevitable (or even typical) in the absence of PDM. Resistance might also develop because the changes are not based on valid reasons, or because the explanations or justifications given for them are unclear or incomplete (Lawrence, 1971). Studies have demonstrated that expert power (authority based on a high degree of knowledge) can lead to both high satisfaction and high performance among subordinates (summarized in Wood, 1973). Hamblin, Miller, and Wiggins (1961) found leader competence to be the single most important factor determining group morale (see also Rosen, 1969, pp. 58ff). It has also been found that status differentiation is quite compatible with both satisfaction and efficiency as long as there is consensus regarding the status structure (Heinicke and Bales, 1953).

Motivation   A number of motivational factors may affect the success of PDM. First, PDM may not satisfy or conversely, directive leadership may not dissatisfy, employees who do not want or expect PDM, who lack independence and want to be told what to do (Berkowitz, 1953; Davis, 1963; Derber, 1963; Dill, 1958; Dill et al., 1961; Foa, 1957; Heller and Porter, 1966; Marrow, 1972; McMurray, 1958; Obradovic, French, and Rodgers, 1970; Singer, 1974; Strauss, 1963; Vroom, 1960, 1969). Second, it may not be effective with those who are not used to it (Carroll and Tosi, 1973; French, Kay, and Meyer, 1966; Ivancevich, 1976; Tannenbaum and Schmidt, 1958); this implies, of course, that with repeated exposure, employees could become used to it.

Third, it has been asserted frequently, on theoretical grounds, that PDM will not be effective among generally unmotivated employees, e.g., those with low job involvement, low need for achievement, or low commitment to organizational goals (Fein, 1976c; McMurray, 1958; Singer, 1974; Tannenbaum, 1974; Tannenbaum and Schmidt, 1958; Vroom, 1969). However, it is precisely among such populations that PDM has often been associated with enhanced motivation (e.g., Carroll and Tosi, 1977; Latham and Yukl, 1975b; Lawler and Hackman, 1969; Steers, 1975). Argyle et al.'s finding (1958) that PDM was related to performance and attitudes only in departments which were *not* on direct incentive pay is congruent with these results. No conclusive explanation for this apparent paradox has been offered. Possibly employees with low motivation feel powerless and unefficacious and PDM gives them a feeling of control which is manifested in setting challenging goals, higher goal commitment, and/or greater job involvement. In contrast, for more highly motivated employees, PDM may be simply redundant.

Organizational Factors
This category defined broadly includes all factors external to the participating employee, or to factors which involve an interaction among the participating members.

Task attributes   It has been asserted that highly complex unstructured tasks require PDM, because of the increased knowledge and flexibility requirements, whereas routine tasks do not (e.g., Morse and Lorsch, 1970; Shaw and Blum, 1966). While this may be true with respect to knowledge requirements, the opposite may be the case with respect to motivation. As noted above, employees on routine jobs may become more committed as a result of PDM while those at higher job levels need no such incentive. Vroom and Mann (1960) have observed that tasks which require extensive coordination among employees are performed more effectively under directive leadership than under participative methods.

Group characteristics   Two possible dangers of group participation have been clearly identified. First, PDM may increase (or release) group conflict (Derber, 1970; Gomberg, 1966; Maier, 1967; Mansbridge, 1973; Sashkin, 1976). Such conflicts may involve personality clashes, actual differences in values and goals between members, or simply resentment over the rejection of some members' ideas (Wood, 1973). In such cases, directive leadership may be an effective method of resolving the disputes (Burke, 1966).

However, this does not necessarily imply that group homogeneity is always beneficial. Hoffman, Harburg, and Maier (1962) found that differences of opinion, if utilized constructively, led to higher-quality decisions than did the absence of conflicting viewpoints. Similarly, Pelz (1956) found that daily group contact helped the productivity of a scientist only when the other scientists had different views than himself.

A second danger is that of group conformity and/or groupthink (Janis, 1972). Groups can be just as autocratic as supervisors, if not more so (McMurray, 1958), and may thereby inhibit the expression of new or unpopular ideas (Jaques, 1964).

It has also been argued that if group goals differ from organizational goals, the use of PDM will lead to poor decision quality (Vroom and Yetton, 1973), although this issue has not been widely studied. PDM advocates might argue, however, that PDM would lead to the development of more responsible group goals than existed before PDM.

Leader attributes   It has been frequently observed that supervisors themselves are often threatened by the introduction of PDM and, as a result, oppose and sabotage attempts to use it (Campbell, 1953; Derber, 1963, 1970; Maslow, 1970; Scheflen, Lawler, and Hackman, 1971). A common reason for the failure of Scanlon Plans is alleged to be the unwillingness of managers to allow PDM by the rank and file (Frost, Wakeley, and Ruh, 1974). Clearly, any successful PDM program must have the support of all levels of management.

A second requirement is that of skill in the use of PDM techniques (Hall, 1971; Maier, 1973; Vroom, 1969). Even a willing leader may not have the capacity to effectively utilize these methods without careful training.

The personality and style of the leader *in relation* to that of the group members must also be considered. There is some evidence that when leader and group have similar values, the members are more satisfied (Haythorn, 1958; Sadler, 1970), but the results with respect to performance are equivocal (McCurdy and Eber, 1953; Pelz, 1956).

Degree of contact with the leader may also affect the success of PDM (Pelz, 1956) especially where information exchange is needed.

Other organizational factors   PDM requires more time to reach a decision than more directive methods (although conceivably time could be saved in the long run if the decision under PDM were better); thus if there is pressure for an immediate decision, PDM may not be feasible (Davis, 1963; Derber, 1970; Mansbridge, 1973; Sadler, 1970; Strauss and Rosenstein, 1970; Vroom, 1969).

Organization (and group) size is pertinent, since an increase in the number of members participating results in a disproportionate increase in the potential amount of interaction. Thus increasing size affects not only the time needed to reach a decision, but increases the problem of regulation and coordination (Heller and Yukl, 1969; Hemphill, 1950), although methods have been suggested for solving this problem (cf. Likert, 1961, 1967).

Finally, it has been argued that PDM is needed most urgently under conditions of rapid or constant organizational (including technological) change (Albrook, 1967; Morse and Lorsch, 1970). Again the argument is made that employees will resist changes which are not introduced participatively. However, this claim cannot be accepted without qualification. We have argued that employees may accept change readily without PDM, especially if logical reasons are given for it and if the employees are already motivated. Furthermore, directive leaders are often in a position to respond more rapidly to change than are participative leaders. However, when organizational change involves complex knowledge requirements which cannot be mastered by a single person, PDM should be superior to unilateral decision making. PDM should also facilitate change when the changes are threatening to employees if it gives them a heightened sense of control.

VI. PARTICIPATION IN RELATION TO OTHER MOTIVATIONAL TECHNIQUES

Participation is not the only method organizations can use to motivate employees. There are at least three other major motivational techniques: money, goal setting with feedback, and job enrichment. It is undeniable that each of these techniques can be successful even when divorced from PDM. For example, incentive plans, in which pay is based upon the amount of work produced, have led to productivity increases as high as several hundred percent (Lawler, 1971); increases between 40 and 70 percent are not uncommon (Fein, 1976b). However, as in the case of PDM studies, the experimental designs are sometimes confounded with variables other than pay (e.g., the introduction of work standards).

There is also impressive evidence supporting the efficacy of assigned goals combined with feedback, as a means of improving job performance (Latham and Yukl, 1975a; Litwin and Stringer, 1968). Although the typical performance increases obtained with goal setting are not as large, on the average, as those obtained with incentives, a performance improvement of close to 50 percent was obtained in one goal setting experiment (Latham and Baldes, 1975).

Numerous successful studies of job enrichment (i.e., delegation of responsibility, modules) have been reported (Ford, 1969; Maher, 1971; Suojanen, McDonald, Swallow, and Suojanen, 1975). Many were done without the use of participation (e.g., Ford, 1969; Paul, Robertson, and Herzberg, 1969). Again the experimental changes in enrichment studies have often been multifaceted, so that the effect of enrichment as such is hard to isolate (Locke, 1975). One recent study attributed the productivity increases observed in job enrichment to goal setting (Umstot, Bell, and Mitchell, 1976) although other factors may also be involved (Locke, Sirota, and Wolfson, 1976).

Since PDM is a technique, with the particular content being optional, it can, of course, be combined with other techniques, including the three described above.

The Scanlon Plan, for example, combines PDM with pay (Frost, Wakeley, and Ruh, 1974). It is not clear whether the results of Scanlon Plans are any better than those which use plant-wide incentives without PDM such as Fein's Improshare (Fein, 1976b, 1977). The effects of PDM within the Scanlon Plan may not be motivational but cognitive. PDM may facilitate the development of useful ideas for improving efficiency, while the monetary aspect provides the incentive to develop and accept the proposed changes. PDM techniques have also been used to *develop* pay incentive plans (e.g., Lawler and Hackman, 1969; Lawler, 1975) with some success. The motivational effect in these cases is probably to increase acceptance of the plans, although cognitive factors (such as better understanding) cannot be ruled out.

Several investigators have argued that PDM will not work *unless* it is combined with or involves monetary incentives (Derber, 1963; Rosenstein, 1970; Strauss, 1963); however, as indicated earlier, the research does not necessarily support this claim.

A number of studies have compared assigned and participative goal setting (e.g., Carroll and Tosi, 1973; Hannan, in press; Ivancevich, 1976, 1977; Latham and Yukl, 1975b, 1976; Latham, Mitchell and Dossett, 1978). The results have been equivocal. In some cases employees set higher goals under PDM conditions than supervisors set for comparable subordinates under assigned conditions. However, when goal level is controlled by yoking the assigned groups to the goal levels set by the PDM groups, differences in goal acceptance rarely emerge. As noted earlier, PDM may be more beneficial if employees are accustomed to it than if they are not (French, Kay, and Meyer, 1966). It seems that in many cases the demand characteristics of the job are sufficient to ensure substantial goal acceptance (Locke, 1978), although if frequent changes in task and goal level occur, resistance to assigned goals may develop (Coch and French, 1948).

PDM has been used in some job-enrichment studies (e.g., Locke, Sirota, and Wolfson, 1976). Although there are strong opinions both in favor of using it (Hackman, 1975) and against using it (Ford, 1969), there is little evidence indicating that PDM necessarily makes enrichment more effective. One simulated field study (discussed earlier) compared the results of enriching jobs with and without PDM (Seeborg, 1978). It was found that the enrichment ideas of the PDM group did not really involve vertical loading at all but rather were focused around social changes. Furthermore, the work quality of the PDM group was poorer than that of the non-PDM, vertically loaded group. When the same changes made by the PDM group were made unilaterally by the plant manager in another experimental group, however, there was a difference in satisfaction in favor the PDM group.

Another way in which PDM and job enrichment are being combined, often promoted by "sociotechnical system" advocates (e.g., Susman, 1976, Trist, Higgins, Murray, and Pollock, 1963), is through the development of autonomous work groups. This system allows PDM among the group members, while the group as a whole is given increased responsibility for decision making. It is claimed that such a procedure is superior to individual enrichment, but there is no evidence to support this claim.

VII. CONCLUSIONS

Our analysis of the issue of employee participation in decision making has led to the following conclusions: (1) the use of PDM is a practical rather than a moral issue; (2) the concept of participation refers to shared or joint decision making, and therefore excludes delegation; (3) there are numerous mechanisms both cognitive and motivational through which PDM may produce high morale and performance; (4) research findings yield equivocal support for the thesis that PDM necessarily leads to increased satisfaction and productivity, although the evidence for the former outcome is stronger than the evidence for the latter; (5) the evidence indicates that the effectiveness of PDM depends upon numerous contextual factors; and (6) PDM is not the only way to motivate employees.

If the effects of PDM depend upon the context in which it is used, it follows that PDM might be not only ineffective in some circumstances, but might be actually harmful. For example, it could lead to excessive intragroup or intergroup conflict caused by such factors as fundamental value differences or the resentment of members whose ideas are rejected. Group cohesion fostered by PDM may work against the goals of the organization instead of for them. Conformity and groupthink fostered by group pressures could lead to poor decision quality, especially if these pressures intimidate the most knowledgeable members or lead the other members to ignore their ideas. The time requirements of PDM could result in harmful delays. The ubiquitous use of PDM could retard the development and emergence of leaders, and the leaders who do emerge may be too emotionally involved in their groups to make objective decisions, especially if the decisions are "tough" or unpopular.

That our claim of possible dangers associated with PDM is not idle speculation is demonstrated by the unfortunate experience of Nonlinear Systems (Malone, 1975). Following 8 years of rapid growth and increasing profitability as a manufacturer of electrical measuring instruments, the company, after consulting with several eminent PDM advocates and years of planning, introduced radical organizational changes aimed at making the company thoroughly democratic. One key change involved removing the authority of upper and middle management by making them merely "advisors." Time clocks, recordkeeping, the accounting department, and the inspection department were all eliminated.

After 5 years, the program was largely abandoned because of increasingly serious problems with respect to sales volume, sales costs, the failure of productivity to rise, managerial frustration, and decreased profitability. Malone writes that: "The seven vice presidents formerly had been vigorously active in the midst of daily problems and were more or less expert in their individual specialties. Under participative management these men were practically immobilized as 'sideline consultants'" (Malone, 1975, p. 58). Lower-level managers were correspondingly frustrated by the lack of guidance and training from above. Only among shop workers was morale high (because of increases in pay, fringe benefits, and job enrichment) and production stable (but not higher).

The key error caused by the overzealous application of PDM was the *separation of responsibility from knowledge.* The attempt to make everyone equal regardless of ability led to the most competent employees being prevented from acting on their judgment.

The issue was put succinctly by a former Westinghouse executive, "Good management is the rule of the best minds. It is anti-democratic [which it is in the Greek sense], although private organizations flourish best in democratic [i.e., free] countries. However, the democratic rule of the majority will frustrate and defeat any management. The crew cannot run the ship" (quoted in Derber, 1963, p. 69).[12]

One reason for our lack of knowledge regarding the conditions under which PDM will be harmful is the widespread pro-PDM bias noted earlier; researchers do not look for consequences they do not think will (or should not) occur. Another reason is the generally neobehavioristic approach to PDM research, which has focused more on stimulus and response, i.e., participation and productivity (or satisfaction), than on the mechanisms which bring the effects about (e.g., the knowledge and values of the participants).

Another unfortunate consequence of the pro-PDM bias has been the establishment of a false dichotomy. It is often implied that leadership must be either authoritarian or participative (or somewhere in between), thus closing the door to the discovery of other dimensions. Authoritarian leadership demands *obedience to authority as such,* regardless of reason or context. Full participative leadership involves joint decision making with one or more subordinates regardless of reason or context. Thus the dichotomy reduces to decision making based on the whim of the leader or the whim of the group. In neither case is the issue of knowledge addressed explicitly, although as noted earlier, PDM practitioners acknowledge its relevance implicitly by typically allowing participation only on issues about which the workers have pertinent knowledge.

The recognition of individual differences in competence implies a third type: knowledge-based leadership. If a leader clearly knows the best solution, then he should properly assert his knowledge and make the decision. *Such a procedure would not be authoritarian but authoritative.* If subordinates do not agree with his solution, such a leader should try to rationally persuade them by giving them the reasons for his position, or, if necessary and feasible, demonstrate the validity of his ideas in some concrete form (e.g., through an experiment, examples, etc.). In the course of such discussions, the leader, of course, may find that he is wrong, in which case he should change his position.

If a leader does not know the best (or any) solution to the problem, then he should properly consult those who do have such knowledge, including competent members of his own subordinate staff, his superiors, and outside experts.

In some cases there may be options; for example, several different solutions may work equally well and have equivalent costs. In such a case, responsibility could be delegated or a straight majority vote could be used.

It should be stressed that managers and experts do not always know more than their subordinates (e.g., see Thorsrud, Sorensen, and Gustavsen, 1976, p. 431). The rule of knowledge does not mean the rule of formal degrees, positions, or job titles, but by those who have the best ideas whatever their position. Human relations theorists could argue, with much justification, that many managers underestimate the knowledge and capacity of their subordinates. However, the solution is not to assume that everyone knows as much as everyone else but to determine who knows what.

The above should not be taken to imply that a competent leader should ignore motivational issues, e.g., getting employees to accept decisions, gaining commitment, promoting satisfaction, etc., but it *should* be taken to imply which goal has logical priority. Knowledge must take precedence over feelings in business organizations (Gomberg, 1966).

A profit-making organization survives by the discovery and application of knowledge relevant to its product and market. In the absence of rational leadership, the effort exerted by employees will be useless. Nor do business organizations exist for the purpose of satisfying their employees since employee feelings have no market price; the goal of such organizations is to satisfy their customers and stockholders.

It must be emphasized that there is no *fundamental* conflict between the interests of employees, stockholders, and customers. If employees are not reasonably satisfied, the organization will be plagued by high turnover, absenteeism, sabotage, strikes, and apathy and thus will not produce a good product at a reasonable cost. On the other hand, if the firm does not make a profit, there will be no jobs at all for the employees—a condition which will cause dissatisfaction!

While the goal of each *individual* is properly to achieve his own happiness, he cannot expect others (e.g., employers) to arbitrarily provide him with what he wants. Nor is what a given person wants always rational. If an organization based its decisions solely on whatever desires its employees happened to have rather than on reason and logic, it would soon go bankrupt. Applied on a wide scale, the result would be mass poverty.

From the point of view of an organization, employee satisfaction must be considered a means to an end (i.e., a necessary condition for long-term profitability), not an end in itself.

In view of this, one must ask what those who advocate PDM *solely* in the name of satisfaction wish to accomplish. For example, Susman (1976), citing various authorities, argues that PDM is consistent with an "organic" world view which is coming to replace the older "mechanical" world view.

The mechanical world view "is characterized by faith in applying rational methods to the betterment of the human condition. Each successful application of rationality builds upon previous achievements, resulting in . . . historical progress. It is also characterized by belief in an objective world that exists independently of any human observer" (Susman, 1976, p. 24).

In contrast, the organic world view holds that "harmony and equilibrium, not progress are the primary end of human activity. History is to be understood as a series of events that are recurrent and eternal rather than successively leading to a progressively better future . . . knowledge is gained through contemplation and revelation to the end of better understanding the relationship of man to the eternal and divine. God or a similar concept is considered the source of all knowledge" (Susman, 1976, p. 24).

The organic view, according to Susman, is partly the result of recent changes in political ideology which include the abrogation of property rights which are to be supplanted by worker control (socialism), the substitution of satisfaction for production as the goal of work organizations, and the replacement of the profit motive with the (undefined) principle of "social utility."

Let us examine exactly what these two world views imply and stand for. The so-called mechanical world view stands for reason, objectivity, production, individual rights, and progress. The organic view advocates feelings, mysticism, collectivism, and stagnation (i.e., poverty). In this context, the term "mechanical" is a rather bizarre label for the description of ideals which, in essence, represent the key values of the Renaissance and the American Revolution. The term "organic," in contrast, is a strangely benign designation for values which represent the essence of tribalism and the Dark Ages. If this is what participation on a wide scale will ultimately lead to, then one must ask why anyone would want it.

If participation is to be used as a tool for the furtherance of man's happiness and well-being, then it must be in a context which recognizes not only individual differences in knowledge and ability, but the primacy of reason over feelings in organizational decision making.

FOOTNOTES

1. Some of the ideas and conclusions in this paper were presented by the senior author at the Academy of Management meetings, August 1977. The authors would like to thank Dena Schneier and Ron Prestwich for their extensive help in collecting, compiling, and verifying the reference material used in this article.

2. This characterization of American intellectuals is not intended entirely as a compliment. While their desire to insure that theories apply to reality is admirable, their skepticism (due mainly to the philosophy of pragmatism) has been carried to the point where most of them believe that there are no general principles of any kind, that reason is basically impotent, and that there is no objective reality.

3. One book written in the United States has asserted explicitly that because the United States is a democracy, the majority should have the right to coerce the minority in the realm of action (White and Lippitt, 1960, pp. 295ff.). This view is now widely accepted.

4. If forced egalitarianism abrogates political and economic freedom and leads to a low standard of living, it remains to explain why some men still favor it. An extremely benevolent interpretation would be that it is due to an error of knowledge, i.e., its advocates do not understand what it implies and entails. However, Rand's (1971a) motivational interpretation is a more likely explanation, especially for many intellectuals. She attributes the advocacy of forced egalitarianism to hatred of the good for being the good, i.e., to hatred of achievement, of values, of competence. This, in turn, stems from the fact that because of their own resentment against mental effort and the resulting arrested cognitive development, they find men of achievement to be a threat to their self-esteem.

5. The claim that Yugoslavian business organizations are run democratically must be taken with an enormous dose of skepticism considering the fact that the Communist Party has absolute control over every facet of life. Sturmthal (1964) notes that limited autonomy has been permitted in Yugoslavia, but only because the Party has not seen the workers' councils as a threat to its authority. A similar experiment in Poland was rapidly terminated because the Party saw the councils as anti-Communist. Sturmthal concludes that "No attempts to 'humanize' totalitarianism . . . can bridge the gap that separates self government from an unlimited dictatorship" (1964, p. 190).

6. In most of Maier's studies, judgments regarding decision quality were based on the experimenter's opinion rather than on an external criterion. The present writers believe that the solutions judged to be best in Maier's studies would not necessarily be the best under all circumstances. The danger of making quality judgments divorced from a specific real-life context was illustrated by an experience of the junior author. He presented a standard decision-making exercise to one of his classes in which the students had to decide upon the best strategies to survive in the wilderness. When presented with the "official" solutions to the exercise, which the author of the exercise had proposed, one student who had spent a considerable amount of time in the military commented that the proposed solutions were absurd and both his survival education and experience had taught him that the best solutions were totally contrary to many of the solutions proposed in the exercise.

7. The term "solved" should be placed in a wider organizational perspective. In the first 10 years after nationalization, the British Coal Industry had a cumulative deficit of $164.6 million (data provided by the Library of Congress). Thus the application of a sociotechnical systems approach could not overcome (nor was it designed to overcome) the problem of organization-wide (or industry-wide) inefficiency.

8. Additional information regarding this study was presented at a lecture given by Dr. Susman at the University of Maryland on October 7, 1976.

9. In a personal communication, Dr. Smith indicated that very little participation actually occurred in the PDM groups; this suggests that the results were probably due to goal setting rather than PDM.

10. It should be noted, however, that while our major conclusion (that PDM is contextual) agrees with that of another survey by Filley, House, and Kerr (1976), we do not agree with their classification of the results of many of the studies they reviewed (see their tables 11-2, 11-3, 11-4). For example, they reported the Vroom and Mann (1960) study as showing a positive relationship between satisfaction and PDM, whereas the actual finding was a positive correlation in one group and a negative correlation in another. We classified this study as "0", meaning the result was contextual. As a result of classification discrepancies like this, Filley, House, and Kerr did not conclude, as we did, that the results with respect to satisfaction were more consistent than those with respect to productivity. The reader will have to judge for himself whose classifications are more accurate.

11. This statement must be qualified to apply only to U.S. workers at this point in time. Dr. Frank Landy, who recently visited Sweden, observed that in that country the ideal of egalitarianism is so strong that the demand for participation by workers is not limited by lack of knowledge. For example, university janitors have demanded (successfully) to participate in the decisions of faculty committees!

12. It should be noted that the principle of the "rule of knowledge" cannot be applied out of context to the running of a government. While a government should be run by qualified people, no amount of superior knowledge would give them the right to enslave the citizens (e.g., like Plato's philosopher kings). Such a policy would negate the right of the citizens to act on their own rational judgment when it disagrees with that of the authorities (and would stifle the discovery of new knowledge). In a private organization, in contrast, when employer and employee disagree, they are free to part company (refuse to trade). Neither has the right to use physical force to make the other comply.

REFERENCES

1. Adams. S. (1952) "Effect of Equalitarian Atmospheres upon the Performance of Bomber Crews," *American Psychologist 7*, 398.
2. Albrook, R. C. (1967) "Participative Management: Time for a Second Look," *Fortune 75*, 166–170, 199–200.
3. Allport. G. W. (1945) "The Psychology of Participation," *Psychological Review 53*, 117–131.
4. Alutto, J. A., and F. Acito (1974) "Decisional Participation and Sources of Job Satisfaction: A Study of Manufacturing Personnel," *Academy of Management Journal 17*, 160–167.
5. Anderson, R. C. (1959) "Learning in Discussions: A Resumé of the Authoritarian-Democratic Studies," *Harvard Educational Review 29*, 201–215.
6. Argyle, M., G. Gardner, and F. Cioffi (1958) "Supervisory Methods Related to Productivity, Absenteeism, and Labour Turnover," *Human Relations 11*, 23–40.
7. Argyris, C. (1955) "Organizational Leadership and Participative Management," *Journal of Business 28*, 1–7,
8. Baumgartel, H. (1956) "Leadership, Motivations, and Attitudes in Research Laboratories," *Journal of Social Issues 12*, 24–31.
9. ———. (1957) "Leadership Style as a Variable in Research Administration," *Administrative Science Quarterly 2*, 344–360.
10. Bennett, E. (1955) "Discussion, Decision, Commitment, and Consensus in 'Group Decision'," *Human Relations 8*, 251–273.
11. Bennis, W. (1966) "A Reply: When Democracy Works," *Trans-action 3*, 35–36.

12. Berkowitz, L. (1953) "Sharing Leadership in Small, Decision-making Groups," *Journal of Abnormal and Social Psychology 48*, 231–238.
13. Blumberg, P. (1968) *Industrial Democracy: The Sociology of Participation*, New York: Schocken Books Inc.
14. Bucklow, M. (1966) "A New Role for the Work Group," *Administrative Science Quarterly 11*, 59–78.
15. Burke, P. J. (1966) "Authority Relations and Disruptive Behavior in Small Discussion Groups," *Sociometry 29*, 237–250.
16. Calvin, A. D., F. K. Hoffmann, and E. L. Harden (1957) "The Effect of Intelligence and Social Atmosphere on Group Problem Solving Behavior," *Journal of Social Psychology 45*, 61–74.
17. Campbell, H. (1953) "Some Effects of Joint Consultation on the Status and Role of the Supervisor," *Occupational Psychology 27*, 200–206.
18. Carey, A. (1967) "The Hawthorne Studies: A Radical Criticism," *American Sociological Review 32*, 403–416.
19. Carroll, S. J., and H. L. Tosi (1973) *Management by Objectives: Applications and Research*, New York: Macmillan Inc.
20. ———, and ———. (1977) "Relationship of Various Motivational Forces to the Effects of Participation in Goal Setting in a Management by Objectives Program," *Industrial Relations Research Association, Proceedings of the Twenty-Ninth Annual Winter Meeting* pp. 20–25.
21. Chaney, F. B., and K. S. Teel (1972) "Participative Management—A Practical Experience," *Personnel 49*, 8–19.
22. Coch, L., and J. R. P. French (1948) "Overcoming Resistance to Change," *Human Relations 1*, 512–532.
23. Cook, T. D., and D. T. Campbell (1976) "The Design and Conduct of Quasi-Experiments and True Experiments in Field Settings," in M. D. Dunnette (ed.), *Handbook of Industrial and Organizational Psychology*, Chicago: Rand McNally & Company.
24. Dachler, H. P., and B. Wilpert (1978) "Conceptual Dimensions and Boundaries of Participation in Organizations: A Critical Evaluation," *Administrative Science Quarterly 23*, 1–39.
25. Davies, B. (1967) "Some Thoughts on 'Organisational Democracy'," *Journal of Management Studies 4*, 270–281.
26. Davis, K. (1957) "Management by Participation: Its Place in Today's Business World," *Management Review 46*, 69–79.
27. ———. (1963) "The Case for Participative Management," *Business Horizons 6*, 55–60.
28. ———. (1967) *Human Relations at Work: The Dynamics of Organizational Behavior*, New York: McGraw-Hill.
29. Derber, M. (1963) "Worker Participation in Israeli Management," *Industrial Relations 3*, 51–72.
30. ———. (1970) "Crosscurrents in Workers Participation," *Industrial Relations 9*, 123–136.
31. Dill, W. R. (1958) "Environment as an Influence on Managerial Autonomy," *Administrative Science Quarterly 2*, 409–443.
32. ———, W. Hoffman, H. J. Leavitt, and T. O'Mara (1961) "Experiences with a Complex Management Game," *California Management Review 3*, 38–51.
33. Donnelly, J. F. (1977) "Participative Management at Work," *Harvard Business Review 55*, 117–127.

34. Dowling, W. F. (1975) "At General Motors: System 4 Builds Performance and Profits," *Organizational Dynamics 3* (Winter), 23–38.
35. Dubin, R. (1965) "Supervision and Productivity: Empirical Findings and Theoretical Considerations," in R. Dubin (ed.), *Leadership and Productivity,* San Francisco: Chandler Publishing Company.
36. Emery, F., and E. Thorsrud (1976) *Democracy at Work,* Leiden, The Netherlands: Martinus Nijhoff.
37. ———. and E. L. Trist (1960) "Socio-technical Systems," in C. W. Churchman and M. Verhulst (eds.), *Management Sciences, Models and Techniques,* Vol. 2, New York: Pergamon Press, Inc.
38. Falcione, R. L. (1974) "Credibility: Qualifier of Subordinate Participation," *Journal of Business Communication 11,* 43–54.
39. Fein, M. (1976a) "Improving Productivity by Improved Productivity Sharing," *Conference Board Record 13* (July), 44–49.
40. ———. (1976b) "Designing and Operating an Improshare Plan," Hillsdale, N.J. (unpublished).
41. ———. (1976c) "Motivation for Work," in R. Dubin (ed.), *Handbook of Work, Organization, and Society,* Chicago: Rand McNally & Company.
42. ———. (1977) "An Alternative to Traditional Managing," Hillsdale, N.J. (unpublished).
43. Filley, A. C., R. J. House, and S. Kerr, *Managerial Process and Organizational Behavior,* Glenview, Ill.: Scott, Foresman and Company.
44. Fleishman, E. A. (1965) "Attitude versus Skill Factors in Work Group Productivity," *Personnel Psychology 18,* 253–266.
45. Foa, U. G. (1957) "Relation of Workers Expectation to Satisfaction with Supervisor," *Personnel Psychology 10,* 161–168.
46. Ford, R. N. (1969) *Motivation Through the Work Itself,* New York: American Management Association.
47. Fox, W. M. (1957) "Group Reaction to Two Types of Conference Leadership," *Human Relations 10,* 279–289.
48. Foy, N., and H. Gadon (1976) "Worker Participation: Contrasts in Three Countries," *Harvard Business Review 54,* 71–83.
49. French, J. R. P. (1950) "Field Experiments: Changing Group Productivity," in J. G. Miller (ed.), *Experiments in Social Process: A Symposium on Social Psychology,* New York: McGraw-Hill.
50. ———, J. Israel, and D. As (1960) "An Experiment in a Norwegian Factory: Interpersonal Dimensions in Decision-making," *Human Relations 13,* 3–19.
51. ———, E. Kay, and H. H. Meyer (1966) "Participation and the Appraisal System," *Human Relations 19,* 3–20.
52. ———, I. C. Ross, S. Kirby, J. R. Nelson, and P. Smyth (1958) "Employee Participation in a Program of Industrial Change," *Personnel 35,* 16–29.
53. Frost, C. F., J. H. Wakeley, and R. A. Ruh (1974) *The Scanlon Plan for Organization Development: Identity, Participation, and Equity,* East Lansing: Mich.: Michigan State University Press.
54. Geare, A. J. (1976) "Productivity From Scanlon-type Plans," *Academy of Management Review 1,* 99–108.
55. Gibb, C. A. (1951) "An Experimental Approach to the Study of Leadership," *Occupational Psychology 25,* 233–248.
56. Gillespie, J. (1971) "Toward Freedom in Work," in C. G. Benello and D. Roussopoulos (eds.), *The Case for Participatory Democracy: Some Prospects For a Radical Society,* New York: Grossman Publishers.

57. Glueck, W., and D. Kavran (1971) "Yugoslav Management System," *Management International Review 11*, 3–17.
58. Gomberg, W. (1966) "The Trouble with Democratic Management," *Transaction 3*, 30–35.
59. Hackman, J. R. (1975) "On the Coming Demise of Job Enrichment," in E. L. Cass and F. G. Zimmer (eds.), *Man and Work in Society*, New York: Von Nostrand-Reinhold Company.
60. Hall, J. (1971) "Decisions, Decisions, Decisions," *Psychology Today 5*, 51–54, 86–88.
61. Hamblin, R. L., K. Miller, and J. A. Wiggins (1961) "Group Morale and Competence of the Leader," *Sociometry 24*, 295–311.
62. Hannan, R. E. (in press) "The Effects of Participative versus Assigned Goal Setting on Goal Acceptance and Performance," *Journal of Applied Psychology*.
63. Haythorn, W. (1958) "The Effects of Varying Combinations of Authoritarian and Equalitarian Leaders and Followers," in E. E. Maccoby, T. M. Newcomb, and E. L. Hartley (eds.), *Readings in Social Psychology*, New York: Henry Holt.
64. Heinicke, C., and R. F. Bales (1953) "Developmental Trends in the Structure of Small Groups," *Sociometry 16*, 7–38.
65. Heller, F. A., and L. W. Porter (1966) "Perceptions of Managerial Needs and Skills in Two National Samples," *Occupational Psychology 40*, 1–13.
66. ———, and G. Yukl (1969) "Participation, Managerial Decison-making, and Situational Variables," *Organizational Behavior and Human Performance 4*, 227–241.
67. Hemphill, J. K. (1950) "Relations between the Size of the Group and the Behavior of 'Superior' Leaders," *Journal of Social Psychology 32*, 11–32.
68. Herzberg, F. (1966) *Work and the Nature of Man*, Cleveland: World Publishing Co.
69. Hespe, G., and T. Wall "The Demand for Participation Among Employees." Sheffield, England: MCR Social and Applied Psychology Unit (unpublished).
70. Hessen, R. (1968) "Campus or Battleground? Columbia is a Warning to All American Universities," *Barron's*, May 20, pp. 1ff.
71. Hoffman, L. R., R. J. Burke, and N. R. F. Maier (1965) "Participation, Influence, and Satisfaction among Members of Problem-solving Groups," *Psychological Reports 16*, 661–667.
72. ———, E. Harburg, and N. R. F. Maier (1962) "Differences and Disagreement as Factors in Creative Group Problem Solving," *Journal of Abnormal and Social Psychology 64*, 206–214.
73. Holter, H. (1965) "Attitudes toward Employee Participation in Company Decision-making Processes," *Human Relations 18*, 297–321.
74. Ivancevich, J. M. (1976) "Effects of Goal Setting on Performance and Job Satisfaction," *Journal of Applied Psychology 61*, 605–612.
75. ———. (1977) "Different Goal Setting Treatments and Their Effects on Performance and Job Satisfaction," *Academy of Management Journal 20*, 406–419.
76. Janis, I. (1972) *Victims of Groupthink*, Boston: Houghton Mifflin Company.
77. Jaques, E. (1964) "Social-Analysis and the Glacier Project," *Human Relations 17*, 361–375.
78. Kahn, R. L. (1974) "Organizational Development: Some Problems and Proposals," *Journal of Applied Behavioral Science 10*, 485–502.
79. ———. (1975) "In Search of the Hawthorne Effect," in E. L. Cass and F. G. Zimmer (eds.), *Man and Work in Society*, New York: Van Nostrand-Reinhold Company.
80. Kaiser, R. G. (1976) *Russia: The People and the Power*, New York: Atheneum Publishers.
81. Katz, D., N. Maccoby, and N. Morse (1950) *Productivity, Supervision and Morale in an Office Situation*, Part I, Ann Arbor, Mich.: Survey Research Center, Institute for Social Research, University of Michigan.

82. ——, ——, G. Gurin, and L. G. Floor (1951) *Productivity, Supervision and Morale Among Railroad Workers*, Ann Arbor, Mich.: Survey Research Center, Institute for Social Research, University of Michigan.

83. Katzell, R. A., C. E. Miller, N. G. Rotter, and T. G. Venet (1970) "Effects of Leadership and Other Inputs on Group Processes and Outputs," *Journal of Social Psychology 80*, 157–169.

84. Kidd, J. S., and R. T. Christy (1961) "Supervisory Procedures and Work-team Productivity," *Journal of Applied Psychology 45*, 388–392.

85. Lammers, C. J. (1967) "Power and Participation in Decision Making in Formal Organizations," *American Journal of Sociology 73*, 201–216.

86. Lanzetta, J. T., and T. B. Roby (1960) "The Relationship between Certain Group Process Variables and Group Problem-solving Efficiency," *Journal of Social Psychology 52*, 135–148.

87. Latham, G. P., and J. J. Baldes (1975) "The 'Practical Significance' of Locke's Theory of Goal Setting," *Journal of Applied Psychology 60*, 122–124.

88. ——, and G. A. Yukl (1975a) "A Review of Research on the Application of Goal Setting in Organizations," *Academy of Management Journal 18*, 824–845.

89. ——, and ——. (1975b) "Assigned versus Participative Goal Setting with Educated and Uneducated Woods Workers," *Journal of Applied Psychology 60*, 299–302.

90. ——, and ——. (1976) "Effects of Assigned and Participative Goal Setting on Performance and Job Satisfaction," *Journal of Applied Psychology 61*, 166–171.

91. ——, J. R. Mitchell, and D. L. Dossett (1978) "Importance of Participative Goal Setting and Anticipated Rewards on Goal Difficulty and Job Performance," *Journal of Applied Psychology 63*, 163–171.

92. Lawler, E. E. (1971) *Pay and Organizational Effectiveness: A Psychological View*, New York: McGraw-Hill.

93. ——. (1975) "Pay, Participation and Organizational Change," in E. L. Cass and F. G. Zimmer (eds.), *Man and Work in Society*, New York: Van Nostrand-Reinhold Company.

94. ——. (1976) "Should the Quality of Work Life be Legislated?" *The Personnel Administrator 21* (January), 17–21.

95. ——, and J. R. Hackman (1969) "Impact of Employee Participation in the Development of Pay Incentive Plans: A Field Experiment," *Journal of Applied Psychology 53*, 467–471.

96. Lawrence, L. C., and. P. C. Smith (1955) "Group Decision and Employee Participation," *Journal of Applied Psychology 39*, 334–337.

97. Lawrence, P. R. (1971) "How to Deal with Resistance to Change," in D. A. Kolb, I. M. Rubin, and J. M. McIntyre (eds.), *Organizational Psychology*, Englewood Cliffs, N.J.: Prentice-Hall, Inc.

98. Leavitt, H. J. (1965) "Applied Organizational Change in Industry: Structural, Technological and Humanistic Approaches," in J. G. March (ed.), *Handbook of Organizations*, Chicago: Rand McNally & Company.

99. Levine, J., and J. Butler (1952) "Lecture vs. Group Decision in Changing Behavior," *Journal of Applied Psychology 36*, 29–33.

100. Lewin, K. (1947) "Frontiers in Group Dynamics," *Human Relations 1*, 5–42.

101. ——. (1952) "Group Decision and Social Change," in T. M. Newcomb and E. L. Hartley (eds.), *Readings in Social Psychology*, New York: Holt, Rinehart and Winston, Inc.

102. ——, R. Lippitt, and R. K. White (1939) "Patterns of Aggressive Behavior in Experimentally Created 'Social Climates,'" *Journal of Social Psychology 10*, 271–299.

103. Ley, R. (1966) "Labor Turnover as a Function of Worker Differences, Work Environment, and Authoritarianism of Foremen," *Journal of Applied Psychology 50*, 497–500.
104. Likert, R. (1961) *New Patterns of Management*, New York: McGraw-Hill.
105. ———. (1967) *The Human Organization*, New York: McGraw-Hill.
106. Lippitt, R., and R. K. White (1958) "An Experimental Study of Leadership and Group Life," in E. E. Maccoby, T. M. Newcomb, and E. L. Hartley (eds.), *Readings in Social Psychology*, New York: Holt, Rinehart and Winston, Inc.
107. Lischeron, J., and T. D. Wall (1974) "Attitudes towards Participation among Local Authority Employees," *Human Relations 28*, 499–517.
108. ———, and ———. (1975) "Employee Participation: An Experimental Field Study," *Human Relations 28*, 863–884.
109. Litwin, G. H., and R. A. Stringer (1968) *Motivation and Organizational Climate*, Boston: Division of Research, Graduate School of Business Administration, Harvard University.
110. Locke, E. A. (1969) "What Is Job Satisfaction?" *Organizational Behavior and Human Performance 4*, 309–336.
111. ———. (1975) "Personnel Attitudes and Motivation," *Annual Review of Psychology 26*, 457–480.
112. ———. (1976a) "The Nature and Causes of Job Satisfaction," in M. D. Dunnette (ed.), *Handbook of Industrial and Organizational Psychology*, Chicago: Rand McNally & Company.
113. ———. (1976b) "The Case against Legislating the Quality of Work Life," *The Personnel Administrator 21* (May), 19–21.
114. ———. (1978) "The Ubiquity of the Technique of Goal Setting in Theories of and Approaches to Employee Motivation," *Academy of Management Review, 3*, 594–601.
115. ———, D. Sirota, and A. D. Wolfson (1976) "An Experimental Case Study of the Successes and Failures of Job Enrichment in a Government Agency," *Journal of Applied Psychology 61*, 701–711.
116. Lowin, A. (1968) "Participative Decision Making: A Model, Literature Critique, and Prescriptions for Research," *Organizational Behavior and Human Performance 3*, 68–106.
117. Macrae, N. (1977) "'Entrepreneurial Revolution' Ahead, According to British Journalist," *World of Work Report 2* (April), 46–48.
118. Maher, J. R. (1971) *New Perspectives in Job Enrichment*, New York: Van Nostrand-Reinhold Company.
119. Mahoney, T. A. (1967) "Managerial Perceptions of Organizational Effectiveness," *Management Science 14*, 76–91.
120. Maier, N. R. F. (1950) "The Quality of Group Decision as Influenced by the Discussion Leader," *Human Relations 3*, 155–174.
121. ———. (1953) "An Experimental Test of the Effect of Training on Discussion Leadership," *Human Relations 6*, 161–173.
122. ———. (1967) "Assets and Liabilities in Group Problem-solving: The Need for an Integrative Function," *Psychological Review 74*, 239–249.
123. ———. (1970) "The Integrative Function in Group Problem Solving," in L. R. Aronson, E. Tobath, D. S. Lehrman, and J. S. Rosenblatt (eds.), *Development and Evolution of Behavior*, San Francisco: W. H. Freeman and Company Publishers.
124. ———. (1973) *Psychology in Industrial Organizations*, Boston: Houghton Mifflin Company.
125. ———. and M. Sashkin (1971) "Specific Leadership Behaviors that Promote Problem Solving," *Personnel Psychology 24*, 35–44.

126. Malone. E. L. (1975) "The Non-Linear Systems Experiment in Participative Management," *Journal of Business 48*, 52–64.
127. Mansbridge, J. J. (1973) "Time, Emotion, and Inequality: Three Problems of Participatory Groups," *Journal of Applied Behavioral Science 9*, 351–368.
128. Marrow, A. J. (ed.) (1972) *The Failure of Success*, New York: AMACOM.
129. ———, and J. R. P. French (1945) "Changing a Stereotype in Industry," *Journal of Social Issues* December: 33–37.
130. ———, D. G. Bowers, and S. E. Seashore (1967) *Management by Participation*, New York: Harper & Row, Publishers.
131. Maslow, A. H. (1970) "The Superior Person," in W. G. Bennis (ed.), *American Bureaucracy*, Chicago: Aldine.
132. Mayo, E. (1924) "Revery and Industrial Fatigue," *Journal of Personnel Research 3*, 278–281.
133. ———. (1970) "The First Inquiry," in H. F. Merrill (ed.), *Classics in Management*, New York: American Management Association (originally published in 1945).
134. McCormick, C. P. (1938) *Multiple Management*, New York: Harper.
135. ———, (1949) *The Power of People*, New York: Harper.
136. McCurdy, H. G., and H. W. Eber (1953) "Democratic versus Authoritarian: A Further Investigation of Group Problem-solving, *Journal of Personality 22*, 258–269.
137. ———, and W. E. Lambert (1952) "The Efficiency of Small Human Groups in the Solution of Problems Requiring Genuine Co-operation," *Journal of Personality 20*, 478–494.
138. McGregor, D. (1944) "Conditions of Effective Leadership in the Industrial Organization," *Journal of Consulting Psychology 8*, 55–63.
139. McInnes, N. (1976) "People's Capitalism: in Europe, Workers Gain Seats on Corporate Boards," *Barron's* July 12, pp. 9, 16–17.
140. ———. (1977) "Boardroom Revolution? In Great Britain, the Rights of Investors Are in Jeopardy," *Barron's* February 14, pp. 7, 12.
141. McMurray, R. N. (1958) "The Case for Benevolent Autocracy," *Harvard Business Review 36*, 82–90.
142. Meyer, H. H., E. Kay, and J. R. P. French (1965) "Split Roles in Performance Appraisal," *Harvard Business Review 43*, 123–129.
143. Miles, R. E. (1965) "Human Relations or Human Resources?" *Harvard Business Review 43*, 148–163.
144. ———, and Ritchie, J. B. (1971) "Participative Management: Quality vs. Quantity," *California Management Review 13*, 48–56.
145. Miller, E. J. (1975) Socio-technical Systems in Weaving, 1953–1970: A Follow-up Study," *Human Relations 28*, 349–386.
146. Mitchell, T. R. (1973) "Motivation and Participation: An Integration," *Academy of Management Journal 16*, 670–679.
147. Morse, C., and E. Reimer (1956) "The Experimental Change of a Major Organizational Variable," *Journal of Abnormal and Social Psychology 52*, 120–129.
148. Morse, J. J., and J. W. Lorsch (1970) "Beyond Theory Y," *Harvard Business Review 48* (May/June), 61–68.
149. Mulder, M. (1959) "Power and Satisfaction in Task-oriented Groups," *Acta Psychologica 16*, 178–225.
150. ———, and H. Wilke (1970) "Participation and Power Equalization," *Organizational Behavior and Human Performance 5*, 430–448.
151. Mullen, J. H. (1965) "Differential Leadership Modes and Productivity in a Large Organization," *Academy of Management Journal 8*, 107–126.

152. Nicol, E. A. (1948) "Management through Consultative Supervision," *Personnel Journal 27*, 207–217.
153. Obradovic, J. (1970) "Participation and Work Attitudes in Yugoslavia," *Industrial Relations 9*, 161–169.
154. ———, J. R. P. French, and W. Rodgers (1970) "Workers' Councils in Yugoslavia," *Human Relations 23*, 459–71.
155. Parsons, H. M. (1974) "What Happened at Hawthorne?" *Science 183*, 922–932.
156. Patchen, M. (1964) "Participation in Decision-making and Motivation: What Is the Relation?," *Personnel Administration 27*, 24–31.
157. ———. (1970) *Participation, Achievement, and Involvement on the Job*, Englewood Cliffs, N.J.: Prentice-Hall, Inc.
158. Paul, W. J., K. B. Robertson, and F. Herzberg (1969) "Job Enrichment Pays Off," *Harvard Business Review 47*, 61–77.
159. Pelz, D. C. (1956) "Some Social Factors Related to Performance in a Research Organization," *Administrative Science Quarterly 1*, 310–325.
160. Powell, R. M., and J. L. Schlacter (1971) "Participative Management: A Panacea?," *Academy of Management Journal 14*, 165–173.
161. Preston, L. E., and J. E. Post (1974) "The Third Managerial Revolution," *Academy of Management Journal 17*, 476–486.
162. Rand, A. (1964) *The Virtue of Selfishness*, New York: New American Library (Signet).
163. ———. (1966) *Capitalism: The Unknown Ideal*, New York: New American Library.
164. ———. (1971a) "The Age of Envy," *The Objectivist 10* (7), 1–13, and 10 (8), 1–11.
165. ———. (1971b) *The "New Left: The Anti-industrial Revolution,"* New York: New American Library.
166. Raskin, A. H. (1976) "The Labor Scene, The Workers' Voice in German Companies," *World of Work Report 1*, (July) 5–6.
167. Rice, A. K. (1953) "Productivity and Social Organization in an Indian Weaving Shed," *Human Relations 6*, 297–329.
168. Roethlisberger, F. J., and W. J. Dickson (1956) *Management and the Worker*, Cambridge, Mass.: Harvard University Press (originally published in 1939).
169. Rosen, N. A. (1969) *Leadership Change and Work-Group Dynamics: An Experiment*, Ithaca, N.Y.: Cornell University Press.
170. Rosenfeld, J. M., and M. J. Smith (1967) "Participative Management: An Overview," *Personnel Journal 46*, 101–104.
171. Rosenstein, E. (1970) "Histadrut's Search for a Participation Program," *Industrial Relations 9*, 70–186.
172. Rubenowitz, S. (1962) "Job-oriented and Person-oriented Leadership," *Personnel Psychology 15*, 387–396.
173. Runyon, K. E. (1973) "Some Interactions between Personality Variables and Management Styles," *Journal of Applied Psychology 57*, 288–294.
174. Sadler, P. J. (1970) "Leadership Style, Confidence in Management, and Job Satisfaction," *Journal of Applied Behavioral Science 6*, 3–19.
175. Sashkin, M. (1976) "Changing toward Participative Management Approaches: A Model and Methods," *Academy of Management Review 1*, 75–86.
176. Scheflen, K. C., E. E. Lawler, and J. R. Hackman (1971) "Long-term Impact of Employee Participation in the Development of Pay Incentive Plans: A Field Experiment Revisited,"*Journal of Applied Psychology 55*, 182–186.
177. Schregle, J. (1970) "Forms of Participation in Management," *Industrial Relations 9*, 117–122.
178. Schuler, R. S. (1977) "Role Perceptions, Satisfaction and Performance Moderated by

Organization Level and Participation in Decision Making," *Academy of Management Journal 20,* 165–169.

179. Schultz, G. P. (1951) "Worker Participation on Production Problems: A Discussion of Experience with the 'Scanlon Plan,'" *Personnel 28,* 201–210.
180. Seeborg, I. S. (1978) "The Influence of Employee Participation in Job Redesign," *Journal of Applied Behavioral Science 14,* 87–98.
181. Shaw, M. E. (1955) "A Comparison of Two Types of Leadership in Various Communication Nets," *Journal of Abnormal and Social Psychology 50,* 127–134.
182. ———, and J. M. Blum (1966) "Effects of Leadership Style upon Group Performance as a Function of Task Structure," *Journal of Personality and Social Psychology 3,* 238–242.
183. Singer, J. N. (1974) "Participative Decison-making about Work: An Overdue Look at Variables which Mediate its Effects," *Sociology of Work and Occupations 1,* 347–371.
184. Smith, H. (1976) *The Russians,* New York: Ballantine Books, Inc.
185. Sorcher, M. (1967) "Motivating the Hourly Employee," General Electric Company, Behavioral Research Service (unpublished).
186. ———. (1971) "Motivation, Participation and Myth," *Personnel Administration 34* (September/October), 20–24.
187. Stagner, R. (1969) "Corporate Decision Making: An Empirical Study," *Journal of Applied Psychology 53,* 1–13.
188. Steers, R. M. (1975) "Task-goal Attributes, n achievement, and Supervisory Performance," *Organizational Behavior and Human Performance 13,* 392–403.
189. Stogdill, R. M. (1974) *Handbook of Leadership: A Survey of Theory and Research.* New York: The Free Press.
190. Strauss, G. (1963) "Some Notes on Power-equalization," in H. Leavitt (ed.), *The Social Science of Organizations: Four Perspectives,* Englewood Cliffs, N.J.: Prentice-Hall, Inc.
191. ———, and E. Rosenstein (1970) "Workers' Participation: A Critical View," *Industrial Relations 9,* 197–214.
192. Sturmthal, A. (1964) *Workers Councils: A Study of Workplace Organization on Both Sides of the Iron Curtain,* Cambridge, Mass.: Harvard University Press.
193. Suojanen, W. W., M. J. McDonald, G. L. Swallow, and W. W. Suojanen (eds.), (1975) *Perspectives on Job Enrichment and Productivity,* Atlanta, Ga.: Georgia State University.
194. Susman, G. I. (1976) *Autonomy at Work: A Sociotechnical Analysis of Participative Management,* New York: Praeger Publishers, Inc.
195. Tannenbaum, A. S. (1962) "Control in Organizations: Individual Adjustment and Organizational Performance," *Administrative Science Quarterly 7,* 236–257.
196. ———. (1966) *Social Psychology of the Work Organization,* Belmont, Cal.: Wadsworth Publishing Co. Inc.
197. ———. (1974) "Systems of Formal Participation," in G. Strauss, R. Miles, C. C. Snow, and A. S. Tannenbaum (eds.), *Organizational Behavior: Research and Issues,* Madison, Wis.: Industrial Relations Research Association.
198. Tannenbaum, R., and F. Massarik (1950) "Participation by Subordinates in the Managerial Decision-making Process," *Canadian Journal of Economics and Political Science 16,* 408–418.
199. ———, and W. Schmidt (1958) "How to Choose a Leadership Pattern," *Harvard Business Review 36,* 95–101.
200. Taylor, F. W. (1967) *The Principles of Scientific Management,* New York: W. W. Norton & Company, Inc. (originally published in 1911).

201. Teague, B. (1971) "Can Workers Participate in Management Successfully?" *Conference Board Record* 8 (July): 48–52.
202. Thorsrud, E., B. A. Sorensen, and B. Gustavsen (1976) "Sociotechnical Approach to Industrial Democracy in Norway," in R. Dubin (ed.), *Handbook of Work, Organization, and Society,* Chicago: Rand McNally & Company.
203. Torrance, E. P. (1953) "Methods of Conducting Critiques of Group Problem-solving Performance," *Journal of Applied Psychology 37,* 394–398.
204. Tosi, H. (1970) "A Reexamination of Personality as a Determinant of the Effects of Participation," *Personnel Psychology 23,* 91–99.
205. Trist, E. L., and K. W. Bamforth (1951) "Some Social and Psychological Consequences of the Longwall Method of Coal-getting," *Human Relations 4,* 3–38.
206. ———, G. W. Higgins, H. Murray, and A. B. Pollock (1963) *Organizational Choice,* London: Tavistock.
207. Umstot, D. D., C. H. Bell, and T. R. Mitchell (1976) "Effects of Job Enrichment and Task Goals on Satisfaction and Productivity," *Journal of Applied Psychology 61,* 379–394.
208. Van de Vall, M., and C. D. King (1973) "Comparing Models of Workers' Participation in Managerial Decision Making," in D. Graves (ed.), *Management Research: A Cross-Cultural Perspective,* New York: Elsevier Scientific.
209. Veen, P. (1972) "Effects of Participative Decison-making in Field Hockey Training: A Field Experiment," *Organizational Behavior and Human Performance 7,* 288–307.
210. Viteles, M. S. (1953) *Motivation and Morale in Industry,* New York: W. W. Norton & Company, Inc.
211. Von Mises, L. (1962) *Socialism,* New Haven: Yale University Press (originally published in 1951).
212. Vroom, V. (1960) *Some Personality Determinants of the Effects of Participation,* Englewood Cliffs, N.J.: Prentice-Hall, Inc.
213. ———. (1964) *Work and Motivation,* New York: John Wiley & Sons, Inc.
214. ———. (1969) "Industrial Social Psychology," in G. Lindzey and E. Aronson (eds.), *Handbook of Social Psychology,* Reading, Mass.: Addison-Wesley.
215. ———, and F. Mann (1960) "Leader Authoritarianism and Employee Attitudes," *Personnel Psychology 13,* 125–140.
216. ———, and P. Yetton (1973) *Leadership and Decision-Making,* Pittsburgh: University of Pittsburgh Press.
217. Weschler, I. R., M. Kahane, and R. Tannenbaum (1952) "Job Satisfaction, Productivity, and Morale: A Case Study," *Occupational Psychology 26,* 1–14.
218. Wexley, K. N., J. P. Singh, and G. A. Yukl, (1973) "Subordinate Personality as a Moderator of the Effects of Participation in Three Types of Appraisal Interviews," *Journal of Applied Psychology 58,* 54–59.
219. White, R., and R. Lippitt (1953) "Leader Behavior and Member Reaction in Three 'Social Climates,'" in D. Cartwright and A. Zander (eds.), *Group Dynamics: Research and Theory,* Evanston, Ill.: Row, Peterson.
220. ———, and ———. (1960) *Autocracy and Democracy,* New York: Harper & Row, Publishers.
221. Wood, M. T. (1973) "Power Relationships and Group Decision Making in Organizations," *Psychological Bulletin 79,* 280–293.

WORKERS PARTICIPATION IN MANAGEMENT:

AN INTERNATIONAL PERSPECTIVE

George Strauss

ABSTRACT

Formal schemes for workers participation in management (WPM) through elected representatives have been the focus of considerable interest and controversy throughout the world. This article reviews the research evidence with regard to how these schemes work in practice. It begins by discussing the difficulties of doing research in this area, particularly given the multitude of reasons for which WPM is introduced. It then examines the experience with WPM in Israel and Yugoslavia, in producers cooperatives, and in cases where employees have bought their plants to save them from being shut down. The discussion then reviews more generally the new role of the participative board member and the changed roles of labor and management. Next evidence is presented as to the impact of technology, values, and rewards on WPM success. Finally the article pulls the various themes together and concludes with an agenda for future research.

Workers participation in management (WPM)—sometimes called industrial democracy—has become a major political, social, and economic issue throughout the world, particularly in Europe. A wide variety of forms of WPM exist, for example, workers' self-management (Yugoslavia), codetermination (Germany), works councils (in much of Europe), Scanlon Plan (United States), and producers cooperatives or PCs (in many countries). These various social experiments have in turn stimulated a growing stream of research utilizing many methodologies.

WPM's centrality as a social issue has made it a major OB research concern outside the United States. For United States scholars it provides a series of test cases for the participative theories so widely accepted in the OB community. After all, WPM has been prescribed as the solution of a wide variety of organizational problems: alienation, low productivity, autocratic management, poor teamwork, power imbalance, opposition to technological change, union–management conflict, and the like. Further, it represents a massive, presumably planned organizational change, which, if successful, introduces alterations not just in structure and attitudes but also in the variable of much current OB interest: power. Finally, for the industrial relations specialist, WPM provides an alternative to the primarily adversary system existing in the United States.

As an introduction to WPM, this article has two purposes. First, an attempt will be made to interpret the experience with WPM to date, with special emphasis on its significance for OB. The article will concern chiefly the problems encountered in making it "work," the extent of its "success" (by a variety of disputed standards), and the conditions favorable for "success." Second, the main research questions in this area and the kinds of research being done will be described.

Except occasionally for purposes of comparison, this article is concerned chiefly with formal schemes for participation at the plant and company levels, and so it largely ignores three other forms of participation that are already familiar to United States students: (1) job enrichment and autonomous work groups, (2) what might be called Likert-type informal participation in which workers preferences are relayed via linking pins from foremen to company president (rather than through elected representatives), and (3) collective bargaining—though this may be the most effective participation form of all.

The thesis of this article is that WPM should be evaluated in terms of its impact on society generally, not just on productivity and worker satisfaction. Thus, this article will view WPM from a variety of perspectives. It will start with two introductory sections. One will list the main forms of WPM and the conflicting reasons for which they are introduced; the other will deal with the difficult question of how WPM is to be researched. Next several forms of WPM in practice will be reviewed. The purpose here is to provide background for the heart of the article, which consists of two sections. The first one will examine how WPM affects the main interested parties; the second will look at various contextual issues affecting how WPM operates. Finally, some implications from the research as a whole will be offered.

FORMS OF WPM AND WHY THEY ARE INTRODUCED

This section will begin with an around-the-world tour, illustrating the range and forms WPM takes in various countries. Then this diversity will be related to the conflicting theoretical and practical justifications for introducing them in the first place. Finally, seeking to provide some illusory order out of this confusion, it erects a taxonomy of WPM forms that should further demonstrate that WPM is not a unitary concept.

International Diversity

Yugoslavia. Workers in each plant elect Workers Councils, which in turn (subject to some restrictions) hire and fire management. Both national law and the prevailing ideology stress active participation by workers in a variety of councils and committees. Important decisions require the consultation of rank-and-file workers in departmental shop floor meetings.

Germany. Codetermination has been a major political issue. Company boards of directors in the steel and coal industries include equal numbers of management and worker representatives. In other large companies, the current compromise calls for almost equal representation, with a management-selected chairman entitled to a tie-breaking vote. At the plant level, the approval of elected works councils is required for some personnel actions, whereas the councils must be consulted with regard to others.

Britain. Here too "industrial democracy" has been controversial. The Bullock Committee, appointed by the Labour Government in 1975, came out squarely for codetermination (Elliott, 1978). Meeting vehement management opposition and only mild union support, the issue was sidetracked and rests dormant under the Thatcher administration. On the other hand, there is a long tradition of at least partly worker-owned and worker-controlled businesses, some founded by paternalistic owners and others organized to forestall plants from being shut down altogether. Furthermore, worker directors sit on the boards of some nationalized companies. For most of industry, however, collective bargaining represents the main form of participation. Plant-wide bargaining through shop stewards has become increasingly important in recent years.

France. There is wide agreement on participation as a symbol, though not on its substance (Bornstein and Fine, 1977). As early as 1946, De Gaulle supported participation as a "third road" between communism and capitalism, although in practice this meant little more than profit sharing. The socialist unions are committed to "autogestion," worker-run enterprises, whereas the communists support indirect participation through a state-owned, centrally planned economy. Works councils, concerned with personnel issues, exist in most enterprises of any size, although they have less power than in Germany.

Sweden. Until recently Swedish unions sought to influence unemployment rates and the distribution of income through governmental policies, although Paragraph 32 of the national labor–management agreement guaranteed employers' rights to hire and fire workers and to direct and allocate work. The famous quality of worklife experiments at Volvo and elsewhere were largely management sponsored, with only union acquiescence. Then, a 1972 law put two union representatives on most company boards of directors; in 1977, the Employee Participation Act repealed Paragraph 32 and required employers to negotiate with unions before "any important . . . change of activity," with the union being given the power to block change before final resolution by strike, arbitration, or Labor Court decision. The union-backed Meidner plan would require 20 percent of company profits to be converted into stock to be given to union-run "wage earner funds" with the expectation that eventually workers would win majority ownership of most companies (Martin, 1977; Logue, 1978).

Norway. The history here parallels that of Sweden, except that, influenced by Thorsrud and Emery (1970), unions began early to concern themselves with ship-level quality of worklife questions, especially autonomous work groups.

Israel. The kibbutzim or agricultural cooperatives are worker owned and managed, with incomes being shared roughly equally. Many kibbutzim also operate small factories. The national union, the Histradrut, owns a substantial percentage of the country's economy. Various attempts have been made to increase worker participation in the management of this sector, but with little success, as we see later.

Spain. At least for its supporters, Mondragon, a system of Basque producers cooperatives, may provide one of the most successful examples of worker-owned and -managed enterprises today (Johnson and Whyte, 1977; Eaton, 1979).

The United States. Aside from UAW President Fraser's election as a Chrysler director, there has been little United States interest in Germany-style codetermination. United States labor leaders are virtually unanimous in their belief that collective bargaining is the best way to protect workers rights. At the shop level considerable interest has been given to "Quality of Worklife" change, although little of this involves participation in management, except at very low levels. More to the point have been several carefully monitored joint union–management experiments in which workers participated in what may be viewed as middle management decisions as to the type of worklife changes to be made (e.g., Goodman, 1979). The Scanlon Plan combines worker participation in production decisions with a group incentive bonus (Driscoll, 1979). Finally, there is a new-found interest in worker-owned producer cooperatives (PCs). As in Britain, some PCs have a long history whereas others were founded recently to stave off plant shutdowns and still others were organized by members of the counterculture. Related to worker ownership, much attention has been given to Employee Stock Ownership Plans (ESOPs).

Australia. There are few examples of WPM in practice; still it stimulates much controversy (Derber, 1978). The union movement has made it a major objective; the two largest political parties support it in principle (though with differing degrees of enthusiasm); and it is the leading subject for articles in the nation's academic industrial relations journal. Further, Australia—land of strange beasts—houses what is perhaps the most radical WPM experiment on earth, Dynavac, a high-technology business totally without formal leaders.

Latin America. The military regime in Peru passed a law requiring self-management in certain firms which it had expropriated, but with indifferent results (Berenbach, 1979; Stephens, 1980). A similar process occurred in Chile under Allende, but reportedly with greater success because there was a political movement at the rank-and-file level to support it (Espinosa and Zimbalist, 1978).

China. The late Maoist period (1968–1976) was marked by "two participations": (1) professional managers were partly replaced by Revolutionary Committees which included shop-floor representatives and (2) the remaining professional managers were expected to "participate" regularly in physical production work. In fact, Revolutionary Committees had little autonomy; however, work groups were allowed some freedom in *implementing* centrally imposed plans. Further, something akin to Japanese style quality circles were utilized to introduce technological change. Since Mao's death the emphasis has shifted toward representative plant-wide Workers Congress and individual election of supervisors and managers. It is still unclear whether the new approach will make any difference (Walden, 1981; Lockett, in progress).

Soviet Union. As in China, "participation" is widely used to mobilize mass support. Soviet workers attend considerably more meetings than do their Western counterparts. But participation consists chiefly of ratifying policies already decided upon, and of making suggestions as to how these policies may be implemented. Russian workers have little power to reject or modify policy itself (Lane and O'Dell, 1978; Little, 1980).

This is but a quick summary of the state of WPM in various countries. Studies have been completed in a number of other countries: Algeria (Clegg, 1971); New Zealand (Young, 1979); Malta (compare Kester, 1980 and Koziara, 1979); Denmark (Westenholz, 1979); Canada (Nightingale, 1979); Belgium (Jain, Vanachter, and Gevers, 1980); and the Netherlands (Mulder, 1971).

Reasons for Participation

Even more varied than the forms of WPM are the reasons for which it is undertaken. Dachler and Wilpert (1978) analyze the main theoretical justifications. The classification in this article is in terms of the interested parties.

WPM has been popular in older states with highly developed technologies, such as Britain, Sweden, and West Germany, as well as in newer nations, such as Israel and Algeria—and in pluralist democratic countries as well as in one-party states where individual freedom is limited. One reason for its popularity is that it represents a happy melding of the ideologies of socialism and human relations (Strauss and Rosenstein, 1970). Also in many cases it meets the political needs of union leaders and national governmental figures. Parenthetically, the situation today is very different from that of the early 1900s, when the idea of PCs "was opposed by capitalists, academicians, government and labor unions, although each held a separate rationale" (Aldrich and Stern, 1978, p. 7).

OB Experts. More of the impetus for WPM has come from intellectuals (both OB experts and socialists) and politicians than has come from the rank-and-file workers who are supposed to do the participating. So the attitudes of intellectuals, as change agents, are worth considering.

Participation is a central tenet in the managerial ideology taught in many capitalistic business schools. Beginning with Hawthorne the human relations (now OB) tradition placed high value on cooperation between subordinates and superiors. This emphasis has been reinforced by the findings of the Michigan school, by almost the entire OD movement, and most recently by advocates of job enrichment, autonomous work groups, and quality of worklife reforms. To be sure, the managerial version of participation assumes that participation will occur on a face-to-face basis, between individual bosses and subordinates; further it largely ignores unions and all issues of power. Nevertheless, in part as a result of the missionary efforts of such pioneers as McGregor and Likert, the ideology of participation is now at least superficially accepted by managers in most parts of the world (Haire, Ghiselli, and Porter, 1966).

The purported advantages of WPM in terms of OB theory have been described often (Lowin, 1968; Strauss, 1977; Locke and Schweiger, 1979). Very briefly they include

- To the extent that WPM improves *communications,* it raises productivity because (1) better decisions are made because (a) WPM allows subordinates to contribute important information and suggestions and (b) it permits a variety of sometimes conflicting views to be aired; (2) decisions are better implemented because (a) workers know better what they are required to do, (b) teamwork is facilitated, and (c) resistance to change is reduced.
- To the extent WPM involves *goal setting,* productivity is also raised because (1) individuals work harder for goals they have committed themselves to reach; (2) once attaining these goals they gain a sense of achievement; and (3) individual efforts are reinforced by group pressures.

Much of the above contributes to satisfaction. Beyond this WPM provides individuals a chance to express themselves and exercise power. Additionally it promotes individual growth, reduces alienation, and provides training for democracy (Pateman, 1970). Industrial relations scholars see it as reducing labor strife and substituting integrative for distributive bargaining. Finally, for some OB theorists, WPM is important because it leads to power sharing (Tannenbaum, Kovcic, Rosner, Vianello, and Wieser, 1974). Democracy, in other words, is a value in itself.

In short, for OB people the main values of WPM are productivity, satisfaction, human growth, and for some, power sharing or democracy. To various degrees of intensity, managers voluntarily instituting WPM share these views. In addition, some view it as a means of keeping unions out.

Socialists. Socialists have theories of their own. Presumably WPM helps eliminate the four causes of alienation that Marx saw as resulting from capitalism; meaninglessness, powerlessness, social alienation, and self-estrangement. "Workers control" has become a common goal of socialists of almost every persuasion, even though there is much difference as to what the term means. Disillusioned by socialism Soviet-style, many younger socialists are looking for a socialism with a "human face." They place a high value on "self-management," that is, freedom for workers to direct their own work on a democratic basis. By contrast Communists reject *shop-level* workers control, as did many older socialists, most notably Sidney and Beatrice Webb (1920). Workers control for these socialists means *public* control of the economy on a fairly centralized basis. Workers self-management, they fear, will be inefficient; further, workers in each shop are likely to favor their own narrow interests rather than those of the working class as a whole. All factions agree that workers control involves a rejection of capitalism and a substantial redistribution of power. As a distinguished Yugoslav scholar puts it, "The goal of self-management is above all the political emancipation of the working class" (Rus, 1979, p. 322; see also Mako, 1978, p. 8). Ironically, once socialists become managers themselves they begin to accept some of the human-relations OB values as their own.

Unionists. Unionists also disagree as to WPM. As mentioned earlier, United States and many right-wing British unions (Elliott, 1978) have generally opposed WPM, largely because they fear being co-opted and believe that collective bargaining better protects their members. United States unions are reluctant to become involved in "Quality of Worklife" programs, such as job enrichment or autonomous work groups, fearing that these will mute the demands for economic gains, lead to speedups, and weaken hard-fought-for work rules (for a more extensive discussion, see Strauss, 1977, p. 80). Interestingly, some left-wing and Communist-dominated unions also reject WPM, viewing it as a form of class collaboration.

In between are unions in Scandinavia, Germany, and some in the Netherlands (Albeda, 1977) and Britain who have come to support WPM with various degrees of enthusiasm. Their motivation for doing so is complex and varied, though, for the most part, it boils down to a desire to extend union power. Swedish unions, reacting to extensive wildcat strikes during the late 1960s, saw WPM as a means of reinvigorating plant-level unions in an era of centralized bargaining. Earlier many Swedish unions opposed WPM on the grounds that stronger plant-level unions would impede the drive toward nationwide wage equalization (Martin, 1977).

In Britain, under the Labour Party, the introduction of worker-directors at the firm level was seen as a means to plug the last gap in the network of industrial democracy, which already included shop steward representation at the shop and plant levels, industry-wide bargaining, and a nationwide social contract (Elliott, 1978).

On the continent, especially in Germany, collective bargaining traditionally has been conducted at the industry, rather than company or plant, level (and many unions have stressed national-level political roles). Further it has been concerned chiefly with overall wage levels. Thus WPM provides the opportunity to extend the scope of bargaining to subjects other than wages and to strengthen the union at the plant level. The German law, which requires management to consult with the works council or get its approval before engaging in discipline, layoffs, or significant technological change, brings to German industry the rough equivalent of United States-style, plant-level collective bargaining. However, codetermination goes beyond this. It allows some worker input into the investment policies that determine the level of employment. As a Swedish unionist put it, "our interest is seeing that capital is used to provide secure jobs, and that's what we need influence for. We can't trust management to do that" (Logue, 1978, p. 12).

Politicians. In many countries WPM has been introduced by law. Therefore, the motives of the politicians and public leaders involved should be examined. Often these combine various mixtures of the practical and the ideological.

In Germany, according to Hartmann (1970), codetermination was introduced after the war because of the fortunate juxtaposition of numerous interests: the British occupying power supported it as a means of curbing industrialists' power, managers hoped it would protect their plants from Allied dismantling, unions viewed it as a means of preventing the reestablishment of a management controlled nationalist party, whereas Catholic liberals found it consistent with papal encyclicals. (Cynically, one might add that Socialist leaders may have perceived support for WPM as a means of preserving their credentials as socialists while at the same time abandoning the class struggle and nationalization of industry as political objectives.)

Attempts by De Gaulle to introduce participation in the waning days of his administration may be interpreted as an effort to devise a new look for his regime and also to win support among increasingly militant students by proposing a seemingly leftist measure. The Giscard government also proposed some mild participatory measures, leading Bornstein and Fine (1977, p. 161) to conclude that "participation schemes function, for conservative governments, as a means of pacifying workers, separating them from their unions, and integrating them into a rationalized neocapitalist institutional framework."

In communist bloc countries, WPM programs existed for a while during the 1960s in Poland and Czechoslovakia; quite recently they have been revived in China and Poland. In all these cases, WPM reflected the intentions of the political leadership to decentralize and liberalize economic life. In Yugoslavia, workers self-management legitimated the return to a semimarket economy at the time of the split with Russia; in this way Tito's reforms could be treated as a new advance into socialism rather than a retreat to capitalism. In Britian (Jones, 1977), the Labour Government offered unions "industrial democracy" in part as a quid pro quo for acquiescence (through the social contract) in incomes policy; roughly the same deal was made in Sweden (Martin, 1977).

In Israel (as we shall see, the Histadrut leaders looked upon WPM as a means of closing the gap between their own ideological convictions and the reality that their union had become a business conglomerate. In Algeria and other developing countries, the problem was to endow economic activity with a patina of socialism and at the same time introduce industrial discipline. In India, government-introduced programs represented, among other things, a carry-over into mass industry of the gentle notions of Mahatma Ghandi.

Conflict Among Objectives. Clearly participation means all things to all people. For some it means increased motivation and productivity or, by contrast, protection of jobs and work rules. For various others it means personal growth, a defeat for capitalism, or the preservation of social peace.

In some cases (e.g., Germany) this very diversity of meaning helped make the formal institutionalization of WPM politically possible. WPM can be a convenient slogan around which many different interests may gather. Politicians especially may view it as a seemingly costless concession that can be made to have considerable symbolic value.

Yet many of the parties' objectives are mutually inconsistent. There is conflict, for example, between those who view WPM as a means of winning greater acceptance of organizational objectives and those who see it as a means of counterbalancing or weakening management. The first group tends to ignore power; for the second, power is the central issue. In a sense the difference is between those who view WPM as an integrative process and those who see it as distributive (Walton and McKersie, 1965).

Thus management may view WPM as a means of eliciting worker suggestions for improving productivity and generally for facilitating change, whereas, for many unionists its purpose is to protect job rights and work restrictions against unilateral management actions (Bull and Barton, 1978). These differences in expectations contribute to differences in their "vocabulary of participation" (Brannen, 1976), that is, the parties differ in the meanings they give to the same words and institutions, thus greatly frustrating communication. There is a tendency to assume that WPM will automatically solve real conflicts of interest, when, in fact, by creating an unrealistic assumption of mutuality, it may only sweep problems under the table. Thus the diversity of expectations that helps facilitate *formal* acceptance of WPM may actually hinder its successful *implementation.*

Objectives and Research Strategy. This diversity of objectives also creates problems for researchers. On what aspects of WPM should they concentrate: attitudes, strike rates, level of employee benefits, distribution of profits, or what? New left academic idealists—seeking a freer society—may stress different points than do hard-headed (hearted?) business school OB types. And by what criteria should WPM be evaluated? Obviously value judgments are involved here. OB reviews that examine participative decision making merely in terms of productivity and satisfaction (e.g., Locke and Schweiger, 1979) may be too narrowly focused. Perhaps the impact of WPM upon society generally should also be considered.

Forms of Participation: A Taxonomy

As the foregoing discussion illustrates, much of the confusion regarding WPM arises from the fact that the generic term covers a multitude of activities. Disagreement extends even to the appropriate name to use. Americans prefer "workers participation in management" (the term used here), whereas for some Europeans "participation" sounds too manipulative. They prefer "industrial democracy," "self-management," or "workers control," all terms that imply that workers have substantial power.

Given that WPM means so many different things to different people, it is understandable that much recent writing has been devoted to constructing taxonomies. This is no idle exercise because the various forms of participation have greatly varying impacts on organizational performance. Although there is as yet little agreement as to terms, most attempts at classification (Globerson, 1970; Walker, 1974; Bernstein, 1980; Espinosa and Zimbalist, 1978) involve one or more of four dimensions, which I shall call: organizational level, degree of control, issues, and ownership. Table 1 outlines the major dimensions.

Table 1.   A Taxonomy of Various Forms of Participation

Classification	Examples
Organizational Level	
Individual	Job enrichment
Small group	Autonomous work group
Departmental	Scanlon Plan production committees
Plant	German works councils
Company	Worker directors
Industry	Much European collective bargaining
National	Labor input into national economic planning
Degree of Control	
Joint consultation	French works councils
Joint decision making	Collective bargaining; codetermination in the German iron and steel industry
Self-management	Yugoslavia; producers cooperatives
Issues	
Wages	Collective bargaining in most countries
Personnel issues (e.g., layoffs, overtime)	Collective bargaining in the United States; works councils in Germany
Welfare benefits	French works councils' control over plant medical services
Production methods, job content	Scanlon Plan, autonomous work groups
Vacation schedules	Yugoslav zbors (shop meetings)
Selecting managers	Yugoslav workers council selecting a manager
Major investment decisions	Supervisory board under German codetermination
Ownership	
No worker ownership	Typical company
Some worker ownership	United States Employee Stock Ownership Plan (ESOP)
Completely worker owned	Producers cooperative

Organizational Level. This dimension requires little explanation. American academic interest in WPM has been at the departmental level and lower. European writing stresses the plant or company levels, with an increasing emphasis occurring at the national level.

Organizational level is related to the often-debated question of *direct* (face-to-face) versus *representative* (indirect) participation. The human relations arguments for WPM apply best to direct participation. Representative participation may be effective in protecting workers' economic interests and perhaps in giving them a sense of power. However, the sense of involvement and participation provided by direct participation is reduced when participation is handled indirectly. In theory, to obtain a fully participative organization, both forms of participation should be integrated. However, aside from the Scanlon Plan, few WPM schemes have successfully integrated the participative efforts of various organizational levels.

Degree of Control. This dimension is concerned with the subordinate's influence over decision making. With joint consultation (the most common form of WPM), management makes the final decisions, but workers have the right to be informed, to offer advice and objections, and even to make proposals. Joint decision making implies that the parties have equal power and that each side's consent is needed before action is taken. Self-management gives workers or their representatives final authority.

Only in joint decision making and self-management do workers have formal power to make or block decisions. Joint consultation depends on management's good will to make it work; management can (and frequently does) merely go through the motions and totally ignores the workers' input.

Each of the main categories can be further subdivided (e.g., IDE, 1981). Walker (1974), for example, notes three forms of what I call joint consultation: "Management decides unilaterally but workers are informed before decision is put into effect"; "Management decides after hearing workers' views"; and "Negotiations take place but management goes ahead if no agreement is reached."

Another distinction can be made between formal decision making and actual decision making. There appear to be numerous instances where one party (either workers or management) has the formal power but usually allows the other party to do what it wants. Thus the decisions of autonomous work groups may be subject to a rarely exercised management veto; by contrast Yugoslav workers councils typically give rubber stamp approval to most of management's recommendations.

As Locke and Schweiger (1979, p. 276) suggest, participative decision making "may be more effective at some stages than others." Motivated by decision-making theory, recently researchers have examined the various stages of the participative decision-making process. The Decisions in Organizations (DIO, 1979) group distinguishes among four stages: initiation, development, finalization, and implementation.

Issues. Compared with other dimensions, there is somewhat less agreement as to how to classify the subject matter covered by WPM. By contrast with the categories indicated for level and degree, which are meant to be fairly inclusive, those for issues are merely illustrative. Distinctions relevant to one country may be irrelevant in another. The main point is that some WPM schemes may be limited to purely personnel or shop-level production problems whereas others may cover the entire gamut of issues. If WPM deals only with personnel issues, it hardly extends beyond United States-style collective bargaining. Some British participative committees deal with such trivial issues that critics call them "tea and toilet" committees.

WPM advocates differ in the issues they stress. Human relationists have focused chiefly on production issues and some are disappointed when workers talk about wages. German and British union proponents of WPM, by contrast, have been interested mainly in long-run employment-related issues.

Obviously levels and issues are related. Different issues are likely to be handled at different levels. Major investments are more likely to be considered at the company level; shop-level WPM is more likely to be concerned with such issues as vacation schedules or production methods.

Ownership. The issue of participation is often connected with that of ownership. Employee Stock Ownership Plans have spread rapidly in the United States in recent years because of favorable tax treatment. Many producers cooperatives are purely worker owned; however, as we shall see, most of the employee-owned firms recently established in the United States to prevent plant shutdowns, in fact, have a high degree of management or outside ownership as well as little employee control. In Europe, employee ownership schemes, such as Sweden's Meidner Plan, have been widely proposed as a complement or even substitute for WPM, particularly to ensure the socially acceptable use of capital (Chamberlain, 1980).

LITERATURE AND RESEARCH

The growth of workers' participation in the real world has been matched by the development of a substantial literature (of uneven quality), only a small portion of which will be cited here. (For bibliographies, see Marclay, 1971; Williams, 1976; Maley, Dunphy, and Ford, 1979). Much of the early writing was speculative and normative, based on hopes and fears, because there was little evidence. Later authors described the background and details of participation schemes in individual countries as these were adopted (e.g., there have been a host of books and articles on Yugoslav self-management, German codetermination, and the British Bullock report). Some of these studies related the introduction of participation to the social, political, and economic conditions in the countries in which participation has been introduced (see especially Garson, 1977). In addition, as research data have accumulated, there have been several important studies that compare the experience of various forms of WPM in a conceptual manner. Pateman (1970), Walker (1974), Dachler and Wilpert (1978), and Bernstein (1980) deserve special note. Finally, there have been some valuable collections of articles (Vanek, 1975a; Hunnius, Garson, and Case, 1973; Windmuller, 1977; Garson, 1977; Lansbury, 1980).

Two streams of specialized normative literature deserve mention. The first, produced largely by trade unionists and academic union sympathizers, debates the question of what the union's attitude toward WPM should be (e.g., Webb and Webb, 1920; Clegg, 1960; Coates and Topham, 1968). The second, chiefly by radical political economists, seeks to determine optimum incentive, price, and investment policies for self-managing organizations (e.g., Wachtel, 1973; Vanek, 1977). Some of the articles involve mathematical economic theory, others analyze empirical data. (For a summary, see Steinherr, 1978.) Much of it appears in an English-language Yugoslav journal, *Economic Analysis and Worker Management*.

Aside from conceptual and normative studies, there is a growing stream of empirical studies. These fall into two main categories, behavioral and attitudinal–cognitive, each of which involves research problems.

Measures of Participation. Before going further, some conceptual questions, which are discussed at greater length elsewhere (Strauss, 1977, 1979a), should be considered briefly. Implicitly or explicitly, most studies (e.g., IDE, 1981) in this area examine aspects of two general questions:

1. To what extent is *proscribed* (intended or de jure) participation associated with *actual* (or de facto) participation?
2. To what extent is proscribed and/or actual participation associated with such *outcomes* as higher productivity, increased worker satisfaction, fewer grievances, or increased power for the working class?

Proscribed participation has been defined as referring to "all formal, written operative norms and rules governing the participation of various groups which result from the implementation of national laws, bargaining contracts, or managerial policies" (IDE, 1979, p. 274). It includes the various participative forms discussed in the taxonomy section.

Regarding actual participation, there are two main schools of thought. The first looks at participation as a resultant, the extent to which subordinates are able to *influence* decisions (or, more frequently, the extent to which they perceive themselves as influencing decisions). Many of the influence studies make use of Tannenbaum control graphs (e.g., Rus, 1970), which are based on respondents' responses to questions asking them how much "say" people at various organizational levels have with regard either to what happens in the organization *generally* or with regard to such *specific subjects* as task assignment. Influence studies typically make use of questionnaires.

The second approach views participation as a *decision-process* and is interested in how decisions are made, for example, by.the boss, by subordinates, or jointly. Process, of course, is a behavior. Though some process studies involve questionnaires, they also include what I call "behavioral research."

Behavioral Research

Behavioral research consists chiefly of intensive studies, each of which looks at how WPM works in a small number of cases (usually just one). A few studies have included observation over years; when combined with interviews and historical records, the evolution of WPM in any one situation can be traced from its inception to the present. Some case studies are based largely on interviews and short plant tours (e.g., Eaton, 1979) whereas others make use also of available "hard" data such as production records or minutes of participative bodies (e.g., Rosenberg and Rosenstein, 1980).

More intensive case studies involve observation of participative bodies in action (for Dutch research, see Mulder, 1971; for a United States example, see Witte, 1980). Thus, Kolaja (1960) spent eight weeks in a Polish factory interviewing workers and managers and attending meetings of the workers council and then (1966) repeated his observation in two Yugoslavian factories, spending 4 weeks in each. Adizes (1971) also studied two factories, but for longer periods. Not only did he attend a broader range of meetings than Kolaja, but in each factory he was given a desk in a key department (legal in one and planning in the other), permitting him to observe decision making on a continuing basis, thus giving perhaps our most intensive view of WPM in action.

Obradovic (1975; see also Bertsch and Obradovic, 1979) and his colleagues observed workers council meetings in 20 companies over a 3-year period, accumulating data on over 900 hours of discussion. Coding their observations in great detail, eventually they were able to analyze 16,941 interactions.

Observational studies of this sort present difficulties. The observer's time is limited, so at best he can sample only a small portion of the activities of the organization being studied. Additionally, entree is always difficult. The most interesting organizations may be the ones that do not let you in; the ones that you can study may well not be representative.

Further, there is the problem of what to observe and record. Obradovic (1975) coded verbal interactions in workers council meetings, but according to Adizes (1971) some of the most important communications at these meetings took the form of low-level murmurs, body language, and facial responses. Finally, many decisions are made informally, in advance, making the discussion at the formal meeting merely a formality. Presumably none of this was recorded in Obradovic's statistics.

In an almost unique study, reminiscent of the Aston research, Espinosa and Zimbalist (1978) examined a stratified sample of 35 presumably worker-run firms that had been either expropriated or worker-seized during the Allende period in Chile. Key union and management informants were asked questions as to relatively objective factors, such as organization structure, attendance at meetings of participative bodies, productivity, accident rates, and the like. Unfortunately this remarkable study may be faulted for (1) relying excessively on somewhat biased observers, (2) mixing dependent and independent variables, and (3) basing its findings on a limited time frame and an unrepresentative sample.

Attitudinal Surveys

By contrast with case studies, which are based chiefly on observation and nonstandardized interviews, attitudinal surveys are based on standardized questions asked (either orally or in writing) of a variety of respondents, often at different organizations. The number of respondents is great enough and the alternate responses are sufficiently structured to permit quantification of the data. Among other issues, the questions relate to how much participation respondents have now, how much they want, their satisfaction with the participation, and their receptions of the behavior of others.

Unfortunately, "the predominant use of questionnaire and interview techniques in the study of mainly attitudinal–cognitive factors precludes deeper insights into the intensity of behavioral" change (Wilpert, 1975; p. 60) or the contingent factors (such as technology) affecting WPM success. Further, only a few studies permit comparisons, either among organizations that enjoy various degrees of participation or within given organizations before and after participation is introduced. Goodman (1979) provides one of the rare examples of a before and after study, here of the introduction of autonomous work groups by a joint union–management committee. In this study questionnaire data collected at five time periods is supplemented by "hard" (production, cost, accidents) data and actual observation.

There have been a variety of studies of desired and perceived actual participation (e.g., Tabb and Galin, 1970; Quinn and Staines, 1978; Wall and Lisheron, 1977; Witte, 1980; Rus, 1979), some of them based on nationwide samples. Nightingale (1979) compares 10 participative with 10 nonparticipative Canadian firms, collecting data from 50 respondents at 3 hierarchical levels in each firm.

More recently there have been several international studies comparing forms and extent of participation in various countries, each making use of an international team. Just organizing these international studies represented a participative triumph itself. Not only did the academicians concerned come from a variety of intellectual traditions, but measures had to be developed that would be appropriate in a wide variety of legal and industrial relations systems and that could be translated so as to be meaningful and equivalent in as many as ten languages.

Perhaps the first of these international teams, Tannenbaum, Kavcic, Rosner, Vianello, and Wieser (1974), made use of a number of measures, particularly the Tannenbaum control graph; thus making it possible to compare participation in three countries utilizing conventional management (the United States, Italy, and Austria) with two forms of WPM (the Israeli kibbutz and Yugoslavian self-management). Ten carefully matched factories were studied in each country. Members of this same team have joined with others in a new project, MPIO (Member Participation in Organizations), to compare matched participative and nonparticipative firms in six countries ($N = 70$ firms and approximately 3,500 respondents).

The Industrial Democracy in Europe (IDE) International Research Group consists of 25 scholars from 12 countries. Their study (IDE, 1981) involves 134 firms (matched as to technology) and nearly 9,000 individual respondents. This is not purely an attitudinal study because certain data were provided by "expert" respondents in each firm. However, respondents at all levels were asked a number of questions probing attitudes regarding issues such as actual and desired participation, satisfaction, and participation by others. A distinctive characteristic of the IDE study (as well as of Tannenbaum et al., 1974) is that WPM is viewed not in isolation but in terms of its impact on the distribution of power among organizational levels.

The work of the Decisions in Organizations group (DIO, 1979) is closely related to the IDE study. It involves overlapping questions and personnel. Its sample is smaller (three countries, seven firms, 988 respondents), but it is looking at some questions in greater depth. It employs longitudinal as well as cross-sectional measures and it observes decision making as well as asking questions about it.

Still another study, conducted by what has become known as the Vienna Center, was confined to automobile manufacturing, but covered 3,200 workers in 135 work places in 15 countries, including six behind the Iron Curtain (P. Jacob, Vez, Koval, Margulies, Rautalaiho, Rehak, and Weiser, in press). Again, though focused more on the impact of automation than on WPM as such, the survey asked numerous questions relating to participation.

Methodological Problems. Attitudinal studies are beset by methodological and conceptual problems. Many ask workers to indicate the extent and form of participation they *desire*. But answers to such questions are heavily subject to priming, salience, and attribution. Workers responses will be influenced by the rhetoric of their leaders, the values of their peers, and even by the way the question is worded (Salancik and Pfeffer, 1977).

Participation often takes on symbolic meanings and so the term evokes a broad range of connotations. As we have seen, in some European circles WPM means victory for the working class; in contrast, many United States labor leaders have learned to suspect it as a form of union busting. A French union, the CFDT, makes self-management a fundamental goal; not surprisingly, 82 percent of its leaders state that their preferred form of management would be one elected by the workers (Smith, 1977). But how deep a feeling is this? For decades the 30-hour week has been a widespread official United States union objective, yet rarely is it given high priority and many members of the few unions to win a 30-hour week have clamoured for guaranteed (but voluntary) overtime or second jobs. Until workers have a *real* need to make a choice, questions about priorities are not very meaningful. For workers who never have had any experience with substantial participation, questions as to desire for participation are essentially hypothetical. By contrast, the attitudes of workers in countries such as Germany or Yugoslavia, which already enjoy forms of participation, may be shaped by their particular experience and not indicate desire for participation in the abstract.

Responses may differ, depending on the context in which they are asked. More favorable responses may be given to formal survey questionnaires than in informal conversations with participant observers (Mulder, 1971). Daniel (1973) shows how workers may resist job enrichment in a collective bargaining context yet react highly favorably when asked about it in a different context 9 months later.

Small differences in the wording of questions may lead to substantial differences in response. Thus, Ramsay (1976) asked four different versions of essentially the same question regarding the desirability of participation at the company-wide level and got seemingly very different responses. Some day research should focus on these small differences, which have so great an effect. Or perhaps projective tests might be useful to uncover underlying perceptions and values.

Cross-national studies pose additional problem. According to Tannenbaum et al. (1974), United States workers report considerably less desire for participation (influence) than do those in Yugoslavia, even though in reported actual influence the two countries are roughly alike (with the United States making up in shop-floor informal participation what it loses in terms of plant-level formal participation). What does this apparent

lesser United States desire for participation reflect? Are Yugoslav workers really so different? Does this difference reflect the fact that WPM
plays a key role in Yugoslav national political ideology whereas it is less
salient in the United States? Or, despite its apparent sophistication, does
the authors' methodology try to compare the incomparable? How can
the researcher determine whether a score of 4 on a seven-point scale
means the same in one country as it does in another?

Questions as to actual (as opposed to desired) WPM face equal problems. If participation is won after a long fight (as codetermination was
won in Germany), it may be more favorably evaluated than if it is merely
a gift from a benevolent management (or a theory Y-oriented OD consultant) or imposed by the government. A good advertising program (or
years of indoctrination, as in Iron Curtain countries) may persuade workers that they have more influence than they really have. Similarly, attention from visiting social scientists or newspaper publicity may make
participation more salient to workers. On the other hand, unrealistic
expectations as to what WPM may bring may lead to frustration and
expressed dissatisfaction (Wilpert, 1975). It is possible, for example, that
ideology has inflated Yugoslav workers' desire for participation, but the
frustration they experience may reduce reported actual participation.

Given these problems, how does the researcher evaluate findings that
Soviet workers report that they have "a lot of opportunity" to influence
wage and production decisions (P. Jacob and Ahn, 1979); that Soviet
unions score 90+ percent on perceived "adequacy," whereas capitalist
unions rank much, much lower (B. Jacob, 1978); or that 80 percent of
Russian auto workers are willing to take part in "decisions affecting the
plant," as compared to 63 percent of Yugoslav workers, 34 percent of
United States workers, and 24 percent of Swedish workers (Jacob and
Jacob, 1979)? This latter study also finds perceived opportunities for
participation to be greater in Czechoslovakia and the United States than
in Yugoslavia and puts Sweden, home of the job-enriched assembly line,
lowest of all. These findings, contrary to normal expectations, are not
easy to explain.

A Caveat. The discussion that follows is based on the available evidence, but this is often sketchy and always incomplete. Many seemingly
"hard" findings (based on large-scale attitude studies) are actually rather
soft; only part of them are directed toward the critical issues. On the
other hand, the behavioral research is often based on small, possibly
nonrepresentative samples. Another problem: many of the original studies, especially of Germany and Israel, are not published in English.
Consequently the discussion is based on English-language summaries.

WORKERS' PARTICIPATION AND OWNERSHIP: FOUR CASES

This section illustrates the chief problems faced by WPM as well as some of the major research approaches in this area. Space permits but four cases: (1) Israel exemplifies the range of WPM possibilities, from the relatively successful kibbutz cooperative farms to the relatively unsuccessful attempts to introduce WPM into firms owned by the country's dominant union. (2) By contrast with Israel's diversity, Yugoslavia has introduced workers self-management on a uniform basis as a matter of national policy. (3) Worker-owned, worker-managed producers cooperatives (PCs) exist in a variety of countries; some have been studied intensively. (4) Finally, we look at some examples of largely worker-owned firms, none of which enjoy substantial WPM; they are included here to illustrate the relative importance of worker ownership as contrasted to worker control.

Israel

Participation has a high value in Israel. Many early settlers were socialists; even nonsocialists were committed to common nation-building sacrifices. The discussion below deals with participation as it exists in three sectors of Israeli society: (1) kibbutzim or agricultural communes; (2) kibbutz industries, manufacturing operations run by the kibbutzim; and (3) manufacturing firms directly owned by Histadrut, the country's labor movement. The other forms of participation that exist in various cooperatives and the state and private sector industries will be ignored.

Kibbutzim. The 4 percent of the labor force who belong to kibbutzim represent the elite of Israeli society, contribute far more than their proportional share of the national leadership, and provide an ideological and behavioral model for the rest of society. In addition, there is a strong commitment to the value of hard physical labor as an end in itself.

Kibbutzim are highly equalitarian. Property is owned in common. Except for a small pocket money allowance, goods and services are allocated according to need. Communal dining rooms and nurseries are the norm. Nasty jobs and leadership positions are rotated, the first to prevent alienation, the second to avoid oligarchy.

Kibbutzim are small (averaging 200–300 members each), thus permitting a considerable amount of direct democracy. Daily work decisions are made either by elected committees (annually 50 percent of the membership serves on one committee or another) or by elected department heads, in consultation with other department members. More basic decisions are referred to weekly or monthly community-wide general assemblies.

Such is the ideal. In practice, there appears to be some erosion of these standards (Fine, 1973; Agassi, 1974). In some kibbutzim a revival of the nuclear family is occurring. Young people often reject their parents' strict ideals, try their wings in the outside world, and many never return. As kibbutz members get better educated, they become less enamored of physical labor. Technical skills are more and more required, and for technical jobs the norm of rotation is often ignored. In fact, most males become specialists, while women are often relegated to lower status domestic jobs. Volunteer and hired temporary laborers are excluded from the participative system.

Nevertheless, the basic ideals are still highly valued, and they are violated only at the cost of guilt, tension, and endless discussion.

Kibbutz Industries. Many kibbutzim engage in manufacturing, in part to earn extra income. Industrial plants are governed much like agricultural branches. Weekly or monthly assemblies of all members working in the plant make the major decisions not requiring approval of the entire community. Managers are elected, averaging 2–3 years in office before being rotated (Leviaton, 1978). Many managers do part-time physical work. Fifty percent of the membership belongs to one committee or another.

In practice, these ideals are violated more frequently than in farming (Agassi, 1974). Somehow factory work is seen as less ennobling than working with the soil. Further, the industrial kibbutz tends to have less of a sense of community than does its agricultural counterpart and it deals with a narrower, more technical range of problems (Rosner, forthcoming). Jobs are more specialized making rotation more difficult. Over 50 percent of the workers in many plants are hired nonkibbutz members who are excluded from self-government (though in some cases they have a separate union-like committee to represent their interests). Consequently "everyday life in some kibbutz plants . . . [is] nearly as undemocratic as the average plant anywhere" (Agassi, 1974, p. 70). Further, there are economic pressures for these plants to grow, despite the recognition that growth will further threaten the democratic ideal.

Despite these problems, kibbutz industries get high grades from Tannenbaum et al. (1974), who, however, confined their studies to plants in which all workers were kibbutz members. Compared to the other four countries studied, the kibbutz industries ranked highest on the Likert System 1–System 4 participativeness scale; its workers were least alienated and psychologically most healthy, and its managers were seen as most participative and supportive. On the other hand, workers felt that they themselves had less influence than did Yugoslav workers and only very slightly more than did American workers.

The kibbutz plants are the only group studied in which the workers "ideal" distribution of influence gives them more power than it gives management. All this means that kibbutz managers suffer: they are seen as having less power than those in the United States, Italy, or Yugoslavia (but more than in Austria).

Two other studies are relevant. On the basis of a comparison between six kibbutz plants and six matched conventionally managed Israeli plants, Melman (1971) concludes kibbutz plants "can be as efficient or more efficient, than managerial controlled units" (p. 212). In analyzing the impact of managerial rotation on kibbutz enterprises, Leviaton (1978) found that firms in which a high percentage of the work force consisted of present and former managers also tended to score high on various measures of economic efficiency, participativeness, and initiative-taking behavior.

Hevrat Ovdim. About 15 percent of the Israeli labor force work for plants owned by the national union, Histadrut. Theoretically this is very democratic. As union members, workers elect Histadrut's national council, which doubles in brass as the council for Hevrat Ovdim, the industrial division. In turn this council selects management. Thus, workers indirectly select their own bosses.

In practice, it doesn't make much difference. Not that elections are pro forma; quite the contrary, they are hotly contested. But the electorate consists of *all* Histadrut members, not just those working in union-owned plants; the issues are national party politics and members must choose from among slates representing the national parties; further, each slate runs at large so that no one person represents Hevrat Ovdim as such (Ben-Porat, 1979). All this reduces top leadership's sensitivity to shop-level concerns. Finally, not only is the union also management, but until the 1977 Begin government, the party controlling the union also controlled the government. The government was interested in reducing inflationary pressures, which in practice meant raising productivity and keeping a tight control over wages—neither typical union objectives. Contrasted with this was the ship-level "feeling that a worker employed in an enterprise that 'belongs to him' should be earning more than workers in other enterprises and not have to work so hard" (Tabb and Galin, 1970).

This might not make much difference were the Israeli industrial culture naturally participative; however, IDE (1981) ranked Israel and Italy as the lowest of the 12 countries studied on practically all of their many measures of worker and supervisory participativeness. Further, according to another study, Hevrat Ovdim managers exhibited a less democratic ideology than did managers of state and privately owned Israeli plants, perhaps because their experience with participation (discussed later) made them "disillusioned about the desirability of participative management" (Vardi, Shirom, and Jacobson, 1980).

In addition to voting for Histadrut's national leadership, workers elect a plant "workers committee" to handle grievances. Collective bargaining contracts themselves are negotiated on a nationwide basis through a process by which one section of the union in effect negotiates by itself, often without input from the workers involved. Workers committees behave like unions elsewhere, negotiating with local management over wages and working conditions and frequently using unauthorized strikes and slowdowns to bolster their position. [During 1960–1969, 76 percent of the strikes in the Histadrut sector were unauthorized, contrasted to only 39 percent in the private sector (Michael and Bar-El, 1977)]. Thus union ownership was irrelevant to shop-level behavior.

The Histadrut leadership was acutely aware of ironies involved: particularly for the older leaders this situation violated the socialist, equalitarian values they continued to espouse. The answer was to experiment with a series of forms of WPM. This would restore commitment to common objectives, raise productivity, and perhaps reconcile workers to the realities of a tough wage restriction policy.

Faced with the new state's need for dramatically increased productivity, in 1952 the order went out to establish shop-level Joint Productivity Councils in each enterprise. These were to seek means of "assuring cooperation between workers and management . . . increasing production and . . . determin[ing] appropriate methods of work." Though duly established, they were soon concerned primarily with negotiating piecework rates. Galin (1980) believes they make an "economic contribution by increasing efficiency and output" (1980, p. 185), but they hardly constitute kibbutz-style participation.

Having failed once, the Histadrut leadership tried again. This time the objective was to "turn the factories into social cells based on communal work, self-management and communal ownership" (Tabb and Galin, 1970, p. 103), the objective being primarily to reduce alienation (Galin, 1980). As a first step, half-labor, half-management Plant Councils were established with the authority "to discuss and decide all matters pertaining to the enterprise, except wages and social conditions" (Tabb and Galin, 1970, p. 104). Management engaged in "passive resistance" while works council discussions "often deteriorated into mutual accusations" (Galin, 1980, p. 186). By 1961 these Councils had petered out. Post mortems ensued, with the final decision being that another effort should be made, this time with more careful preparation.

The new attempt was called Joint Management. Again there were to be plant-level joint boards, this time accompanied by worker representatives on company-wide boards and some profit sharing. The first experiment with Joint Management largely failed (Tabb and Galin, 1970). Undaunted, Histadrut's top political leadership plowed on. By 1975, 32 Joint Managements has been set up. Galin and Tabb (1978, p. 20) summarize the results of two case studies: "The employees of both plants did not believe that there were any improvements due to the participating management, and even the most ardent supporters . . . could not point to a contribution of the joint managements to labour–management relations, worker morale or economic achievements."

So the experiment continues. Rosenstein (1977), once a sharp critic of Israeli participation, now concludes more moderately that "the program . . . reveals considerable variation in implementation. . . . Some boards are active and deal with important issues, while others merely have formal meetings and deal with marginal questions" (p. 119). But Agassi (1974, p. 78) calls it "an empty formality—if not . . . a bad joke."

What have been the main problems all along? Almost everything (Rosenstein, 1977; Tabb and Galin, 1970; Galin and Tabb, 1978). The various plans were initiated entirely by the top political leadership. Neither operational managers nor workers showed much enthusiasm. By the third time around, lack of enthusiasm turned to skepticism. Even at the beginning the expectations of the various parties differed; nevertheless, managers, engineers, technicians, and workers council members all suspected that participation would dilute their authority. Initial difficulties were compounded by political and ethnic rivalries. Rank-and-file workers were uninvolved. Unresolved differences arose with regard to distribution of profits.

"Yet participation plans are turned to repeatedly. One reason is undoubtedly the extent to which the residues of traditional ideology are yet part of Israel's political mythology" (Fine, 1973). Participation has become almost an exercise in nostalgia, an attempt to return to the days when Israel was smaller, its technology less complex, and its society more homogeneous. Alas, "the pioneering and intensely idealistic workforce of the early days has been replaced by newcomers for whom a Histadrut-owned plant is just another work place" (Rosenstein, 1977).

Some Lessons. Why was WPM more successful in the kibbutzim than in the Histadrut? Provisionally let me suggest that (1) kibbutzim were more autonomous and perhaps smaller; (2) WPM was introduced by the workers themselves, rather than from top-down; (3) plant-level WPM was extended to the shop; (4) there was no union to act as a rival power center; (5) workers rotated as managers; and (6) kibbutz members were much better educated and more ideologically motivated than the largely oriental workers in the Histadrut firms.

Yugoslavia

Yugoslavia is of interest not only because it involves an attempt to run an entire economy on a self-management basis but because of the exceptionally broad freedom given researchers during the 1960s and early 1970s. Yugoslav WPM research is probably richer than that of any other country.

Yugoslav self-management originated at the time of Tito's break with Russia in 1948. In an effort to win popular support for the break, Tito sought to reduce the typically tight centralized Stalinist controls that had been placed on the country immediately after the war.

Self-management initially meant that firms were allowed a certain amount of freedom in implementing plans set nationally. Over the years this freedom was enlarged. Individual enterprises were given increased discretion to choose what they would produce, to set prices, to allocate profits, and to select their own management. The share of profit claimed by the government declined, and each enterprise was set free to compete in a fairly unrestricted market—and increasingly against foreign competition. The main restriction was that since business property was "socially owned" by the *entire* society, individual enterprises were not permitted to sell their assets. To obtain money for expansion, they had to turn to the banks, thus making banks a major instrument of national planning.

Structure of Self-Management. Most of the published research was conducted during 1968–1973 (even if some is dated later), and the discussion that follows is based largely on this period.

During 1968–1973, the typical enterprise was organized as follows: The governing body is the Workers Council, of 30 to 120 members, elected on a rotating basis for 2-year terms, with (as in Israel) some restrictions to reelection that prevent oligarchy. The Council meets at least monthly. It elects a smaller Management Board and also appoints the plant Director, after an advertised search and some consultation with local authorities. In theory, the Council makes basic decisions, the Management Board the more routine ones, and the Director implements both. By contrast with the kibbutz, Directors are professionals, and many move from job to job.

Yugoslav firms tend to be larger than kibbutzim. Large enterprises are divided in Economic Units; each Unit elects its own Council, which makes Unit decisions (e.g., setting vacation schedules) and in some cases selects Unit management. Really important decisions, such as the annual production and investment plans, require successive approval of the Workers Council, the Unit Councils, and finally mass meetings of individual workers, often assembling on a department-by-department basis. In addition, the various councils spawn a number of committees, with perhaps 30 percent of the work force serving on some committee in any given year. Perhaps the most important of these is the Personnel Committee, which has the power to hire and discipline workers.

Finally, there are two other moderately important bodies: the League of Communists (the local unit of the governing party) and the union. Though most of the top enterprise leaders in fact belong to the League, the League as such played a rather low-keyed role in the plant during the early 1970s. Theoretically representing the interests of the larger society, it occasionally acts as a trouble-shooter, but mostly its role is to espouse values. Workers typically reported that it had much less influence than either the Workers Council or management (Rus, 1970). Unions, as we shall see, have less influence yet (Rus, in press).

Thus, except for fairly weak party and union organizations, the Yugoslav self-management structure closely approximates that of the kibbutz. The major differences relates to pay. The kibbutz is equalitarian. Yugoslav enterprises have pay differentials of 5 to 1 or more. Yugoslav pay consists of a number of complex elements: (a) base pay, set by job evaluation or by Council vote; (b) *individual* bonuses, based on performance; and (c) *Unit* and *enterprise* bonuses, depending on their respective profits. Each Unit serves as an accounting profit center; as production moves from one Unit to another, the sending Unit charges the receiving Unit a transfer price. Base pay, the allocation of profits among various uses, and inter-Unit transfer prices are all democratically determined, the latter technically requiring the concurrence of both sending and receiving departments (with elaborate provision for resolving deadlocks). All these details generate much paperwork and give participative bodies much to discuss.

How Workers Councils Operate. There is a voluminous evidence here. The ideal is that the Council's membership would reflect that of the work force generally. But, as Yugoslavian scholars keep rediscovering, skilled workers, managers, staff experts, League members, and well-educated people are more than proportionally represented—further, this disproportion increases over time (e.g., Jovanov, 1978; Baumgartner, Burns, and Sekulic, 1979). Actual participation tends to be even more elitist than membership in the Council itself. Though but 6 percent of the work force in the plants studied had college training, this group held the Council floor 65 percent of the Council time (Obradovic, 1975); similarly League members constituted but 13 percent of the workforce, but did 70 percent of the talking.

Actually different groups participate regarding different subjects, depending on their knowledge and interests. In a typical meeting, according to Kolaja (1966; see also Riddell, 1968), rank-and-file workers listened passively through management's presentation of the next year's production plan, then displayed a "lively reaction" to some new rules regarding incentive rate payments, but developed real enthusiasm only when debating the allocation of newly available apartment houses. More quantitative data confirms these observations (Obradovic, 1978). Marketing experts and top management dominate deliberations regarding marketing; participation regarding compensation issues is more evenly distributed with almost no correlation (.029; N = 1,825 individuals, 16,941 interactions) between the length of time any one individual spends discussing marketing and the time he spends discussing compensation (see also Wachtel, 1973: 91). Especially with regard to marketing and economic issues, the worker councillor's role is chiefly to ratify management's proposals (Ramondt, 1979).

Council sessions are often overloaded with trivia. The issues are often too complex for the average member to understand and rapid turnover of membership makes expertise difficult to develop. Sessions may last for up to 6 hours, well past dinner time. Council members become bored and side conversations are frequent. Attendance is often spotty, particularly because a high percentage of workers have second jobs. Except for a few activists who develop expertise, there are few rewards for Council membership. Further, fellow workers are likely to feel resentful when the Council votes against them. Given these frustrations, it is understandable that Obradovic (1970) found that Council members were more alienated than rank-and-file workers. Similarly, Yugoslav Council members have less "interest" in WPM and evaluate it less favorably than do their German counterparts; just the reverse is true at the rank-and-file level (IDE, 1981, Figures 8.6 and 8.7).

Contrasting Decision-Making Patterns. It would be misleading, however, to concentrate just on the Council's formal deliberations. As with legislative bodies everywhere, many of the important decisions are made behind the scenes. Further, there are sharp differences in decision-making patterns among organizations. Adizes (1971) provides a fascinating contrast between two textile firms that were similar in size and technology but very different in decision-making practices.

The Director of one firm, XYZ, was somewhat self-effacing. Major proposals were initiated in the Collegium, a group of top management officers, who might debate an issue for months in regular sessions before a rough consensus was reached. It would then be sent consecutively to (1) the Extended Collegium, a somewhat larger group including lower-level managers; (2) the Politikal Aktiv, which included key leaders from management, the Workers Council, the League, and the union; (3) meetings in the affected units; and finally to (4) the Workers Council for ratification. Substantial opposition at any level would hold the proposal up until appropriate modifications were made. But once a decision was made at one stage, those participating felt committed to defend it at later stages. Progress was slow, meetings were lengthy, and ideas were often dropped because consensus was not obtained. Agreement was particularly difficult regarding such issues as production work rates, transfer prices, and the transfer of work or workers from one department to another, all of which related to relative status and income.

To make the system work required political skills, manipulation of agendas, and much patience. Decisions were often delayed until crises made their logic overwhelmingly compelling. At worst, it sounds much like faculty self-governance; at best, like Japanese management.

The advantages of this system included high commitment and excellent communications (workers were observed debating plant investment issues on the bus and in social gatherings). Among the disadvantages were slow reactions to external pressures, perhaps heightened tension between groups, and decisional saturation (Alutto and Belasco, 1972) for some people. (Supervisors had to exert considerable pressure to round up workers for unpaid, after-work Zbor meetings.)

At a second firm, ABC, a young, charismatic director had important political connections in the community and with the local bankers. He initiated key decisions. His contacts with subordinates were on a one-to-one basis (rather than as a group), and he hired a much larger college-trained staff than in XYZ. Although decisions went through the same stages as in XYZ, meetings were formally conducted, with status differences much more obvious (top management had special, gold-plated coffee cups). The Director made his presentation, questions were answered, formal consent was obtained, and the meeting was fairly quickly adjourned. Though the Director was easily available to all levels of the work force, his rapid decision making short circuited the formal participatory process.

The results were as one might expect: quick decisions, but less development of middle management, poorer communications, technological change occurring faster than workers could be trained to handle, a high disciplinary rate, and a strike (by night-shift workers who failed to understand that their paycheck was low because the company had incurred a loss).

Which plant was more typical? To read Yugoslav sociologists, it was ABC. In several well-publicized cases (Adizes, 1971, p. 209–213), the Workers Council entered into a "contract" with its Director according to which the Council relinquished its power to interfere in operational management, in return for which the Director agreed to have this performance (and even compensation) judged strictly on results.

Staff and Middle Management. Self-management downgrades the legitimacy of the formal management hierarchy and makes managers uncertain of their roles. Even though workers councils can be manipulated, this takes time. Being weak in reward, coercive, and legitimate power, managers must rely heavily on their expert power. However, staff people resent being forced to make the often vain attempt to explain technical questions in language that the average worker can understand (Broekmeyer, 1977).

The Yugoslav system is highly legalistic. Each firm has a legal department. A "self-management lawyer" is normally present at every meeting to ensure that the rules are observed. Of the 12 countries studied by IDE (1981), Yugoslavia scored *by far* the highest on formalization, functional differentiation (Pugh, Hickson, Hinings, and Turner, 1968), and in the number of rules regulating participation.

Rather than undergo the frustration to make the rules work, managers are tempted either to pass the buck to the Council or to give only lip service to the rules (as Director ABC did). Either approach generates cynicism. Functional differentiation (i.e., the division of responsibility among middle managers) plus the need to use "illegitimate" means has the result that "effective influence and formal responsibility have been separated . . . top management remains the dominant group; it exerts influence without being subject to satisfactory control" (Rus, 1970, p. 160). (Although IDE, 1981, reports that Workers Councils exercise more influence than do directors, at least five others studies, including Tannenbaum et al., 1974, put directors first.)

Labor Relations. In theory, as a workers' state, Yugoslavia should be free of strikes. In fact, they are fairly common and have been extensively studied (Jovanov, 1978; Arzensek, 1978; Zupanov, 1973; Rus, in press). Strikes are often caused by the failure to consult a work group sufficiently before instituting a change (e.g., the night-shift strike at ABC). But on several occasions an entire plant (even management) has struck to protest high material costs or low prices for the product it makes.

From the Yugoslav point of view, strikes are illegitimate. Why should workers strike against themselves? On the other hand, given management's own shaky legitimacy and the ideological priority given workers' interests over management's, it becomes illegitimate for management to crush these strikes. Strikes are viewed as being caused by "bureaucratic deformations" (Rus, in press) and are an embarrassment all around. (There is some similarity between Yugoslav and OD theory: both treat strikes as pathological occurrences to be cured by better communications.)

As a consequence neither side seeks an all-out battle. Most strikes are settled quickly. Few last more than a day; some consist merely of mass attendance at Workers Council meetings. Usually management concedes most of the workers' demands; sometimes all that is required is that management listens.

How about the union? As in other communist countries, Yugoslav unions are concerned chiefly with welfare and ceremonies, and at times the union and the personnel department are almost indistinguishable. Thus, the union plays little part in settling strikes; neither does the Workers Council. Third-party mediation, if any, comes from the political leadership in the outside community.

Attitudinal Impacts. Despite the problems mentioned earlier, self-management gave Yugoslav workers a sense of power and influence. Both Tannenbaum et al. (1974) and the IDE (1981) group placed Yugoslav workers first in terms of influence among the countries these groups studied. (Tannenbaum et al., 1974, put them even above kibbutz workers.) Apparently shop-floor ratification of major policy pays off, because of the 12 work groups studied by IDE, only Yugoslav workers were perceived to exert substantial influence on long-run issues. (Norwegian workers ranked higher on short-term, shop-level issues.) Yugoslav plants have the flattest control curves (Tannenbaum et al., 1974), and Workers Councils were the most influential of IDE's 12 national forms of participative bodies.

Though Yugoslav workers rank high on perceived influence, participation with regard to big issues does not translate into a participative immediate boss–subordinate relationship. Yugoslav managers are reported as being less participative than Danish (IDE, 1981), kibbutz, or United States managers (Tannenbaum et al., 1974). Neither has the opportunity to participate eliminated alienation or dissatisfaction. Yugoslav workers were the most alienated of those studied by Tannenbaum et al. (1974) and their job satisfaction is quite low compared to other countries (Jacob and Jacob, 1979, p. 35; Tannenbaum et al., 1974). Despite their relative sense of power and influence, few knew or cared much about what workers councils did (Riddell, 1968, p. 65–66; Kolaja, 1966, p. 60; Sachs, 1975). When asked how frequently they participated, the average response lay between "very seldom" and "seldom" (Rus, 1979, p. 226).

Although, as do workers in most other countries, Yugoslav workers expressed an abstract desire for more participation than they actually had, their aspirations for equality declined during the experiences of the 1960s (Burt, 1972, p. 166). When asked *how* they would like to participate, over two-thirds wished "to be informed only" or "to discuss"; the percentage who wanted " to decide" or "to control implementation" ranged from 12.5 to 31.1, depending on the issue (Rus, 1979, p. 232–233). Although Yugoslav workers rate the consequences of participation higher than do workers in other countries and a higher percentage of them are willing to serve on participative bodies generally (IDE, 1981), the possibility of serving on such bodies was ranked as either fifth or sixth of six possible sources of satisfaction (wages and physical conditions being highest) (Obradovic, 1970). Further, the most frequently mentioned advantage of WPM was more equitable distribution of income (Burt, 1972).

Epilogue. During the early 1970s, self-management and Yugoslav society generally went through a crisis. As the economy became more competitive and turbulent, it became increasingly obvious that the self-management system had become too cumbersome. There was mounting criticism that "technocrats" were usurping the power properly belonging to workers. Competitive pricing and enterprise autonomy was widening income differentials, not just within individual firms, but among firms and above all among regions. (Income in the richest region was five times per capita that of the poorest, and inequality was growing.) The capitalist ethic of self-interest was triumphing over the socialist ethic of equality. On top of this, Yugoslav leadership had additional concerns: student unrest, rapid inflation, Tito's approaching death, and rivalry among regions.

The early 1970s saw a substantial reassertion of central power. Censorship was tightened and dissidents were discharged or imprisoned. In the economic sphere, the party's power was strengthened, plant autonomy was reduced, and measures of national planning (in the form of "social compacts") were introduced to constrain unrestricted free market competition. The shop Units, now renamed BOALs (Basic Organizations of Associated Labor) were reorganized and in theory given more autonomy to plan their activities. The power and size of the enterprise-level Workers Councils was cut back: now they were responsible chiefly for coordination. Presumably BOALs' smaller size—ideally 300 workers or so—would weaken the "technocracy" and permit direct democracy. Finally, an effort was made to distinguish more sharply between the executive responsibilities of management and the legislative responsibilities of the Workers Councils (Sachs, 1975). Overall, the net effect was to weaken enterprise-level management (Wachtel, 1973, p. 95) and to redirect participation to the shop level, where presumably it might be more effective.

Reports to date (Sachs, 1975; Stephen, 1977; Miller, 1978) suggest that internal decisions are made faster under the new setup, but that coordination with other units is more complex and that the already existing paperwork and legalism has increased. Unfortunately, along with these changes, restrictions were placed on social scientists' freedom to operate in Yugoslav plants, thus stemming the flow of research.

Conclusion. Despite its problems, the Yugoslav experiment was fairly successful, at least up to 1972. It did much to transform a traditional, hierarchical society. GNP expanded rapidly. Growth was achieved with less stress than in most rapidly developing countries (Warner, 1975). Self-management acted as a safety valve, co-opting many potential dissenters and directing their energies toward safe plant-level issues. Further, self-management trained a whole generation of managers (Dunlop, 1958), a considerable accomplishment, even if homegrown managers become less needed as a college-trained generation takes over. Even if there was not "complete participative management," there was "managed participation" (Warner, 1975).

WPM may have given an opportunity to participate in a fairly meaningful way for most of those who wanted it. Perhaps we should be more impressed by the substantial numbers of rank-and-file workers who participated actively (or even learned silently) during workers council meetings—than by data suggesting these meetings were in fact controlled by small elites. Even for those with little desire to participate, WPM may have had an important symbolic meaning. Possibly "participation diminishes the meaninglessness of work, although it does not diminish the powerlessness of the worker" (Broekmeyer, 1977, p. 139)—this, despite findings of high alienation and dissatisfaction among these very workers.

Yet as of 1973, Yugoslav self-management still had some serious problems to solve: (1) The relationship between bottom-up participation and top-down management had yet to be resolved. All roles were diffuse and conflict ridden (though Rus, in press, calls this a strength). Councils still had not learned to develop an independent expertise. Workers still viewed managers as all powerful, even though managers themselves felt hamstrung by participative red tape. (2) There was little evidence of participation with regard to shop-level problems. (3) Communications between Workers Council members and their constituents remained poor. (4) Inadequate mechanisms had been developed for resolving the conflicting interests of individual workers, the enterprise, and society generally. (5) Yugoslav self-management seemed to work best in a stable environment where product mixes and prices changed infrequently. Under these circumstances, production efficiencies could accumulate. With a rapidly changing environment, the WPM system became overloaded.

(6) Finally, Yugoslavia may have been suffering from what OD people call "plateauing," a loss of initial enthusiasm after early problems are solved and more difficult ones emerge.

Producers Cooperatives

Producers Cooperatives (PCs) are worker-managed, worker-owned organizations (the terms "worker-managed" and "worker-owned" are both somewhat fuzzy and, as shown later, there are numerous cases that are only marginally PCs).

Israeli kibbutz are PCs and, in a way, so is Yugoslav self-management; but our concern here will be chiefly with PCs in the United States and Britain, plus two fairly unique PCs, Mondragon in Spain and Dynavac in Australia. PCs also exist in France and Italy (Oakeshott, 1978), and others were sponsored by revolutionary regimes in Peru (Berenbach, 1979), Chile (Espinosa and Zimbalist, 1978), Algeria (Clegg, 1971), and elsewhere.

American PCs date back to the early pioneers. Jones (1979) has identified 458 manufacturing PCs about which some data are available. Many were established as social or religious communes (with all property shared) whereas others had more purely economic ends. Most were short-lived, but some lasted 20 years or more.

Scholarly attention has been devoted to two sets of surviving "old" cooperatives: a group of plywood companies established in the Pacific Northwest during 1939–1955 (Bellas, 1972; Berman, 1967; Bennett, 1979) and a group of San Francisco scavenger companies (Perry, 1978; Russell, Hochner, and Perry, 1979). The PC approach also has been utilized to prevent plant shutdowns. These "plant rescue" cases have been intensively studied and will be discussed separately. Also, there is IGP (International Group Plans), an insurance company in which workers own half the shares, elect half the company board, help select managers and have extensive democratic rights regarding office-level problems (Zwerdling, 1979). Finally, there have been a number of generally short-lived "alternative institutions" or communes, such as food and farming cooperatives, legal collectives and craft communes. Generally these participant owned and managed organizations have been founded by counterculture members. They are highly equalitarian and antibureaucratic (Rothschild-Whitt, 1979; Berger, 1981).

PCs have an equally long history in Britain, and British scholars have found them of continuing interest (e.g., Jones, 1977; Oakeshott, 1978; Pateman, 1970). The early PC movement peaked around 1905, but one firm founded in 1874 still survives (Jones, 1977). Two of the better-known, more recent firms, the John Lewis Partnership (Flanders, Pomeranz, and Woodward, 1968) and the Scott Bader Commonwealth (Blum, 1968) were founded by paternalistic owners who transferred formal ownership to their workers. Under the recent Labour Government, three new PCs were established, as in the United States, to prevent depressed firms from being shut down (Oakeshott, 1978). Despite some government support, two of these have died and the third, Triumph Meriden, barely survives.

Mondragon is the great PC success story (Johnson and Whyte, 1977). Founded in 1956 under the guidance of a Basque priest, this PC federation is highly profitable and growing rapidly. It now has over 18,000 workers and is continually spawning new offshoots. Besides its success, three things make Mondragon unique. In the first place, it is a "pure" PC in that all employees (and only employees) are owners. Second, each new employee must make a significant investment (some of which may be borrowed) when hired; afterwards each employee's share of the profits is kept in a reserve fund until he leaves or retires. Finally, Mondragon is supported by a "shelter" organization (Vanek, 1975a) consisting of three affiliates: (1) a large, growing credit union that generates capital for investment, develops new PCs, and provides general technical assistance, (2) a school system to provide managerial and technical training, and (3) a League for Education and Culture, to provide ideological support.

Mondragon's governmental structure is less unique. The members annually elect a small Managing Board, which in turn selects the general manager and other key members of management. A somewhat larger elected but ineffective Social Council is supposed to advise the Management Board. Shop-level supervision is somewhat traditional, although there have been some experiments with autonomous work groups.

Finally, there is Dynavac, a 30-employee firm specializing in vacuum equipment (Cupper, 1980), with a highly unconventional government structure. There are no managers. Each member has a job description or "responsibility list." Within his area of responsibility, he is the boss. Anyone with a problem or suggestion that concerns the organization as a whole indicates this on a centrally posted "agenda" sheet. On Thursday, those who are interested in the week's supply of agenda items meet to discuss these. (Attendance varies from 0 to 20 employees.) The Group (as it is called) passes its recommendations on to a weekly General Meeting of all employees, which in turn makes the final decisions. Roughly, this procedure is applied to all organization decisions, including performance evaluation, salary setting, and discipline. The norm is that all members actively participate in the management process (not just sit through meetings). Those who fail to do their share receive a negative performance evaluation from their peers. Three individuals have been expelled for inability to work without close supervision and others have found self-management so distasteful that they have resigned. So this is a self-selected group, but it seems to work.

Purity and Degeneration. One could argue that in "pure" PCs (1) *all* workers should be owners, *only* workers should be owners, and ownership should be equally shared; (2) management should be democratically elected with each member having an equal vote, and (3) there should be a high level of participation in all decisions, big or little (Jones, 1980). Bernstein (1980) adds several additional requirements: (4) profit sharing among workers; (5) widespread dissemination of essential information; (6) guaranteed "basic political liberties"; (7) an independent appeals board to handle grievances; and (8) a "democratic consciousness." In practice, PCs vary greatly. Only Mondragon and some counterculture PCs appear to meet the first two criteria and none meet all eight.

Beginning with the Webbs (Webb and Webb, 1920), it has been widely argued (Bernstein, 1980; Vanek, 1975a; McGregor, 1977) that PCs have a tendency to "degenerate" over time, that is, to abandon the principle of worker ownership and control, and also to become economically less successful. These separate but related problems are discussed in the following sections.

Ownership. Many PCs have considerable nonworker ownership. Even where ownership is originally widely distributed among the work force, the percentage of nonowners in the work force tends to rise over time. Present owners are reluctant to share the profits with newcomers. As in the Israeli kibbutz, nonowners are hired, initially on a temporary basis but eventually permanently. Nonowners become second class citizens and eventually the spirit of cooperation is lost. This process may be accelerated by technological changes, which increase status differences within the work force. Thus, technological changes in San Francisco scavenging, such as centralized billing and containerized collection, contributed to the decision to retire stock, as owners left the business, rather than to sell it to newcomers who would work only on unskilled jobs.

On the other hand, the percentage of owners who are not workers may also increase. If PCs are successful, the value of their stock goes up, making it harder for new owners to buy in; eventually retiring owners may be allowed to sell their interests to outsiders. A partial solution to this problem is a requirement that only workers may own stock. Stock of retiring members can be bought out at a fixed price, and new workers may buy their stock on an installment plan. Alternatively, ownership may be held by some sort of trust (as in Dynavac, Scott Bader, and IGP), which eliminates individual ownership altogether. Ownership, of course, helps foster commitment. Beyond this, without selling some sort of stock, it may be difficult to obtain the capital to start the business or to permit growth. Retained profits may be insufficient (and at first are zero) and outside financing is often problematical.

Present Earnings Versus Investment. According to some observers, PCs tend to underinvest (Jones and Backus, 1977; Vanek, 1975b). Workers vote themselves high wages or take out their profits as dividends, rather than invest the substantial capital required for growth and modernization. In economic terms, capital is underrewarded and undersupplied; thus, labor is substituted for capital and the firm operates at a point of increasing returns to scale.

As a partial solution to this problem, the constitution of some British PCs requires that most profits be reinvested (Oakeshott, 1978). Another partial solution is not to rely so exclusively on owner investment and instead to obtain outside financing. Yet commercial banks are reluctant to invest in strange organizational forms. So "shelter organizations" that can provide financial (and also technical) support become important. Mondragon's success is due in part to its allied credit union, which generates the steady stream of capital its factories require. There are somewhat similar financial and advice-giving organizations in several European countries.

Governance. To what extent do worker–owners really run their companies? To what extent are they able to fend off Michel's iron law of oligarchy? The evidence we have is very limited (Abell, forthcoming). Dynavac suggests that town-meeting participation is possible in small, technologically advanced firms. In plywood PCs, all directors are worker–owners; these in turn appoint a manager who typically is not an owner. The fact that there is a high turnover of such managers suggests that the worker–owners retain control. All major decisions are made by a general membership meeting. Communications between directors and rank-and-file workers appear good and there is continuous shop-floor discussion of production problems (Greenberg, 1978; Bennett, 1979). In both Dynavac and the plywood PCs, workers take on substantial responsibility both for making difficult personnel decisions and for keeping themselves informed about organizational matters generally. By contrast, managerial level employees now dominate the boards in scavenger PCs, though elections may be hotly contested and worker–owners feel they have considerably more "say" than do comparable workers in other firms (Russell et al., 1979).

Scott Bader and John Lewis, the two well-known British PCs founded by benevolent owners, both provide an elaborate framework of committees, councils, and assemblies in which workers could take part (e.g., Scott Bader holds semiannual meetings for all members at which any subject of interest can be *discussed*). However, the power of these participatory bodies is so restricted that their role in primarily advisory. The Managing Director appoints a majority of the board in both cases. Limited and perhaps outdated evidence (Pateman, 1970), suggests that in neither case is there much worker participation in shop-floor or company-wide problem solving. In fact, white-collar workers and management seem to dominate the elaborate constitutional apparatus (Jones, 1977).

Similarly, Bradley (1980) concludes that worker directors had limited communications with the rank and file in two recent PCs established by the radical left: Manuest in France and *Scottish Daily News* in Britain. In both cases there was also "considerable doubt" whether even the directors controlled the firms' daily activities.

Communications between the rank and file and the Management Board in Mondragon's largest unit were reported as poor; the Social Council "serves mainly as a channel of communications from management to workers and does not provide a channel through which workers can influence management" (Johnson and Whyte, 1977, p. 25). But even the Management Board was powerless "because the managers have a near-monopoly of knowledge. . . . It is impossible for [the Management Board] which meets monthly to keep abreast . . . and provide any countervailing power" (Eaton, 1979, p. 36). So, in the largest Mondragon unit, "the ostensibly very democratic governing structure has become a sick joke" (Eaton, 1979, p. 34). But changes may be underway (Stern, private communication).

The situation at IGP, the insurance company, is somewhat different. Corporate-wide decisions regarding finance and marketing are made rather conventionally, but there are hot contests for the board of directors. Decisions regarding discipline and work procedures (e.g., installation of computers) are made democratically and somewhat chaotically (Zwerdling, 1979).

U.S. counterculture communes place high values on democracy, equality and decision-making by consensus. The typical commune spends countless hours discussing problems of governance (Rothschild-Whitt, 1979) yet few last long. Among their main problems (Gamson and Levin, 1980) are (1) inability to agree on common and appropriate decision-making norms, especially with regard to the legitimate use of authority, the handling of deviant behavior, and the productive use of meeting time, (2) lack of a common culture, and (3) lack of technical skills.

Evaluation. How successful have PCs been? The picture is somewhat mixed. Many of the more profitable ones have transformed into more conventional companies as ownership has fallen into the hands of non-workers and as higher management has eliminated democratic controls.

PCs remaining loyal to their principles have had problems of their own. Many have been slow to expand, either by investing new capital or by hiring new workers. On the other hand, Mondragon, spurred on by its credit union staff experts, has grown rapidly and even established a research lab.

How about technological change? Back in 1920 the Webbs argued that PCs were "perpetually tempted to maintain existing processes unchanged" (Webb and Webb, 1920, p. 68). The evidence (summarized in Jones, 1980) as to this is mixed. Certainly PCs tend to be small, many are in labor-intensive industries, and some utilize obsolete equipment and technology. On the other hand, the United States scavenger and plywood PCs have generally adjusted to technological changes in their industries. Still, Aldrich and Stern (1978) may be right: PCs may survive best in stable industries, with little technological change, where craftsmen predominate.

PCs' reluctance to accept either new members or new risks may contribute to "self-strangulation" (Jones, 1980). According to Jones (1979), the typical United States PC goes through a three-stage life cycle: first, both total employment and the number of worker–owners increases; second, the number of worker–owners declines, while total employment continues to grow; finally, employment also decreases and the firm dies. Some observers note a tendency to self-strangulate at age 20–30, though this has not been systematically demonstrated (Abell, forthcoming).

Nevertheless, comparisons between PCs and capitalist forms "do not seem to indicate a markedly different failure rate" (Abell, forthcoming). After all the mortality rate of small firms is always high. A number of cases (e.g., Bellas, 1972; Jones, 1980) suggest that at least in their earlier years PCs' labor productivity, profitability, and income per worker is higher than their capitalist counterparts; so is their owner–workers commitment to the organization (Russell et al., 1979; Greenberg, 1978).

Finally, there is fairly good evidence (Bellas, 1972; Jones, 1979, 1980) that, comparing PCs as a whole, those that come closest to the "pure" PC ideal tend to survive longer and to be more successful by a variety of economic criteria (but see Abel, forthcoming).

To conclude, PCs probably meet important noneconomic needs for *some* workers. Preserving worker ownership and control may be a more difficult problem than the maintenance of economic efficiency (Chaplin and Cowe, 1977). With some care, PCs may work, at least in some niches of the economy. But IGC, Dynavac, and the plywood PCs are among the few cases in which workers substantially contribute to management decision making.

Finally, I should emphasize that the data with regard to PCs is sketchy, noncomparable, and in some cases (e.g., with regard to Scott Bader, John Lewis, and perhaps Mondragon) out-of-date. Some of the findings (e.g., regarding PC life cycles) are based on historical data that are particularly sketchy. Only the plywood PCs have been studied in any real depth.

Ownership Without Control

PCs involve worker ownership *and* control. What is the relative significance of these two elements? We already have evidence as to the attitudinal and behavioral impacts of various forms of worker control. Here we examine the impacts of ownership, taken alone.

Theory suggests that even without control, worker ownership should lead to improved motivation, productivity, satisfaction, and labor relations. (1) Presumably the interests of the worker owners will be congruent with those of the organization itself. Thus, greater efforts will lead to greater economic rewards. (2) Ownership should lead to greater commitment, particularly if workers have voluntarily sunk some of their savings into the firm. Commitment should lead to greater efforts to prove the commitment decision was a right one and also to beliefs supportive of this commitment. (3) If other workers are owners, peer pressure should lead to harder work. (4) Resistance to change should be reduced. (5) Participation in decision making will be viewed as more legitimate by both workers and management. (6) Finally, because workers have a vested interest in company success, labor–management relations should improve.

Some data as to the impact of worker ownership is provided by six well-studied cases in which employees have helped buy plants that parent countries had threatened to shut down. Four are in the United States: Vermont Asbestos Group (Johannesen, 1979), a furniture factory (Stern, Wood, and Hammer, 1979; Hammer and Stern, 1980), a knitting mill (Zwerdling, 1979), and a lathe manufacturing company (Survey Research Center, 1977); the fifth, a trucking firm, is Canadian (Long, 1978a, 1978b, 1979); and the last, Hart, a solar heating firm, is Australian (Goldstein, 1978). (For summary articles, see Zwerdling, 1979 and Long, 1980.) Unfortunately, different variables were studied in these six plants, so detailed comparisons are difficult.

The six companies varied considerably as to the proportion of stock owned by blue-collar workers, white-collar workers, managers, and outside interests. Two firms were 100 percent *employee* owned, but much of this ownership was by managers. Of the five cases about which data are available, only at Vermont Asbestos was a majority of the stock *worker* owned, and there only 51 percent. In none of these cases did the money to buy the plant come primarily from workers. Most of it was loaned by banks and government agencies, subject to various restrictions, including specifically in one case that professional management keep control.

In none of the six cases were plans made for worker participation. In fact, the new arrangements were put together with such haste that little thought was given to internal governance. The motivation was to save jobs and radical new ideas might have scared off financial supports. Though workers were elected to three of the company boards, in no case were they in the majority. Even those who were elected were subject to co-optation. The seven hourly paid workers on the asbestos board kept its deliberations secret, despite some rank-and-file desire to know how each director voted (Johannesen, 1979). None of the reports suggest any special effort to involve rank-and-file workers in decision making.

Under these circumstances, these companies provide a fairly good test of the impact of ownership without control. But note that except for Hart, worker ownership had lasted for less than 2 years at the time of the studies. The initial results may be biased by worker euphoria: even though they may not have participated in management, they had participated in a successful effort to save their jobs. Interestingly, the study at Hart, conducted in the fourth year of worker ownership, when the plant was losing money, showed some signs of disillusionment.

What are the results of the various studies? Profits improved initially in all six cases, in some cases dramatically (Long, 1980; Goldstein, 1978; Survey Research Center, 1977; Johannesen, 1979). Worker productivity improved in four cases, turnover declined in two (Long, 1980; *Wall Street Journal,* May 31, 1978; Survey Research Center, 1977), with evidence as to the other plants not being available. Of course, part of the reported improvement may be explained by the fact that these plants had been neglected by the old management and the new managers had more independence. Yet, comparing three plants with varying degrees of employee ownership, Long (1980) concludes that improved economic performance is directly related to the degree of ownership.

Conte and Tannenbaum (1978; Survey Research Center, 1977) studied some 98 employee-owned firms. In 21 of these, workers owned half the equity; in 47, employees were on the Board of Directors. Profits, as a percentage of sales, in this group were 50 percent higher than for comparable firms in their respective industries. Further, the higher the proportion of equity owned by workers, the higher the profits. However, once employee ownership was controlled, there was a small, insignificant negative relationship between profitability and having employee directors.

Attitudes were reported to have improved in three firms (Long, 1980; Survey Research Center, 1977), but not in a fourth (Long, 1980). Most workers felt that conditions had become better under the new arrangements and that teamwork had increased. Managers were seen to communicate better and to be more considerate. Half the workers in one case perceived some increase in influence (Long, 1979); by contrast, 68 percent of the lathe company workers saw no changes in decision making (Survey Research Center, 1977, p. 54).

Two studies find that shareholders have more positive attitudes regarding such dimensions as involvement, integration (Long, 1980), challenge, and responsibility (Goldstein, 1978) than do nonshareholders. But in one company this difference in attitude depended largely on holding $100 or more of stock (Goldstein, 1978). The attitudes of small holders were much like those of nonshareholders.

Though workers generally believed that change in ownership had increased their influence, there was general agreement that management's influence remained higher than theirs (Long, 1979; Hammer and Stern, 1980). Managers were felt to "own" the plant more than did workers, with little correlation between worker sense of ownership and their actual ownership of stock (Hammer and Stern, 1980). There was little feeling of psychological partnership. Interestingly, management perceived greater change in the power relationship than did workers (Survey Research Center, 1977; Long, 1979).

Are workers satisfied with their relative lack of power? As do workers almost everywhere, the workers studied here would like some slight increase in their influence (Long, 1979); nevertheless, they felt that management should retain the greatest power regarding production and policy decisions while the union should be most powerful regarding wages (Hammer and Stern, 1980). Indeed the less alienated workers were, the more they wanted management to be powerful. Blue-collar workers preferred to exert their power through their union, not through a participative group; white-collar workers had greater interest in participation as such.

Why didn't blue-collar workers give higher priority to participation? One possible reason is that most of the workers were fairly skilled; perhaps they already had all the shop-floor autonomy they wanted (Hammer and Stern, 1980). A second reason is that there was little preparation for participation in higher level decision making. Neither management nor the institutional arrangements encouraged it. The workers had no available model of self-management. Nor had they any training in making the technical decisions self-management requires.

As mentioned earlier, the behavioral science research on the United States and Canadian cases was based on the first 2 years of workers ownership. Zwerdling (1979, p. 78), a journalist dedicated to self-management, reports recent signs of disillusionment in several of these cases. His (possibly unrepresentative) respondents are unhappy because the change in ownership has not led to greater change in worker–management relations. "People are happy their jobs were saved and the company is doing well . . . and there is no great drive for change. . . . On the other hand, insiders say, many workers *do* have a vague if inarticulated demand for greater involvement in participation—and they feel frustrated they've been denied it."

At the Vermont Asbestos Group, the Board of Directors ignored a negative stockholder vote and invested company money in a new subsidiary; whereupon a number of workers sold their stock to an outside investor. The outside investor became president and the workers earned a large profit. The lathe company suffered a 9-week strike in 1979. The union is suing the company to restore the workers' rights in a conventional pension plan, which they had surrendered in return for worker ownership. "Productivity in the plant has steadily declined during the last two years after a 25 percent spurt at first" (*Wall Street Journal,* December 8, 1980, p. 22).

To conclude, while there is some evidence that worker-owned companies can be more efficient than conventionally owned companies, at least in their first years, there are few signs that worker ownership generates an inevitable dynamic for greater participation. Indeed after the effect of the initial participative act of assuming ownership has been dissipated, plateauing and disillusionment may set in. Because many of the arguments for ownership assume participation, unless some special efforts are made to gain participation, the payoff from worker ownership may be limited. An effort is being made to avoid these problems at Rath, the packinghouse firm, now being launched into worker ownership. Here a variety of techniques are being utilized to increase participation at various organizational levels (Gunn, 1980).

WPM AND THE AFFECTED PARTIES

This section seeks to draw some generalizations from the four sets of case studies just discussed and also from the experience in other countries, especially Germany, Sweden, and Britain.

If representative participation is really to increase worker influence over managerial decisions, a whole series of new formal and informal relationships must be developed. A new organization is required, the joint worker–management participatory body (PB); and a new role must be created, that of worker representative on the participatory body. Older roles must change, too, particularly those of union and management.

What Participatory Bodies Do

Except for the smallest organizations, every WPM scheme has a participatory body, which includes worker representatives that are either directly elected by the workers themselves or appointed by the unions. Most of the participation in representative WPM occurs in PBs, yet most reports describe formal charters or attitudes toward WPM rather than what actually happens in PBs themselves. Often there is a wide gap between the PB's formal function and authority, as described in its charter, and what it does in practice. Some PBs are almost inert; others are in fact quite powerful.

PC boards and Yugoslav Workers Councils have been discussed already. Here we deal with three other PB forms: (1) Joint Consultative Committees (JCCs), whose function is primarily advice and consultation; (2) Works Councils—the best examples of which are in Germany—operating at the plant level, which have joint decision-making power (e.g., the power to block specific personnel actions); and (3) company boards containing worker directors selected to represent the rank-and-file workers. Each type varies in its effectiveness and each has unique problems.

Joint Consultative Committees. JCCs are common in a number of countries; (for British cites, see Jones, 1977; for a United States case, see Witte, 1980). Typically their mandate is open-ended: to deal with subjects of common interest to labor and management. Worker representatives may make suggestions whereas management is expected to keep the committee informed about important developments affecting the work force generally and sometimes to seek the committee's advice before taking action.

Some committees have broad formal jurisdictions but real power in only limited subsidiary areas. "Enterprise committees" in France have merely consultative and information-getting power over most topics but are solely responsible (with a budget) for certain welfare activities (e.g., canteens) and jointly responsible for company medical services (Sturmthal, 1964; Harrison, 1976). Scanlon Plan committees in the United States provide another example of successful limited-purpose committees. Their function is to process worker suggestions for increasing productivity, and their success results largely from the associated bonuses, which provide a strong economic incentive to make the Plan work.

By and large, general purpose JCCs have exerted little influence. In the first place, in unionized companies their jurisdiction is typically confined to non-"strategic" matters not subject to collective bargaining (but collective bargaining tends to be less all-encompassing in Europe than in the United States). By contrast, in nonunion companies, JCCs may perform some of the personnel-representative functions of a union (Witte, 1980).

Second, because JCCs lack the power to block management's actions, their influence may depend on management's faith and good will. Given management's interest in preserving its prerogatives, it often restricts the committee's scope to trivial matters of no great importance to either workers or management. (For a discussion of techniques management uses to downgrade committees, see Lammers, 1967, p. 210.)

A third reason for JCCs' limited success is that the parties fail to agree on their mission. Management expects them to help solve production, safety, housekeeping, and similar problems, whereas workers want them to deal with grievance and labor relations issues not subject to collective bargaining. Because neither side is interested in what the other is saying, not much gets done (de Bellecombe, 1968; Tabb and Galin, 1970; Legendre, 1969).

Thus, although committees are often established with high hopes, there is a tendency over time for fewer significant topics to be assigned to them, for attendance to drop, and for meetings to be convened less often until finally the committee becomes completely inactive. This was seen to occur in Israel. Much the same happened in India (Tanic, 1969). In England, committees flourished during the two world wars, but atrophied afterward as shop steward committees took over their functions (Clarke, Fatchett, and Roberts, 1972; Bullock Report, 1977). Production committees in the United States during World War II suffered the same fate, although there have been some efforts to revive these, especially in steel and autos (de Schweinitz, 1949; Gold, 1976). Kochan, Dyer, and Lipsky (1977) report that it is difficult to keep health and safety committees going in the United States.

These union–management constraints help explain United States and British studies finding "that the consultative machinery was of prime importance [only] where union organizations were weak and management was human-relations oriented" (Clarke et al., 1972, p. 80; see also Derber, 1955, p. 80). Indeed JCCs play a key role in several paternalistic examples of qualified industrial democracies, such as Glacier (Jaques, 1951; Kelley, 1968), Scott Bader, and John Lewis (previously discussed).

The implicit assumption behind most consultative systems is that the subjects with which they deal are those regarding which workers and management share common interests and that, therefore, committee deliberations will occur in a nonadversary atmosphere. Recently, however, as European unions have become more assertive, many have attempted to transform consultation into bargaining. Thus, in Sweden, purely advisory committees largely atrophied during the 1960s (Peterson, 1968), but now that they have been given some real power they work reasonably well. At Kockums and Fiskeby, for example, shop- and plant-level committees participate in such decisions as the introduction of new equipment and even in the selection of management (Gunzberg, 1978). To the extent such committees in fact exercise joint control, they transform themselves into what I call works councils.

Works Councils. The distinction I have drawn between JCCs and works councils is that the former are primarily advisory whereas the latter have significant power to block management's actions (i.e., management cannot go ahead without the PB's approval). Like many other WPM distinctions, this one may be more theoretical than practical because many PBs are advisory with regard to some subjects and have veto powers with regard to others. Further, we have the Swedish case where management is merely required to "negotiate" with the labor–management committees; presumably after negotiating it has the right to go ahead without committee approval, but it rarely does so.

Works councils in Germany have been studied more intensively than in other countries (for summaries, see Furstenberg, 1981; Wilpert, 1975). In Germany, the works council assent is required before management can make major changes in a wide variety of personnel areas: work and leave schedules, piece rates and other pay schemes, selection, training, safety, suggestion systems, and welfare services. Its approval is also required before management can introduce technological change affecting the "work place, work flow, or work environment" (Furstenberg, 1981). The jurisdiction of Swedish committees is even broader. It includes "any important change of the working or employment conditions."

Apparently some works councils are largely ineffective, but others, particularly those in larger plants and with better trained council members, tend to be quite powerful (Logue, 1978; Hartmann, 1979). In fact, they and management jointly make all decisions likely to affect workers' welfare. "As time passes, interaction between management and the works council seems to have gained in scope and depth" particularly with regard to managements' "drive toward advanced mechanization and attendant measures of personnel administration. Councillors are now drawn increasingly into functional committees established by management to cope with major problems" (Hartmann, 1979, p. 79). "The administration of social welfare services, supervision of working conditions . . . and, in particular, the selection of workers who have to be discharged in cases of lack of work are examples of works council's activities which management considers to be useful" (Furstenberg, 1981, p. 15).

Technically, at least in Germany, works council members are elected by the workers, not appointed by the unions. In practice, a majority of most works council members have close union ties. Nevertheless, as we shall see, the relationship between works councils and the union is not free from tension.

In powerful works councils, being a works council member in practically a full-time job and works council members have offices and even staffs of their own on company premises (Hartmann, 1979). To the United States observer, their function seems somewhat like that of the shop committeeman in the United States auto industry, who also has a full-time, company-paid position. Indeed, German works councils deal with matters that are subject to plant-level collective bargaining in the United States. The main difference is that United States plant-level labor relations are covered by company-wide and plant-wide contracts, usually negotiated at 3-year intervals. Because these contracts cover most major issues, in theory at least the parties merely interpret them. Works council labor relations tend to be more ad hoc, dealing with each problem on its merit as it comes up. Regardless, works councils may have more control over production rates than have United States unions (Herding, 1972).

Worker Directors. In seven European countries (Germany, France, Luxembourg, Austria, Norway, Sweden, and Denmark), the law requires some sort of worker representation on the boards of directors of at least some large companies (in most of these countries, the representatives sit on *supervisory boards;* these in turn elect *management boards* that run the company on a day-to-day basis). In all cases except the German iron and steel industry, the worker directors constitute only a minority of the board; in France, they are merely observers. In Britain, worker directors serve on the boards of several nationalized industries and in some private companies.

Worker directors have received a good deal of research attention (see particularly Batstone, 1976) with individual studies being done in Germany (Furstenberg, 1978), Norway (Engelstad and Quale, 1977), Sweden (National Swedish Industrial Board, 1976), Denmark (Westenholz, 1979), and Britain (Brannen, 1976; BSC Employee Directors, 1977; Chell and Cox, 1979).

How effective are worker directors? There is little agreement here, perhaps in part because the researchers begin with different expectations and value systems and in part because there may be in fact a wide difference in effectiveness among various companies and countries. Batstone (1976, p. 35) may take an extreme position: "Two conclusions can be easily reached: first, worker directors have generally had little effect on anything, and second and consequently, they certainly had no catastrophic effect on anything or anybody."

It is readily understandable why worker directors can be ineffective. With or without worker representation, many boards act merely to rubber stamp management decisions. They meet infrequently, sometimes for only a few hours a year. Management sets the agenda and controls the information flow. Even in those companies in which the board plays an important role, the discussion frequently relates to financial and other issues of little direct interest to workers. The addition of worker directors may do little to change this.

Once on the board, the new worker directors felt seriously handicapped. They lacked the background information to evaluate management's proposals. Even when this information was provided, they lacked the skills to evaluate it. Some were awed by management's wealth, experience, and status (Englestad and Quale, 1977; Adams and Rummel, 1977). They tended to discuss those issues about which they had some personal expertise and to keep silent when anything else was considered.

But worker directors may be less ineffective than such observers as Batstone have claimed. European unions themselves look upon the worker director scheme as an important, if sometimes only a symbolic, victory. Just as works councils institutionalize union power at the plant level, so worker directors ensure their role at the company level. But in many cases the impact of worker directors has extended well beyond the symbolic. They serve to provide unions with early warning as to management intentions. They constitute an alternate form of input into top management decision making. In some circumstances they have successfully delayed plant closings until appropriate plans have been developed to relocate or otherwise protect the displaced workers. They have affected investment decisions, for instance, holding up Volkswagen's decision to build plants in the United States. At Porsche, they successfully opposed the appointment of an allegedly autocratic managing director. In Norway, they have raised issues, such as health and safety, never before given board-level attention. Indeed, in Scandinavia, "changes in board composition have had a 'shock effect' on both corporate management and boards, tightening up board procedures, turning boards into real decision-making bodies rather than 'rubber stamp' institutions, and making management and labor more responsive to the needs of the other interest group" (Hammer and Stern, 1981, citing Engelstad and Quale, 1977).

Even though workers are typically in the minority, voting is rarely used to resolve differences. Instead, contested issues are often assigned to special study committees or resolved by off-board bargaining (Fogarty, 1964). The net result is that board representation results in delay, bargaining, and compromise but rarely complete stalemate (Wilpert, 1975, p. 61).

By a variety of measures, worker directors are relatively more effective in the German iron and steel industry, where workers and management have equal board membership, than they are in other situations (Furstenberg, 1981; Fogarty, 1964, p. 106). For example, in iron and steel (and in the British Steel Corporation), worker directors often sit on board subcommittees (Batstone, 1976; BSC Employee Directors, 1977); this occurs less commonly elsewhere. Where worker directors are relatively effective in other industries, they hold premeeting caucuses, prepare their own agenda, and often speak through a single spokesman.

In German iron and steel, workers nominate a full-time "labor director" who sits on the management board and is responsible for the industrial relations department. The consensus is that such labor directors become co-opted by management. They have done much to humanize personnel administration, but few act as workers representatives (Furstenburg, 1978).

To conclude, worker directors must have some (at least symbolic) significance because some companies try to restructure themselves to get around the law. Still German, Swedish, and some British unions view them more as a source of information than as a means of equalizing power. For power equalization these unions look to works councils or collective bargaining (Martin, 1977; Furstenberg, 1978; Chell and Cox, 1979, p. 27).

What Subjects Do PBs Handle? One of the assumptions behind the Human Relations–OB approach to WPM is that WPM permits workers to make greater inputs into how they do their jobs and the way the company is run. Outside of Yugoslavia there has been little analysis of the content of PB meetings (but see Witte, 1980). The evidence is largely anecdotal. As mentioned earlier, PBs deal with numerous personnel issues. But, beyond this, they touch on nonpersonnel issues (such as plant layout, manufacturing processes, new equipment, and investment policies) only when these affect job security, income distribution, and physical working conditions. An early British study (National Institute of Industrial Psychology, 1952) found that JCCs functioned more effectively when dealing with matters of joint interest, such as work rules and safety, than with purely managerial issues, such as training and quality. By and large, in Rus's (1979, p. 231) words, PBs have been "defensive and protective" rather than "offensive and active." They are reactive, not proactive in their relationships to management. Only in the Scanlon Plan and possibly in some Swedish consultative systems and a few German works councils have PBs been much concerned with how the work is done.

The Role of the PB Member

On the one hand, the PB member represents workers; on the other, he helps run his company. As a partner in management, he may be asked to assent to actions that, as a representative of the workers, he should oppose. "If he is effective, he may lose the confidence of his constituents by becoming too closely identified with management" (Bullock, 1977, p. 39). Thus the more power he accumulates, the more difficult his role becomes. The greater his opportunity to influence management, the more likely he will be co-opted himself. (For an excellent case, see Whyte, 1955. Batstone, 1976, reviews the literature, and BSC Employee Directors, 1977, is sheer good reading. See also Drenth, 1973; Jaques, 1951; Bullock, 1977, p. 39.)

Alternative Roles. In dealing with this dilemma of representation, PB members are likely to take a variety of roles (see also Westenholz, 1979).

1.   PB members may be *inactive,* possibly because they lack the skills, information, or initiative to take part in PB meetings or because they think being participative would be fruitless. This is the response of some worker directors and perhaps the majority response in "tea and toilet" JCCs.

2.   PB members may view themselves as primarily *adversaries:* they represent interests of workers regarding subjects about which there is a clear difference of interest and remain largely silent regarding others. To the extent that WPM's purpose is to provide workers immediate bread-and-butter economic interests, such behavior is functional. But in terms of larger objectives, such as increasing workers' involvement in work processes or improving the organization's long-range economic efficiency, the primarily adversary role is dysfunctional. Among other drawbacks, it induces management to take an equally adversary role and makes it harder for PB members to exert influence regarding noneconomic issues.

3.   By contrast, PB members may view themselves as *comanagers* and put the long-run interests of the organization as a whole above the immediate interests of their constituents. In so doing they agree to such unpopular actions as cutting pay rates, reducing employment, and raising individual production quotas. Having helped make these unpalatable decisions, they may also try to sell them to their constituents.

In several United States cases (Strauss and Rosenstein, 1970, n. 23), the union agreed to cooperate to raise productivity to save the company from bankruptcy. The union's cooperation consisted of (a) informing workers about changes introduced by management, and by implication rejecting in advance any grievance against them, (b) negotiating changes in contractual provisions that hindered production, and (c) pressing workers to work harder. Individual workers had little chance to make suggestions or to participate in the key decisions. Understandably these workers began to view their officers as management stooges and eventually voted them out of office.

4.   PB members may participate in joint decision making regarding subjects about which they possess *expert* knowledge but confine their

activities largely to the conference room, making little effort either to discern rank-and-file opinions or to communicate to them. Under these circumstances management uses the PB member to legitimate decisions and to obtain what it considers to be typical worker opinions (even, though, in fact these may not be representative). The worker director in one British company was viewed as one

who would contribute to board business as one functional specialist among equals—his specialism being knowledge of shop values and opinions . . . his role was to contribute something new to management information resources rather than to make the shop floor aware of how the board works, or be responsible for putting forward or reporting back the progression of new or alternative plans derived from shop floor concerns (Chell and Cox, 1979, p. 29).

All four roles are dysfunctional when performed alone. Ideally, perhaps, the advocate, comanager, and expert roles should be somehow combined.

The Knowledge Gap. On the basis of experimental evidence, Mulder (1971) argues that when participants differ considerably in their expertise, participation accentuates rather than reduces differences in perceived power. This may well be the case with regard to much WPM. Management frequently fails to provide PB members with the information they need to make a meaningful contribution. Even when this information is provided, the members may lack the skills to evaluate it.

This knowledge gap is particularly serious for worker directors. After all, it is a big jump from work floor to boardroom. The role of worker director is very new and there are few role models to follow. The new director is unsure of how to handle himself at board meetings; more important, he typically lacks the skills to deal with legal, accounting, and marketing issues. Part of the blame for WPM failures in Peru (Berenbach, 1979) and Vermont Asbestos (Johannesen, 1979) is laid on the fact that the worker directors were insufficiently trained to perform their roles.

The knowledge gap helps explain the disillusionment and apathy reported in a number of cases, particularly in Yugoslavia. This apathy, in turn, leads to control of PBs by management, along with a small elite of PB members who are capable of bridging the gap.

To ease the bridging process, WPM rules in some countries (e.g., Sweden) specify the information PB members should receive. To help evaluate this information, training programs for PB members have been established in Britain, Germany, Yugoslavia, Sweden, and Norway. Even this is not enough. To match management at its own game and to avoid dependence on management's briefing, PB members must develop information sources of their own (BSC Employee Directors, 1977). All this takes time. To become really effective, many German works councillors converted their positions to full-time jobs.

But knowledge comes at a price. The more familiar PB members become with management problems and the more involved they become in dealing with them, the less sensitive they are likely to be to their constituents' needs and the more dependent they become on the management, which provides them their information. As Slichter (1941, p. 559) commented with regard to an early case of United States WPM, "Union–management cooperation turned out to be a process by which leaders gained such a thorough appreciation of the problems of the company that proposals that seemed unreasonable to the rank-and-file seemed reasonable to leaders." In some instances the co-optation process may be so effective that the workers' representative becomes little more than another member of management (Furstenberg, 1981, p. 14). Even where this does not happen, PB members "once elected and equipped with better access to information from 'the other' management) side begin to see 'both sides' and start to behave and/or appear as 'compromisers'" (Wilpert, 1975, p. 61).

Social Pressures. Social pressures, both within and without the PB, also foster co-optation. In the case of worker directors, there are strong, frequently explicitly stated expectations that they will represent the organization as a whole, not just their immediate constituents (Brannen, 1976; Thorsrud and Emery, 1970). "Existing board members" pressure them "to adopt an elite status and remove themselves socially, politically, and psychologically from a possible labor constituency" (Hammer and Stern, 1981).

> The company is seen in unitary terms. Worker directors in all [Western European] countries bear similar responsibilities to other directors. Their task is to look after the interests of the enterprise, although the responsibility for looking after workers' interests is often seen as one aspect of this general task. Accordingly there is little differentiation between the role of shareholder and worker representative; both are expected to defend the interest of the company as a whole. Court rulings in Germany have reinforced [this] view (Batstone, 1976, p. 14).

These expectations may be further reinforced by management-oriented training programs to which worker directors are sent; to counteract these, unions in a number of European countries offer training programs of their own.

Confidentiality. By custom or rule, company board members are expected to keep board deliberations confidential. This custom applies to worker directors as well. In theory, it could be a major block to communications. Certainly it provides an excuse for those who do not want to communicate. Thus, in the United States, the seven hourly paid workers serving on the Board of Directors of the partly worker-owned Vermont Asbestos Company kept the board's deliberations secret, despite rank-and-file workers desire to know how each director voted (Johannesen, 1979). Bradley (1980) argues that the perceived need to protect the company from outside competition will inevitably lead PB board members to withhold important information from the rank and file.

Nevertheless, most observers agree that confidentiality is not a serious problem in practice (BSC Employee Directors, 1977; Furstenberg, 1978; Batstone, 1976, p. 33; National Swedish Industrial Board, 1976), at least because PB members use discretion in what they reveal (Gunzburg, 1978). True secrets are generally respected, the few exceptions involving serious threats to workers well-being (Paul, 1979). Perhaps more of a problem is that PBs often deal with technical matters, at times in a somewhat legalistic manner. Even if the PB members understand what is happening, rank-and-file workers may not.

PBs Unrepresentative. Another block to communications is the fact that PB members often come from different occupations and reflect different values than the people they represent (Furstenberg, 1978; Batstone, 1976, p. 23–24; Berenbach, 1979). Better educated, skilled, male workers and union members tend to be overselected and "guestworkers" (in Germany) are underselected. White-collar workers hold more than their proportionate share of PB membership in Yugoslavia and Peru, but are underrepresented in Germany. A Norweigian study suggests that those who seek PB membership may be "management oriented" and suffer from blocked aspirations for upward mobility (Holter, 1965). Yugoslav workers council members have considerably greater interest in becoming managers than do nonmanagers (Obradovic, French, and Rodgers, 1970).

Professionalism and Elitism. As PB members develop expertise, they become more "professional" (Furstenberg, 1969). Indeed, in Germany (and perhaps elsewhere) a wholly new career path, that of full-time PB member, seems to be developing. In any case, the greater the influence PB members feel they have, the more anxious they are to be reelected (IDE, 1981: Table 8.6). Further, their superior knowledge and skills help them win reelection. Turnover in office is low, at least in Germany (Hartmann, 1979). In Yugoslavia and Israel, there are limits to tenure, but these can be evaded. The net result may be that the "representatives from an elite, and most members of the organization resign from actual participation" (Mulder, 1971, p. 36).

Breakdown in Communications. Whatever the cause, communications between PB members and the rank and file tend to break down. Council members fail to report what happens in PB meetings (Kolaja, 1966, p. 71; Sachs, 1975; Galin, 1980, p. 190; Gunzberg, 1978, p. 25; Adams and Rummel, 1977, p. 12; Johannesen, 1979). Even where PB members do hold meetings to report to constituents, such meetings are poorly attended (Adams and Rummel, 1977; Gunzberg, 1978). Perhaps PB members have good reasons for not making such reports; anyway, a German study (Hartmann, 1979) finds no relationship between works council "efficiency" (power) and the extent to which their members communicate with the rank and file.

Understandably, workers report that they know little about what happens in PBs and that PB members fail to represent their interests. Such attitudes are reported throughout Europe (Matejko, 1976, p. 921; Wilpert, 1975; Kolaja, 1966; IDE, 1981) and in United States Scanlon Plan companies (Driscoll, 1979). In turn, at least in Germany, workers are more likely to bring their problems to their supervisors and their colleagues than to their works councillors (Furstenberg, 1981, p. 9). As Wilpert (1975, p. 61) explains it, the "professionalization of representative functions could easily create an estrangement from the constituency. Representatives may now appear part of 'them,' the upper management. The cognitive dissonance of basic agreement with the idea of co-determination and dissatisfaction with its practice is then resolved by stating that 'the right people' were not available."

Obviously, this process can reinforce itself, as some PB members react to worker hostility by withdrawing into "safer" relationships with management, while, to alleviate suspicion, others behave less cooperatively than they might have otherwise (Goodman, 1979, p. 364).

How can PB member responsiveness be retained? Later I consider some of the suggestions that have been made for dealing with this difficult problem.

The Role of the Union

As we have seen, union attitudes toward WPM, as a *principle*, differ greatly. On one side we have French Communist and United States unions, who view WPM as weakening the adversary relationship and inviting cooptation. On the other side are German and Scandinavian unions, who see WPM as extending collective bargaining to the plant level. In between are schemes, such as the Scanlon Plan in the United States and works council control of welfare benefits in France, where WPM is the side show, concerned with integrative bargaining issues regarding which the parties have common interests; meanwhile, in the main tent, adversary distributive bargaining continues over economic conditions.

Related to the union's attitude toward WPM as a principle are questions concerned with the union's role once WPM has been introduced. Here we see a rough continuum.

No Union Role. Under self-management the union is either weak or absent. Although kibbutz members are nominally also union members, there is no independent union presence. Yugoslav unions are little more than welfare agencies. Mondragon had no union until apparently quite recently. In each case there was at least an implicit assumption that because the workers already managed themselves there was no need for separate union representation.

Unions and PBs are Rivals. The union may largely deny the PB's legitimacy as workers' representatives and treat management like any other management, and even strike against it (as it did in the worker-owned lathe company). This kind of relationship was a fairly common occurrence in Britain, where JCCs existed alongside increasingly militant stewards and where worker directors played an "expert" role, making no pretense of speaking for the workers as a whole (Chell and Cox, 1979).

Such a relationship appears viable chiefly when either the union or the PB is rather weak. If both are strong, rivalry is likely to develop between the two bodies, both claiming to represent workers interests. In Britain and Italy, the shop steward system existed alongside independent JCCs, just as long as the shop stewards were weak. Once the stewards gained strength, JCCs atrophied (Batstone, 1976). By contrast, German works councils quickly coopted and contained a union-sponsored movement for independent shop stewards (Hartmann, 1979).

Division of Labor. The union may accept WPM and the PB as legitimate, but keep collective bargaining and WPM distinctly separate. This separation may be required by law or occur because of management insistance or trade union preference. Often unionists fear that too close connection with WPM will result in the unions being coopted. To take an extreme example, union leaders were allowed to take only a limited role in Chilean self-management under Allende, purportedly because "if the union assumed management functions, then it would cease to lead the workers effectively in the class struggle" (Zimbalist, 1976: 50). From a very different perspective, Kochan et al., (1977: 83) argue that union and management contract negotiators should not sit on safety committees "because essentially different kinds of behaviors are required to make a problem-solving process work compared to the roles that must be played in contract negotiations.'' McGregor and Knickerbocker (1942) make a similar argument regarding the Scanlon Plan.

In some situations, as in German work councils, PB members are elected directly by the workers. In other cases they are appointed by the union, but the union makes sure that different people serve in each role. Worker directors in many British nationalized and private companies are expected to resign their union office once elected to the company board (Chell and Cox, 1979). Except for the union president, Scanlon Plan PB members in the United States may not hold positions in either the grievance or safety complaint mechanisms; neither may the PB discuss grievances or safety problems. A similar distinction exists in the Histadrut industries.

This separation occurs more frequently where collective bargaining occurs chiefly at the industry-wide level whereas works councils and co-determination are concerned chiefly with company- and plant-level personnel problems or where WPM covers the jurisdiction of several unions or both union and nonunion workers (BSC Employee Directors, 1977, p. 49).

In other instances active union officers may be appointed to PBs (particularly as worker directors) but abstain from discussion or absent themselves when collective bargaining issues are discussed. This is what President Fraser of the UAW announced he would do when he was elected to the Chrysler board. It occurs in Sweden, too (Batstone, 1976, p. 13).

The PB as a Union Instrument. The union may seek to use WPM as a form of plant-level bargaining and thus treat the PB as the rough equivalent of a United States plant-level grievance committee. This is what German unions intended works councils to become, though in fact the councils have maintained considerable independence. Swedish unions hope to do better in their new plant-level joint decision scheme.

The Union Runs Self-Management. At Kirby Manufacturing, a now-defunct British PC, the two trade union conveners (chief stewards) served also as the company's entire legal board of directors and as full-time company executives (Edelstein, 1979). In the state-owned Israel Electric Company, the union appointed three stewards to be full-time company officers (one as Personnel Director) while also serving as stewards. Eventually one steward was appointed general manager. (Galin and Tabb, 1978).

In a sense this last approach is like the first. Workers have no independent body to which to appeal. Indeed union, management, and the WPM scheme are rolled up into a single institution.

Tensions Among Roles. The third approach—that of separating the WPM and traditional bargaining roles—is probably the most common. Nevertheless the relationship between the adversary and collaborative functions is never easy. By fostering competitive power structures, such an approach makes conflict difficult to avoid (Peterson, 1968; Tanic, 1969; Hartmann, 1979; Galin, 1980). If nothing else, the leaders on the two sides may become political rivals. Driscoll (1979) observes that sometimes Scanlon Plan PB members may challenge incumbent union office holders. (But in plants where the Plan worked relatively successfully, PB members and union officers each tended to stay in their own "career paths," with the PB path often leading to a job as a supervisor.) On the other hand, in Germany, "works council election is generally the first step in a union career (Adams and Rummel, 1977, p. 19).

Beyond this, the two institutions represent different interests. From the union's point of view, PB members are too concerned with the economic success of their own firms. The union's focus is either narrower (*immediate* benefits for workers in the particular plant) or broader (the welfare of workers in the industry as a whole or of the working class generally). To take one example, union stewards in an Israeli plant fought for immediate wage increases while PB members argued for deferring these until the firm became more profitable (Rosenstein, 1977).

As unions "are organized on an industry-wide level they are much more interested in the progress within the whole industry than within a single factory"; so there are frequent complaints that PBs engage in "plant egotism," putting the interests of their own plant above those of the union movement generally (Furstenberg, 1978, p. 15; 1981). Indeed, in Germany, if there are separate union and works-council representatives on the company board of directors, the two sets of worker representatives may take conflicting positions (Batstone, 1976, p. 27).

To reduce this independence, German unions exert considerable influence to insure that the "right" persons win the works council elections (Furstenberg, 1978). Further, worker representatives on company boards are frequently key unionists (Batstone, 1976). It is partly to reduce possible union–PB conflict that British unions argued for "single channel" selection of worker directors (i.e., union appointment), a position supported by the Bullock Report (1977), and some British unions have reconsidered their opposition to having current union officers serve on company boards (BSC Employee Directors, 1977).

The Need for Union Support. Though unions are ambivalent toward WPM, union support seems quite important for WPM success. "In the last resort [the works council's] effectiveness is dependent on union power," even on the threat of strike (Adams and Rummel, 1977, p. 21).

Espinosa and Zimbalist (1978) found a significant ($r = .37$) relationship between union attitude toward WPM and WPM success. Without union support, the PB has little clout, a point that Kochan et al. (1977) demonstrate with regard to health and safety committees. With union opposition (or if the union or unions are divided by political rivalry) WPM will become a battleground, rendering cooperation difficult.

The Need for Checks and Balances. Much of the foregoing discussion assumes the existence of three competing power centers: the union, management, and the PB. But under workers self-management, the three parties may merge into one. Even where the parties maintain their institutional separation, the more cooperative they become, the less they check up on each other. The habit of working together leads the parties to assume that their interests are mutual.

The danger is that, to the extent this assumption of mutuality blocks consideration of problems where there is genuine conflict of interest, WPM may well increase discontent by preventing it from being brought out into the open. Unless discontent is adequately expressed through regular union or WPM channels, participation may lead workers to become alienated from their union as well as from management. It may also lead to strikes, as in Yugoslavia and Mondragon. As Whyte (1967, p. 25) puts it,

> Since conflicts are an inevitable part of organizational life, it is important that conflict-resolution procedures be built into the design of organizations. . . . [Cooperative relationships] do not arise when underlying conflicts of interest are ignored, but rather when the two parties have worked out procedures whereby the problems each faces are argued vigorously with each other.

Even under self-management there may be numerous instances where individual workers require separate representation.

1. Individual supervisors may be tyrannical, engage in favoritism, violate organizational policy, or just make stupid decisions.
2. The governing elite (top management, the PB, and the union, if present) may represent the long-run interests of the organization as a whole (as they tend to do in Yugoslavia); often these interests are inconsistent with the short-run interests of individual members. Quite often, for instance, the individual wants increased pay now, although the organization's long-run interest calls for investment; this conflict occurs particularly when, as in Yugoslavia, individual workers are not allowed to sell their share of the organizational assets.
3. Regardless of the organizational form, individuals and groups may compete for status or scarce resources, yet the "common good"

may not be clear. Under these circumstances vigorous argument may be required before a satisfactory solution can be reached.

If the union doesn't maintain its independence, then perhaps some independent institution is needed to expose inefficiency, to increase the range of solutions considered in decision making, to uncover new sources of leadership, to protect the rights of minorities, and generally to provide checks and balances. This point will be discussed later.

The Role of Management

Management support is critical to WPM success (for reviews, see Walker, 1974, p. 24; Espinosa and Zimbalist, 1978), yet it is easy to see why such support is difficult to achieve. WPM can be a bitter pill for top managers, who must now consult and negotiate before winning acceptance of the kinds of decisions that they once made entirely on their own. But it is even harder for middle managers and first-line supervisors who find that representative participation bypasses them completely.

There have been relatively few studies of how managers react to the *experience* of WPM (as opposed to their attitudes toward WPM in the abstract) and fewer still suggesting what the manager's role should be in a smoothly operating WPM system.

Top Management. According to the Webbs, "The relationship set up between a manager who has to give orders all day to his staff, and the members of the staff who, sitting as a committee of management, criticize his action in the evening, with the power of dismissing him if he fails to conform to their wishes, has been found by experience to be an impossible one" (Webb and Webb, 1920, p. 72).

Nevertheless, management tends to keep the upper hand, even in Yugoslavia. (Among the few exceptions to this rule: the kibbutz, where managers are rotated by design, and plywood PCs, where they are frequently fired.) With proper "handling," WPM may even increase management's effectiveness. Note, for example, how German management sometimes enlists works councils to handle difficult personnel chores and how Yugoslav workers councils help legitimate management decisions. Lammers (1967, p. 211) summarizes a common view when he says that WPM "can contribute toward employee motivation in the sense of heightened trust on the part of employees that their interests and views are well represented at top levels. Joint consultation can release relevant information to top executives, not primarily in the form of productivity suggestions, but rather in the form of insight into possible resistance to or alternatives for the managerial actions under consideration."

Still, WPM changes management's task and may lower its status. There is weak evidence (IDE, 1981, Tables 7.5 and 7.10) that WPM reduces top management's *absolute* influence and stronger evidence that it reduces it *relatively* (IDE, 1981, Figure 9.3; Tannenbaum et al., 1974; Nightingale, 1979). Managers of plywood PCs report lower job satisfaction than do capitalist plywood managers, even though PC managers are better paid (Bellas, 1972). Similarly Yugoslav and kibbutz top managers are less satisfied (and have more ulcers) than their United States, Italian, and Austrian capitalist counterparts. Further, workers in participative organizations are relatively less interested in being promoted to management than are workers in capitalist organizations (Tannenbaum et al., 1974, pp. 132, 83).

Supervisors and Middle Management. WPM threatens supervisors' power (Mako, 1978). In some cases their jobs are eliminated altogether, as in Dynavac, or substantially altered, as at Triumph Meriden (Edelstein, 1979) and Bolivar (Goodman, 1979). The power to discipline may be taken from them and handed to a workers' committee, as in Yugoslavia, Chile, and IGP (but in Yugoslavia supervisors are still the ones to initiate most disciplinary changes, Rus, in press).

WPM may also lead to the bypassing of lower levels of management. Workers belonging to PBs have contacts with higher management that are denied to their immediate bosses. German works councillors, for example, are more likely to communicate directly with higher management than with lower management (Furstenberg, 1978). The Scanlon Plan's suggestion system permits inefficiencies on the part of foremen, middle management, and staff to be brought directly to top management's attention, and many PB members do this with gusto (Driscoll, 1979; Strauss and Sayles, 1957)!

Not only do PB members bypass their bosses, but they become privy to information not available to them. (Somewhat the same problems occur when union members serve on plant-level or company-wide grievance committees. Sayles and Strauss, 1967.) As a British steel worker director put it, "Management below board level . . . became unsure of themselves, realizing that now I had access to levels of information they didn't have. . . . One day the department manager is my boss. . . . The next day I'm off to a board meeting, and its a meeting he'd love to go to" (BSC Employee Directors, 1977, p. 24).

Representing Managers' Interests. Middle and lower management participation may be especially important when WPM schemes are introduced. Enthusiastic top management support for WPM may not be enough, especially if this support inhibits frank expression of lower management concerns. Opposition from foremen at Rushton, whose power was reduced, and who were not sufficiently represented on the QWL steering committee, may have contributed to that QWL program being abandoned (Goodman, 1979). Schrank (1978) reports that management at Philips Eindoven in the Netherlands feared that extension of job enrichment would lead unionized foremen to strike. Ironically, Chilean evidence suggests that managerial policies that decentralize power to the supervisory level may actually inhibit WPM because supervisors may be reluctant to share their power with workers (Espinosa and Zimbalist, 1978, p. 52).

Managers need to participate, too. As organizational stakeholders, they have perspective and information to contribute. Further, beyond their links as links in the managerial chain, managers have personal and economic interests of their own. But how should their interests be represented? Trade unions, especially in Britain, have generally argued for "single channel" representation—through unions. If lower level managers want representation, they should join unions. Otherwise top management can speak for their interests. Essentially this was the position adopted by the Bullock Report (1977, p. 113) which said, "We do not think a special seat should be reserved for [professional and managerial employees]. . . . It would be unfortunate . . . to give the impression that certain employees had a special and presumably higher status in the law than other employees." By contrast, in some continental countries, works council members are elected on a "one man, one vote" principle, which gives managers representation equivalent to their number. Over strong union objection, the 1976 German Codetermination Act guarantees that senior executives will be given at least one of the seats on the "worker" side of the supervisory board. Norwegian middle managers, backed by their union, have shown much interest in serving on PBs (IDE, 1981).

In Yugoslavia, managers and staff not only serve on the workers council, they dominate it. On the other hand, PC boards typically exclude managers.

Foreman–Worker Relations. There is conflicting evidence as to whether WPM changes day-to-day managerial behavior. Insofar as there has been change, it has been toward making managers more participative. Nightingale (1979) compared managerial practices in ten participative and ten nonparticipative Canadian firms. In the more participative firms, workers perceived greater emphasis being placed on rules (as in Yugoslavia) and less on surveillance. Opportunities for initiative were greater and the hierarchy of authority was weaker. Communications were better and conflict was more often resolved by "problem solving" and less by "ignoring." (A caveat: Nightingale's sample included some forms engaged in direct participation only. In part, he may be measuring direct WPM itself, not the impact of representative participation.)

On the other hand, codetermination has done little to expand German workers' ability to influence what they do on the job. "On the job itself, management's discretion is hardly restricted" (Herding, 1972, p. 330). Many supervisors at Mondragon are autocratic and jobs are structured along traditional Tayloristic lines (Johnson and Whyte, 1977), though this may be changing. As we have seen, supervisors in union-controlled industries in Israel may be less participative than those in the private sector. Bellas (1972) found no significant difference in Initiating Structure and Consideration (Fleishman, 1957) between plywood PC managers and a small matched sample of their capitalist plywood counterparts. Further, Yugoslav and kibbutz industry managers may be less participative than their United States counterparts (Tannenbaum et al., 1974, p. 58), despite the Yugoslav and kibbutz participative superstructure.

The picture changes a bit when we look at quantitative studies. According to IDE (1981), influence of rank-and-file workers is positively correlated with both PB influence (Table 7.5) and perceived participative supervisory leadership (Table 7.22). Espinosa and Zimbalist (1978, p. 66) found a .70 correlation between shop- and plant-level extensiveness of WPM (though the two levels specialized in different subjects). Despite the limited efforts to formalize shop-floor WPM in Yugoslavia and Germany, the two countries with most extensive plant- and company-level participation, they ranked among the top five (of 12) countries in shop-floor *managerial* participative leadership (IDE, 1981, Table 8.8).

Few studies relate managerial behavior to WPM success. Ruh, Wallace, and Frost (1973) report that managers of plants that have discontinued Scanlon Plans tend to have less confidence in their employees and place lower value on participation than do managers in plants where the Scanlon Plan continues and is therefore presumably successful. Bellas (1972) looked at managers of plywood PCs ($n = 15$), finding a negative relationship between organizational performance and Initiating Structure but no significant relationship between performance and Consideration.

Aside from these studies, there has been almost no research as to how managers should behave under WPM. Conventional wisdom suggests that managers in WPM organizations should be patient, be good listeners and politicians, make decisions by consensus rather than by edict, and attend a lot of meetings. Beyond this, what should they do? Recall Adizes's (1971) two very different Yugoslav directors. Director XYZ acted chiefly as a facilitator of democratic decision making; decision making in XYZ was slow and cumbersome. By contrast, the more charismatic Director ABC took full advantage of his political power, social skills, and control over information to push through quick decisions.

Which form of management was more appropriate for WPM? This depends in part on the criteria one uses. Similar issues have been long debated in political science. Can government be run on a town-meeting basis? Or does effective democracy require strong leaders who initiate action and take responsibility for organizational success? Can the plant manager of a self-managed plant be a charismatic leader or should he be little more than a secretary to the works council? Or is there some viable compromise in between? Some argue that the most the electorate and the electorate's representatives can do is to react to initiatives, to criticize, reject, accept, or change them, and eventually to decide whether to retain the current leadership. Questions such as this have been barely raised by vestigial WPM theory.

TECHNOLOGY, VALUES, SKILLS, AND REWARDS

Having examined the role problems faced by people involved in WPM, I now turn to what might be called "contextual" variables that may affect WPM success: technology, values, skills, and rewards. As will be noted, many of these variables impact on WPM but are themselves changed by WPM. Each section begins with the relevant theories and then examines the somewhat scanty research that tests these theories.

Technology, Environment, and Size

Arguably, WPM will work best—in terms of increased employee influence—in small firms, with simple labor intensive technologies, where the work force is relatively homogeneous, where the work layout permits communications, and where the external environment is stable and predictable. This section considers some of these factors under three headings: size, production technology, and environmental turbulence.

Size. Theory suggests that WPM should be more successful in smaller organizations. In small organizations communications are easier, workers know more about the organization as a whole, and contacts between PB members and their constituents are more direct. The "knowledge gap" between management and workers should be less. Further, jobs are more likely to be homogeneous in terms of duties, salary, and status—thus making consensus easier. Finally, the smaller the group, the greater the social and economic incentive for the individual to work for the collective good (Olson, 1965).

Successful self-managing firms tend to be small (Bernstein, 1980). Kibbutzim and PCs rarely exceed 500 workers each. Mondragon, a decentralized organization, has over 15,000 members, but the participatory mechanism at Ulgor, its largest 3,000 member unit, seems to be largely ineffective (Johnson and Whyte, 1977). Yugoslavia shifted the emphasis of participatory mechanism to the shop level, justifying this as an attempt to strengthen participation. On the other hand, Scanlon Plan success appears unrelated to company size as long as the company has fewer than 600 employees (White, 1979).

Surprisingly, quantitative studies fail to support the hypothesized relationship between size and participation. Tannenbaum-type studies in Yugoslavia find no relationship between size and the slope of the influence gradient (Rus, 1970; Tannenbaum et al., 1974). IDE (1981) finds a nonsignificant but small positive relationship between size and two measures of direct and representative participation. Espinosa and Zimbalist (1978, p. 65) come to the same conclusion, using one composite measure. IDE (1981, p. 203) suggests that opposing forces may be at work here in small organizations "power sharing is achieved mainly through greater direct cooperation between workers and management"; in larger firms the PB acts as a counterbalance to management. An alternate explanation of the attitudinal data is that direct, face-to-face participation actually occurs in small organizations. Larger organizations, however, are more likely to establish formal participative schemes, at least on paper; once these are publicized, workers attribute to them greater influence for themselves. Relevant to this issue, works councils are more likely to be established in large German firms than in small ones (Wilpert, 1975, p. 60). Furthermore, works councillors in large firms tend to be better trained; and the better trained they are, the more "efficient" (in terms of accomplishment and "degree of participation") they become (Hartmann, 1979). On the other hand, voter turnout is proportionally higher in smaller firms (Furstenberg, 1981).

It may be that size places a restraint on self-managing organizations but not on forms of WPM that act chiefly to represent workers' interests with management.

Production Technology. Hypotheses abound here, but there is little firm evidence. Arguably, complex technology should widen the knowledge gap and reduce the homogeneity among workers, thus making participation more difficult (Walker, 1974). For example, as scavenging expanded from just garbage collecting to complex waste processing, control of the scavengers' PCs fell out of rank-and-file hands into those of technicians and managers (Russell et al., 1979). By contrast, Israeli agricultural kibbutzim do relatively little stoop or hard manual labor. They prefer growing crops which make use of mechanical equipment and their own technical skills.

On very simple work, workers may have very little to contribute. By contrast, craft work would seem suited for WPM because craftsmen are themselves a repository of critical production knowledge. Further, craftsmen are accustomed to exercising discretion and are less likely to be alienated from the entire system. Indeed, United States PCs have been especially common in industries involving the skilled crafts (Jones, 1979). Goldthorpe, Lockwood, Bechhofer, and Platt (1968, p. 108), found craftsmen to be the only occupational group to approve of WPM as a primary union goal. Finally, labor intensive production technology processes are more likely to be favorable to WPM (especially PCs; Aldrich and Stern, 1978), in part because in capital intensive processes workers' suggestions may be expensive to implement.

Espinosa and Zimbalist (1978) are among the few scholars to discover a statistical relationship between technology and WPM success. Their study of Allende-era Chilean self-management found artisan work was most favorable to the development of high levels of WPM, followed, in descending order by machine tending, continuous process, assembly, and assembly line work ($R^2 = .151$). Similar technological considerations moderated the relationship between intensity of participation and productivity. By contrast, Edlung (private conversation) found that in Sweden, process workers were most active in WPM, primarily because they had most time to talk. (The difference may be that Chilean WPM was driven by frustration, whereas Swedish workers responded to opportunity.)

Once more IDE data (1981, Tables 7.12, 7.13, 7.21, 7.22) are inconclusive, with different measures giving different results. Further White (1979) finds little relationship between technological factors and Scanlon Plan success. Two Yugoslav studies by Rus (1970, p. 154; 1979, p. 236) come to similar findings.

There has been little study of the impact of professionalism on WPM. I would hypothesize that professionalism would foster participation within a professional group but would legitimate efforts by such groups to protect their decision-making turf against the participative demands of nonprofessionals (Poole, 1975; Batstone, 1976).

Environmental Turbulence. Theory suggests that turbulence—rapid market changes, scientific advances, new laws—should inhibit WPM. WPM takes time, and turbulence requires both more and quicker decisions. Turbulence also increases the knowledge gap: The power of boundary spanners (many of whom are in management) is increased, whereas technological changes may make workers' traditional knowledge obsolete. Often, too, the effects of shop-floor decisions (e.g., those raising productivity) may be swamped by external changes over which workers have no control. Turbulence may even require PBs to keep decisions secret from the rank and file (Bradley, 1980).

Adizes (1971) describes how turbulence affected Yugoslav self-management. Prior to 1965, the twin objectives were to maximize productivity and participation. These goals were reasonably consistent, as participation mobilized workers' efforts toward clear productivity goals. After 1965, as the country switched to market economy, the emphasis changed from production to profits, and profits depended on selling the right goods for the right price. But with regard to sales and pricing, the workers could contribute little. Under the new system flexibility was all important, but "the democratic process, appropriately adhering to the system of maximum participation, made flexibility almost impossible" (p. 216). As in PCs (see previous discussion), self-management units were reluctant either to expand or contract employment. Even the United States Scanlon Plan may inhibit rapid technological change (Northrup and Young, 1968).

Zimbalist (1976, p. 53) reports that in Cuban farms and factories, "The uncertainty of the market is replaced by the clearness of the production plan. . . . Management at the farm and factory level thus is straightforward and largely demystified to the production worker. This facilitates a more equal distribution of power and more active participation by production labor in management." In other words, take the difficult questions out of workers' hands, and they can make a go of it.

Nevertheless self-management is not inconsistent with considerable technological change. Yugoslavia has enjoyed one of the world's highest rates of investment and economic growth (Batstone, 1976, p. 380). Mondragon has rapidly expanded into new technologies (but how efficiently will it abandon old ones?). In Chile, Espinosa and Zimbalist (1978, p. 165ff) found a positive relationship between extensiveness of WPM and various measures of technological change.

Once we move from self-management to codetermination, we find additional evidence that WPM *can* facilitate change. In Germany (Adams and Rummel, 1977; Batstone, 1976) and Sweden (Gunzburg, 1978, p. 22), WPM has been described as slowing down the decision-making process but making implementation much smoother. Indeed it may have increased adaptiveness and encouraged risk taking (for citations, see Batstone, 1976, p. 37). WPM is widely credited for Germany's peaceful run-down of employment in coal and steel.

Conclusion. The issues discussed here may more sharply constrain self-management than other forms of WPM. Self-management may be capable of handling only simple problems. Large size, complex technology, or environmental turbulence may easily swamp the fragile self-management vessel. However, to the extent that the function of forms of WPM other than self-management (e.g., codetermination) is not to run the organization but merely to represent workers' interests, the factors mentioned may be less constraining. Similarly I would hypothesize that technology would have less of an impact on representative WPM than on direct WPM.

Values and Skills

Logic suggests that if participation is to "work" (1) participants should want to participate, which requires that participation should be perceived to provide them with some rewards, whether economic or noneconomic, concrete or symbolic; (2) participants should have the knowledge and skills required to participate effectively; and (3) both management and workers should view participation as legitimate, a perception that itself is influenced by the parties' cultural and ideological values. Values and skills are discussed in this section, economic rewards in the next one.

Appropriate values and skills facilitate WPM's acceptance and sustenance. On the other hand, successful WPM helps develop values and skills.

The Impact of Values and Skills on WPM. Hypothetically, values and ideologies affect both the likelihood that (1) participative efforts will be perceived to pay off in terms of valued rewards and (2) WPM will be perceived as legitimate. The socialist ideologies in Yugoslavia, the kibbutz, and certain plants in Allende's Chile all taught that WPM would lead to a better world. Working for this world was socially legitimate. Further, participation made the organization "normative" and led to "moral" involvement (Etzioni, 1975) in working for superordinate organizational goals. In each case there was widespread initial acceptance of the values associated with participation, such as equality, a belief in the value of group decision making and responsibility, and organizational identification. In short, making participation work became an end in itself. Early religious communes had a similar involvement, although religiously rather than politically motivated. Professional organizations have an "ideology" of their own. WPM, as long as it is confined to professionals, is widely accepted as legitimate in universities, in many hospitals, and in scientific and welfare organizations.

Beyond this, WPM may be more easily accepted in societies where participation is valued generally. Johnson and Whyte (1977, p. 21) credit much of Mondragon's success to Basque society's equalitarian values, "associative spirit," and general atmosphere of trust. Similarly, the largely Scandinavian Pacific Northwest communities in which plywood PCs have developed are known for their support of consumer cooperatives. The kibbutz principles, with which children are indoctrinated— "voluntarism, cooperatism, and equalitarianism—aim at the complete identification of the individual with society" (Fine, 1973, p. 210). By contrast, we would expect strong hierarchical culture, such as in Peru (Whyte, 1969:chapter 32), to be somewhat less hospitable to WPM.

Finally, we should expect WPM to work better in situations where union–management relations were already harmonious.

Earlier sections stressed the importance of PB members developing at the least the minimum skills necessary to evaluate management's proposals. PB members need to learn management's language and management needs to learn to make reports intelligible to PB members. Thus, both parties need education. Even rank-and-file workers need education so they can evaluate PB members' effectiveness and prevent their cooptation.

Members of kibbutzim and counterculture communes in this country would argue that ability to evaluate PB effectiveness is not enough. Workers should be able to make basic decisions themselves. This means that knowledge should not be concentrated among a few high status experts. To help equalize knowledge and status, such organizations emphasize job rotation and continual training (Rothschild-Whitt, 1979).

The Impact on WPM of Values and Skills. Still, the importance of antecedent values and skills for successful WPM should not be exaggerated. German management ideology is supposedly autocratic; Yugoslav workers possessed few managerial skills in 1950. Yet WPM seems to have survived tolerably well in both seemingly unhospitable environments. Thus although it can be argued that appropriate ideologies and skills are required to make WPM work, just the reverse may be true. Participation (at least in its superficial forms) has been used in many developing countries to mobilize support for modernization, to legitimate change, and to manufacture consensus (Delacroix and Ragin, 1978). Numerous authors see, as one of WPM's main virtues, its enhancement of the values and skills necessary for a larger democratic (Pateman, 1970) or socialist (Vranicki, 1965) society. Yugoslav workers councils may be viewed as a massive management development scheme. The kibbutz trained a nation's leadership. At the very least, service on PBs helps develop management skills (Cupper, 1980). Experience in lower level PBs trains people for higher levels. Finally, motivation for participation "is learned; actual exertion of influence leads to a stronger motivation for further exertion of influence" (Mulder, 1971, p. 35). Experience with WPM may even change a worker's orientation from instrumental to expressive (Goldthorpe et al., 1968), thus in turn intensifying his interest in WPM.

This brings us to an old question bedeviling OD: Which should change *first,* structure or attitudes? Must attitudes change before structure can be altered, or will attitudinal change follow as an inevitable concomitant of change in structure? To be more specific: Could the Bullock Committee's recommendation—that British boards of directors be restructured to include equal representation of labor and management (plus some neutrals)—change Britain's disastrous labor relations? The Committee argued that the way to raise "the level of productivity and efficiency in British industry" was "not by recrimination or exhortation but by putting the relationship between capital and labour on a new basis which will involve not just management but the whole workforce in sharing responsibility for the success of the enterprise" (Bullock Report, 1977, p. 160). Would such a structural change transform years of bloody-minded, class-conscious, shop-level guerilla warfare into German-style harmony? Would British unions "accept a share of responsibility for the increased efficiency and prosperity of British companies" (p. 161) or would this structural change merely extend collective bargaining into the boardroom without substantially changing attitudes?

Social science research to date provides little ground for a firm answer. The IDE study (1981) suggests that formal participative schemes do indeed lead to perceptions of changed power and to greater satisfaction with the participative process. But we should note substantial differences between the German and British situations. German codetermination had widespread support during the late 1940s. Even management felt it was better than the total dismemberment of large plants. Both unions and management were weak, and the war-time experience gave everyone a desire to start anew. In contrast, British industrial democracy would have been crammed down management's throat; it would have had the support of only a few unions; and there was a long tradition of bitter, zero-sum gain bargaining. Further, even in Germany, unions have accepted very little "responsibility for . . . increased efficiency and prosperity."

Clearly this is not an either–or issue. Although favorable ideology and adequate skills facilitate WPM at first, it is the skills that workers develop and the economic and noneconomic rewards that they obtain that keep WPM going.

Economic Rewards

The role of rewards is rarely mentioned in the WPM literature (but see Wachtel, 1973; Bernstein, 1980). Yet for workers to exert the effort to keep WPM going they need to perceive that their efforts will be rewarded. Rewards can serve two purposes: they satisfy needs and, properly designed, they serve a form of feedback as to the participative effort's success. Rewards can be economic and/or noneconomic (moral). Economic rewards are discussed here. The role of rewards generally is considered in the concluding section.

Where participation is related to wages, fringes, or job security, successful WPM may carry its own reward (e.g., saving one's job). But where WPM is concerned with production decisions, workers in capitalist "utilitarian" (Etzioni, 1975) firms feel it only fair that if they produce more they should be paid more. Bernstein (1980) argues persuasively that such compensation should be (1) by right, (2) given everyone concerned, (3) apart from wages, (4) frequent, and (5) related to the success of the activities under workers control. Thus, if participation is at the shop level, then the bonus should depend on shop effectiveness.

The Scanlon Plan is among the few WPM schemes to meet most of Bernstein's requirements. It pays a bonus based on the previous month's production. Most United States job redesign programs (e.g., autonomous work groups) rely on moral rewards alone. This may be among their biggest weaknesses (Strauss, 1979b). In Hungary, as probably elsewhere, workers resist opportunities for more influence and independence unless this greater responsibility also leads to higher pay (Mako, 1978, p. 7).

In designing a WPM reward system, three questions are involved: (1) How equalitarian should the basic pay scale be; (2) How should the "profit" from increased efficiency be divided between present compensation and investment; and (3) how should the portion of the profits available for present compensation be divided among various claimants?

Pay Equality. Some PCs pay all workers alike, with some possible adjustment for need. Among these are the kibbutz, Triumph Meriden, the plywood PCs, and (for a while) the scavenger PCs (Edelstein, 1979). Other self-management schemes, such as Dynavac and Mondragon and those in Yugoslavia, provide for pay differentials, though there is some evidence that these have been narrowed by WPM (Cupper, 1980, p. 96; Oakeshott, 1978; Espinosa and Zimbalist, 1978). In Yugoslavia, the years 1956–1967 were associated with some decline in interskill differentials, perhaps due to WPM, and some increase in interfirm differentials, perhaps due to market factors (Wachtel, 1973). Arguably, pay differentials reflect power differentials, though the cause–effect relationship may be uncertain. Nevertheless, it may be no coincidence that some equal-pay PCs (kibbutz and plywood) have been among the most successful WPM schemes in terms of involving ordinary workers in WPM decisions.

Investments. The theory of investment under WPM has been heavily debated (Steinherr, 1978). The conventional view is that workers will prefer present consumption to some rather uncertain claim on future earnings, especially if present sacrifice is not directly related to future rewards. As we have seen, United States and British PCs provide some— not entirely consistent—support for this hypothesis (e.g., Jones, 1979, 1980). On the other hand, Scott Bader employees have voted for high investment levels (Bernstein, 1980), and Yugoslavia and Mondragon have enjoyed very high growth rates. Similarly Batstone (1976) concludes that codetermination has had no adverse effect on investment in Germany.

In Yugoslavia, total compensation (wages plus bonuses) tends to be set by labor market considerations; what is left is invested (Wachtel, 1973).

The Division of Rewards. The distribution of differential economic rewards is a prime cause of divisiveness in WPM systems. It has caused trouble in Yugoslavia, Dynavac, and in some United States union–management programs (Strauss, 1979b). Workers may resist creating divisions among themselves. In a Hungarian experiment, 14 work groups accepted management's offer to set their own wage scale but made it more equalitarian; the remaining five, who happened to be more cohesive, refused the offer altogether (Mako, 1978).

Conclusion. Economic rewards for greater efficiency may be necessary, at least in utilitarian organizations; and these rewards should be distributed in a manner that workers view as equitable. However, it should also be remembered that one presumed advantage of WPM is that it can also provide important moral rewards. A group bonus for high productivity can provide a concrete symbol of group success (Whyte, 1955) and thus serve intrinsic and extrinsic functions. But excess emphasis on monetary rewards alone may kill intrinsic motivation.

CONCLUSION

This concluding section seeks to pull together several themes which may help us evaluate WPM as a social intervention.

Outcomes

Is WPM a success? This depends on which of the many criteria one accepts. Productivity and satisfaction, the criteria mentioned by Locke and Schweiger (1979), are not the only relevant ones.

Survival. Those who say that WPM violates human or economic nature have been proven wrong. By the organization ecologists' test of survival a number of forms of WPM have taken root: German codetermination, Israeli kibbutz, Mondragon, plywood PCs, and Scanlon Plans have all survived for at least 25 years. Some of these successes have shown signs of degeneration or creeping bureaucratization; however, WPM as an institution has not yet been shown to be inherently unstable.

On the other hand, it is too early to predict the ecological niches in which WPM is most likely to be successful. Indeed WPM has survived in seemingly inhospitable cultures such as Germany and Yugoslavia.

Economic Variables. The evidence relating WPM to indices of economic success (e.g., productivity, profits, and worker earnings) is somewhat spotty. Because WPM is often accompanied by other forms of change, the impact of WPM alone is difficult to decipher. A few studies suggest that more participative firms function better than do their less participative counterparts (Rus, 1970; Melman, 1971; Bellas, 1972; Espinosa and Zimbalist, 1978; Svejnar, 1981); others find no significant impact (e.g., Batstone, 1976). Aside from a few PCs approaching "degeneracy" (Jones, 1980), there is almost no evidence that WPM firms do less well. In some instances, workers in PCs and in Yugoslavia have worked so hard as to engage in "self-exploitation" (Rus, in press; Eaton, 1979).

In theory, one would not expect representative WPM to have a substantial impact on productivity, especially because (except in the Scanlon Plan) effective PBs rarely discuss production questions or, if they do discuss them (as in Yugoslavia), management dominates the discussion. The main impact of representative WPM on productivity may be through reducing resistance to change and facilitating the handling of personnel grievances.

Job Satisfaction. Most studies of participation, formal or informal, show a positive relationship between extent of participation and overall job satisfaction (Locke and Schweiger, 1979). WPM research confirms this for direct, shop-level participation and personal participation on participative bodies. But there is little evidence that job satisfaction is higher in organizations enjoying representative WPM. The latter finding is a bit surprising, as one might expect positive relationships because of response biases and attribution effects.

IDE (1981, Table 8.18) found a positive correlation between job satisfaction (three measures: correlations .25, .23, .27; $n = 134$ companies) and extent of direct WPM but no relationship between satisfaction and various measures of representative participation. Rubenowitz, Norgren, and Tannenbaum (unpublished) report somewhat similar findings in a study of ten Swedish companies. Similarly, job satisfaction was no higher in worker-owned scavenger companies than in their capitalist or public-sector counterparts (Russell et al., 1979). By contrast, Nightingale (1979) does find that satisfaction is higher in participative than in matched nonparticipative firms, but his measure confounds direct and indirect measures of participation.

Industrialization and Management Development. As previously mentioned, self-management in the kibbutz, Yugoslav industry, and Mondragon has trained management and facilitated industrialization.

Management and Change. As we have seen, there is some evidence that workers' self-management may inhibit the organization's ability to adjust to change. Arguably, self-management works better when the goal is efficiency (making optimum use of current technology) than when it is effectiveness (successful adjustment to external stress). By contrast, codetermination, at least in Sweden and Germany, may facilitate rapid technological change. Nevertheless there is the prospect that, if our society becomes ever more turbulent, more and more decisions will be made externally by forces over which plant- or company-level WPM may have little impact. Employees may gain "more and more freedom for participation within a less and less free system" (Rus, 1979, p. 240).

WPM, whether self-management or codetermination, requires the development of some sort of consensus, at least with regard to major decisions. Commitment may take the place of control as the primary management tool (at least at the levels where WPM occurs). Responsibility may be shared, diffused, and blurred. Hypothetically, political skills may become more important for the manager than analytic ones. Nevertheless, Adams and Rummel (1977, p. 17) conclude, "There is general consensus that, due to codetermination, management has become more rational, more professional, and more efficient." (In fact, the requirements of successful management under WPM have been scarcely studied.)

Labor Relations. Codetermination has been part of the strategy of European unions to increase their power at the plant and company levels and to extend collective bargaining's coverage beyond wages. In part, codetermination merely brought United States-style labor relations to Western Europe. But European unions have gone beyond this: They can now significantly influence company investment decisions. They have been able to block layoffs, at least temporarily. Although they have not prevented plant shutdowns altogether, most observers agree they have significantly slowed the process down (Batstone, 1976, p. 34 summarizes the literature).

WPM is designed to change the predominantly adversary character of labor relations. To some extent it has been successful. This does not mean that differences have been obliterated, but their mode of expression is less ritualized. Though more research is necessary, it seems that PB members (and PB membership somewhat overlaps union leadership) have accepted considerable responsibility for overall organizational success. All this may have contributed to Germany's good postwar record of labor peace, especially in iron and steel (Batstone, 1976, p. 36). Strikes have not been eliminated in Yugoslavia, but all parties seem to accept the responsibility to keep them short.

Co-optation. It is widely charged that PB members will inevitably be co-opted. Co-optation is, of course, a standard technique by which the organization gains resources and neutralizes opposition (Pfeffer and Salancik, 1978). Hammer and Stern (1981) suggest that PBs serve three functions for management: (1) as an information *conduit,* upward and downward, between workers and management; (2) as a means of winning *support* for (or legitimating) management's decisions; and (3) as *appeasement,* that is, to control labor–management conflict. However,

> the success of cooptation as a strategy . . . depends on the ease with which targets can be coopted. . . . An offer to share power through board representation does not mean that an actual trade takes place. For cooptation strategies to work, it is necessary that a formal action like board representation . . . *not* evolve into real power whereby the worker representatives take full advantage of their positions to actually control board decisions. This means that the worker representatives have to be controlled informally (Hammer and Stern, 1981, p. 5).

The record suggests that a considerable amount of co-optation occurs, but that in many cases PB members also exert "real power" and influence, if not "actually control board decisions." Instead of being fully co-opted, they develop into a quasi-independent interest group that has interests (or at least perspectives) of its own. They are less interested in immedite profits or efficiency than is management and more concerned with the general welfare of the organization whole than are specific groups of subordinates.

Conflict. Earlier it was suggested that WPM—especially workers' self-management—might squash and hide interest group differences. Though this may occur in some cases, there is some evidence that on balance WPM helps bring such conflict out into the open. According to IDE (1981, Table 7.8), "frequency of conflicts" is positively correlated ($r = .26$) with PB power but negatively correlated with supervisors' power. The difference may be in the way conflicts are settled. Nightingale (1979) reports that, compared to nonparticipative organizations, participative organizations are more likely to use problem-solving as a conflict resolution technique and less likely to use ignoring or forcing. Rus (1982) concludes that diffuse social relations plus the "higher order" ideology prevailing in Yugoslavia combine to permit conflicts to be more easily surfaced and resolved.

Power Distribution. For some of its proponents, WPM's major objective is to equalize power. Clearly, in such countries as Germany, WPM has increased the power of unions at the company and plant levels, even though the power has to be expressed through the union's membership on PBs. Indeed unions have become the partner of management (albeit junior partner) in the operation of the economic sphere. PB members have gained power of their own, to some degree independent of that of the union. The impact of WPM on management is less clear. If we view total power as a fixed amount, as some socialists do, then management's relative power has been reduced. But Tannenbaum and others (see especially Lammers, 1967) argue that effective participation increases total power. By this standard WPM has increased management's power in many instances.

Reaction of Workers to WPM. Whether WPM in fact increases the power of lower participants, workers enjoying WPM *report* having more power than do workers not enjoying WPM (Nightingale, 1979; Russell et al., 1979; Tannenbaum et al., 1974).

Attitudes toward WPM as such have been extensively studied (IDE, 1981; Furstenberg, 1981; DIO, 1979; Adams and Rummel, 1977). The findings are a bit hard to interpret. By and large, they suggest that most workers support WPM as an institution, even though few report receiving direct benefit from it. Support tends to be positively correlated with both direct involvement with participation and with the PB's power, both formal (de jure) and actual (IDE, 1981, chapter 8). Satisfaction with participation is highest in Yugoslavia and Germany, the two countries with the strongest PBs in the IDE sample. Satisfaction with participation is also correlated with various demographic characteristics, although not consistently across countries. Insofar as there are negative reactions to WPM, they are directed either toward WPM in practice or toward individual PB members.

> A major difficulty with German participation is that it seems to provide the individual worker with little sense of involvement . . . the worker, although satisfied with the representation scheme, feels that he has little ability to affect his own destiny. Decisions are taken mostly at distant places and, although the worker may benefit from them, he has little perceived capacity to notably influence them (Adams and Rummel, 1977, p. 22).

Support for WPM as a concept is always stronger than desire to participate personally (Holter, 1965). In capitalist countries, the percentage of workers willing to serve on PBs ranges from 14 to 28 (IDE, 1981, Table 8.6) though it may be higher in Communist countries (Jacob and Jacob, 1979). Interviews suggest that the reasons for not participating in WPM are much the same as those for not participating in unions or democracy generally. According to a Hungarian report, participation is time consuming as well as a "new and hazardous affair . . . a worker . . . risks making himself ridiculous or even provoking social conflict. . . . [It] entails passing judgment, intentional or unintentional, on the work of others" (Hethy and Mako, 1977, p. 16).

This lack of involvement is readily understandable. Apathy is common in unions, governmental politics, and even in universities. A few people participate actively because they feel a responsibility for the larger organization and/or because they get their kicks from participative activity. But most people participate only with regard to subjects important to them and about which they feel some competence to affect the final result.

Desire to participate personally often consists of little more than the wish to be informed or to have the opportunity to discuss matters (Rus, 1979; IDE, 1981). Even in Yugoslavia, only 31 percent of the workers wish to "decide" the criteria for income distribution, and with regard to other issues desire to participate is less (Rus, 1979, pp. 232–233).

Even aside from personal participation, most studies indicate a greater desire for "influence" or "say" with regard to shop floor rather than higher level problems (Wall and Lisheron, 1977; Holter, 1965; Hethy and Mako, 1977; Ramsay, 1976). On the other hand, Yugoslav workers show equal desire to participate at shop and plant levels, perhaps because they are already familiar with plant-level participation (Rus, 1979).

What do workers want to have influence about? Generally, desire for WPM at the plant or organization level is with regard to topics directly affecting their pocketbooks: pay, bonuses, and layoffs. Concerns for participation at the shop level are broader: worker assignments, holiday schedules, personal equipment, safety and physical working conditions (Rus, 1970, 1979; IDE, 1981; Ramsay, 1976; Wall and Lisheron, 1977; Heller, Wilders, Abell, and Warner, 1979; Witte, 1980). There is some suggestive evidence that workers who have already enjoyed some WPM, as in Yugoslavia and Hungary, have different sets of preferences than do United States workers who have had none (compare Rus, 1979, with Witte, 1980 and Quinn and Staines, 1978, p. 178). The limited research suggests that United States workers appear to be more interested in participating in such subjects as work procedures than do their Yugoslav counterparts but much less interested in selecting co-workers or managers.

Pateman (1970), Mulder (1971), and Rus (1979) all argue that participation is addictive: the more one has, the more one wants. There is some evidence that perceived and desired participation are positively correlated (IDE, 1981; Rus, 1979). Nevertheless, just the opposite is possible: if experience with participation is disillusioning, desire for further participation may decline.

Impact on Shop-Floor Activities. As we have seen, there is some evidence that supervisors tend to be more participative in dealing with their subordinates in plants with strong PBs (IDE, 1981). On the other hand, except for a few cases in Scandinavia, there has been little reported effort to link plant-level representative WPM with shop-level job redesign efforts, such as autonomous work groups. (Indeed, Furstenberg, personal communication, tells how one German works council opposed the development of autonomous work groups, fearing that they would lead to the development of rival power centers, some of which might be dominated by guestworkers.) Except in United States plywood PCs (Bennett, 1979), there are few reports of shop-level discussions of production problems.

Similarly, only a few examples can be given of WPM involving more than one level with regard to the same topic. Among the exceptions, the Scanlon Plan deals with suggestions generated by individual workers, which are discussed by shop and plant committees successively. Here participation typically starts at the bottom (though occasionally management may use Plan channels to obtain advance reactions to proposed technological changes). In contrast, important initiatives start at the top in Yugoslavia but normally are at least cleared through shop meetings. Shop-level meetings are frequently asked to deal with plant-wide problems in plywood PCs (Bennett, 1979).

Aside from these perhaps significant exceptions, representative WPM seems to have had little impact on the shop. Indeed, German "codetermination has been least effective in providing shop-floor control" and "in humanizing immediate shop conditions" (Adams and Rummel, 1977, pp. 14–15, citing Herding, 1972). Given workers' propensity to participate only with regard to matters salient to their interests and about which they have some expertise, WPM is unlikely to involve large numbers of workers or to affect how they feel about their jobs unless it is extended to the shop-floor and job-design levels.

Requirements for Effective WPM

Knowledge of expectancy theory may be helpful in preparing a summary of the conditions under which WPM is most likely to be "successful." If workers are to invest effort into participation, they must expect (a) that these efforts will not be wasted and will in fact affect decisions (valence), which in turn depends on their ability (skills and power) to make their voices heard, and (b) that the decisions so made will lead to valued rewards (instrumentality).

Power. If workers are to exert the effort to participate, they must believe that their efforts will have some impact on managerial decisions. In short, that they must have power (see especially Poole, 1975). With so-called "managerial participation," management listens to workers' suggestions but retains the right to make final decisions. Or it may even grant workers the right to make final decisions, but only with regard to topics it feels are unimportant (even if some such topics, e.g., vacation

schedules, happen to be important to workers). But management is unlikely voluntarily to give workers extensive powers over subjects important to it. Even the paternalistic ex-owners of John Lewis and Scott
Bader retained a large measure of final say for themselves. Joint consultative committees in various countries have had little impact largely
because management has had the right to ignore their input.

For power to be securely in workers' hands, they must be able to have
the final say themselves (or at least to block management's action) with
regard to some significant topics. One source of such power is a formal
charter or law. But charters are not self-enforcing. Workers need independent sources of power to enforce their legal rights, for example,
a strong non-co-opted union or the credible threat of going on strike.
Power can also be drawn from status and control over resources, the
most important of which may be knowledge and having a key position
in the communications channel.

The major dilemma with regard to power is that one must have power
to exercise it. Union power is often controlled by its leadership. Experts
and other resource controllers have power. But how will WPM help the
powerless? Too often WPM is confined to a small elite.

Knowledge. As Mulder (1971) dramatically pointed out, putting people
with unequal knowledge together in a formally participative structure
actually increases the power differential between them and leads to
frustration.

Two kinds of knowledge are required: first, the organizational skills
to function well in meetings or a bureaucracy, and second, content skills
necessary to contribute to problem solving. The second is obvious, but
inability to function as a board member has been a problem in numerous
contexts.

It is hardly surprising that the totally untrained workers in Peru and
Algeria proved unequal to the demands of WPM or that the knowledge-
elite dominated Yugoslav workers councils. German PB members have
positioned themselves to gather knowledge; indeed their quasi monopoly
of it has increased strains with the rank and file.

Yet, as with power, there are limits as to the extent to which knowledge
may be equalized. As organizations become more complex, specialists
may increasingly outsmart generalists (at best, PB members are generalists). Indeed, by weakening top management's power, WPM may
strengthen that of the experts. "The end result of attempts at democratization could therefore be an extension of the autonomy and power
of experts whose perspectives and skills run counter to the interests of
workers, and this may be legitimized by apparently democratic structures" (Batstone, 1979, p. 256; see also Bradley, 1980).

Rewards. The outcomes or rewards of WPM take many forms: saving one's job, protecting oneself against tyrannical supervision, demonstrating one's political or technical problem-solving ability, reducing class differences. Rewards may derive either from the *results* or the *process* of participation (because participation will right a grievance in one's favor or because one just enjoys talking). Rewards may also be extrinsic (economic) and/or intrinsic (moral). Though there has been considerable analysis of the relative roles of extrinsic and intrinsic motivation among both psychologists (Staw, 1976) and socialist economists (e.g., Bernardo, 1971), little of this analysis has been applied to WPM.

Ideologically oriented WPM, as in the kibbutz and in the early days in Yugoslavia, can make organizational (or even national) welfare a superordinate goal. Unfortunately, the strength of such superordinate goals is likely to decay. The provision of other superordinate goals that will be of interest to more than a small, politically oriented group of activists is among the most difficult of WPM's problems.

Whatever the reward—intrinsic or extrinsic—it should be significant for the workers involved, and it should satisfy *their* needs (not the needs that liberal-minded consultants think they should have).

Introducing and Sustaining WPM

Not enough attention has been given to viewing WPM as an OD intervention, a form of planned change. WPM has been introduced for a variety of idealistic and materialistic reasons. Similarly it has been introduced in a variety of ways: by starting from the bottom up, as when individual San Francisco scavengers joined together to form their PC; from the top down, as in Yugoslavia, and in PCs formed by paternalistic owners; or through the instigation of intellectuals, as in some recent British PCs. None of these factors seem to have made much difference for eventual WPM viability. Only one firm conclusion seems justified: it helps to have a "shelter organization" (as at Mondragon), namely, an institution (or institutions) that can provide financing, technical advice, and ideological support. Such organizations now exist in several European countries.

Among the major findings of the IDE (1981) group is that the existence of formal (de jure) rules for WPM has a strong influence on workers' influence and involvement: in other words, that laws requiring participation in fact increase participatory behavior (at least perceived participatory behavior). But, as just discussed, laws are not enough; power and knowledge are also important. Beyond this, it seems to help if workers have a psychological sense of "owning" WPM (Gunzburg, 1978). (This is different from actual ownership of the firm, although clearly actual ownership encourages psychological ownership.) For psychological ownership to be felt, it may be necessary that the workers (or at least their representatives) make a substantial psychological investment to introduce WPM in the first place. This facilitates commitment. For example, the German and Swedish labor movements committed a considerable proportion of their political clout in the campaign to get WPM introduced. This heavy investment may have helped codetermination succeed. WPM success in Chile was closely related ($r = .50$) with whether plant nationalization was preceded by a struggle (Espinosa and Zimbalist, 1978, p. 103).

Theory would suggest that for WPM to be truly accepted, it needs some initial success. Once such success is achieved, WPM begins to develop the kinds of participative skills and ideologies that help sustain it. Participation may become addictive, at least for a while.

Plateauing. But early success cannot maintain WPM indefinitely. Even if early efforts richly pay off, without adequate reinforcement—continued triumphs—initially favorable ideology may decay. The first problems to be solved may be the easiest ones; later problems may be more difficult. Further, if expectations are too high, they become easily dashed. The state of perpetual mobilization for collective goals may become exhausting; the relative values of collective, superordinate, noneconomic rewards may decline and that of economic goods may increase. If the real reward system diverges too far from that proscribed by the participative ideal, faith in the ideal may erode. Along with this, the actual practice of WPM may increasingly be restricted to a small elite, and management may take over. All of this may have occurred in Yugoslavia. Finally, a new generation that lacks even their parents' initial commitment may emerge.

If plateauing is so likely a danger, how can WPM's initial verve be sustained? Hypothetically, a continuing effort might be made to widen WPM to cover more issues and levels. For example, if WPM begins at the plant level, it might be extended to the shop (e.g., autonomous work groups). If it initially deals primarily with personnel issues, it might be extended to production problems or investment. To the extent that more and more people gain success experiences for personally making participative decisions, the participative momentum may continue, at least for a while.

However, workers' willingness to participate directly in workplace decisions is limited. Except perhaps for short periods, the responsibility for daily decisions is likely to be delegated to a small elite (either by plan or by practice). Usually the elite is concentrated on the PB. The trick, therefore, is to keep the PB responsive.

Maintaining PB Responsiveness. The PB role is a new one and its incumbents are still learning to play it. Nevertheless, the members' role problems, arising largely from the conflicting requirements of expertise and responsiveness, are not that different from those of union leaders and congressmen. In each case they must deal with technical issues about which they know less than does management and more than does the rank and file. They frequently must make decisions to which some of their constituents greatly object; they must compromise when their constituents think they should hold fast.

Some members thrive under their conflicting role as part-worker, part-manager. "Being twin-hatted isn't a problem for me," one British worker director explained. "If you can't ride two horses at once, you don't belong in the circus" (BSC Employee Directors, 1977, p. 47). It takes courage, but it is not impossible to be adversary, comanager, and even partly expert, all at once. Essentially all this requires is that one agrees with management, when one thinks its proposals are in the workers' best long-run interests—and disagree when they are not. As do experienced legislators, wise PB members know how to keep experts "on tap, not on· top." (Some of the more effective worker directors in Britain had prior service on elected local legislative bodies. Handling management experts, they said, was not much different from handling civil service experts. BSC Employee Directors, 1977.)

To be effective, communications with the rank and file should be two way. PB members need to listen carefully to their constituents but also to educate them (Whyte, 1955). Face-to-face communication may be supplemented by news bulletins of various sorts (Bernstein, 1980). Attendance at shop meetings may improve if the PB member uses this opportunity to seek workers opinions rather than merely to make a speech (Bennett, 1979). Above all, the PB member needs to function like Lawrence and Lorsch's (1967) "integrator," sensitive to the values of both workers and management.

As in democracy generally, the PB member's responsiveness may increase when there is competition for his job. Furstenberg (conversation) reports that some of the most effective German workers councils exist in plants where there is an organized communist opposition. Perhaps WPM requires contested elections and even a party system. If this happens, will WPM be immobilized by pressure group politics? Does it need a strong executive?

But even a two-party system may leave the question of responsiveness unresolved. The United States political system has not been particularly successful in developing courageous political leaders who act only in the best interests of the country as a whole and who fearlessly educate their constituents to sacrifice their own special interests. For the most part, the rank-and-file member, whether voter or worker, tends to ignore the governmental process except when his own ox is being gored. Further, the task of industrial democracy may be even more difficult than that of political democracy. The political government may pass new laws that bother us *personally* only several times a year. Industrial democracy (whether self-management or joint decision making) involves the supervision of our daily activities. Being closer to us, it affects us more directly. Democratic determination of our daily behavior may be more difficult than democratic determination of general codes of social conduct.

Protection of Minority Interests. Democratic elections alone may not protect the interests of individual workers. The bulk of the membership may be apathetic; even with contested elections, the majority may tyrannize the minority; and both PB and union may be co-opted by management.

Bernstein (1980) argues that an enforceable bill of rights may help protect individual opportunities to dissent. But this is not enough unless there is some formal institution through which individuals *and* groups may express their viewpoints when the primary participatory channel becomes blocked. Without such an institution, self-managing organizations may be prone to oligarchy.

Even under worker ownership, United States workers prefer the union to preserve its separate role (Hammer and Stern, 1980). But if the union won't fulfill this function, perhaps some other agency, at least an ombudsman or appeals system, should. Mondragon's separate Social Council is supposed to represent workers' interests but does so with only moderate effectiveness (Johnson and Whyte, 1977). The John Lewis Partnership has a grievance committee, a separate appeals body, and a newspaper in which individual employees may publish anonymous complaints, which management must answer. Triumph Meriden has a grievance committee, Scott Bader an appeals board, and IGP a "community relations board", all of which serve as independent power centers outside the main WPM hierarchy (Bernstein, 1980; Edelstein, 1979; Zwerdling, 1979). Yugoslav firms (Adizes, 1971) and plywood PCs (Bennett, 1979) have disciplinary committees to protect individual workers against unfair discipline.

Considerably more attention is needed with regard to these essentially political questions of responsiveness and protecting workers' rights.

A Last Word

In terms of some of its proponents' objectives, representative WPM has had only limited success. It has involved top leadership more than the rank and file, and it has almost ignored middle and lower levels of management. It has not brought substantial power or influence to the ordinary worker; nor has it unleashed workers' creativity or even actively involved them in making production decisions. The division of labor between decision-makers and those who carry out decisions has not been abolished. Workers are not more involved in their work than before. WPM has not created a juster, more equal society.

WPM (or organizational democracy) has many of the strengths and weaknesses of political democracy. Despite the dreams of eighteenth century philosophers, it is difficult to show that political democracy has made our citizenry any more happy, law abiding, patriotic, or considerate of others. Similarly, there is little evidence that WPM has reduced workplace discontent, increased productivity, or created self-actualized workers. Perhaps all that either political or organizational democracy provides are orderly procedures for effecting compromises, developing consensus, and legitimating decisions. But this alone may make democracy of either sort worthwhile.

APPENDIX

A Research Agenda

For my taste, studies investigating such issues as desire for participation have reached the point of declining returns. Perhaps, too, some time should be spent digesting the results of recent international comparative large-sample, cross-section studies before undertaking a new wave. For the moment, researchers are long on data but short on explanatory hypotheses. Without further hypotheses as to the dynamics of WPM, further data gathering may be undirected.

Case studies may prove little, but they do suggest hypotheses. So my first priority would be for a series of carefully monitored longitudinal case studies that would follow the evolution of WPM in specific organizations from (or before) the date of its initial implementation for at least 5 years. Nonparticipant observation (as practiced, for example, by Adizes) would be the heart of each study. The observer would be concerned chiefly with how WPM (especially the PB) affects decision making, politics, and industrial relations within each affected organization. These observations might be supplemented by several waves of questionnaires (or interviews) designed to examine the changing perceptions of the principle parties (rank-and-file workers, union officers, PB members, supervisors, top managers, etc.) as to how participation is affecting their own behavior and the behavior of others.

Five years should be long enough to permit researchers to observe the dynamics of co-optation and plateauing. Aside from time and cost, the major danger with research of this sort is that the intensity of observation may affect the behavior being studied.

A second priority would be for cross-section, probably cross-national, studies examining how decisions are made regarding each of a small number of specific topics (e.g., layoffs, new investment, or discipline) under various forms of WPM. For example, researchers might compare a set number of (and reasonably equivalent) new investment decisions in 20 companies in 5 countries. Each study would examine the decision-making process in detail (as did the DIO group). It should report anecdotal material and not merely answers to questions such as, "How much say do you have with regard to. . . ." The emphasis in this research should be on WPM as a decision-making (or conflict resolution) process occurring over time, not on its psychological meaning.

A third priority would be to learn more about workers' attitudes toward engaging in WPM *themselves*. Years ago Sayles (1954) used projective tests to discover that though most union members supported their union as an institution, they evidenced a generalized hostility toward their leaders and a deep-seated reluctance to cause trouble by filing grievances. Are workers equally reluctant today to take part in shop-floor participative efforts or to initiate action through their PB member? Do workers ever gain a vicarious sense of participation through identification with their representatives' actions? Strikes provide an opportunity for active, physical participation. Are there psychological equivalents of the strike in WPM?

Projective techniques might also help researchers explore the differences in the meaning of various forms of participation across cultures. It might be fascinating to study the different meaning given to various forms of consultative actions by Japanese, United States, Yugoslav, and German workers.

REFERENCES

Abell, Peter. An evaluation of industrial co-operatives, the successes and failures. *International Yearbook of Organizational Democracy,* (forthcoming) *1.*

Adams, R. J., & Rummel, C. H. Workers participation in management in West Germany. *Industrial Relations Journal,* 1977, *8,* 4–22.

Adizes, Ichak. *Industrial democracy: Yugoslav style.* New York: Free Press, 1971.

Agassi, Judith. The Israeli experience in democratization of work life. *Sociology of Work and Occupations,* 1974, *1,* 82–109.

Albeda, Wil. Changing industrial relations in the Netherlands. *Industrial Relations,* 1977, *16,* 133–145.

Aldrich, Howard, & Stern, Robert. Social structure and the creation of producers' co-operatives. Paper presented to the IX World Congress of Sociology, Uppsala, Sweden, August 14–19, 1978.

Alutto, Joseph A., & Belasco, James A. A typology for participation in organizational decision making. *Administrative Science Quarterly*, 1972, *17*, 117–125.

Arzensek, Vladimir. Managerial legitimacy and organizational conflict. In Josip Obradovic & William N. Dunn (Eds.), *Workers' self-management and organizational power in Yugoslavia*. Pittsburg, PA: University Center for International Studies, University of Pittsburg, 1978.

Batstone, Eric. Industrial democracy and worker representation at board level: A review of the European experience. In Eric Batstone & P. L. Davies (Eds.), *Industrial democracy*. London: Her Majesty's Stationery Office, 1976.

Batstone, Eric. Systems of domination, accommodation and industrial power. In T. R. Burns, L. E. Karlsson, & V. Rus (Eds.), *Work and power*. London: Sage, 1979.

Baumgartner, Tom, Burns, Tom R., & Sekulic, Dusko. Self-management, market, and political institutions in conflict: Yugoslav development patterns and dialectics. In T. R. Burns, L. E. Karlsson, & V. Rus (Eds.), *Work and power*. London: Sage, 1979.

Bellas, Carl J. *Industrial democracy and the worker owned firm: A study of twenty-one plywood companies in the Pacific Northwest*. New York: Praeger, 1972.

Bennett, Leamon. When employees run the company. *Harvard Business Review*, 1979, *57*, 75–90.

Ben-Porat, A. Political parties and democracy in the Histadrut. *Industrial Relations*, 1979, *18*, 237–243.

Berenbach, Shari. Peru's social property: Limits to participation. *Industrial Relations*, 1979, *18*, 370–375.

Berger, Bennett. *The Survival of a Counterculture*. Berkeley: University of California Press, 1981.

Berman, K. F. *Worker-owned plywood companies: An economic analysis*. Washington: Pullman, 1967.

Bernardo, Robert M. *The theory of moral incentives in Cuba*. University, AL: University of Alabama Press, 1971.

Bernstein, Paul. *Workplace democratization, its internal dynamics*. New Brunswick, NJ: Transaction Books, 1980.

Bertsch, Gary K., & Obradovic, Josip. Participation and influence in Yugoslav self-management. *Industrial Relations*, 1979, *18*, 322–329.

Blum, Fred H. *Work and community: The Scott Bader Commonwealth and the quest for a new social order*. London: Routledge and Kegan Paul, 1968.

Bornstein, Stephen, & Fine, Keitha. Worker control in France: Recent political developments. In G. David Garson (Ed.), *Worker self-management in industry: The West European experience*. New York: Praeger, 1977.

Bradley, Keith. A comparative analysis of producer cooperatives: Some theoretical and empirical implications. *British Journal of Industrial Relations*, 1980, *18*, 155–168.

Brannen, P. *The worker directors: A sociology of participation*. London: Hutchinson, 1976.

BSC (British Steel Corporation) Employee Directors. *Worker directors speak*. Westmead, England: Gower Press, 1977.

Broekmeyer, Marius. Self-management in Yugoslavia. *Annals of the American Academy of Political and Social Science*, 1977, *431*, 133–140.

Bull, P. E., & Barton, G. A. Attitudes towards worker participation. *Journal of Industrial Relations*, 1978, *20*, 303–310.

Bullock, Lord Alan. *Report of the Committee of Inquiry on Industrial Democracy*. London: Her Majesty's Stationery Office, 1977.

Burt, W. J. Workers participation in management in Yugoslavia. *International Institute for Labour Studies Bulletin*, 1972, *9*, 129–172.

Chamberlain, Neil W. *Forces of Change in Western Europe*. London: McGraw-Hill, 1980.

Chaplin, P., & Cowe, R. A survey of contemporary British worker cooperatives, Manchester Business School Working Papers, 1977.
Chell, Elizabeth, & Cox, Derek. Worker directors and collective bargaining. *Industrial Relations Journal*, 1979, *10*, 25–31.
Clarke, R. O., Fatchett, D. J., & Roberts, Ben C. *Workers participation in management in Britain*. London: Heinemann, 1979.
Clegg, Hugh A. *A new approach to industrial democracy*. Oxford: Basil Blackwell, 1960.
Clegg, Ian. *Workers' self-management in Algeria*. London: Allen Lane, 1971.
Coates, Ken, & Topham, Anthony (Eds.), Industrial democracy in Great Britain. London: MacGibbon and Kee, 1968.
Conte, Michael, & Tannenbaum, Arnold. Employee owned companies: Is the difference measureable? *Monthly Labor Review*, 1978, *101*, 23–28.
Cupper, Les. Self-management: The Dynavac experiment. In Russell Lansbury (Ed.), *Democracy in the work place*. Melbourne: Longman Cheshire, 1980.
Dachler, H. Peter, & Wilpert, Bernhard. Conceptual dimensions and boundaries of participation in organizations: A critical evaluation. *Administrative Science Quarterly*, 1978, *23*, 1–39.
Daniel, W. W. Understanding employee behaviour in its context. In J. Child (Ed.), *Man and organization*. New York: Wiley, 1973.
de Bellecombe, L. Greyfie. Workers participation in management in Poland. *International Institute of Labour Studies Bulletin*, 1968, *5*, 188–220.
Delacroix, Jacques, & Ragin, Charles. Modernizing institutions, mobilization, and third world countries: A cross-national study. *American Journal of Sociology*, 1978, *84*, 123–150.
Derber, Milton. *Labor-management relations at the plant level under industry-wide bargaining*. Urbana, IL: University of Illinois Press, 1955.
Derber, Milton. Advancing Australian union democracy. *Industrial Relations*, 1978, *17*, 112–116.
de Schweinitz, Dorothy, *Labor and management in a common enterprise*. Cambridge, MA: Harvard University Press, 1949.
DIO (Decisions in Organizations). Participative decision making: A comparative study. *Industrial Relations*, 1979, *18*, 295–309.
Drenth, P. The works council in the Netherlands. In Eugene Pusic (Ed.), *Participation and self-management*. Zagreb: 1973.
Driscoll, James W. Working creatively with the union: Lessons from the Scanlon Plan. *Organizational Dynamics*, 1979, *8*, 61–80.
Dunlop, John T. *Industrial relations systems*. New York: Holt, Rinehart, and Winston, 1958.
Eaton, Jack. The Basque workers' cooperative. *Industrial Relations Journal*, 1979, *10*, 32–40.
Edelstein, J. David. Trade unions in British producers' cooperatives. *Industrial Relations*, 1979, *18*, 358–363.
Elliott, John. *Conflict or cooperation: the growth of industrial democracy*. London: Kogan Page, 1978.
Engelstad, Per, & Quale, Thoralf. *Innsyn og innflytelse i styre og bedritsforsamling* (Understanding and influence in boards of directors). Oslo: Tiden, 1977.
Espinosa, Juan G., & Zimbalist, Andrew S. *Economic democracy: Workers' participation in Chilean industry, 1970–73*. New York: Academic Press, 1978.
Etzioni, Amitai. *A comparative analysis of complex organizations*. New York: Free Press, 1975.

Fine, Keitha. Workers participation in Israel. In Gerry Hunnius, G. David Garson, & John Case (Eds.), *Workers control*. New York: Vintage Books, 1973.

Flanders, Allan, Pomeranz, Ruth, & Woodward, Joan. *Experiment in industrial democracy*. London: Faber & Faber, 1968.

Fleishman, E. A. A leader behavior description for industry. In R. M. Stogdill & A. E. Coons (Eds.), *Leader behavior: Its description and measurement*. Columbus, OH: Bureau of Business Research, 1957.

Fogarty, M. Co-determination and company structure in Germany. *British Journal of Industrial Relations*, 1964, 2, 79–113.

Furstenburg, Fredrick. Workers' participation in management in the Federal Republic of Germany. *International Institute for Labour Studies Bulletin*, 1968, 6, 94–148.

Furstenberg, Fredrick. *Workers' participation in management in the Federal Republic of Germany*. Geneva: International Institute for Labour Studies, Research Series No. 32, 1978.

Furstenberg, Fredrick. Co-determination and its contribution to industrial democracy. *Proceedings of the thirty-third annual meeting of the Industrial Relations Research Association*, 1981, 185–190.

Galin, Amira. An evaluation of industrial democracy schemes in Israel. In Russell Lansbury (Ed.), *Democracy in the workplace*. Melbourne: Longman Chesire, 1980.

Galin, Amira, & Tabb, Jay. *Workers participation in management in Israel, successes and failures*. Geneva: International Institute for Labour Studies, Research Series No. 29, 1978.

Gamson, Zelda, & Levin, Henry. *Obstacles to the Survival of Democratic Workplaces*. Unpublished manuscript, 1980.

Garson, G. David. *Workers self-management in industry: The West European experience*. New York: Praeger, 1977.

Globerson, Arie. Spheres and levels of employee participation in organizations: Elements of a conceptual model. *British Journal of Industrial Relations*, 1970, 8, 252–262.

Gold, Charlotte. *Employer-employee committees and worker participation*. Ithaca: New York State School of Industrial and Labor Relations, Cornell University, 1976.

Goldstein, S. G. Employee share ownership and motivation. *Journal of Industrial Relations*, 1978, 20, 311–330.

Goldthorpe, J. H., Lockwood, D., Bechhofer, F., & Platt, J. *The affluent worker: Industrial attitudes and behavior*. Cambridge: Cambridge University Press, 1968.

Goodman, Paul, *Assessing organizational change: The Rushton quality of work experiment*. New York: Wiley, 1979.

Greenberg, Edward S. *Producer cooperatives and democratic theory: the case of the plywood firms*. Unpublished manuscript, 1978.

Gunn, Christopher. Towards workers' control. *Working Papers for a New Society*, 1980, 7, 4–7.

Gunzburg, Doron. *Industrial democracy approaches in Sweden: An Australian view*. Melbourne: Productivity Promotion Council of Australia, 1978.

Haire, Mason, Ghiselli, Edwin E., & Porter, Lyman W. *Managerial thinking: An international study*. New York: Wiley, 1966.

Hammer, Tove, & Stern, Robert. Employee ownership: Implications for the organizational distribution of power. *Academy of Management Journal*, 1980, 23, 78–100.

Hammer, Tove, & Stern, Robert. *Worker members on company boards of directors*, unpublished manuscript, Cornell University, 1981.

Harrison, Roger, *Workers' participation in Western Europe, 1976*. London: Institute of Personnel Management, 1976.

Hartmann, Heinz. Codetermination in West Germany. *Industrial Relations*, 1970, *9*, 137–147.

Hartmann, Heinz. Works councils and the iron law of oligarchy. *British Journal of Industrial Relations*, 1979, *17*, 70–82.

Heller, Frank, Wilders, Malcolm, Abell, Peter, & Warner, Malcolm. *What do the British want from participation and industrial democracy?* London: Anglo-German Foundation for the Study of Industrial Society, 1979.

Herding, Richard. *Job control and union structure*. Rotterdam: Rotterdam University Press, 1972.

Hethy, L., & Mako, C. Workers direct participation in decisions in Hungarian factories. *International Labour Review*, 1977, *116*, 9–21.

Holter, Harriet. Attitudes towards employee participation in company decision-making processes. *Human Relations*, 1965, *18*, 297–321.

Hunnius, Gerry, Garson, G. David, & Case, John (Eds.). *Workers' control: A reader on labor and social change*. New York: Random House, 1973.

IDE, Industrial Democracy in Europe International Research Group. Participation: Formal rules, influence and involvement. *Industrial Relations*, 1979, *18*, 273–294.

IDE, Industrial Democracy in Europe International Research Group. *Industrial democracy in Europe*. London: Oxford, 1981.

Jacob, Betty M. The effective trade union. In *Automation and industrial workers*, 2. Oxford: Pergamon, 1978.

Jacob, Betty M., & Jacob, Philip E. *Automation and humanization*. Honolulu: Research Corporation of the University of Hawaii, 1979.

Jacob, Philip, & Ahn, Chungsi. Around the world on the automated line. *The Wharton Magazine*, 1979, 64–67.

Jacob, Philip, Jez, V., Koval, B., Margulies, F., Rantalaiho, L., Rehak, J., & Wieser, G. (Eds.). *Automation and industrial workers: International comparisons*. Oxford: Pergamon, (in press).

Jain, H., Vanachter, O., & Gevers, P. Success and problems with participative schemes—the case of Belgium. In Hem C. Jain (Ed.), *Worker participation: Success and problems*. New York: Praeger, 1980.

Jaques, Eliot. *The changing culture of the factory*. London: Tavistock, 1951.

Johannesen, Janette Eadon. VAG: A need for education. *Industrial Relations*, 1979, *18*, 364–369.

Johnson, Ana G., & Whyte, William F. The Mondragon system of worker production cooperatives. *Industrial and Labor Relations Review*, 1977, *31*, 18–30.

Jones, Derek C. Worker participation in management in Britain. In G. David Garson (Ed.), *Worker self-management in industry*. New York: Praeger, 1977.

Jones, Derek C. U.S. producer cooperatives: The record to date. *Industrial Relations*, 1979, *18*, 342–357.

Jones, Derek C. Producer cooperatives in industrialized Western economies. *British Journal of Industrial Relations*, 1980, *18*, 141–154.

Jones, Derek C., & Backus, David K. British producer cooperatives in the footwear industry: An empirical evaluation of the theory of financing. *Economic Journal*, 1977, *87*, 488–510.

Jovanov, Neca. Strikes and self-management. In Josip Obradovic & William Dunn (Eds.), *Workers' self-management and organizational power in Yugoslavia*. Pittsburgh, PA: University of Pittsburgh, 1978.

Kelley, Joe. *Is scientific management possible? A critical examination of Glacier's theory of organization*. London: Faber & Faber, 1968.

Kester, Gerard. *Transition to workers' self-management: Its dynamics in the decolonizing economy of Malta.* The Hague: Institute for Social Studies, 1980.

Kochan, Thomas A., Dyer, Lee, & Lipsky, David. *The Effectiveness of union-management safety and health committees.* Kalamazoo, MI: Upjohn, 1977.

Kolaja, Jiri. *A Polish factory: A case study of workers' participation in decision making.* Lexington, KY: University of Kentucky Press, 1960.

Kolaja, Jiri. *Workers' councils: The Yugoslav experience.* New York: Praeger, 1966.

Koziara, Edward C. Workers' participation in Malta. *Industrial Relations,* 1979, *18,* 381–384.

Lammers, Cornelius J. Power and participation in decision-making in formal organizations. *American Journal of Sociology,* 1967, *73,* 201–216.

Lane, David, & O'Dell, Felicity. *The soviet worker: Social class, education, and control.* New York: St. Martin's Press, 1978.

Lansbury, Russell (Ed.), *Democracy in the work place.* Melbourne: Longman, 1980.

Lawrence, Paul R., & Lorsch, Jay W. *Organization and environment: Managing differentiation and integration.* Boston: Division of Research, Harvard Business School, 1967.

Legendre, M. *Quelques aspects des relations professionnelles.* Paris: Service d'Etudes pour le Developpement, 1969.

Leviaton, Uri. Organizational effects of management turnover in kibbutz production branches. *Human Relations,* 1978, *31,* 1001–1018.

Little, D. Richard. *Political participation and the soviet system. Problems of communism,* 1980, *29,* 62–67.

Locke, Edwin, & Schweiger, David M. Participation in decision-making: One more look. In Barry Staw and L. L. Cummings (Ed.), *Research in organizational behavior,* 1. Greenwich, Conn.: JAI Press.

Lockett, M. Organizational democracy and politics in China. *International Yearbook of Organizational Democracy,* (in progress) *1.*

Logue, John. On the road toward worker-run companies? The employee participation act in practice. *Working Life in Sweden,* 1978, *9.*

Long, Richard. The effects of employee ownership on organizational identification, employee job attitudes, and organizational performance. *Human Relations,* 1978a, *31,* 29–48.

Long, Richard. The relative effects of share ownership vs. control on job attitudes in an employee owned company. *Human Relations,* 1978b, *31,* 753–764.

Long, Richard. Desires for and patterns of worker participation in decision-making after conversion to employee ownership. *Academy of Management Journal,* 1979, *22,* 611–617.

Long, Richard. Job attitudes and organizational performance under employee ownership. *Academy of Management Journal,* 1980, *23,* 726–737.

Lowin, Aaron. Participative decision making: A model, literature critique, and prescriptions for research. *Organizational Behavior and Human Performance,* 1968, *3,* 68–106.

Mako, Csaba. *Shopfloor democracy and the socialist enterprise.* University of Turko, Sociological Studies Series A:3, 1978.

Maley, Brian, Dunphy, Dexter, & Ford, Bill. *Industrial democracy and worker participation.* Adelaide, South Australia: Unit for Industrial Democracy, 1979.

Marclay, Annette. *Workers participation in management—a selected bibliography, 1950–1970.* Geneva: International Labor Organization, 1971.

Martin, Andrew. Sweden: Industrial democracy and social democratic strategy. In G. David Garson (Ed.), *Worker self-management in industry: The West European experience.* New York: Praeger, 1977.

Matejko, Alexander. Work and management in Poland. In Robert Dubin (Ed.), *Handbook of work, sociology, and society*. Chicago: Rand McNally, 1976.

McGregor, Andrew. Rent extraction and the survival of agricultural production cooperatives. *American Journal of Agricultural Economics*, 1977, *59*, 478–488.

McGregor, Douglas, & Knickerbocker, Irving R. Union-management cooperation: A psychological analysis," *Personnel*, 1942, *19*.

Melman, S. Managerial vs. cooperative decision making in Israel. *Studies in Comparative International Development*, 1970–71, *6*, 47–58.

Michael, Avraham, & Bar-El, Rafael. *Strikes in Israel: 1960–69: A quantitative approach*. Ramat-Gan: Bar-Ilan University, 1977.

Miller, Richard F. Worker self-management in Yugoslavia. *Journal of Industrial Relations*, 1978, *20*, 264–285.

Mulder, Mark. Power equalization through participation. *Administrative Science Quarterly*, 1971, *16*, 31–38.

National Institute of Industrial Psychology. *Joint consultation in British industry*. London: The Institute, 1952.

National Swedish Industrial Board. *Board representation of employees in Sweden*. Stockholm: LiberForlag, 1976.

Nightingale, Donald V. The formally participative organization. *Industrial Relations*, 1979, *18*, 310–321.

Northrup, Herbert R., & Young, Harvey A. The causes of industrial peace revisited. *Industrial and Labor Relations Review*, 1968, *22*, 31–47.

Oakeshott, Robert. *The case for workers' co-ops*. London: Routledge & Kegan Paul, 1978.

Obradovic, Josip. Participation and work attitudes in Yugoslavia. *Industrial Relations*, 1970, *9*, 161–169.

Obradovic, J. Workers' participation: Who participates? *Industrial Relations*, 1975, *14*, 32–44.

Obradovic, Josip. Participation in enterprise decision-making. In Josip Obradovic & William N. Dunn, *Workers' self-management and organizational power in Yugoslavia*. Pittsburgh, PA: University Center for International Studies, University of Pittsburgh, 1978.

Obradovic, Josip, French, R. P. John, & Rodgers, Willard L. Workers' councils in Yugoslavia: Effects on perceived participation and satisfaction of workers, *Human Relations*, 1970, *23*, 459–471.

Olson, Mancur. *The logic of collective action*. Cambridge: Harvard University Press, 1965.

Pateman, Carole. *Participation and democratic theory*. London: Cambridge University Press, 1970.

Paul, Bill. Germany's requiring of workers on boards causes many problems. *Wall Street Journal*, 1979, December 10, p. 1.

Perry, Stewart. *San Francisco scavengers: Dirty Work and the pride of ownership*. Berkely, CA: University of California Press, 1978.

Peterson, Richard B. The Swedish experience with industrial democracy. *British Journal of Industrial Relations*, 1968, *6*, 185–203.

Pfeffer, Jeffrey, & Salancik, Gerald R. *The external control of organizations*. New York: Harper & Row, 1978.

Poole, Michael. *Workers participation in industry*. Boston, MA: Routledge & Kegan Paul, 1975.

Pugh, D. S., Hickson, D. J., Hinings, C. R., & Turner, C. Dimensions of organizational structure. *Administrative Science Quarterly*, 1968, *13*, 65–105.

Quinn, Robert P., & Staines, Graham. *1977 quality of employment survey*. Ann Arbor, MI: University of Michigan, Institute for Social Research, 1978.

Ramondt, Joop. Workers self-management and its constraints: The Yugoslav experience. *British Journal of Industrial Relations*, 1979, *17*, 83–94.

Ramsay, Harvie. Participation: The shop floor view. *British Journal of Industrial Relations,* 1976, *14,* 128–141.

Riddell, D. S. Social self-government: The background and theory in Yugoslavian socialism. *British Journal of Sociology,* 1968, *19,* 47–75.

Rosenberg, Richard, & Rosenstein, Eliezar. Participation and productivity: An empirical study. *Industrial and Labor Relations Review,* 1980, *33,* 355–367.

Rosenstein, Eliezar. Worker participation in Israel: Experience and lessons. *Annals of the American Academy of Political and Social Science,* 1977, *431,* 113–122.

Rosner, Menachem. Political and organizational democracy in the Israeli kibbutz. *International Yearbook of Organizational Democracy,* (forthcoming) *1.*

Rothschild-Whitt, Joyce. The Collectivist Organization: An Alternative to Rational-Bureaucratic Models. *American Sociological Review,* 1979, *44,* 509–527.

Rubenowitz, S., Norgren, F., & Tannenbaum, A. S. Some social psychological effects of direct and indirect participation in ten Swedish companies. Unpublished manuscript, 1980.

Ruh, Robert A., Wallace, Roger L., & Frost, Carl F. Management attitudes and the Scanlon Plan. *Industrial Relations,* 1973, *12,* 282–288.

Rus, Veljko. Influence structure in Yugoslav enterprise. *Industrial Relations,* 1970, *9,* 148–160.

Rus, Veljko. Limited effects of worker participation and political counter-power. In Tom Burns, Lars E. Karlsson, & V. Rus (Eds.), *Work and power.* London: Safe, 1979.

Rus, Veljko. Conflict regulation in self-managed Yugoslav enterprises. In Richard Peterson & Gerard Bommers (Eds.), *Conflict management and industrial relations.* Boston: Kluwer-Nijhoff, 1982.

Russell, Raymond, Hochner, Arthur, & Perry, Stewart E. Participation, influence, and worker-ownership. *Industrial Relations,* 1979, *18,* 330–341.

Sachs, Stephen M. *Implications of recent developments in Yugoslav self-management.* Unpublished manuscript, 1975.

Salancik, Gerald R., & Pfeffer, Jeffrey. An examination of need-satisfaction models of job attitudes. *Administrative Science Quarterly,* 1977, *22,* 427–456.

Sayles, Leonard R. Field use of projective techniques. *Sociology and Social Research,* 1954, *38,* 169–173.

Sayles, Leonard R., & Strauss, George. *The local union,* rev. ed. New York: Harcourt, Brace, & World, 1967.

Schrank, Robert. *Ten thousand working days.* Cambridge, MA: MIT Press, 1978.

Slichter, Sumner. *Union policies and industrial management.* Washington, D.C.: The Brookings Institution, 1941.

Smith, W. R. Attitudes toward workers control in France. *Sociological Review,* 1977, *25,* 877–885.

Staw, Barry M. *Intrinsic and extrinsic motivation.* Morristown, NJ: General Learning Press, 1976.

Steinherr, Alfred. The labor managed economy: A survey of the economics literature. *Annals of Public and Cooperative Economy,* 1978, *49,* 129–148.

Stephen, Frank H. Yugoslav self-management 1945–74. *Industrial Relations Journal,* 1977, *7,* 56–65.

Stephens, Evelyne. *The politics of workers' participation: The Peruvian approach in comparative perspective.* New York: Academic Press, 1980.

Strauss, George. Managerial practices. In J. R. Hackman & Lloyd Suttle (Eds.), *Improving life at work.* Santa Monica, CA: Goodyear, 1977.

Strauss, George. Can social psychology contribute to industrial relations? In Geoffrey Stephenson & Christopher Brotherton (Eds.), *Industrial relations: A social psychological approach.* New York: Wiley, 1979a.

Strauss, George. Quality of worklife and participation as bargaining issues. In Hervey Juris & Myron Roomkin (Eds.), *The Shrinking Perimeter*. Lexington, MA: Lexington Books, 1979b.

Strauss, George, & Rosenstein, Eliezer. Workers participation: A critical view. *Industrial Relations*, 1970, *9*, 197–214.

Strauss, George, & Sayles, Leonard R. The Scanlon Plan: Some organizational problems. *Human Organization*, 1957, *16*, 15–22.

Stern, Robert, Wood, K. Haydn, & Hammer, Tove. *Employee ownership in plant shutdowns*. Kalamazoo, MI: Upjohn, 1979.

Sturmthal, Adolf. *Workers' councils*. Cambridge, MA: Harvard University Press, 1964.

Survey Research Center, University of Michigan. *Employee Ownership*. Unpublished manuscript, 1977.

Svejnar, Jan. Relative wage effects of unions, dictatorship and codetermination: Economic evidence from Germany. *Review of Economics and Statistics*, 1981, *43*, 188–197.

Tabb, Jay, & Galin, Amira. *Workers participation in management*. Oxford: Pergamon, 1970.

Tanic, Zivan. *Workers participation in management*. New Delhi: Siri Ram, 1969.

Tannenbaum, Arnold S., Kovcic, Bogdan, Rosner, Menachem, Vianello, Mino, & Wieser, Georg. *Hierarchy in organizations*. San Francisco, CA: Jossey-Bass, 1974.

Thorsrud, E., & Emery, F. E. Industrial democracy in Norway. *Industrial Relations*, 1970, *9*, 187–196.

Vanek, Jaroslav (Ed.). *Self-management: Economic liberation of man*. Baltimore, MD: Penguin, 1975a.

Vanek, Jaroslav. The basic theory of financing of participatory firms. In Jaroslav Vanek (Ed.), *Self-management*. Baltimore, MD: Penguin, 1975b.

Vanek, Jaroslav. *The labor-managed economy*. Ithaca, NY: Cornell University Press, 1977.

Vardi, Yoav, Shirom, Arie, & Jacobson, Dan. A Study of the leadership beliefs of Israeli managers. *Academy of Management Journal*, 1980, *23*, 367–374.

Vranicki, Predrag. Socialism and the problem of alienation. *Praxis*, 1965, *1*, 307–317.

Wachtel, Howard M. *Workers' management and workers' wages in Yugoslavia: The theory and practice of participatory democracy*. Ithaca: Cornell University Press, 1973.

Walder, Andrew. Participative management and worker control in China. *Sociology of Work and Occupation*, 1981, *8*, 224–251.

Walker, Kenneth F. Workers' participation in management: Problems, practice, and prospect. *International Institute for Labour Studies Bulletin*, 1974, *12*, 3–35.

Wall, Toby, & Lisheron, Joseph. *Worker participation: A critique of the literature and some fresh evidence*. London: McGraw-Hill, 1977.

Walton, R. D., & McKersie, R. B. *A behavioral theory of labor negotiations*. New York: McGraw-Hill, 1965.

Warner, Malcolm. Whither Yugoslav self-management? *Industrial Relations Journal*, 1975, *6*, 65–72.

Webb, Sidney, & Webb, Beatrice. *A constitution for the socialist commonwealth of Great Britain*. London: Longmans, 1920.

Westenholz, Ann. Workers' participation in Denmark. *Industrial Relations*, 1979, *18*, 376–380.

White, J. Kenneth. The Scanlon Plan: Causes and correlates of success. *Academy of Management Journal*, 1979, *22*, 292–312.

Whyte, William F. *Money and motivation*. New York: Harper, 1955.

Whyte, William F. Models for building and changing organizations. *Human Organizations*, 1967, *26*, 22–31.

Whyte, William Foote. *Organizational behavior: Theory and application.* Homewood, IL: Irwin, 1969.

Williams, Carol. *Workers' participation: A bibliography.* Kingston, Ont.: Industrial Relations Centre, Queens University, 1976.

Wilpert, Bernhard. Research on industrial democracy: The German case. *Industrial Relations Journal,* 1975, *6,* 65–72.

Windmuller, John (Ed.). Industrial democracy in international perspective. *Annals of the American Academy of Political and Social Science,* 1977, *431.*

Witte, John F. *Democracy, authority, and alienation in work.* Chicago, IL: University of Chicago Press, 1980.

Young, F. John. Workers participation in management in New Zealand: A survey. (mimeographed), 1979.

Zimbalist, Andrew. The dynamic of worker participation. In G. David Garson & Smith, Michael P. (Eds.), *Organizational democracy.* London: Sage, 1976.

Zupanov, Josip. Two patterns of conflict management in industry. *Industrial Relations,* 1973, *12,* 213–223.

Zwerdling, Daniel. Employee ownership: How well is it working? *Working Papers for a New Society,* 1979, *7,* 15–27.

THE MEETING AS A NEGLECTED
SOCIAL FORM IN ORGANIZATIONAL
STUDIES

Helen B. Schwartzman

ABSTRACT

This paper presents an overview of the uses of meetings and the available
studies of meetings that have been conducted by anthropologists, psychologists, sociologists, political scientists, business administrators, and others.
It is argued that researchers have made meetings a *tool* of analysis, when
they should have been the *topic* of investigation. To reverse this situation,
a framework for a theory of meetings is presented here, and this framework
is used to set a research agenda for the study of meetings in organizations.

Gibbon observes that in the Arabian book *par excellence,* in the Koran, there are no camels; I believe that if there were any doubt as to the authenticity of the Koran, this absence of camels would be sufficient to prove it is an Arabian work. It was written by Mohammed, and Mohammed, as an Arab, had no reason to know that camels were especially Arabian; for him they were a part of reality, he had no reason to emphasize them.

Jorge Luis Borges

At first glance, it would seem that meetings are one of the most well-understood phenomena in organizational life; they are certainly one of its most common events. This chapter takes a second glance at meetings and finds that although meetings are much maligned, we really know very little about them. This is so because meetings in organizations are like camels are to Arabs—they are a taken-for-granted part of reality and few researchers have had reason to emphasize them. Researchers, however, have had reason to *use* them, and so meetings provide the background context for a variety of investigations, especially small-group and decision-making studies. In this chapter, an overview of the uses and studies of meetings that are available, as they have been conducted by anthropologists, psychologists, sociologists, political scientists, business administrators, and others is presented. In addition, a framework for a theory of meetings, is outlined and then used to set a research agenda for the study of meetings. The overall purpose of this chapter is to move meetings into the foreground and to suggest that they are a legitimate topic of research in their own right.

THE STUDY OF MEETINGS: A BRIEF REVIEW

It will be argued here that meetings are so pervasive and taken for granted in organizations that often they have been overlooked by researchers. Textbook indexes provide one window on the topics of concern to investigators. Therefore it is interesting to discover that entries for meetings (or conferences, boards, councils, committees) rarely appear in the subject indexes of several frequently used textbooks on organizational behavior (e.g., Kerr, 1979; March & Simon, 1958; Nadler, Hackman, & Lawler, 1979; Schein, 1980; Szilagyi, 1980). The exclusion of such an obvious topic suggests that the authors consider meetings to be either too general or too familiar a subject to merit inclusion in the index. Meetings do, however, make their appearance in various ways in the organizational literature. For the most part, meetings appear *as they have been used* by researchers, consultants, and others for the examination or investigation of other topics. Following Bittner's (1974) insight about organizational structure, it can be said that researchers have made meetings a *tool* of analysis, although they should have made them the *topic* of investigation. Parkinson (1957) suggested this some time ago by noting that researchers have paid scant attention to committees, which led him to playfully call for the development of a science of "comitology." This call, however, has been only sporadically answered, as will be evident in the following review.

Meetings as Tools for Research

Meeting groups such as boards, conferences, councils, committees, and staffings have been used by researchers to investigate a variety of topics. For example, the extensive literature on small-group dynamics has used meeting groups to examine several issues. During the 30 years of its existence, the small-group field has focused on approximately 12 major topics, according to a recent review by Zander (1979).[1] Researchers in each of these topical areas have used meetings in one way or another to pursue their specific interests, which include the following:

1. Interest in the power of groups and group norms to determine the behavior of members[2] (e.g., Janis's 1972 analysis of the effect of "groupthink" on committees in the federal government; see also Flowers' 1977 experimental investigation of this phenomenon).
2. A long-standing concern with the study of leadership style and effects on group productivity and/or member satisfaction. For example, both leader style and situational studies have used meeting groups, especially discussion groups, to assess leadership traits and processes (see Hollander & Julian, 1969).
3. Sources and effects of interpersonal power and the effect of social networks on communication within groups (e.g., Blau and Scott's 1962 analysis of formal status and interaction in weekly meetings in a county welfare bureau, or Caudill's 1958 study of interaction processes in administrative conferences in a mental hospital).
4. The study of cooperation and conflict in groups (e.g., Levit and Benjamin's 1976 use of a conference between Jews and Arabs to examine ways to resolve conflict in groups, or Fenno's 1962 study of integrative mechanisms operative in the United States Congress House Appropriations Committee).
5. Structural effects (such as group size) on group performance and productivity (e.g., the 1976 study by Paulus, Annis, Setta, Schkade, and Matthews of group size, room size, interpersonal proximity, and their effect on group performance).

Meetings also have been used as a "testing ground" for the variety of theoretical models developed by small-group researchers. A study by Fiedler, Godfrey, and Hall (1957) of boards of farm cooperatives, undertaken to validate a contingency model of leadership effectiveness, illustrates this approach. Similarly, meetings or meeting-like events have been used to develop and refine several small-group observational methods and instruments, e.g., Interaction Process Analysis (IPA) as developed by Bales and colleagues (see Bales, 1950).

In all of these studies the purpose of the research has been to achieve knowledge about the nature of groups as a general phenomenon or to develop more effective ways to study groups. The nature of meetings as a specific group form has not been the subject of investigation.

One of the most recent interests of researchers is the process of decision making in groups and organizations. There is now an immense literature on this subject and once again meetings figure prominently as the background structure for investigations of those topics of specific interest to the decision researcher. These interests include:

1. Studies of particular types of decision processes, such as diferences between consensus and majority voting for achieving decisions, e.g., Bailey's (1965) comparison of councils and committees in India and in Western universities and Olsen's (1972) examination of differences between confrontation vs. "sounding out" procedures for making organizational choices.
2. Analysis of the impact of the decision environment on the decision reached, e.g., comparisons of decisions made under the differential conditions of certainty, risk, and uncertainty (Bowman 1958).
3. Studies and comparisons of different types of decisions, e.g., budgeting decisions (Hofstede, 1968), strategic/innovative decisions (Mintzberg, Raisinghani, & Theoret, 1976; Pettigrew, 1973), and crisis decisions (Janis & Mann, 1977).
4. Investigations of leadership and decision making (Vroom & Yetton, 1973).
5. Studies of problems associated with reaching a decision, especially communication problems (see Argyris, 1975), and evaluations of new decision techniques, e.g., the nominal group approach that involves a highly structured group meeting or the Delphi technique that involves no meetings (see Van de Ven & Delbecq, 1974; Delbecq, Van de Ven, & Gustafson, 1975).
6. Illustrations and evaluations of specific decision models, for example, Wallace and Schwab's (1976) use of a university committee to test five decision models and their ability to predict committee

decisions, or March and Olsen's (1976) studies illustrating the value of a "garbage can" model of decision making.

7. Case analytic investigations that trace (or reconstruct) the natural history of momentous, as well as routine, decisions, e.g., Allison's (1969, 1971) study of decisions concerning the Cuban missile crisis, or March and Olsen's (1976) investigations of specific decisions made in organized anarchies.

Like small-group studies, many decision-making investigations suffer from the problem of artificiality because they often are conducted in laboratories with groups of individuals (generally college students) who have had no previous experience working together. One of the most extensive decision studies attempting to overcome this problem is also one of the most detailed investigations of the process and structure of government committees. In this study, Barber (1966) examines the nature of power and power relationships as these affect decisions made in meetings of 12 different Connecticut boards of finance observed at the Yale Interaction Laboratory in 1952. Guetzkow and colleagues (see Guetzkow, Alger, Brody, Noel, & Snyder, 1963) also have observed actual government officials in several controlled decision-making and role-playing experiments. Field studies of actual decision-making groups invariably require the investigator to attend meetings, as is the case in March and Olsen's (1976) studies.

Meetings as Symptoms, Meetings as Cure

A second tradition in the literature treats meetings as if they are either the symptoms of or the cure for a host of organizational problems. This literature generally is not oriented toward researchers, as it is written by and/or for organizational members, especially managers and administrators. In this case, meetings may be seen as symptomatic of problems such as ineffective leadership, ambiguous or conflicting goals, lack of clear job definitions, and communication problems of all sorts (see Drucker, 1974). Along with being symptomatic of "malorganization," Drucker (1974) suggests that:

> meetings should be considered as a concession to organizational imperfection. The ideal is the organization which can operate without meetings—in the same sense in which the ideal of the machine designer is to have only one moving part in his contraption. In every human organization there is far too much need for cooperation, coordination, and human relations to have to provide for additional meetings. And the human dynamics of meetings are so complex as to make them very poor tools for getting any work done. (p. 548)

In contrast to this view, a number of consultants have suggested that meetings are actually useful diagnostic tools for understanding organizational activity and events. In this tradition, meetings are used to correct certain problems; therefore, a manager may be instructed to monitor his or her meeting performance in order to evaluate changes in his or her leadership style (see Argyris, 1975), or the manager may be advised to use meetings to let people "get things off their chest" (see Lee, 1952; Johnson, 1953), or to study expressive movements and nonverbal behavior in conferences as signs of commitment to the company, interest in the meeting, the development of alliances among subordinates, etc. (see Caplow, 1976).

In the human relations tradition, meetings were used in many instances to encourage "open communication" between managers and workers (see Chapple, 1953). Participative management techniques and the current enthusiasm for "quality circles" (see Greenberger, 1981) also represent this tradition. In these instances, the meeting form is introduced to an operating or production level of an organization that typically does not rely on the scheduled meeting as a context for gathering people together.

One of the dominant themes in much of this literature is the *use* of meetings, as a management tool, as well as for the development of suggestions for improving meeting effectiveness. This specific interest has inspired its own genre of management literature, the "how to make meetings better" book (see Bradford, 1976, Carnes, 1980, Doyle & Straus, 1976, Dunsing, 1976, Hon, 1980, Strauss & Strauss, 1951, Tropman, 1980, Zander, 1977). These books make two basic points. First, they assume that most meetings in most organizations are ineffective, unproductive, inept, chaotic, incompetent, wasteful, ridiculous, boring, tedious, silly, and so forth. Second, they suggest that the solution to these problems is either tighter structuring of meeting procedures (e.g., more pre-meeting preparation, developing a structured agenda, following a strict series of steps, adhering to time frames, setting meeting priorities and goals) or more attention to group dynamics (e.g., recognizing the importance of involving all members, developing effective leadership skills, using a meeting "facilitator" and "recorder," developing trust and shared responsibility, becoming familiar with techniques for resolving conflict, and the importance of self-examination).

Recent developments in the field of telecommunications have made possible a variety of alternatives to the face-to-face meeting—all of which are forms of the so-called electronic meeting. In order to enhance and expedite the relay of information, and also to avoid the problems and burdens of travel, a variety of teleconferencing techniques exist, including audio teleconferences (the most well-known approach), computer-based teleconferences, and video conferences. Over 100 studies assessing the advantages and disadvantages of various types of electronic meetings currently exist. This literature has been reviewed by Johansen, Vallee, and Spangler (1979). Changing the medium of group communications by using the electronic meeting is seen to be a way to improve communication and at the same time avoid unnecessary travel and expense. In this case the *medium* of the meeting is *used* as a way to improve organizational functioning.

The literature which treats meetings as either the symptom of or cure for organizational problems continues the tradition of using meetings—in this case, they are used by managers and consultants to diagnose or improve organizational functioning. Unfortunately, even though this approach focuses directly on the meeting form, it also takes this form for granted by assuming either that meetings transparently reveal the problems in an organization, or that meetings are naturally ineffective, unproductive, etc., and therefore in dire need of improvement. This approach tells us something about what managers/consultants think about meetings, but it does not constitute a study of the meeting form itself.

Meetings as the Topic of Research

So far in this review it has been found that those areas of organizational research (small-group and decision-making studies) that would most be expected to have examined meetings have instead overlooked them. This has happened, it has been argued, because researchers and others have taken meetings for granted and have used them as a convenient form for the study or examination of other topics. This analysis is not meant as a critique of the substantive issues organizational researchers have chosen to study (decision making is indeed a central issue for investigators' consideration). The argument here is that instead of ignoring meetings, researchers should give them equal time as a topic worthy of investigation. Fortunately, there are some researchers who have already done this.

Meetings, conferences, committees, boards, and councils have been the subject of some researchers' attention in several disciplines. A number of specific issues come into focus here that are not emphasized (or sometimes even considered) in other studies. The change that is most evident is a switch from using meetings as a tool for researching other topics, to researching the uses of meetings, and examining the reasons for and process of constructing a "meeting" event in organizations. Questions of concern include the following: How do meetings impact on individuals in an organization? (see Bales, 1954 and Mintzberg, 1973) How do individuals use meetings in organizations, and what do they get out of them? (see

Guetzkow & Kriesberg, 1950; also Brinkerhoff, 1972; Kriesberg & Guetzkow, 1950[3]) What do meetings mean to organization or community members? (see Moore, 1977; Silverman, 1977) How do meetings function
in specific organizational and cultural settings? (see Bailey, 1977; Dalton, 1959; Smith, 1979) Ideas suggested in many of these studies are used
below in the development of a theoretical framework for the study of
meetings.

One of the most specific studies of the meeting event itself adopts an
anthropological and ethnomethodological concern with the taken-for-
granted features of social life by examining specific taken-for-granted features of meetings as settings for multi-party talk. In this study, Atkinson,
Cuff, and Lee (1978) examine "how people talk in a meeting to achieve
and sustain the meeting as a social setting" (p. 133). This issue is specifically considered by investigating how participants in a meeting of a
local radio station make the transition from a "coffee break" back to a
"meeting." The researchers are concerned with the recommencement of
the meeting. It is suggested that participants in a meeting orient to the
following three taken-for-granted features of the structuring of interaction,
in order to achieve and constitute an event as a meeting. The researchers
argue that meeting talk can be examined for the ways in which this orientation is displayed and secured (p. 149).

1.   Those present orient to meetings and to the course of events and
     activities in meetings as being episodic in nature.
2.   Those present orient to the scheduling and controlling of these ep-
     isodes and the talk within them.
3.   Those present orient to meetings as having purposes that can be
     used to frame the business, and the episodic organization of the
     business. (Atkinson et al., 1978, p. 149)

This specific study is used in the following section to develop a working
definition of meetings in formal organizations.

Summary

It has been argued in this review that meetings have been *used* by researchers to study other topics, but generally they have not been viewed
as a legitimate topic of investigation in their own right. In order to move
meetings out of the background and into the foreground of organizational
research, the next section of this chapter presents a definition and typology
of meetings and outlines a framework for a theory of meetings in organizations.

DEFINITIONS AND A TYPOLOGY

Although the literature may lack research on meetings, dictionaries offer a multitude of definitions for the word *meeting(s)*. According to Webster's *Third New International Dictionary* (1976), a meeting is an "act or process of coming together that may be a chance or a planned encounter." A meeting may also be an "assembly for a religious worship, a congregation of religious dissenters or their house of worship, the permanent governing organization of a congregation of the Society of Friends or that of a regional group of congregations, a gathering for business, social or other purposes, a horse- or dog-racing session extending for a stated term of days at one track, a joint in carpentry or masonry," or a meeting may be a "place of meeting." A meeting, in these terms, seems to involve a confluence, intersection, or joining of people and/or things. The implication is that meetings are face-to-face interactions.

A meeting is understood here to be a type of gathering or encounter that, in Goffman's (1961) words, is characterized by *focused interaction*.

> Focused interaction occurs when people effectively agree to sustain for a time a single focus of cognitive and visual attention, as in a conversation, a board game or a joint task sustained by a close face-to-face circle of contributors. (p. 7)

A meeting is a specific type of focused interaction that for the purposes of this chapter may be defined as follows:

> A meeting is a *social form* that organizes interaction in distinctive ways. Most specifically a meeting is a gathering of three or more people who agree to assemble for a purpose ostensibly related to the functioning of an organization or group (e.g., to exchange ideas or opinions, to make a decision, to formulate recommendations). A meeting is characterized by multi-party talk that is episodic in nature and participants develop or use specific conventions for regulating this talk. The meeting form frames the behavior that occurs within it as concerning the 'business' of the group or organization.

Conferences, assemblies, talks, discussions, moots, buzz sessions, "musters" (see Hon, 1980) are understood here as synonyms for the word *meeting,* i.e., they denote the form of encounter defined herein. Another way to describe the meeting as it is defined here is to say that it is a form that falls between a "chat" and a "lecture." A meeting is more formal than a chat, which may also be characterized by multi-party talk but does not necessarily involve a discussion of the business of a group or organization. A meeting, however, is less formal than a lecture, which is characterized by single-party talk directed to an audience.

Figure 1.

	Unscheduled Meetings	*Scheduled Meetings*
Time	No Set Time	Set Time
Formality	Low	High
Representation	Not Formally Responsible to Another Group	Formal Responsibility or Sovereign

Meetings are found in all societies and frequently they occur to provide direction, to govern, or to regulate activity in some way. In the United States, meetings are used by all types of groups—business, community, religious, political, professional—as a form for conducting what they define as their business. These groups have in turn developed a number of specific types of "meeting groups" that vary in the degree to which they formalize and schedule the meeting event, structure and control the meeting talk, and represent or are responsible to other groups.

Meetings may be classified along a series of three continua—time, formality, and representation. Two very general types of meeting events may be identified using this classification (see Figure 1):

1. *Unscheduled meetings* are those in which the gathering of individuals has not been planned in advance and the meeting talk generally is loosely regulated. A group that holds an unscheduled meeting usually does not have a clear-cut responsibility to represent or report back to a larger group. Groups engaged in unscheduled meetings generally are smaller in size than those involved in scheduled meetings (although this is not always the case). An unscheduled meeting may be called because of a need to exchange information or to make decisions quickly as in a crisis situation; however, these events also may occur quite spontaneously to consider routine matters, as when a "lunch" is transformed into a "quick meeting" because several individuals with common interests happen to be together. Groups engaged in unscheduled meetings generally do not have specific names attached to them.

2. *Scheduled meetings* are those events in which a group's gathering has been scheduled in advance and also often recurs over time. Scheduled meetings differ greatly in the degree to which the meeting talk is itself scheduled and regulated. For example, a discussion or study group may hold numerous working meetings to exchange ideas or opinions about a specific subject, to draft policy or procedures, etc. Talk in these meetings is likely to be moderately scheduled, and there is not always a clear expectation that the group will produce tangible results or reports (sometimes

a "good discussion" will be counted as a result) (see Hon, 1980). Meetings that are routinely called in an attempt to coordinate intra- or intergroup activities or to relay information of some sort (such as staff meetings, division director meetings, professional society meetings) also share the above characteristics (although in the case of professional society meetings, the talk generally is structured in a lecture mode, except for the business meetings that also take place during these events).

Committees are more formalized meeting groups that may be defined following Wheare (1955):

> The essence of a committee is . . . that it is a body to which some task has been referred or committed by some other person or body. It may be asked or required or permitted to carry out this task. . . . The notion of a committee carries with it the idea of a body being in some manner or degree responsible or subordinate or answerable in the last resort to the body or person who set it up or committed a power or duty to it[4]. . . . There is inherent in the notion of a committee some idea of a derived or secondary or dependent status, in form at least; it lacks original jurisdiction. It acts on behalf of or with responsibility to another body. (pp. 5–6)[5]

As committees use them meetings tend to be somewhat more formal than those held as unscheduled events. Talk in these meetings is moderately to very scheduled, and there is the definite expectation that something should be produced by the committee to be brought back to the group that established it.

Councils, cabinets, parliaments, and conventions are all examples of meeting groups that are sovereign instead of responsible to a parent body (Bailey, 1977, p. 83). Meetings of these groups generally are formal (sometimes very formal) occasions and meeting talk is almost always scheduled and controlled, sometimes to a very great degree (as when Robert's Rules of Order are meticulously invoked).

The definition and discussion of meetings that has been presented so far suggests an important research question for consideration: Does the structure of a meeting as a social form contradict its presumed function in organizational settings? Episodic talk and the conventions that have been developed to regulate this talk may not be conducive to the sharing of ideas and opinions, or to the making of decisions or the resolution of problems. In some very important ways, it appears that the meeting form may be ill-suited for its purpose. However, groups and organizations persist in holding meetings—so meetings must do something. This raises an obvious question: *What do meetings do?* In order to begin to answer this question, an examination of what happens at a typical meeting is presented. It is suggested that all meetings progress through stages that serve various functions for individuals and organizations and have little to do with the actual content of a meeting event.

THE NATURAL HISTORY OF A MEETING

Meetings and meeting groups (especially committees) are most maligned in the literature because it is believed that they involve individuals in futile, impossible, useless, and often ridiculous discussions. Humorous descriptions of meetings and meeting groups illustrate this approach.

> A committee is an aggregation of the unwilling appointed by the incompetent to do a task that is unnecessary. (Carnes, 1980, p. 61)
> A camel is a horse assembled by a committee. (Carnes, 1980, p. 65)
> [A cartoon] shows two men bending over their date books. One is saying, "Gee, if I can get in one more meeting this week I won't have to do any work"! (Tropman, 1980, p. 7)

Researchers need to take these descriptions seriously because they are comments on the contradictory nature of the meeting as a social form (meetings are a place to "work," but they do not work) and because they describe meetings playfully. It will be argued and illustrated below that researchers and members of organizations have, for the most part, examined the meeting only as an instrumental social form, although it may be that meetings are expressive forms that serve expressive functions much better than they serve instrumental ones; when looked at from this perspective, their persistence in organizations makes sense. These expressive qualities, which are sometimes obvious and sometimes subtle, are suggested in the following natural history of a meeting.

Negotiating a Meeting: The Play and Display of Status

In order to have a "meeting," it is first necessary to arrange one. This can be as simple as suggesting that a "conversation" become a "quick meeting," as in the case of an unscheduled meeting. However, the seemingly inconsequential (although often annoying) process of arranging a scheduled meeting contains innumerable possibilities for displaying status, as well as finding out about one's status in the organization (e.g., whose time takes precedence in setting the meetings, who "needs" to be there and who does not, who knows about which meetings, etc.). In some cases, this may be the only way that individuals learn about their place in the organizational hierarchy. In the process of negotiating a meeting, other meetings can be used as a dodge or excuse to get out of a meeting that one does not want to attend. Along with this, once a meeting time is set, the organizer can cancel it because of other "pressing" matters, or an individual can cancel out of any specific meeting for the same reason, and both of these are effective status rebukes.

Meeting Arrivals and Departures

Once a meeting has been set, the meeting enters a new phase as an event, and a number of new possibilities are created for status display. For example, the issue of who arrives first, who arrives with whom, the seating pattern that is chosen, and, finally, whose arrival signals the start of the meeting are all indirect but important communications about status, as well as alliance and friendship patterns. Among the Merina (in the Malagasy Republic), as reported by Bloch (1975), meetings become very important places for "prestige auctions" of this sort.

> The actual time of the meeting (*kabary*) was always set three or four hours too early, and as for many Merina occasions, great skill was required by those who wanted to arrive at the right time, in the right place. Nobody wanted to arrive too early, but obviously it would not do to arrive too late. The influence of a person is at stake in manoeuvres of this kind, and his effectiveness at such a meeting depends on his arriving at the right time to give the impression that the meeting is starting because of his arrival. This involves a lot of waiting about in nearby houses and sending children to spy out the land and report back. As if by magic the *raiamandreny* (elders) all appear at once at a time little related to the originally appointed hour. This custom (infuriating for the anthropologist) is part of the prestige auction which . . . characterizes these meetings. (p. 48)

The times surrounding the start and finish of a meeting (and also breaks within it) also are quite significant, as they provide individuals with opportunities to exchange gossip, trade information, and hold "mini-meetings." In fact, scheduled meetings generally produce a kind of unscheduled meeting "ripple effect" that is probably very important for structuring interaction and relaying information—perhaps more important than the scheduled meeting itself. Dalton (1959) discusses the significance of pre- and post-meeting "confabs," and Mintzberg (1973) describes the importance of "side-issue" discussions that occur at the beginning and end of formal meetings. He refers to this as the "ritualistic" phase of a meeting.

> Gossip about peers in the industry is exchanged; comments are made on encounters the participants have recently had or on published material they have recently read; important political events are discussed and background information is traded. It seems reasonable to conclude that the manager collects much information in these discussions, and that this fact alone makes the formal, face-to-face meeting a powerful medium. (1973, p. 43)

Meetings also provide individuals with an opportunity for making strong symbolic statements of disagreement by choosing to break the meeting frame (e.g., by dramatically walking out of a meeting). This effect can sometimes backfire, as was the case for New York's Mayor Edward Koch.

The QCO (Queens Citizen Organization) got off with an Alinsky-style flourish. In what now is a celebrated incident, New York's Mayor Edward Koch, then newly elected, *stormed out of a meeting* [italics added] with the fledgling QCO when the group refused to allow him five minutes for a speech, instead of the two minutes that had been scheduled. The mayor's action received considerable criticism, and the QCO received abundant attention. With a certain coyness, the QCO now refers to Mayor Koch as one of our "founding fathers." (*The Wall Street Journal*, May 13, 1981, p. 20).

In this case, the mayor chose to break the meeting frame in an effort to disqualify the organization, but instead this action served to disqualify the mayor and legitimate the meeting and therefore the organization.

Individuals can also make less dramatic exits from meetings, underlining their status, the need for their time, or the importance of some other event e.g., a phone call, an emergency meeting, or a crisis. Interruptions of this kind are another example of the way a meeting unobtrusively facilitates status displays.

The Meeting Frame

According to March and Olsen (1976, p. 11), a decision process transforms the behavior of individuals into organizational action. Unfortunately, the researchers do not say how, in fact, this happens. It will be suggested here that it is actually "the meeting" (and not the decision process) that accomplishes this transformation, because as a social form it frames the behavior that occurs within it as being concerned with the "business" of a group or organization. As soon as a meeting begins, this transformation takes place. However, what is perhaps most important about this transformation is that the episodic nature of meeting talk creates the possibility for individual and group social relationships, agreements and disagreements, to be discussed and framed as a discussion of business. For example, this occurs when individuals juggle for status via the placement of items on the meeting agenda, or when the presentation of reports becomes a context for disagreement among individuals, as illustrated in a description by Bradford (1976) of a company meeting.

The president of a company holds his weekly Monday morning meeting with his vice presidents. After he makes a few comments urging redoubled efforts, he asks the several vice presidents to report on their operations. All reports generally are favorable. However, the vice president for engineering says offhandedly that some of his staff feel the research people have no idea how difficult it is to retool for new products. Somewhat heatedly, the vice president for production adds that no one has any idea how hard it is to retrain workers for new tasks. It might be cheaper, he says, to fire old workers and hire new ones. At that, the face of the personnel director reddens, but he says nothing. The vice president for marketing complains that one of the problems his people face is selling new products. Finally the president interrupts in a soothing voice, saying that the company must keep ahead of the field and he is certain they will work it all out. (p. 2)

In this way, the meeting form provides participants with a way "to challenge or reaffirm friendships and antagonisms" (Sproull, Weiner, & Wolf, 1978), and to engage in power struggles (and be assured of an audience), all in the guise of discharging business or work. This is the way that meetings become a (possibly the) form for merging formal and informal systems in organizations, as suggested some time ago by Dalton (1959, p. 227). The meeting frame, however, disqualifies itself as performing this function because it indicates that the meeting is merely a facilitating event. This makes the meeting an invisible, but very powerful social form.

It also seems to be crucial that organizations have a means to *express* the natural conflict that can be expected to develop among individuals living and/or working together, in a way that ultimately minimizes or diffuses this conflict. Meetings provide a perfect form for doing this because discussions of social relationships can always be framed as "business"— and therefore conflict is legitimated and framed as "business." In this way the social relationships acted out in the meeting are legitimated, and conflicts that may occur also are legitimated and framed as interactions that are "for the group/organization/business."

The fact that something like the process just described occurs in meetings is generally recognized by saying that individuals at meetings act in certain ways because they have "hidden agendas" (see Bradford, 1976) that for the most part are seen as dysfunctional for the purposes of a meeting. I am suggesting that the opposite may be the case, i.e., that "hidden agendas" are functional for the purpose of the meeting, because the purpose is to reconcile the formal with the informal system and to legitimate this merger as "the business" of the organization (see also Schwartzman, 1981). In this way, meetings come to symbolize the organization, because they are frequently the only context that creates this link.

Post-Meetings

When a meeting is concluded, individuals may move into a series of other events, including "post-meetings" (where information may be exchanged on a more informal basis, as discussed previously) and "post-mortems" of the meeting that has just occurred. After the fact, a meeting is objectified and becomes tangible evidence of organizational activity or inactivity (depending on the assessment of the meeting that has just occurred). When meetings become jokes in an organization, what transpires within them is discounted as not-serious. In this way a meeting may negate itself and the information that is relayed within it. This may be one reason why many organizations operate on a weak information base (see Cohen & March, 1974), and find themselves constantly replicating ideas and information (the "reinventing the wheel" phenomenon). On the other hand, it may be that this effect is actually valuable for individuals in an organization because it makes it always possible to recast (and reinvent) history. If meetings symbolize the organization, criticism and jokes about them may also be one way to criticize the organization indirectly.

Meetings, as suggested by several investigators (e.g., Tropman, 1980), are also one way to shift responsibility for actions or decisions from individuals and even from groups onto the meeting itself. This shift is evident in Allison's (1971) reconstruction of decisions concerning the Cuban Missile Crisis, for example, in the statement, "*That meeting* [italics added] decided to shy away from the Western end of Cuba (where SAMs were becoming operational) and modify the flight patterns of the U-2s in order to reduce the probability that a U-2 would be lost" (p. 713). The tactic of blaming the meeting, after it has occurred, as in "the meeting made me do it," is another example of this shift. Individuals at one mental health center I studied frequently reported that it was the meeting and its dynamics that *led them to a decision or action*. As one informant stated:

> There's the dynamics of the meeting that leads you to a certain decision and people on the outside wonder, "How in hell did you decide that?" and if you weren't at the meeting, you really can't appreciate how it was done.

TOWARD A THEORY OF MEETINGS

In this paper I have suggested that meetings are valuable to organizations, as well as to researchers of organizations, because they are not what they seem to be. They seem to be a sort of "blank slate" that individuals can use to make decisions, discuss issues, and resolve conflicts, but a form that in itself has no effect on an organization. This blank slate view treats the meeting task (e.g., the decision) as something extraordinary and therefore in need of explanation, but it places the meeting form itself in the background, because it has not been defined as a proper subject of study. Therefore, although the literature is crowded with decision-making models, studies of conflict resolution and negotiations, and investigations of small-group dynamics, only a few researchers have given serious attention to the study of the meeting as the social form which shapes all of these activities.

In this paper, I have suggested that it is time for researchers to change their blank slate view of meetings. The specific change I am suggesting requires that the meeting form be moved into the foreground, placing some of the more traditional topics of organizational research (e.g., decision making, leadership, conflict, and change) at least temporarily into the background. This shift is suggested not because I believe these topics are irrelevant to our understanding of organizations. However, our exclusive focus on topics such as decisions and leadership has obscured other equally important aspects of organizations, especially those features that most members of organizations and organizational reseachers typically take for granted. I have suggested here that meetings are an example of such a taken-for-granted social form, and also that in many ways researchers have put the cart before the horse by developing decision-making models or theories of small-group dynamics without first developing a theory of meetings in formal organizations.

In order to correct this emphasis, I suggest that what is needed in this field are intensive fieldwork studies as well as theoretical work that elucidates the structure and function of the meeting form in organizations. We need to produce field studies that examine what naturally occurring meetings do for individuals in specific organizations, how individuals use meetings in their day-to-day organizational life, and how meetings affect individuals in specific settings. We need to try to understand why meetings and complaints about meetings are so prevalent in American organizational life. What does this tell us about meetings and organizations? In this regard, we also need to begin to examine relationships between individuals and meetings, and to compare the structure and uses of meetings across organizations and cross-culturally. Toward the development of such studies, I briefly propose and discuss three images of meetings. These images suggest ways to view the form and function of meetings that directly challenge the conventional blank state image that has been so influential in directing our thinking about this topic.

Meetings as Rituals

Anthropologists consider rituals and ceremonies to be important forms in all societies because they "structure and present particular interpretations of social reality in a way that endows them with legitimacy" (Moore & Myerhoff, 1977, p. 4). These forms are also important because they convey certain messages *as if* they were unquestionable, and they may do this in secular as well as sacred contexts (see Moore & Myerhoff, 1977, for a detailed analysis of secular rituals). Moore (1977) in particular has suggested an analogy between meetings, specifically political meetings held by local Tanzanian African National Union (TANU) party leaders among the Chagga of Tanzania, and religious rites. She suggests this analogy because it "draws attention to the general symbolic and doctrinal representations made in the course of business. It keeps the analytic focus from being entirely on the practical purposes listed on the agenda'' (p. 151).

This emphasis on the ritual-like quality of meetings has been echoed as well by organizational researchers such as Olsen (1970) and Mintzberg (1973). For example. Mintzberg suggests that all scheduled meetings follow a particular pattern or series of stages which include ceremony, strategy making, and negotiation (p. 42). In his terms, the ritual phase of the meeting is preliminary to the "core issue" of the meeting. I will suggest later that the ritual significance of the meeting may, in fact, be its core issue. A growing interest in the symbolic aspects of organizational life is evident in the organizational behavior research field in general, as illustrated by recent studies of organizational culture (see Jelinek, Smircich, & Hirsch, 1983), and specifically by studies of organizational rituals and ceremonies (e.g., Trice, Belasco, & Alutto, 1969).

The symbolic significance of meetings is tricky to analyze because everything about them suggests that it is what goes on *within* a meeting (their explicit purpose as formalized in some meetings by an agenda) that is important. However, when we turn attention to the meeting as a symbolic and ritual-like form, new questions, including the following, emerge: What does the meeting symbolize? How does it do this? What are the functions of meetings for organizations as well as individuals? Some preliminary answers to these questions are suggested below.

Meetings are important social symbols for organizations because they are or may become the organization *writ small*. There may be other competing symbols for an organization, such as individual leaders, a building, an organizational chart, a technological process, a logo, etc., but a meeting is a powerful and ongoing symbol for an organization because it assembles a variety of individuals and groups together and labels the assembly as "organizational action." In this way, a meeting does more than just symbolize the organization—it also may be the major social form that constitutes and reconstitutes the organization over time. It is most effective at doing this because it conveys the message that it is *not* doing this (this is one of the most important unquestionable messages conveyed by the meeting frame). As a collective ritual, meetings provide participants with a way to both negotiate and interpret their social reality and, at the same time, in certain organizations (e.g., organized anarchies) the meeting may be the major evidence of organizational action. This suggests a reversal of the standard view that meetings exist in order to facilitate making a decision, solving a problem, or resolving a crisis. What I suggest here instead is that at least at one level, decisions, problems, and crises occur in organizations *because they produce meetings,* and organizations need meetings, because it is through meetings that the organization creates and maintains itself.

Meetings as Social Metaphors

Related specifically to the above image of meetings, I also suggest that meetings operate as social metaphors for individuals in organizations. This view highlights the way that meetings provide individuals with a structure to use to metaphorically mix their formal and informal relationships and feelings with organizational issues, problems, and solutions. March and Olsen (1976) refer to this as the "garbage can" quality of choice situations, but it is the nature of the meeting form, more than the choice to be made, that is the best structure for this mix, because in this context one thing can always be talked about in terms of something else. In this sense, meetings may be viewed as metaphors where the "associated implications" (see Black, 1962) of a subsidiary subject (e.g., the informal social structure) may be applied to a principal subject (e.g., the need to solve a particular problem as a manifestation of the formal structure). This is how, as discussed earlier, meetings are able to reconcile the formal and informal systems which occur in all organizations. Because this application or mix occurs in the public arena of the meeting, it will always be framed as "the business" of the organization. In this way the meeting allows individuals to engage in a variety of expressive activities while they appear to be engaged in instrumental behavior. When this "metaphoric" process of meetings takes precedence in an organization, it is not surprising to find that they produce confusing or contradictory results, e.g., decisions that are not decisions, unpredictable decisions, action that leads to inaction, inaction that is defined as action, and organization that is disorganization. When meetings are found to last inordinate amounts of time, to elicit a high degree of involvement from participants, and to produce unpredictable decisions or no decisions, I suggest that the metaphorical nature of the meeting form as described here is being emphasized by individuals and the organization. It is my hypothesis that this particular use of meetings is more prevalent in organized anarchies (March & Olsen, 1976), but this needs to be investigated cross-culturally and cross-organizationally in order to spell out those contextual conditions that do or do not emphasize this feature of meetings.

Meetings as Homeostats

The metaphorical and ritualistic qualities of meetings have other effects as well, and lead directly to the third image of meetings to be proposed here. A focus on meeting content contributes to the view that meetings are events that advance (or "meet") organizational goals, facilitate discussions and decisions, and improve the organization. However, a focus on the meeting form suggests that although meetings may facilitate decision making and organizational improvement and change, in a very fundamental sense their most important function may be to serve as homeostats in the system to validate the current social structure and to regulate and maintain the status quo. This is the "tradition-celebrating" role of meetings as secular rituals as discussed by Moore and Myerhoff (1977, p. 7). This is why it is so difficult to use meetings within organizational systems to change an organization—they *look* like they will be a context in which to take action, change events, or solve problems, but they often produce solutions that only maintain problems, or change that leads to no change.

If the meeting form actually is a kind of homeostat for organizations, it could be expected that an organization (or a subsystem of it) faced with a crisis, or with internal or external pressures to change, would see a rise in the number of meetings held as the organization struggles to regain or maintain itself. (There is some evidence for this view, but this topic basically has not been investigated.) If this is the case, it also is not surprising to find that many organizations, especially those that experience severe ambiguity in all areas of their operation (i.e., organized anarchies as described by March and Olsen, 1976), would turn to meetings as the best means available to disguise and yet at the same time maintain organizational ambiguity. In my own research in a community mental health center (see Schwartzman, 1981, 1984a), meetings clearly had this effect. The meeting as a homeostat helps to explain the frustrations that organizational actors state about meetings that "get nowhere," "never seem to accomplish anything," "just go round and round." In fact, these are all appropriate comments on the homeostatic function of meetings.

An Agenda for Research on Meetings

A number of general and specific avenues for research on meetings have been suggested in this paper. In particular, fieldwork investigations that will allow researchers to examine the meeting form as it exists in and affects the day-to-day life of individuals in specific organizational settings has been recommended. In conjunction with these studies, theoretical work that attempts to elucidate the structure and function of the meeting form in organizations must also be undertaken. A number of specific types of studies have been suggested in this chapter.

1.   It is very important to gather basic information on the time individuals spend in meetings. The need to collect such information was suggested some time ago by Bales (1954). Mintzberg's (1983) detailed study of the work of five chief executive officers in large organizations contains the most interesting information collected on this topic. For example, he

found that 59% of a manager's time was spent in scheduled meetings, and another 10% was spent in unscheduled meetings.[6] Given the amount of time that some individuals devote to the meeting form, it seems clear that researchers must devote a similar amount of time and energy to attempting to understand this activity.

2. Instead of focusing on how (or whether) decisions are made in a meeting, researchers should attempt to document how organizations generate meetings, and how meetings crosscut organizational units as well as confuse organization–environment relationships. One way to initiate this approach is for researchers to reconceptualize the way that organizational authority relationships typically are depicted (e.g., the organization chart which locates authority in individuals or offices). If the typical organizational chart is redrawn to depict the types of meeting groups (e.g., boards, committees, task forces) and the authority relationships that exist between these meeting contexts, it is possible to see how an organization and the time of the individuals in it may be structured and controlled by various large- and small-scale meetings. This approach specifically challenges theoretical constructs in the organization literature that locate the source of control and power in organizations in individuals (see Schwartzman, 1984b).

3. The form and function of meetings should be compared across organizations and cross-culturally. In this regard, it is particularly useful for researchers studying meetings in Western societies to consider recent work by anthropologists in non-Western societies on traditional as well as changing meeting forms. Taken-for-granted features of our views about meetings may be specifically revealed in these comparisons. In fact, some of this work (especially Moore, 1977) was very useful in developing ideas for this chapter. In addition, features of meetings that may be universal may also be revealed by these studies. Research by anthropologists that should be of interest in this regard includes studies by Bloch (1975), Duranti (1983), Irvine (1979), Moore (1977), Pinsker (1981), Richards and Kuper (1971), Rosaldo (1973), Salmond (1974), and Silverman (1977).

4. Finally, it is important to investigate how meetings may serve as homeostats for organizations, and in this regard studies of organizations in crisis or faced with internal or external pressures for change would be particularly interesting to pursue. It is, however, also important to examine how meetings can "traditionalize new material as well as perpetuate old traditions" (Moore & Myerhoff 1977, p. 7). Pinsker (1981) is initiating research in this area by examining the role that meetings of the Congress of the Federated States of Micronesia play in the invention of a "Micronesian tradition." Moore's (1977) research on political meetings held by local TANU party leaders among the Chagga of Tanzania also emphasizes this aspect of meetings.

CONCLUSION

The most important feature of the studies suggested here is that they should be studies of meetings—*not* studies of decisions, or leadership, or conflict resolution, and the like. All of these are worthy subjects, and researchers have in fact given these activities considerable attention over the years. However, if we are really looking for ways to question current assumptions and theories in the field of organizational behavior, I believe it is important to reverse some of our standard research practices. We can begin by using decisions to study meetings, or by observing leaders because their activities will necessarily lead us to meetings, or by focusing on crises and conflicts in organizations because these are interesting contexts for the study of meetings. In undertaking this research, we may find significantly challenged some of our traditional assumptions about the importance of decisions, the influence of leaders, and the accepted vehicles for organizational change (to name just a few of the issues which may be illuminated by studies of meetings). Meetings have been taking place for a long time, but we have just begun to recognize their significance to members of organizations and to organizational researchers.

ACKNOWLEDGMENTS

I would like to thank John Schwartzman, L. L. Cummings, and Barry M. Staw for their comments and criticism on this paper, and Andrea Dubnick for typing several drafts of it.

NOTES

1. According to Zander one of the by-passed topics of small-group research is the study of ways to help committees have more efficient meetings. He specifically addresses this issue in his book, *Groups at Work* (1977).

2. A variety of controversies concerning the advantages and disadvantages of individual vs. group activities animates this particular topic for researchers. The committee man vs. the lone individual is a dichotomy that often is made in discussing this issue. Whyte's (1956) well-known discussion and critique of "the organization man" and the group mentality one must achieve in this setting is a good example of this theme in the literature, as is Festinger's work (Festinger, Pepitone & Newcomb, 1952) on "deindividuation" in groups.

3. Credit for recognizing the significance of meetings in organizations must certainly go, in part, to researchers such as Guetzkow and Kriesberg (1950) (also see Berkowitz, 1953; Collins & Guetzkow, 1964; Kriesberg and Guetzkow, 1950; Marquis, Guetzkow, & Heyns, 1951), who were involved with the "Conference Research" project at the University of Michigan between 1947 and 1951. Although the emphasis of this research was on the conference as a context for the investigation of group problem solving and decision making,

the researchers also chose to make conferences/meetings the subject of research in their own right. In this project, the researchers studied actual meeting events and also interviewed a wide range of administrators to see how conferences were used day to day.

4.　Bailey (1977) notes that a committee bears a strangely ambivalent relationship toward its parent body. It reports back, and etiquette usually demands that the committee indicate a subordinate position by referring to itself as "your committee . . ." and ending the document with the phrase "respectfully submitted." Parent bodies may debate the report and accept or reject its recommendations, but when they choose to reject it there certainly is a feeling that matters are not as they should be. (p. 64)

5.　Self-constituted organizations created for the promotion of some common objective may sometimes call themselves committees (e.g., the Wildlife Preservation Committee), in which case the committee *is* the organization—this is the case as well with "committees of the whole" (i.e., a committee consisting of the whole membership of a legislative house).

6.　It is interesting to note that managers, according to a recent review by McCall, Morrison, & Hanna, (1978, p. 17–18), consistently *underestimate* the time they spend in meetings. Managers estimated they spent 49% of their time in meetings, but according to observations they actually spent 69% of their time in this activity. Managers also consistently *overestimate* the time they spend reading and writing and thinking. Managers estimated 32% but observations found they spent 25% of their time reading and writing, and that they estimate 19% of their time is spent thinking, versus 5% observed.

REFERENCES

Allison, G. T. (1969). Conceptual models and the Cuban Missile Crisis. *American Political Science Review, 63*(3), pp. 689–718.

Allison, G. T. (1971). *Essence of decesion: Explaining the Cuban missile crisis.* Boston: Little, Brown and Co.

Argyris, C. (1975). Interpersonal barriers to decision-making. In *Harvard Business Review, On Management* (pp. 425–445). New York: Harper & Row.

Atkinson, M. A., Cuff, E. C., & Lee, J. R. E. (1978). The recommencement of a meeting as a member's accomplishment. In J. Schenkein (Ed.), *Studies in the organization of conversational interaction* (pp. 133–153). New York: Academic Press.

Bailey, F. G. (1965). Decisions by consensus in council and committees. In M. Banton (Ed.), *Political systems and the distribution of power* (pp. 1–20). London: Tavistock.

Bailey, F. G. (1977). *Morality and expediency: The folklore of academic politics.* Chicago: Aldine.

Bales, R. F. (1950). *Interaction process analysis.* Reading, MA: Addison-Wesley.

Bales, R. F. (1954). In conference. *Harvard Business Review, 32,* 44–50.

Barber, J. D. (1966). *Power in committees: An experiment in the governmental process.* Chicago: Rand McNally.

Bateson, G. (1972). *Steps to an ecology of mind.* New York: Ballantine.

Berkowitz, L. (1953). Sharing in small, decision-making groups. *Journal of Abnormal Social Psychology, 48,* 231–238.

Bittner, E. (1974). The concept of organization. In R. Turner (Ed.), *Ethnomethodology* (pp. 69–81). Harmondsworth: Penguin.

Black, M. (1962). *Models and metaphors.* Ithaca, NY: Cornell University Press.

Blau, P. M., & Scott, W. R. (1962). *Formal organizations.* San Francisco: Chandler.

Bloch, M. (Ed.). (1975). *Political language and oratory in traditional society.* New York: Academic Press.

Bowman, M. J. (1958). *Expectations, uncertainty, and business behavior.* New York: Social Science Research Council.

Bradford, L. P. (1976). *Making meetings work.* San Diego, CA: University Associates.

Brinkerhoff, M. B. (1972). Hierarchical status contingencies and the administrative staff conference. *Administrative Science Quarterly, 17,* 395–407.

Caplow, T. (1976). *How to run any organization.* New York: Holt, Rinehart & Winston.

Carnes, W. T. (1980). *Effective meetings for busy people.* New York: McGraw-Hill.

Caudill, W. (1958). *The psychiatric hospital as a small society.* Cambridge, MA: Harvard University Press.

Chapple, E. D. (1953). Applied anthropology in industry. In A. Kroeber (Ed.), *Anthropology Today* (pp. 819–831), Chicago: University of Chicago Press.

Cohen, M. D., & March, J. G. (1974). *Leadership and Ambiguity: The American college president.* New York: McGraw Hill.

Collins, B. E., & Guetzkow, H. (1964). *A social psychology of group processes for decision-making.* New York: Wiley.

Dalton, M. (1959). *Men who manage.* New York: Wiley.

Delbecq, A., Van de Ven, A., & Gustafson, D. (1975). *Group techniques: A guide to nominal and delphi processes.* Glenview, IL: Scott, Foresman.

Doyle, M., & Straus, D. (1976). *How to make meetings work.* New York: Wyden Books.

Drucker, P. (1974). *Management.* New York: Harper & Row.

Dunsing, R. J. (1976). *You and I have simply got to stop meeting this way.* New York: AMACOM.

Duranti, A. (1983). Samoan speechmaking across social events: One genre in and out of *Fono. Language in Society, 12,* 1–22.

Fenno, R. F., Jr. (1962). The House Appropriations Committee as a political system: The problem of integration. *American Political Science Review, 56,* 310–324.

Festinger, L., Pepitone, A., & Newcomb, T. (1952). Some consequences of deindividuation in a group. *Journal of Abnormal Social Psychology, 47,* 382–389.

Fiedler, F. E., Godfrey, E. P., & Hall, D. M. (1957). *Boards, management, and company success.* Danville, IL: Interstate Printers & Publishers.

Flowers, M. L. (1977). A laboratory test of some implications of Janis' group-think hypothesis. *Journal of Personality and Social Psychology, 35,* 888–896.

Goffman, E. (1961). *Encounters.* Indianapolis, IN: Bobbs-Merrill.

Greenberger, R. S. (1981, September 22). Quality circles grow, stirring union worries. *The Wall Street Journal,* p. 1.

Guetzkow, H., Alger, C. F., Brody, R. A., Noel, R. C., & Snyder, R. C. (1963). *Simulation in international relations.* Englewood Cliffs, NJ: Prentice-Hall.

Guetzkow, H., & Kriesberg, M. (1950). Executive use of the administrative conference. *Personnel, 26,* 318–323.

Hofstede, G. H. (1968). *The game of budget control.* London: Tavistock.

Hollander, E. P., & Julian, J. W. (1969). Leadership. In E. F. Borgatta (Ed.), *Social psychology: Readings and perspectives* (pp. 275–284). Chicago: Rand McNally.

Hon, D. (1980). *Meetings that matter.* New York: Wiley.

Irvine, J. T. (1979). Formality and informality in communicative events. *American Anthropologist, 81,* 773–790.

Janis, I. L. (1972). *Victims of groupthink.* Boston: Houghton Mifflin.

Janis, I. L., & Mann, L. (1977). *Decision making.* New York: The Free Press.

Jelinek, M., Smircich, L., & Hirsch, P. (Eds.). (1983). *Administrative Science Quarterly,* (Special Issue on Organizational Culture), *28,* 331–501.

Johansen, R., Vallee, J., & Spangler, K. (1979). *Electronic meetings.* Reading, MA: Addison-Wesley.

Johnson, W. (1953). The fateful process of Mr. A. talking to Mr. B. *Harvard Business Review, 31,* 49–56.

Kerr, S. (Ed.). (1979). *Organizational behavior*. Columbus, OH: Grid.

Kriesberg, M., & Guetzkow, H. (1950). The use of conferences in the adminstration process. *Public Administration Review, 10*, 93–98.

Lee, I. (1952). *How to talk with people*. New York: Harper.

Levit, A. M., & Benjamin, A. (1976). Jews and Arabs rehearse in Geneva: A model of conflict resolution. *Human Relations, 29*, 1035–1044.

March, J. G., & Olsen, J. P. (1976). *Ambiguity and choice in organizations*. Bergen, Norway: Universitetsforlaget.

March, J. G., & Simon, H. A. (1958). *Organizations*. New York: Wiley.

Marquis, D. G., Guetzkow, H., & Heyns, R. W. (1951). A social psychological study of the decision-making conference. In H. Guetzkow (Ed.), *Groups, leadership and men* (pp. 62–64). Pittsburgh, PA: Carnegie Press.

McCall, M. W., Jr., Morrison, A. W., & Hanna, R. C. (1978). *Studies of managerial work: Results and methods* (Technical Report No. 9). Greensboro, NC: Center for Creative Leadership.

Mintzberg, H. (1973). *The nature of managerial work*. New York: Harper & Row.

Mintzberg, H., Raisinghani, D., & Theoret, A. (1976). The structure of "unstructured" decision processes. *Administrative Science Quarterly, 21*, 246–275.

Moore, S. F. (1977). Political meetings and the simulation of unanimity: Kilimanjaro 1973. In S. Moore & B. Myerhoff (Eds.), *Secular ritual* (pp. 151–172). Amsterdam: Van Gorcum.

Moore, S. F., & Myerhoff, B. (Eds.). (1977). *Secular ritual*. Amsterdam: Van Gorcum.

Nadler, D. A., Hackman, J. R., & Lawler, E. E., III. (1979). *Managing organizational behavior*. Boston: Little, Brown.

Olsen, J. P. (1970). Local budgeting—Decision making or ritual act? *Scandinavian Political Studies, 5*, 85–115.

Olsen, J. P. (1972). Voting, "sounding out" and the governance of modern organizations. *Acta Sociologica, 15*, 267–283.

Parkinson, C. N. (1957). *Parkinson's law*. Cambridge, MA: Houghton Mifflin.

Paulus, P. B., Annis, A. B., Setta, J. J., Schkade, J. K., & Matthews, R. W. (1976). Density does affect task performance. *Journal of Personality and Social Psychology, 34*, 248–253.

Pettigrew, A. M. (1973) *The politics of organizational decision-making*. London: Tavistock.

Pinsker, E. C. (1981). *Constituting the constituting of a constitution: The 1975 Micronesian constitutional convention and the genesis of "the Micronesian way."* Unpublished master's thesis, Department of Anthropology, University of Chicago.

Richards, A., & Kuper, A. (Eds.). (1971). *Councils in action*. London: Cambridge University Press.

Rosaldo, M. (1973). "I have nothing to hide": The language of Ilongot oratory. *Language in Society, 2*, 193–223.

Salmond, A. (1974). *Hui: A study of Maori gatherings*. Wellington, New Zealand: A. H. & A. W. Reed.

Schwartzman, H. B. (1981). Hidden agendas and formal organizations or how to dance at a meeting. *Social Analysis, 9*, 77–88.

Schwartzman, H. B. (1984a). Stories at work: Play in an organizational context. In E. M. Bruner (Ed.), *Text, Play, and Story: The Construction and Reconstruction of Self and Society*, Proceedings of the American Ethnological Society (pp. 80–93) Washington, DC: American Ethnological Society.

Schwartzman, H. B. (1984b, September). *Research on work group effectiveness: An anthropological critique*. Paper presented at the Conference on Work Group Effectiveness, Carnegie-Mellon University, Pittsburgh, PA.

Schein, E. H. (1980). *Organizational psychology* (3rd ed.). Englewood Cliffs, NJ: Prentice-Hall.

Silverman, M. G. (1977). Making sense: A study of a Banaban meeting. In J. L. Dolgin, D. S. Kemnitzer, & D. M. Schneider (Eds.), *Symbolic anthropology* (pp. 451–479). New York: Columbia University Press.

Smith, M.D. (1979, November–December). *"Tribal" councils: Traditional and modern.* Paper presented at the Annual Meeting of the American Anthropological Association, Cincinnati, OH.

Sproull, L., Weiner, S., & Wolf, D. (1978). *Organizing an anarchy: Belief, bureaucracy and politics in the National Institute of Education.* Chicago: University of Chicago Press.

Strauss, B., & Strauss, F. (1951). *New ways to better meetings.* New York: The Viking Press.

Szilagyi, A. D., Jr., & Wallace, M. J. (1980). *Organizational behavior and performance* (2nd ed.). Santa Monica, CA: Goodyear.

Trice, H. A., Belasco, J., & Alutto, J. A. (1969). The role of ceremonials in organizational behavior. *Industrial and Labor Relations Review, 23,* 40–51.

Tropman, J. E. (1980). *Effective meetings: Improving group decision-making.* Beverly Hills, CA: Sage.

Van de Ven, A., & Delbecq, A. (1974). The effectiveness of nominal, delphi and interacting group decision-making processes. *Academy of Management Journal, 17,* 605–621.

Vroom, V. H., & Yetton, P. W. (1973). *Leadership and decision making.* Pittsburgh: University of Pittsburgh Press.

Wallace, M. J., & Schwab, D. P. (1976). A cross-validated comparison of five models used to predict graduate admission committee decisions. *Journal of Applied Psychology, 60,* 559–563.

Wheare, K. C. (1955). *Government by committee: An essay on the British constitution.* London: Oxford University Press.

Whyte, W. H., Jr. (1956). *The organization man.* New York: Simon & Schuster (Touchstone).

Zander, A. (1977). *Groups at work.* San Francisco: Jossey-Bass.

Zander, A. (1979). The psychology of group processes. *Annual Review of Psychology, 30,* 417–451.

UNDERSTANDING GROUPS IN ORGANIZATIONS

Paul S. Goodman, Elizabeth Ravlin, and
Marshall Schminke

ABSTRACT

The central thrust of this chapter is to examine some of the basic concepts,
assumptions, and models we use to think about work group effectiveness.
Our orientation is not simply to critique current modes of thinking, but rather
to unfreeze how we currently think about work groups and to propose some
alternatives. A detailed analysis of model specification, variable selection,
and the meaning of work group effectiveness is presented. Then, the focus
changes to three central concepts—technology, cohesiveness and norms.

Problems with current conceptualization are explored and new alternatives
are presented. The last section examines a series of methodological issues
in studying work group effectiveness. These include selecting the appropriate
level of analysis, designing studies on work group effectiveness, describing
work groups, and sampling strategies.

This chapter is about groups in organizations. The central thrust is to examine some of the basic concepts, assumptions, and models we currently use to think about groups. One goal is to challenge how we think about groups in organizations. In some sense we may have become intellectually complacent in the tools we use to describe and explain group performance. Concepts such as group norms, cohesiveness, group task, and performance represent some of the conceptual currency used in understanding groups. In many cases these and other concepts move from study to study without careful examination of their meanings. In this chapter we review the basic models and concepts used in understanding groups in organizations. Our orientation is not simply to critique current practices but rather to unfreeze how we currently think about groups and to propose some alternatives.

The rationale for examining groups in organizations is straightforward. Groups are pervasive phenomena in society; they touch everyone. In organizations they are central building blocks for getting work done. Policy committees, staff groups, loan committees, quality circles, work crews, and new-product committees are only a few of the many groups that permeate organizations. We have all participated in a multitude of groups in our organizational lives. Sometimes we have experienced the excitement, enthusiasm, and power of groups in getting things done. Other times we have experienced the inefficiency and ineffectiveness of groups. One simple rationale for trying to learn more about groups is that they are pervasive in organizations, determine in part the effectiveness of organizations, and greatly affect our own lives as well as organizational participants.

Another rationale is that over the last 8 to 10 years there has been a renewed interest in groups. One source of this renewed interest comes from the quality of working life (QWL) movement, which became influential in the mid 1970s. The group has been a central unit of analysis for these work innovation projects. Quality circles, autonomous work groups, labor-management teams, and QWL groups are a few examples of the types of groups that have emerged in organizations because of the interest in enhancing quality of working life. At the same time that this action research perspective was growing, development of theory for understanding groups in organizations reemerged. The work of Cummings (1981), Hackman (1976), Kolodny and Kiggundu (1980), and Gladstein (1984) are a few examples of attempts to develop new theoretical perspectives in this area. Given this renewed interest in both practical and theoretical perspectives on groups in organizations, it seems appropriate to step back and examine our conceptual apparatus for thinking about groups in organizations and to offer new perspectives.

Because the literature on groups is vast, we need to place some boundaries on our inquiry. McGrath's (1984) recent review of the literature clearly demonstrates the large volume of studies over time and the breadth of research over different types of groups. To make our work manageable we will focus on groups in organizations. Next we will concentrate on groups that produce something. The "something" could be a ton of coal, a manufactured part, an approved bank loan, the sale of a good or service, and so on. We acknowledge that there are many other types of groups and group functions in organizations (e.g., receiving information, politically legitimizing acts), but some boundaries are necessary so we can do a more intensive analysis. By implication we will focus more on permanent versus temporary groups, groups that have formal structure and objectives, and groups where the environment, in this case the organizational context, is key to understanding group functioning. We acknowledge the vast literature on groups (cf. McGrath, 1984), but can not effectively incorporate that into this analysis.

This chapter opens with a set of assumptions that characterize how we think about groups in organizations. Because the goal of this chapter is to change how we think about groups, focusing on critical assumptions seems to be a useful organizing device. The analysis begins with how we specify models of group effectiveness. Then, we turn to the selection of variables in these models as well as the meaning of effectiveness. The analysis becomes more specific as we examine in detail the meanings used to characterize three critical variables in the groups literature: technology, cohesiveness, and norms. The chapter closes with a section on methodology and a discussion section. In each of these areas we will identify current modes of thinking, present a critique, and then present an alternative strategy.

CRITICAL ASSUMPTIONS

In any body of literature there are a set of beliefs or assumptions that either explicitly or implicitly drive how people think and do research in a particular area. In this introductory section we will briefly list a set of assumptions about groups in organizations and examine them individually as the chapter unfolds. It is clear that other assumptions could be generated and examined, but practical considerations such as chapter length dictate that we should look at a few assumptions, and the following assumptions represent areas in which we have worked.

Assumption 1. Current models of group effectiveness represent appropriate model building strategies.

Assumption 2. The classes of variables in current models represent appropriate specification of factors that affect group performance.

Assumption 3. The effect of variables such as technology and organizational context are mediated through their impact on group process.

Assumption 4. Social psychological factors such as leadership and group interaction significantly affect group effectiveness.

Assumption 5. A common set of determinants can explain variation in different types of work group effectiveness criteria.

Assumption 6. Current ways of conceptualizing and operationalizing task and technology are useful in understanding the impact of these variables on performance.

Assumption 7. Creating cohesive work groups should enhance group effectiveness.

Assumption 8. Norms are critical factors in explaining variation in group performance.

MODELS OF GROUP EFFECTIVENESS

Because we want to examine some of the assumptions about how we think about group effectiveness, some models of group effectiveness are briefly presented to set the stage for our analysis. We tried to select models that have been influential, are current, and to some extent are different from each other. Figures 1 and 2 present illustrative models. Kolodny and Kiggundu (1980) developed a model out of the social–technical tradition that focuses on the interaction between leadership skills, technical skills,

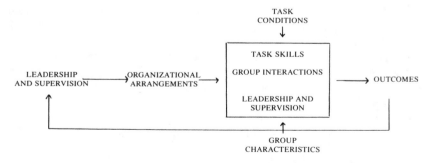

Figure 1.   Kolodny and Kiggundu (1980) A Sociotechnical Systems Model and Its Key Variables

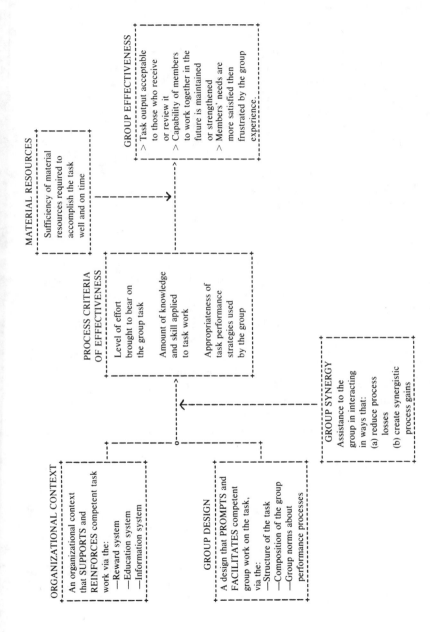

MATERIAL RESOURCES

Sufficiency of material
resources required to
accomplish the task
well and on time

GROUP EFFECTIVENESS

> Task output acceptable
to those who receive
or review it
> Capability of members
to work together in the
future is maintained
or strengthened
> Members' needs are
more satisfied then
frustrated by the group
experience.

PROCESS CRITERIA
OF EFFECTIVENESS

Level of effort
brought to bear on
the group task

Amount of knowledge
and skill applied
to task work

Appropriateness of
task performance
strategies used
by the group

ORGANIZATIONAL CONTEXT

An organizational context
that SUPPORTS and
REINFORCES competent task
work via the:
—Reward system
—Education system
—Information system

GROUP DESIGN

A design that PROMPTS and
FACILITATES competent
group work on the task,
via the:
—Structure of the task
—Composition of the group
—Group norms about
performance processes

GROUP SYNERGY

Assistance to the
group in interacting
in ways that:
(a) reduce process
losses
(b) create synergistic
process gains

Figure 2.   Hackman (1983) An overview of the normative model of group
effectiveness

and group interaction. Hackman's work (1983) has been a major influence in shaping current thinking about work groups. A new model by Shea and Guzzo (1984) focuses on three determinants of group effectiveness: task interdependence, outcomes interdependence or the contingency between rewards and group performance, and potency or the collective belief that the group can be effective (see Figure 3). Recent work by Gladstein (1984) must be incorporated in this status report because it represents one of the first attempts to pose and to test a comprehensive model of work-group effectiveness. The general model (Figure 4) is divided into inputs, processes, and outputs. A different type of model of work-group effectiveness (Goodman, 1986a, Figure 5) has been proposed, which is derived from an economic–technological perspective rather than from the psychological perspective underlying the other models. It focuses on group performance as a function of the mix between labor and technological variables. Although there are other models of work group effectiveness, the above representation provides a fairly broad picture of current thinking about work-group effectiveness.

A brief review of similarities and dissimilarities of these models should highlight some of the issues we will discuss in more detail concerning construction of such models. In terms of similarities there are some obvious commonalities, although our rule in selecting the preceding models is to illustrate diversity. First, the models are very general in nature. That is, they provide a "flow chart" of variables that impact on group effectiveness. For example, outcome interdependence affects task-related interactions (cf. Guzzo, 1986), but we do not know how. Second, all of the models acknowledge that variables at the individual, group, and organizational level of analysis bear on work-group effectiveness. Third, most of the models view psychological and organizational factors as the primary determinants of work-group effectiveness, an assumption that will be reviewed in the next section. Fourth, the concept of process plays a major

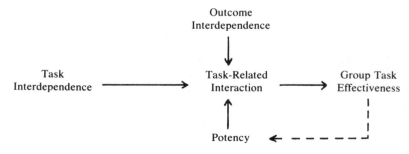

Figure 3.   Guzzo (1984) A model of group task effectiveness

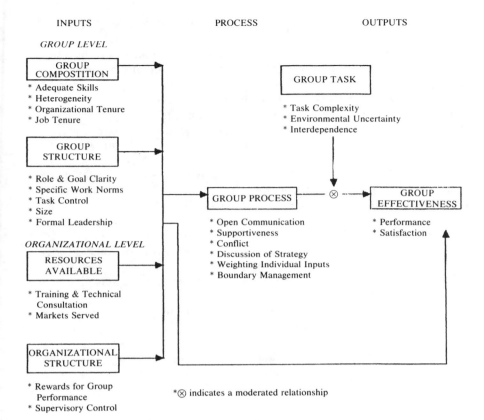

Figure 4.   Gladstein (1984) General model of group behavior: Constructs and measured variables

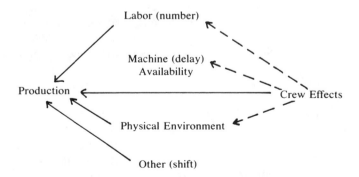

Figure 5.   Goodman (1986a) A production model

role in most models. That is, group process is the link to group effectiveness, and the effect of determinants of work-group effectiveness gets translated through group process.

In terms of differences, some of the models introduce concepts that have not typically appeared in the work-group literature. The potency variable (Guzzo, 1986), and the use of an endogenous and exogenous classification system (Gladstein, 1984) are some examples. In other cases it is not so much the introduction of a new variable but the emphasis on or functional role of a variable that distinguishes some of the models from others. The major role of technology in the production function model (Goodman, 1986a) is an example. Some other differences among the models include:

1. Some models focus on explaining effectiveness whereas others focus on specific criteria (e.g., group performance or output).
2. One model (Hackman, 1983) uses intermediate as well as final criteria of group effectiveness.
3. Some of the models emphasize the importance of feedback loops between variables (Guzzo, 1986).

We now turn to a more specific analysis of the appropriateness of current model specification, variable selection, and conceptualization of group effectiveness.

ISSUES IN MODEL SPECIFICATION

All of the models discussed (Figures 1–5) are very general in nature. Indeed, it may not be appropriate to classify them as models. At best they represent general classes of variables that bear on work-group effectiveness. There is no clear specification of the critical variables in the models nor do the interrelationships among variables get specified. It is true some hypotheses are generated but these seem more illustrative of what can be derived from the model than of any comprehensive specification of the interrelationship among variables in the model. The most typical hypotheses concern the moderator effects of the task variable on group effectiveness.

Why do we find this display of general or heuristic models? One reason is that groups are complex phenomena and these models provide nice intellectual maps for arranging the conceptual data. In this sense, these heuristic models are probably the best way to start untangling the intellectual complexity surrounding work-group effectiveness. A second reason why these heuristic models dominate the group literature is that this approach to theory is common in much of the organizational literature. If we look at other topics such as individual performance, leadership, or organizational–environment relationships, we find the same kinds of heuristic models. Thus, the level of theorizing in groups is no different than in other areas in our field.

Now there are two obvious questions to be addressed. Why should we change this level of theorizing, and what form should it take? Our basic position is that we should move toward more fine-grained specifications of models of group performance. Our first rationale for this position is fairly straightforward. First, we already know some things from the general research literature on groups that could be incorporated in our models. For example, reviews of past research (cf. Goodman, Ravlin, & Argote, 1986, p. 11) indicate an inverted U-shaped relationship between size and group performance. Also, the effect of size may affect certain criteria and not others. The question is, why cannot this empirical literature lead to more specific theoretical development? We know more than we include in our models of work-group performance. One observation we made in a recent review of the literature (Goodman et al., 1986), is that much of the current empirical research on groups is not tied closely to current developments in models of groups. This may happen because (1) researchers in the empirical literature often focus on testing specific variables (e.g., size, uncertainty, leadership) rather than on testing some general models of effectiveness, and (2) testing models of effectiveness, particularly in a field setting, is an expensive and complicated task.

A second rationale for more fine-grained specification of models is that it will improve construct specification and subsequent measurement. Most of the constructs in Figure 1 are very broad in nature. Group context (cf. Gladstein, 1984) has many meanings. Organizational arrangements (cf. Kolodny & Kiggundu, 1980) includes a whole host of variables. Group composition includes many factors, one of which is skill. But *skill* can refer to general education, general job experience, and specific sets of skills. The point is that these models are valuable in the sense that we learn that skill is an important variable. However, what *skill* means and how it interacts with other variables in the model, is not clear. Unless we move to a finer grained level of theory, our constructs will remain general, and the map from these general constructs to operational measures will remain ambiguous.

A third rationale for finer theoretical specification is that it will aid in testing our models of group effectiveness. Most of the models (cf. Gladstein, 1984, for an exception) discussed so far are not in a form to assess their validity.

The general message is that our current models are too general. Through finer specification we can reflect more what we know and we can uncover relationships that are new and exciting. At the same time our constructs will be more refined and our measurement procedures more robust.

The next logical question is the following: How can more fine-grained models be developed? Our basic position is that in building models of group performance one will move through three models: A heuristic model, a technological model, and an organization-specific model. We have already discussed the heuristic model. These characterize our current view of group effectiveness. An important assumption in the heuristic model is that we can generate a model of effectiveness across different types of groups. The question is whether that assumption is reasonable. Would a model that explains sales team performance (e.g., Gladstein, 1984) be generalizable to wood harvesting teams (Kolodny & Kiggundu, 1980)? At one level of abstraction the answer to that question will always be yes. The issue is whether at that level of abstraction we will advance our level of theory or practice in improving group effectiveness. We think not. Professional sales teams are very different from wood-harvesting crews. In the latter, equipment, technological arrangements, and physical conditions dominate what goes on in the group. That is, the technology determines to a large extent the structure of the group. Therefore, to understand group effectiveness, one needs to develop a model in the context of a specific technology, not in terms of groups in general.

Technology in our research (Goodman, 1986a) is defined as the system of four components—equipment, materials, physical environment, and programs—involved in acting on and/or changing an object from one state to another. These four components, once determined, provide constraints and patterns for the group's activity. To develop a viable model of group performance, we need to acknowledge the importance of the technological system. The nature of the system provides the basis of developing a more fine-grained model.

Therefore, the next level of theoretical specification should be bounded by the unique technologies in question. We can illustrate this type of specification from our work on coal mining crews. Coal mining crews are a good illustration of work groups because they are clearly defined social aggregates that work together to produce a group-level output—tons of coal. Crews typically have 8 to 10 workers. The basic production process is transporting coal from the face to an end user (e.g., utility) company. There are three major pieces of equipment (continuous miner, bolter, and shuttle cars) and the work flow is highly interdependent across these machines. (See Goodman, 1986a, for more description.)

At the heuristic level of specification, our own work has viewed group production as a function of technology (capital) and labor. That level of abstraction could fit most, if not all work groups. At the technological level of specification we need to translate the independent variables in a way that reflects the technological conditions. To simplify our discussion, let's focus on the equipment and physical conditions alone for the moment. To specify a model of effectiveness for coal mining crews we need to specify how the equipment, physical environment, and labor will affect performance. There are a variety of ways to think about equipment. We could think about capacity (i.e., how much it can produce) or availability (i.e., downtime). We have chosen to think about availability. Next we can think about what types of equipment can affect production and the relative impact of one type of equipment over another on production. Given our knowledge of the technology in this setting we know that the equipment will have a direct effect on production. Causes of equipment downtime are in part exogenous to the group. Some equipment has a greater impact on production variation (e.g., the continuous miner); therefore, the effects of downtime may not be linearly related to production. We also know that bad physical conditions should directly affect production, independent of crew composition. Further, given the interdependent nature of the production process, we know that all the machinery has to be manned. Absenteeism without replacement should lower productivity; overmanning will not increase productivity. We also know that there may be direct and indirect effects. For example, poor physical conditions can decrease productivity and increase downtime, which can lower production. Under favorable conditions there may be no differences among these teams because the physical conditions and quality of equipment may dominate the production process.

The purpose of this illustration is to suggest that if we thoroughly understand the processes by which groups perform their work, we can develop more specific theoretical specifications that identify critical variables, nonlinearities, interaction effects, and so on. Our motivation is not simply to make theories more complicated, but rather to push our thinking to a more detailed level so we can understand the process that makes some groups more effective than others. In our own work, we have formalized a more specific model incorporating the preceding qualitative description of coal mining crews, and we have empirically assessed the effectiveness of these models (cf. Goodman, 1986a).

This example of theoretical specification at the technological level is not unique to our production function model. We could take any of the heuristic level models in the literature and restate them at the technological level. Consider, for example, the sociotechnical model proposed by Kolodny and Kiggundu (1980). They postulate that group interactions, leadership, and task skills as a system of variables relate to group effectiveness. However, these variables and their interrelationship are stated at such a general level that it is not clear how these variables might operate on effectiveness. However, if we understand the technological system it is possible to translate these variables into a more testable system. Consider the concept of group interaction. In coal mining there are two critical dyads—between the maintenance and the continuous miner operator, and between the continuous miner operator and his helper. If we want to understand differences in coal mining crew effectiveness, the nature of these dyads, for example, their level of cooperation as opposed to that of any other of the 28 possible dyads, explains variation in crew effectiveness. The purpose of this illustration is to demonstrate that testable models and hypotheses can be generated from any of the heuristic level models, once one has an intimate knowledge of the technology.

The process of theoretical specification can move to a third level—groups within an organization. At this level, we generate a group model for a particular class of technology in a specific organizational context. The rationale for moving to an organization "case study" is twofold. First, the technological system of any work group is made up of a complex set of components. There are multiple possible combinations of those components that can yield the same result. Two organizations can have the same basic technology, but variations in maintenance or inventory policy can lead to different constraints on group behavior, and how the group manages these constraints can lead to differences in group effectiveness. The second reason for developing a model at the organizational level is that different organizations create different contexts in which work groups operate. The different contexts can be represented by different management philosophies, reward systems, and so on. This context represents another constraint on group activity, and how the groups respond to these constraints will bear on their effectiveness. If we want to understand what work groups do and why some are more effective than others, we must understand (1) the specific technological configuration, and (2) the specific organizational context in which the groups operate. The better we understand these two factors the better we will be able to develop more precise models of group performance.

The development of the third level of specification—the organizational level—is by definition an idiographic approach to understanding work groups. Although this approach will provide a more detailed account of the relationship among the technological system, the organizational context, and group process, critics (McGrath, 1986) rightly point out that such models will not be generalizable and thus will not contribute to developing uniform knowledge about groups. We agree with this criticism but note that the organizational level requires the researcher to develop an intimate knowledge of what the group actually does in a particular environment. This level of detail should provide more insights into group processes *and* inform our model development at the technological level, which is in the nomothetic tradition.

We can emphasize the need for this third level of specification with a personal research lesson. When we started our research on work groups our strategy was to generate a homogeneous sample of work groups across different organizations, so we developed a sample of coal mining crews who all mine in the same general way across different firms. We developed and tested a model at the technological level. Two general findings emerged from this work. (1) We explained a reasonable portion (R^2 = .60) of variation of crew performance across the different firms; that is, the R^2 for the same model of group performance estimated for different firms was the same. (2) There were major differences in the coefficients among the specific models for each firm; that is, coefficients of the predictors in the group model differ across firms. The work groups were homogeneous at one level, but there was a substantial amount of between firm heterogeneity. This finding indicates that it is necessary to understand how the unique technological configuration in a particular firm and organizational context affects crew performance.

We conclude this discussion of model specification by restating Assumption 1:

- Current models of group effectiveness are specified in too general a fashion. Lists of loosely connected variables will not generate new insights into group functions. Most current models are not generated in a testable form. We need to move beyond the heuristic level of specification to more fine-grained analysis. Specifications at the technological and organizational levels should provide new insights into why groups are differentially effective.

ISSUES IN VARIABLE SELECTION

Another issue in developing models of groups concerns the types of variables selected in the models. A cursory review of the variable selection in the models in Figures 1–5 indicates three important points. First, there is a major emphasis on psychological–organizational variables versus technological–economic variables. Role clarity, group interaction, size, leadership, and potency are examples of such variables. The second observation is that effects of the major determinants of group effectiveness are usually translated through group process. This means that variables such as role clarity or leadership first affect group process, which in turn affects group effectiveness. The third point is that the role of technology or group task is to serve as a moderator. This means that under certain task configurations certain processes are more important than others.

The reason for this type of variable selection and ordering of variables seems quite clear. A large portion of the group literature has been generated in a laboratory setting. In that setting it is easier to focus on process variables versus technological- or organizational-context variables. In addition, quite apart from the laboratory setting, there has always been a strong intellectual tradition in examining process, so it is not surprising to see that tradition passed on to the work-group literature. Another contributing factor is the fact that most of this research is done by psychologists or sociologists who are not "experts" in technology; therefore, one would not expect much focus on equipment or other production-policy variables. An additional reason for the primary focus on social–psychological-type variables is that most of the investigations of work groups are done in a particular organization as opposed to sampling across organizations. By examining groups within a single organization, variations in the contextual variables will not be observed.

Although we can understand the emphasis on psychological variables and the focus on group process, the question is whether the current models underspecify the major variables that affect group performance. We think they do. The set of variables exogenous to the group are critical in explaining group performance. The company policy about equipment allocation will explain differences in group performance. Maintenance and inventory policy will also explain variation in group effectiveness. Kolodny and Kiggundu (1980) report that the physical area where the wood harvesting crews worked had a main effect on how much wood the crews cut. Similarly, we would expect sales team performance (Gladstein, 1984) to be affected by the territory assigned to each team.

In our work on coal mining (Goodman, 1986a), we adopted a different strategy for variable specification. First, we adopted a fairly simple assumption that variation in group performance can be explained by whether people come to work (the number of people in the group) and whether the machinery works. We label this a "simple assumption" because we make no inferences about the quality of the labor (e.g., ability), the group process among labor, or any unique interaction between labor and technology. Using rather crude models that examine the direct impact of labor size, and technology (measured in terms of machine availability), we were able to explain a reasonable portion of production variance across different organizations ($R^2 = .60$). Our next analytic strategy was to examine a more complex model. For example, we found that recognizing different technological procedures improved our ability to explain group differences in performance. In addition, introducing nonlinear approximations in the model improved its explanatory power. The point is that we did a reasonable (actually better) job in explaining production variation, compared with other studies, merely by focusing primarily on a simple labor variable and a simple specification of technology.

Another issue is that the focus on leadership, cohesive groups, and autonomous work groups all speak to the belief that changing these human variables in groups makes a difference in group effectiveness. Our argument is that these human variables are important in some group situations and not in others. The unmodified assumption that these human variables make a difference is misleading. The issue is the relative importance of these classes of variables. This assumption is highlighted because we want researchers to be more sensitive to the role of human *and* nonhuman factors in understanding group performance.

Perhaps an example will highlight this issue. The Rushton experiment (Goodman, 1979) was one of the early quality-of-work experiments designed to find new ways to restructure work and organizational forms. Rushton is a medium-size coal mine in Pennsylvania and the object of change was the work group or the mining crew. The basic focus of the change team was on the human aspects of the group and the basic intellectual focus was to redesign the human or social system to better fit the technological system. Although the total intervention was fairly complex, a major thrust was to develop autonomous groups or self-managing teams. The initial results of the change effort were successful in the sense that highly cohesive self-managing teams were created. The question is whether these changes affected performance. The answer is that there were small positive effects. The lesson, however, is that while some change was successfully initiated, the magnitude of the changes was highly constrained by the technological system. These nonhuman factors (for example, physical conditions, equipment reliability, market factors) varied independently of the intervention, and they explained a large portion of the variance in performance. In this case the nonhuman factors were dominant. They created the constraints by which other systems (for example, the human or team component) could function. They created a "ceiling effect" on the impact of the team intervention.

We conclude this discussion of variable specification by restating Assumptions 2–4.

- Current models of work-group effectiveness overstate the role of human variables such as cohesiveness and leadership and understate the importance of technology and organizational-context variables.
- The variables such as technology and organizational context are not simply moderator variables or variables that interact with other variables to affect performance. These variables have direct impacts on performance. Coal mining crews with better equipment produce more. Sales teams operating in "rich environments" probably sell more.
- Under certain technological and organizational contexts, the social

psychology variables, which dominate the groups literature, may have very little impact on group performance.

ISSUES IN UNDERSTANDING EFFECTIVENESS

The third issue in this analysis of models of work-group effectiveness is the nature of the criterion variables. Two questions will be reviewed. What do we mean by *work-group effectiveness,* and what is the implication of the structure of work-group effectiveness for developing models?

There is no commonly accepted meaning of *work-group effectiveness.* Different researchers use different criteria. The selection of criteria sometimes reflects theoretical viewpoints; in other cases it is driven by convenience of operational measures. Table 1 illustrates some ways researchers represent effectiveness. The list is not meant to be comprehensive, but rather to illustrate some current ways researchers view work-group effectiveness. Most researchers seem to think about effectiveness as a multidimensional concept. In general, we do not find researchers aggregating across different dimensions to come up with a single indicator of effectiveness. Also, one can observe that many of the dimensions of group effectiveness clearly represent a managerial point of view.

There are a number of problems with the current usage of the term group effectiveness that need to be resolved if we are to improve our overall theories. First, there is no clear definition of what effectiveness

Table 1.   Meanings of effectiveness

Author	*Effectiveness Criterion*
Goodman (1986a)	Group Output
Fry & Slocum (1984)	Organizational Commitment
	Supervisor Performance Ratings
Argote (1982)	Promptness of Care
	Quality of Nursing Care
	Quality of Medical Care
Tziner & Vardi (1982)	Overall Performance Effectiveness
Middlemist & Hill (1981)	Customer Satisfaction
	Speed of Service
	Complaints
	Efficiency
	Etc. (23 Criteria)
Hackman & Oldham	Group Performance
(1980)	Satisfaction of Members
	Ability of the Group to Exist Over Time

means. Identifying dimensions of effectiveness is not the same as defining effectiveness. For example, performance can be an attribute of work-group effectiveness, but we do not know what the relationship is between variations in performance and variations in effectiveness. Implicit in most of the literature is the "unmodified" linear assumption (Kahn, 1977) that more of X means more effectiveness. Of course, there is no reason why this should be true. To define effectiveness one must specify the referent for comparison and the relevant constraints (Goodman, 1986).

The second problem concerns the domain of effectiveness. That is, what dimensions should be assessed? Although there is no simple answer to that question (cf. Goodman, 1986), the different constituencies surrounding a group provide one avenue for generating dimensions. From the members' point of view, satisfaction of their own needs could be one class of criteria. Most of the criteria in Table 1 represent the constituency point of view of the manager of the group. Another managerial perspective is at the intergroup and/or organizational level. Here the question is how the performance of one group affects other groups or the organization. An example is the classic case of intergroup conflict or subgroup optimization. In this case, it is possible for a group to be a high performer, but this level of performance negatively effects other aspects of the organization. In coal mining, unless crews cooperate in performing both indirect and direct production activities, total production effectiveness will decrease. The point is, looking at effectiveness solely from the work group's perspective or from only one constituency's perspective will lead to biases in assessment. A related issue is whether one should use concepts of both effectiveness and efficiency. At least in a performance context, viewing effectiveness only in the context of performance variation, without reflecting the cost or input side, also leads to biases in understanding work groups.

Another issue in determining the meaning of effectiveness concerns its temporal dimension. That is, what time period we use to assess group effectiveness bears on the meaning of effectiveness. Hackman and Oldham's (1980) definition of effectiveness is the only one that acknowledges the temporal dimension.

We have loosely constructed the group effectiveness concept. Much emphasis has been placed on the effectiveness concept in the organizational literature. Unless we sharpen this concept at the group level it will be difficult to advance our knowledge about groups.

The last issue concerns the relationship between the determinants of effectiveness and the measures of effectiveness. The general strategy in the literature is to begin with a general concept of work-group effectiveness. Some researchers (e.g., Hackman, 1983) delineate the general concept into a set of subdimensions. Other researchers go from the general conceptualization to specific measures of different aspects of effectiveness.

In either case effectiveness is viewed as a multidimensional construct. What is curious is that the models (determinants) of effectiveness are not further refined to relate to the different dimensions of effectiveness. *The assumption appears to be, even at the heuristic level of specification, that a common set of determinants relate to different effectiveness criteria.* The rationale for this assumption is never supported. The implication is that determinants of group output are the same as the determinants of group quality or satisfaction.

There is no theoretical reason to believe that this assertion is true. In production groups, the quantity of output will be largely affected by the type and reliability of the machinery, and the extent to which this equipment is properly manned. The satisfaction of group members will be largely affected by the degree to which rewards are equitably allocated and the degree to which these rewards are consistent with individual expectations or needs. Output and satisfaction are driven by different theoretical processes so we would expect different models for different dimensions of effectiveness. Empirical evidence indicating that different determinants are related to different effectiveness criteria can be found in Cheng (1984).

We conclude this discussion of work group effectiveness by restating Assumption 5.

- Our ability to understand models of group effectiveness depends on how we delineate the concept of effectiveness. We need to delineate the dimensional structure of work-group effectiveness, its temporal nature, and the perspective of different constituencies.
- More important, implicit in the literature is that a common set of determinants can explain different effectiveness dimensions. An appropriate strategy may be to select one dimension of effectiveness and model it carefully, before moving to other dimensions or more global representations of effectiveness. We need to develop different models for different effectiveness dimensions.

ASSUMPTIONS ABOUT CRITICAL CONCEPTS

We continue this exploration of group effectiveness by examining some critical concepts commonly used in the literature. Specifically we present the basic assumptions underlying these concepts, evaluate the viability of these assumptions, and then suggest some new "intellectual handles" for thinking about these concepts. This orientation reflects the basic theme of the chapter of reevaluating our current strategy for viewing groups and looking for new directions.

The following concepts will be reviewed: task and technology, group cohesiveness, and norms.

We selected these variables because they are central variables in the group literature and appear in most of the current models of work group effectiveness. Our concern is that these concepts get passed on from researcher to researcher without a careful review of the assumptions underlying these concepts.

There are obviously other variables that might be considered, but space provides a real constraint on examining other variables, so we asked which variables would be in our parsimonious model of work-group effectiveness. We think that technology is one of the most important variables in understanding work groups in organizations. It is the key link in understanding the role of the social–psychological determinants of group performance. Technology provides the constraints around the role of human variables in group-effectiveness models. Cohesiveness is selected because it is the best summary representation of the social–psychological variables. That is, cohesiveness can be thought of as representing the human energy of the group, and most designers of groups strive to develop high cohesive groups. We introduced the concept of group norms because they are critical to whether cohesive groups are indeed effective (i.e., norms channel the group's energy), and the concept of norms in work groups has received little critical attention.

Task and Technology

Any review of the group literature will uncover the pervasiveness of task and technology variables. Their primary role has been as a moderator variable. That is, the effects of some variables such as size or group composition are affected by, or moderated by, the type of group task.

Definitions and dimensions. Although the concepts of task and technology are both used as moderator variables, the description of these concepts and the traditions from which they arise differ. Describing tasks is not a new activity. Table 2 provides a picture of some representative group-task dimensions. McGrath's (1984) recent book identifies four dimensions—generate, choose, negotiate, and execute—which he uses to effectively organize much of the literature on groups. Steiner's (1972) classification of tasks has had a dominant influence on the field.

Table 3 provides a list of some of the major technological dimensions. Much of the earlier work on technology by Thompson (1967), Perrow (1967), and Hickson, Pugh, and Pheysey (1969) was clearly focused at the organizational versus group level of analysis. However, more recent work on technology (e.g., Schoonhoven, 1981, and Argote, 1982) has focused at the group level. One is struck by the dominance of the uncertainty concept in all of the categories. Some researchers use different names such as manageability (Mohr, 1971), but the underlying concept is the

Table 2. Group Task Dimensions

Carter, Haythorn, & Howell (1950)	Clerical, Discussion, Intellectual Construction, Mechanical Assembly, Motor Coordination, and Reasoning
Shaw (1981)	Intellectual versus Manipulative Requirements; Task Difficulty; Intrinsic Interest; Population Familiarity; Solution Multiplicity versus Specificity; Cooperation Requirements
Steiner (1972)	Unitary, Divisible, Conjunctive, Disjunctive, Additive
McGrath (1984)	Generate, Choose, Negotiate, Execute
Herold (1976)	Task Complexity, Social Complexity
Tushman (1979)	Routine, Environmental Uncertainty, Interdependence

same. The dominance of the uncertainty term in one sense is surprising, in another sense not. On one hand, technology is a complex concept and is unlikely to be primarily described by one dimension. On the other hand, forms of contingency theory have been a major intellectual force in organizational studies. The driving mechanism of that "theory" is the concept of uncertainty. That is, given certain levels of uncertainty, some organizational structures are more appropriate than others. Given the

Table 3. Technology Dimensions

Thompson (1967)	Long-Linked, Mediating, Intensive
Perrow (1967)	Number of Exceptions, Nature Search Process
Hickson et al. (1969)	Level Automation Rigidity of Work Flow Specificity of Evaluation Continuity of Throughput
Mohr (1971)	Manageability, Uniformity, Analyzability, Complexity
Comstock & Scott (1977)	Task Predictability
Schoonhoven (1981)	Technological Uncertainty
Argote (1982)	Input Uncertainty
Fry & Slocum (1984)	Number of Exceptions, Analyzability, Interdependence
Cummings (1981)	Work Flow Interdependence Work Flow Predictability Boundary Transaction Predictability Spatial and Temporal Relationships Mechanization

correctness of the fit between uncertainty and structure, we should find different levels of effectiveness. The pervasiveness of that theory even in the light of varied criticisms (cf. Schoonhoven, 1981) explains in part the pervasiveness of uncertainty dimensions. The reader should note that while contingency theory is often considered an organizational–level theory, it has been used at the group level, as indicated by the research cited here.

A comparison of Tables 2 and 3 indicates that the task and technology variables have been described differently, although their function is the same—to moderate the effects of organizational variables on group performance. The micro perspective of Shaw or Steiner is quite different from the more macro focus on uncertainty in the work of Mohr or Schoonhoven. These differences reflect in part the different origins of the dimensional schemes. The task dimensions originated from a social–psychological perspective grounded in a laboratory setting. The technology dimensions originated in macro-organizational theorizing and most of the research was grounded in the field setting. The basic premise in the literature is that task and technology are moderators of group performance. We will now examine the viability of these concepts.

Definitional problems. *Task* and *technology* are used almost interchangeably. However, the dimensional structures in Tables 2 and 3 would indicate they are different. In our review of this literature we found little if any work trying to untangle these two concepts. Although much work has been done attempting to define *technology* (cf. Goodman, 1986a), there are few comparable attempts to define *group task*. Task is defined by an attribute such as interdependence. However, an attribute of task is not the same as the definition of task. Unless we can clearly define task and technology, their role in understanding group effectiveness will remain ambiguous.

In none of the accounts of task or technology are we presented with intellectual guidelines about how to define the construct space of these concepts. Some characterizations of tasks describe what they do (e.g., generate, choose), whereas others generate attributes of tasks (e.g., interdependence) that could cut across what groups do. Which of these types of taxonomies are appropriate? Consider the technological dimensions in Table 3. *Uncertainty dominates the way we think about technology.* Is that the only central dimension? Technology seems much too complicated to expect that a single attribute will be adequate. There is nothing in the research literature to show that it dominates other dimensional characteristics of technology. Technology is more likely a multidimensional construct and we need a way to understand the construct space if we are to understand its relationship with effectiveness. The heritage of contingency theory has restricted our ability to think about new ways of characterizing technology in groups.

Implicit in most analyses of the effects of group task or technology on performance is the assumption that there is a single group task. This assumption permits characterizing the task in terms of dimensions such as interdependence or complexity. Although clearly one can construct a single homogeneous task in the laboratory setting, infrequently work is done on single homogeneous tasks in organizational settings. Consider the coal mining crews. Most coal mining crews do developmental and retreat mining. While the product of both these activities is tons of coal, the configurations of machinery, procedures, and group patterns are different. In addition, all crews perform direct and indirect (e.g., safety related) mining activities. We believe that most work groups have multiple sets of tasks. Each task or technological system must be understood separately. Aggregating across all these tasks with descriptive dimensions (Tables 2 or 3) confounds marked differences within these groups and how they operate.

For the moment let's assume that all groups perform single homogeneous tasks so we do not have to worry about aggregating across different tasks to some common dimension. Another question to consider is whether the type of descriptors that appear in Tables 2 and 3 are useful ways to describe task activities. *The assumption implicit in these tables is that a few general abstract descriptors such as task predictability and number of exceptions represent the appropriate strategy to characterize groups or technology as they relate to group effectiveness.* The existence of a small number of descriptors also enhances our ability to do research on these variables. Hence, the use of these general descriptors has gone unchallenged. The consequence of this conceptual and measurement strategy is that when you review the literature on work groups *you never learn what the groups do.* We have data on police groups (Fry & Slocum, 1984), health departments, (Mohr, 1971), hospital groups (Argote, 1982), and so on. But we learn about these groups in terms such as uncertainty or manageability not in terms of how the group operates and transforms objects from one state to another. An interesting exception is a paper by Kolodny and Kiggundu (1980). The paper gives a detailed description of machinery, employees, organizational arrangements, and task conditions, and how they interrelate. For example, there is a detailed discussion of the main type of machinery in the harvesting operation and how this machinery affects production. Downtime was a major problem that directly affected production. The authors identify some specific skills of the operator to assess and diagnose downtime and some specific types of exchanges between the operator and mechanic that had a significant impact on downtime and group performance. That description, which is unique to that machinery, is very informative. It identifies the critical points (or levers) for understanding and changing group performance. In general, we need to question whether the abstract dimensions (for example, uncertainty) that we use to describe technology are really useful.

An alternative position.   Task and technology are major variables in most research on group effectiveness. There are a number of definitional issues and assumptions underlying these concepts that have not been explored in the literature. We have made these assumptions explicit and pointed out their limitations. Before we leave this discussion, an alternative approach to thinking about task and technology and Assumption 6 are explored (see Goodman, 1986b, chap. 4, for a more detailed discussion).

Technology is defined as a system of components directly involved in acting on and/or changing an object from one state to another. There are four classes of components—equipment, materials, physical environment, and programs. *Task* is a subcomponent of technology. It is a program or set of operating rules, heuristics, and criteria, for the transformation process. Tasks describe activities in a particular job or activities that must be accomplished between jobs. Technology is the system of components at the group level that transforms objects from one state to another. Task represents the specific programs to accomplish the transformation process.

The four components—equipment, materials, physical environment, and programs—define the construct space of technology. We view these concepts as interrelated. All will appear in any technological system with varying effects on performance and, alternative combinations of these components can produce the same product or service.

- Technology is viewed as a main effect variable versus a moderator variable. That is, variations in equipment, materials, physical environment, and programs directly affect group performance.
- Most groups use multiple technologies. The assumption of homogeneity of group activities is not accepted.
- Because the four components in the technological system can be combined in multiple ways to produce the same product, it is important to examine the alternative configurations in detail in order to understand the role of technology and task on group performance.
- More emphasis should be placed on describing different configurations of technology versus using the abstract dimensions currently being used in the literature. The description would be organized around the four components of technology.

Cohesiveness

In any discussions of groups and performance, cohesiveness is a central concept. From the seminal work of Festinger in the 1950s (Festinger, 1950) to current interests in autonomous work groups, there has always been interest in designing groups where members are friendly toward each other, where loyalty exists, where everyone is ready to take responsibility and work toward some common goal. A cursory review of the research literature or of current textbooks in organizational behavior reveals the stylized fact that cohesiveness affects performance. The nature of this effect varies by the different literatures. People who are involved in changing groups and organizations view greater levels of cohesiveness as a contributing factor to greater productivity. The research literature indicates that cohesiveness will affect the variance of production, and the direction of the effect may be positive or negative performance. The key idea is that changing the cohesiveness of a group changes the nature of the group's output. In this section we will challenge some of the current thinking on cohesiveness. The basic target will be the link between the conceptualization of cohesiveness and the process by which it affects performance. We think cohesiveness can be a useful variable in summarizing the effects of different social–psychological variables, but the existing conceptualization needs to be changed.

Definitions.   There are a variety of definitions of *cohesiveness* (see Table 4.) We selected definitions that reflect both past and current thinking and those that emanate from the social–psychological laboratory tradition and the organizational behavior literature. Among these definitions there appear several different orientations. Some definitions focus on forces to remain in the group, whereas others focus on the attractiveness of the group to its members. Sometimes attractiveness is defined in terms of member attractiveness toward each other. Although there have been several debates about the definitions of cohesiveness (Gross & Martin, 1952; Cartwright, 1968), a careful examination of these definitions indicates they are quite similar. Attractiveness of the group for its members, or forces to remain in the group, are really the same. Both focus on the valences moving members toward, rather than away, from the group.

Definitional problems.   There is common agreement that cohesiveness is a group-level phenomena. What is surprising is that the definition is at the individual level. The attractiveness of the group to its members is the essence of the definition of cohesiveness. The summation of individual responses represents the level of cohesiveness. Implicit in this kind of definition is that the sum of the parts equals the whole.

Another problem is that the attractiveness of the group to the individual

Table 4. Definitions of Cohesiveness

Author	Definition
Festinger et al. (1950, p. 164)	The total field of forces that act on members to remain in the group.
Back (1951, p. 9)	The attraction that [A] group has for its members.
Gross & Martin (1952, p. 553)	The resistance of a group to disruptive forces.
Libo (1953, p. 2)	The resultant forces acting on each member to remain in the group.
Lott (1961, p. 279)	The group property that is inferred from the number strength of mutual positive attitudes among the members of the group.
Steers (1981, p. 199)	The extent to which individual members of a group are motivated to remain in the group.
Organ & Hamner (1982, p. 325)	The degree to which [the group's] members are attracted to the group, are motivated to remain in the group, and mutually influence one another.
Cartwright (1968, p. 74)	The resultant of all forces acting on all members to remain in the group.

is a very diffuse concept. There is no reason to believe that group members would find the group attractive for the same reasons. If this is true, then the impact of attractiveness on members' subsequent behavior is likely to differ. This would make prediction of the effects of cohesiveness very difficult.

In the literature, the common definition of cohesiveness is in terms of attractiveness of members. That is, the more members that like each other, the higher the group cohesiveness. Many of the laboratory studies on cohesiveness adopt this definition. The induction of cohesiveness is generated by telling the subject that others like him. In field studies, sociometric measures capture levels of cohesiveness. The issue is that this is a very narrow view of cohesiveness. It is really a measure of interpersonal attraction (Lott & Lott, 1965). There is nothing in this conceptualization that speaks to group-level phenomena. In addition, let's say that group members like each other—what does this say about group members orientation to perform group tasks?

The last problem with the current *attractiveness* definition is that it focuses solely on whether one will stay or not stay in the group. That is, the greater the valence of staying, the more likely the individual will remain. The focus is on the decision to participate rather than the decision to produce (March & Simon, 1958). However, the general fact or belief in the literature is that cohesiveness affects the decision to produce. The anomaly then, is that the conceptualization of the concept focuses on the decision to participate, but the theory concerns the decision to produce. Some reconciliation is necessary.

Theory.   The theoretical connection between cohesiveness and performance has been more assumed than theoretically explored. Seashore's (1954) classic study of cohesiveness provides the best explication of this relationship. The basic premise is that high-cohesive groups have more power over their group members than do low-cohesive groups. This power is exercised to induce members to conform to group standards. The power could be exercised through various forms of communication to modify social reality. That is, the group could create a social reality where low production is not a base for discharge. By removing this penalty from members' social reality, one could move the members toward lower production levels. Another form of power may be in disciplining members who deviate from group norms. This exercise of uniformity leads to the low variance prediction that is associated with high-cohesive groups. Another stream of theorizing deals with the direction of production rather than simply the variance. Seashore argues that the individual employee is subjected to continual pressures from the company for higher productivity. He also assumes that there are forces within the individual toward minimal productivity. Some equilibrium is reached between these two forces. Whether the highly cohesive group performs more depends on the perceived supportiveness of the external agent (the company). Given a perception of supportiveness, cohesive groups will exert more power on influencing members to conform to the higher standards set by the external agents.

Issues in theoretical argument.   This basic theoretical argument has not been critically examined. It is based on the assumptions that group standards are visible, member deviation from the standards can be observed, the group is motivated to pressure deviant members, deviant members conform, and conforming leads to greater productivity. It is not obvious that all of these links will occur.

The first major assumption is that groups have visible standards about performance. Visible standards mean that members are aware of a group standard and members consider this standard appropriate. Those two conditions are quite stringent. There is nothing inherent in groups to generate visible standards that are supported by members. Whether members are aware of some goal would partly depend on the visibility of group output, which in turn is affected by the type of technology. However, even if group output is visible, that does not insure that members will define some level of output as appropriate. If we look at the empirical studies, particularly the field studies (e.g., Seashore, 1954; Terborg, Castore, & DeNinno, 1976; Schriesheim, 1980), there is no acknowledgement theoretically or operationally that some standard must exist before group performance comes into play.

The second issue concerns whether deviant behavior can be observed. That is, given some standard, will group members identify and collectively agree on what constitutes deviant performance? The visibility of deviant behavior will be again affected by technology. For example, the greater the degree of interdependence the more difficult it will be for most group members to assess the deviancy of a particular member. Everyone is doing a different piece of the total task. Or, if the workers are not in close proximity it will be difficult to determine deviancy. The point is, the identification and consensus about deviant behavior in a work setting is a complicated process that has not been reflected in the theoretical or empirical literature on cohesiveness.

Given the identification of deviance, there is an assumption that the group will exert power on the members to conform to the group standard. The central question is whether the modal definition of cohesiveness will evoke this type of behavior. If cohesiveness is defined as members' attractiveness to staying in the group, it is not obvious why the group would exert pressure on members from deviating from task standards. If, on the other hand, group cohesiveness is based on attractiveness to completing the task, we would expect pressures to be exerted on members who diverge from task standards. The connection between the modal definition of attractiveness to the group and exertion of pressures is not obvious.

Another assumption is that members conform to group pressures. Although the Asch (1951) studies are often cited to validate this point, the fact is that the Asch study showed that groups can induce members to conform, but not all members respond to conformity pressures. Indeed in the Asch experiment a minority of the subjects actually changed.

The last assumption that we examine here concerns whether conformity would actually affect productivity. If we take a simple case of five workers who each produce an object (an additive task), then, if a deviant worker conformed, we would expect less variation in production and higher average rates. However, most work tasks are not in that form; they are divisible and interdependent. In addition, at work there are a variety of ways to do particular tasks. So if the deviant member received more pressures to conform, it does not follow that the individual would select the correct performance strategies, and group performance would improve. That is, on an interdependent task, greater pressure on a member to conform does not mean total performance will increase.

The basic argument is that the theoretical process underlying the cohesiveness–group output hypothesis is complicated. It has not been explored theoretically or empirically. There are many factors working against finding any relationship. Research needs to explore these linked assumptions previously described. Why then has the literature taken its present form? One reason is that the early work underlying the consequences of cohesiveness focused on attitudes (cf. Festinger, 1950). The research was designed to show that groups with certain characteristics can influence members who hold deviant attitudes. The form of that work was translated to work-group output as the dependent variable. A priori, however, we have no reason to believe that these variables operate in the same way. First, the definition of cohesiveness as the attractiveness of members to staying in a group may be more closely related to whether members want others to hold similar attitudes than to whether members should conform to some task standard. Also, the whole process of identifying deviant performance on an interdependent task and relating that to some standard seems considerably more complicated than whether an individual member's attitude about Y conforms to the modal group attitude. Whether or not this explanation for the current state of affairs is accurate, the major point is that neither the theoretical or empirical work on cohesiveness and group output has carefully examined the critical processes that underly this relationship.

Given some of these definitional and theoretical problems, it is not surprising that the empirical literature on the relationship between cohesiveness and productivity is somewhat ambiguous. Stogdill (1972) provides one of the best reviews of this literature. He reports that out of 34 studies, 12 indicated positive relationships, 11 indicated no relationships, and 11 indicated negative relationships between cohesiveness and productivity. The picture then is very mixed. Even in single studies (Terborg et al., 1976) we find positive, zero, and negative relationships reported.

Some researchers have tried to make sense of this relationship by looking for moderator variables. Seashore (1954) reports that the perceived supportiveness of the external agents (e.g., the company) should predict high levels of productivity. Although this result is a much cited finding from his work, a close examination will show that the supportiveness variables in his study do not always produce significant results. Stogdill (1972) hypothesizes that drive is the key variable. That is, high-cohesive groups with high drive produced more. However, an examination of his empirical findings does not support clear, significant support for this hypothesized relationship.

We can conclude the section with the following observations. Problems with the conceptualization of cohesiveness have led to biases in the operationalization of that concept. In addition, there are other methodological problems not tied directly to the conceptual definition of cohesiveness. All of these problems confound our understanding of how cohesiveness affects group performance.

Cohesiveness—An alternative view. In this section we outline some alternative ways to think about cohesiveness and Assumption 7.

- We define *cohesiveness* as the commitment of members to the group task. The greater the level of commitment among group members, the greater the cohesiveness. *Commitment,* following from the work of Kiesler (1971) and Salancik (1977, p. 4) refers to the binding of the individual to behavioral acts. Commitment is increased to the extent that the act is (1) explicit, (2) irrevocable, (3) public, and (4) done freely.
- The *group task* refers to the set of activities the group must do to achieve the group's goal. Because our interest is in groups in organizations that produce goods or services, our focus is on those activities that produce the group's output (e.g., tons of coal produced, sales revenues, etc.). In a less formal sense, the images we relate to this definition of cohesiveness include "group members work hard as a team on the group task," "they work well together on the group task," "they help each other complete the group task," and so on.
- The proposed definition differs from the modal definition of cohesiveness, which refers to the attractiveness of staying or leaving the group. That definition focuses on the decision to participate; our proposed definition focuses on the decision to produce. In addition, the proposed definition acknowledges that group members can be committed to a common task but not necessarily attracted to each other. So the concept of attractiveness is not an essential ingredient in our definition of cohesiveness.
- There are some other characteristics of the definition we should note. First, there is nothing inherent in the definition to indicate how cohesiveness and group output are related. That is, we do not assume highly cohesive groups are high producing groups. This point will be elaborated shortly. Second, we acknowledge that groups serve many other goals besides producing goods and services, and to that extent our definition of cohesiveness is narrow. However, our position is to move away from very general definitions of phenomena to clear definitions tied to specific research problems.
- *Theoretical assumption:* In the current view of cohesiveness, the relationship with productivity is based on a conformity assumption. That is, deviancy from group standards is observed and pressure is exerted from the group to bring the deviant member in line. In the proposed conceptualization of cohesiveness, there is no single theoretical assumption that links cohesiveness and group output. There is no specific prediction about level or the variance of production. Cohesiveness is seen as one of a series of variables that may bear

on group production. To understand the impact of cohesiveness one must understand its impact in the context of other variables.

- A model of effectiveness that incorporates cohesiveness must reflect the following: First, the technology and task configurations may mitigate any impact of cohesiveness. In configurations that provide little opportunity for human discretion or effort allocation, one would expect little relationships between cohesiveness and group production. Second, even under conditions where the group's activities are highly determined by technological considerations, there are situations where there are unanticipated external events (e.g., emergency, demands by a customer) or internal events (e.g., machine breakdown). In these cases, uncertainty is introduced into the production process, and how the group responds should impact on group performance. For example, if a machine breakdown occurs in coal mining, the total production process will be affected. Crew members in this situation can wait for a mechanic (reactive) or try to solve the machine problems (proactive), or do other work to facilitate the production process. A high-commitment (cohesive) group is more likely to adopt the proactive strategies. A third scenario is when the group operates in an environment where human effort and discretion play a major role in determining the group's output. However, even here we must be careful in the assumption that cohesiveness will lead to high group output. Groups with high commitment to doing the group task should be better producers when there is an opportunity for group effort and discretion to make a difference. However, for that connection to occur, those groups must (1) allocate their effort on the appropriate tasks, (2) apply the correct mix of skills to the task, and (3) understand and implement the appropriate performance strategies. These three conditions (cf. Hackman & Morris, 1975) for group effectiveness are necessary and sufficient conditions for effective group performance. However, they are not caused by high cohesiveness. It is possible to have groups committed to a task that have not met these three conditions. It may be easier for highly cohesive groups to learn these three conditions through trial and error or leadership direction. However, they are not automatic correlates of cohesiveness. The task for the researcher studying cohesiveness is to determine both the extent to which these conditions are present and the process by which they become present in high- and low-cohesive groups.

Norms

Norms represent another central concept in understanding groups and group effectiveness. Our focus on group norms seems to be a natural follow-up from the above discussion on group cohesiveness. Norms and co-hesiveness are the two central social–psychological concepts in a model of group effectiveness. Cohesiveness captures the energy and effort members will allocate to the group task and norms identify the ways to channel that effort. In this section we (1) represent the current set of beliefs or stylized facts about norms that appear in the literature, (2) carefully examine the viability of these beliefs, and (3) provide an alternative conceptualization.

In the social–psychological and organizational literature there is a general espoused principal that norms are viewed as standards that regulate group-member behavior. Norms are expected behaviors sanctioned by the group that control and create uniformity in member behavior. In the context of group effectiveness, standards exist concerning output. That is, the norm regulates the amount of output or effort generated by the group. Or, norms can focus on the input side. For example, there are norms about appropriate ways to do the group task (Hackman & Morris, 1975). Norms also focus on group maintenance issues (versus instrumental or task behavior). In this case, norms develop to regulate the social interaction among group members and not to regulate instrumental task activities. The basic theme in the literature is that norms are pervasive in groups and important in regulating group activities. Our view is that norms exist in work groups, but they may not be as pervasive as is assumed in the literature. The theoretical delineation of norms in a work-group effectiveness model is not well developed. The empirical evidence supporting the role of norms in work-group effectiveness is all but nonexistent.

Definitions of norms. Table 5 presents a set of possible definitions of *norms*. The list is representative of some of the classics in the field as well as current textbook viewpoints. It is not meant to be exhaustive. There appears to be a fairly clear consensus on the definitional attributes of a norm. First, norms specify a set of expected behaviors. The word *behaviors* is used generally to refer to attitudes, beliefs, and behaviors. The expected behaviors are either pre- or proscriptions. That is, they refer to attitudes, beliefs, and behaviors that should or should not be held or performed. Second, these expectations are held and accepted by group members. Most writers feel that the norm does not have to be held by all members but it should be held by at least a majority. The third attribute is that the group members will enforce the performance of the expected behaviors. Deviation from these expectations leads to punishment. The fourth attribute concerns the range of acceptable behaviors. Most writers acknowledge that for most norms there is an acceptable range of behaviors. For some norms that range is narrow, for other norms there is a broad range of behaviors. Jackson's Return Potential Model (1965) represents a theoretical and empirical way to define norms in terms of the distribution

Table 5.   Definitions of Norms

Author	Definition
Thibaut & Kelley (1959)	Norms are some sequential pattern of interactive behavior developed between two people.
McGrath & Altman (1965, p. 65)	Norms are behavior that is anticipated and expected by the group of its members.
Katz & Kahn (1978)	Norms are common beliefs of an evaluative type which constitute a coherent interrelated syndrome. They refer to the expected behavior sanctioned by the system and thus have a specific "ought" or "must" quality.
Steers (1981)	Norms are a standard that is shared by group members and which regulates member behavior.
Hellreigel et al. (1983)	Norms are generally agreed upon standards of behavior that have emerged as a result of member interaction over time.
McGrath (1984)	Norms are sets of expectations about what someone "ought" to do under a given set of conditions. Violation is negatively sanctioned.

of potential approval and disapproval for various behaviors performed by others in a specific situation.

Norms are viewed as different from values, which are more generalized statements about how people ought to behave. Thus, we could have a norm that crews should communicate with each other during shift interchange; a parallel value is that workers should cooperate with each other. Some norms focus on a particular position and how the incumbent of that position should behave. Most researchers in the field would characterize this as a role specification. Roles specify expectations for incumbents in a dyadic relationship; norms specify standards of behavior for groups and larger social systems.

Definitional issues.   The initial definition of *norms* seems clear and there is reasonable consensus across different researchers. However, further conceptual elaboration of the attributes of norms are necessary before we can know what it means to assert that a group norm exists, and understand the relationship of norms to models of work-group effectiveness. Three attributes are considered: the distribution of norms, their enforcement, and their transmission.

An important issue that has not been well delineated by researchers of norms in work groups concerns the acceptance or distribution of a norm. We propose that the distribution of a norm can be specified in terms of the extent of the knowledge of the norm, the extent of the acceptance of agreement with the norm, and the extent of the actual application or performance of the normative behavior. Uniformity of application of a particular behavior among group members does not indicate the existence of a norm. The extent of knowledge about the norm and of the acceptance of the norms must precede the behavior before we can make inferences about the existence of a norm. The distribution of a norm needs to be understood in terms of these three content areas and the frequency of group members in these three content categories. That is, the existence of a group norm must be understood in terms of the number of group members knowledgeable about the norm, who accept the norm, and whose behavior is consistent with the norm. We introduce this more elaborate view of *distribution* because the definitional attribute of "acceptance by group members" is too general and not informative in terms of determining the existence of a norm.

Another issue concerns the attribute of enforcement or sanction, which appears in most definitions of norms. We think that there are three dimensions of enforcement that need to be articulated. First, the enforcement agent is critical in the definition of norms. In the context of this paper, the agent would be other group members. However, there are many other possible enforcement agents, such as a supervisor, higher level management, union officials, and so on. The concept of agent is important because it identifies whether the norm resides in other forms of social aggregation or is unique to the group. For example, most work groups have standard operating procedures. These specify the nature of job activities and the methods of coordination across job activities. Work-group members might perform these behaviors and consider them appropriate. However, this would not necessarily point to the existence of group norms, if the enforcing agent for these behaviors resides primarily in the supervisor or other outside organizational members. Other enforcement dimensions include the consistency of punishment and the severity of punishment. The greater the consistency of punishment by group members and the greater the severity, the more likely the norm exists.

A third attribute concerns the transmission of norms, that is, how norms are passed on to members. Of particular interest is the agent of transmission. Norms may be transmitted to new members by the group or by agents external to the group. Norms that are transmitted by group members are more likely to fit into our definition of group norms. Norms that are transmitted by agents outside the group may or may not be norms unique to a particular group. In general, we think that norms transmitted by outside agents would identify organizational norms (which are general to a variety of groups) versus norms unique to a particular group. We do recognize that norms transmitted from outside agents could be embraced and enforced by the group.

The point of this discussion is that the definitions of norms in the literature reflect a reasonable degree of consensus. At one level, the definition is clear and useful in distinguishing norms from other aspects of social structure. However, terms such as *enforcement* and *acceptance by the group* are very general. They provide little theoretical structure for understanding the conceptual nature of norms or for developing a method to determine the existence or nonexistence of norms. One of the current problems in the literature is that the loose definitional structure of norms makes it difficult to know when norms are in effect. In much of the literature, norms are asserted to exist without any basis. One contribution in this section is to delineate (1) the three-dimensional structure of distribution; (2) the three factors of enforcement, and (3) the transmission process. These concepts should sharpen our understanding of group norms and guide our operational procedures in determining the existence of norms.

Theoretical rationale.   There is no single theoretical position that links norms to group effectiveness. Rather, there seem to be a number of factors one should consider in relating norms to group effectiveness. First, there is a general argument that the existence of norms is a way of cutting costs and increasing profits. Basically, this argument focuses on the function of norms in routinization of sequences that are strategically important to the group (McGrath, 1984). Specifically, norms function to (1) provide group members with an easy frame of reference for understanding the complicated world of work, (2) provide uniformity of action, necessary if a group is to survive (Festinger, 1950), and (3) eliminate the need to use personal power to induce uniformity or predictability in others behavior. The underlying assumption in this argument is that the existence of norms in a group increases the effectiveness of that group's functioning.

The second perspective focuses on types of norms (cf. McGrath, 1984, p. 201). The argument is that certain types of norms have a direct impact on group effectiveness. Two specific types of norms are generally identified. One type focuses on performance strategies. These strategies concern the choices group members make about how to perform the task. The second type focuses on output standards such as the level of effort or actual output. To the extent that appropriate performance strategies are identified and norms for effort and output are set high, then these norms should contribute directly to group effectiveness (Hackman, 1976).

The third theoretical argument comes from the conformity literature and has already been examined under the cohesiveness discussion. The basic argument is that if a norm about group standards (for output) is in place, deviations from the standard will be observed, members will exert pressure on the deviant to move toward the group standard, and the greater level of conformity will affect variability of group performance.

Theoretical limitations. The three arguments linking norms to effectiveness are very general and do not lead to very precise hypotheses. The essence of the functional argument is that norms are efficient mechanisms to create predictability in group activities. Because less time is needed on coordinating activities, more time can be spent in task work. However, there is nothing inherent in this argument that suggests that this extra time will be spent in an appropriate way to increase group effectiveness. Similarly, the argument (about performance strategies) is helpful to the extent to which it identifies a class of norms that should bear on effectiveness. However, there is nothing in the argument that tells us which performance strategies are more appropriate than others. Also, the argument that traces the effects of group pressure on members deviating from group standards is based on a set of assumptions that may not be valid. We have discussed this point earlier (see pp. 147–148).

We have reviewed many articles and books but have not found any clear theoretical arguments linking norms and effectiveness. There are many assertions that norms affect effectiveness, but there are no developed arguments that link these two concepts.

Empirical evidence. The evidence concerning the relationship between norms and work-group effectiveness is very sparse. A few studies do frequently get referenced, but many of these are more than 40-years-old. We acknowledge that there is a large laboratory literature on group norms and conformity, but much of this is conducted on ad hoc temporary groups and the focus is on attitudes or beliefs. This chapter is about permanent groups working in a complex technological environment (at least compared to laboratory tasks) and operating in a complex organizational setting. Although this laboratory work is informative about how groups induce conformity, that process must be understood in the complex setting of groups in organizations.

One major class of field studies deals with rate restriction. One classic study is the Bank Wiring Room of the Western Electric studies. Homans reports, "They had a clear idea of a proper day's work: about two completed equipments, or 6,600 connections, for a man working on the connectors, 6,000 for a man working on the selectors" (Homans, 1950, p. 60). Although there was some variability around these numbers, workers exceeding this criteria became known as "rate busters" or "speed kings" and were punished, as were the "chiselers" who produced below this figure.

Collins, Dalton, and Roy (1946) reported similar output restrictions across three factories under a piece-rate system. Roy (1960) provides similar examples of output restrictions under piece rate and day rate. In the classic experiment on participation and introduction of change, Coch and French (1968, p. 348) report that "the most important force affecting recovery under the no-participation procedure was a group standard . . . restricting production to 50 units an hour." Seashore's (1954) work is also cited to demonstrate the efforts of norms on production—high–cohesive groups exhibited less variability in production.

In general, all these studies suggest that group members adhere to standards that restrict production. It is important, however, to understand what output restriction means. *In most of these studies the researchers report that workers performed a fair day's work by company standards; that is, they produced well.* The interpretation of these studies is that they often demonstrate that workers performed poorly. That is not the case. They could have (i.e., have the capacity to) produced more. They did not because higher production might have led to lower piece rates, working out of a job, and so on. Also, in most of the cases cited here there were feelings of distrust and conflict between the workers, the engineers, and management.

The preceding studies represent the major evidence for the prevailing belief that norms exist in groups and that they shape group performance. Some questions, however, must be raised concerning the quality of this evidence. First, there are not a lot of studies. Second, it is not clear that all of these studies are about work groups. In the Seashore (1954) study, data is collected from organizational units but it is not clear that these units are work groups. Even in the Bank Wiring Room, we find nine wiremen who are all working on individual jobs. They are a group in the sense that they are located together, the payment system is in part tied to everyone's performance, and a number of informal exchanges take place among the wiremen; but there is no interdependence among these individuals in terms of work. Third, in most of the cited studies, output was at the individual level, homogeneous in nature and visible. In this context it is easy to see how some common meaning can be developed about a "fair day's work." However, there are many other situations where group output is not simply the aggregation of individual output; work is interdependent, there is uncertainty in the technological environment, and determining a "fair day's work" is difficult. Fourth, most of the studies do not provide any independent evidence of the existence of the norms. Most of these early studies were participant observation studies where the researcher was a full-time employee. Although his observations about the existence of the norms may be valid, there is no independent confirmation. We know little about the distribution of norms in terms of how extensively the group standards were accepted and obeyed. In the Seashore (1954) and Coch and French (1968) studies, low variability in production is used to infer the existence of a norm, but there is no independent confirmation. There are a variety of reasons (e.g., similar abilities), why a group could exhibit low variability without expecting that an agreed-upon standard about output existed. Fifth, in some of the studies, if a norm about output restriction did exist, its origins were in the organization, not in the group per se. For example, the "norm" in the Bank Wiring Experiment did not originate in the Bank Wiring Group under observation. Its origin was in the department from which this group came or in the larger organization. To assert that a norm about equity or a fair day's pay resides in the organization versus the group does not make it less important. But our interest is in discovering the impact of group norms on effectiveness. All groups exist in any organization, so that context will bear on group effectiveness. However, we should distinguish between organizational and group norms so we can better trace their impact on the group. Most of the studies we discuss do not distinguish between a general norm of equity, which gets translated into a fair day's work for a fair day's pay versus norms that are specific to a particular group.

There are a few other empirical studies that deal with norms about doing work versus work output. Horsfall and Arensberg (1949) describe a method adopted in a shoe factory to allocate work among four teams in a way that each team received work of equal difficulty and could earn equal pay. Roy's (1960) account of "banana time" demonstrates how regularities of social behavior are developed and supported by the group as a means of reducing boredom at work. These studies are important in that they demonstrate how norms develop to regulate some of the maintenance activities of groups. It would be interesting to see how these norms contribute to the satisfaction of the groups. Unfortunately, these studies do not deal with that outcome variable.

There are some more recent studies on norms and effectiveness. Georgopoulous (1965) examined the effect of normative consensus (the degree of group agreement about various norms) and normative complementarity (the extent to which interacting groups agree about norms on effectiveness). He found a positive correlation between these two norm variables and effectiveness. However, his measures of norms are very questionable. For example, normative complementarity is measured in terms of whether or not the employee thinks his or her boss expects too much from him or her. This measure hardly reflects any of the acceptable definitional attributes of norms. Janis' (1972) work on group think is frequently cited as a way that group norms affect the quality of decision making. He argues in his analysis, of the "invasion of Cuba," that the cohesive policy group developed, for example, illusions of invulnerability and illusions of unanimity. Then he shows how these illusions, carried in the heads of group members, led to dysfunctional thinking. Even if we accept this analysis it is not clear that these illusions are norms. Norms are proscriptions or prescriptions about behaviors that are enforced by the group. The illusion of unanimity is a belief held by the cohesive group that everyone else agrees to a particular position; it is a form of pluralistic ignorance, not necessarily a norm. In addition, we should point out that there has been mixed support for the relationship among cohesiveness and dysfunctional processes that affect quality of group decision making (Fodor & Smith, 1982; Flowers, 1977; Manz & Sims, 1982).

The last example of empirical evidence for norms comes from an evaluation of a major quality of working life experiment designed to introduce autonomous work groups into coal mining crews (Goodman, 1979). In this study, the researcher tracked a set of groups over 3 years, using observational techniques, methods surveys, and company records. It represents one of the most comprehensive evaluations of an organizational change project. What was learned from this study? First, the intervention led to the development of high-commitment teams. Members were very aware of themselves as a group and invested a great deal of energy in the group task. Second, there were many new behaviors exhibited by the crews compared to the situation before the change implementation, such as planning and coordinating behaviors. These represented individual initiatives not supported by any normative consensus. Third, there were new institutions such as labor management teams that directly contributed to improvements in safety and productivity. By definition, these new institutions were accepted by the group. But the institutionalization of a new form of work organization is not the same as a group norm about performance strategies or output. Fourth, a number of norms did appear, but they focused on indirect production activities. For example, there was a norm about intershift communication and one about job switching. But no norms were developed about group standards or group performance strategies. What was striking was that despite the high level of task commitment by the members, very few norms emerged to guide the group in the performance of its task.

In the literature there is a fairly pervasive belief that norms affect group performance. In our review of the empirical literature we find (1) very few empirical studies on this relationship, (2) the quality of some of this research is questionable, at least in terms of verifying the existence of norms, and (3) very little evidence on the pervasiveness or the effects of norms on group performance indicators.

An alternative position. In this section we look at some alternative approaches to studying norms and a restatement of Assumption 8.

- *Definition.* We advocate extending the conceptualization of norms to include the dimensions of distribution, enforcement, and transmission. Determining the existence of norms is a critical research task. Simply assuming that norms exist—a pervasive assumption in the literature—is unacceptable. The concept of distribution, for example, includes knowledge of, agreement with, and performance of the normative behaviors. Using this conceptualization to guide the operationalization procedures is a systematic approach to determining the existence of norms in a group. None of the literature we reviewed provides the conceptual guides or the operational procedure to determine the existence of norms.
- *Typology of Norms.* There are many different types of norms operating in group and organizational settings. Developing a typology of norms might provide some guidance on how norms are linked to group effectiveness. Here are some suggestions. We think there are a set of norms dealing with the *production process.* These include norms about group standards (e.g., output), norms about instrumental task behaviors (how to get the job done), and norms about indirect production activities. Indirect production may include norms about communication, coordination, or helping behaviors. For example, the Rushton Quality of Work Study norms about intershift coordination (Goodman, 1979) would fall into this class. These various types of norms are probably differentially related to group output. Norms about standards will explain more variance about production than will indirect norms, although the latter may be more prevalent.

Another class of norms concerns *informal social arrangements.* These norms emanate from informal groups located in formal workgroup structures and primarily regulate the social exchanges within the group. Norms in this class could regulate lunchtime behavior, friendship exchanges, social games, and other activities relative to the maintenance of the social group. Descriptions of these norms can be found in Roy's (1960) description of "Banana Time" and Homan's (1950) discussion of the Bank Wiring Room.

Another class of norms concerns the *allocation of resources.* These norms could have their origin in the group or in the organization. Horsfall and Arensberg (1949) examine a norm that allocated work across teams to insure equality in job difficulty and pay. Similar allocation roles can develop within a group. In examining this particular class of norms it is important to determine whether their origin is in the organization or the group. In addition, it is important to determine the basis of the allocation role: equity, equality, need, and so on. In the Horsfall and Arensberg study, if there is a norm at the *organizational* level that allocates tasks *equally* across groups then this norm will not account for effectiveness differences between groups. If the norm has its origin within the group, and uses an allocation basis different from the other groups, this norm should explain differences across groups. We think the relative conformity to norms in this class will first affect worker satisfaction about resource allocation. In addition, these norms may have an indirect effect on group output.

We think developing a typology along these lines is useful in organizing the multitude of different norms and identifying which norms are related to which dimensions of effectiveness.

- *Types of Groups.* Another issue that needs some exploration is the relationship between types of groups and types of norms. Most of the empirical literature about norms focuses on groups where individuals work independently and their work is aggregated into a group output. In other groups, individuals work interdependently and there is a group output. In the former group it is easy to see why group standards emerge. Everyone is doing the same task and output is visible. In groups exhibiting high interdependence and group-level output, it will be more difficult for norms about group standards to emerge. Rather we would expect to find norms focusing on indirect production activities such as more effective communication or coordination. There has been no exploration in this literature of the effect of the interaction between types of norms and types of groups on the emergence and effect of group norms.

- *Development of Norms.* Another way to better understand the impact of norms on groups would be to take a developmental perspective. That is, we want to trace the emergence, institutionalization, and decay of norms in group settings. This longitudinal approach should provide a more precise way to understand the existence and impact of norms, at least compared to a cross sectional perspective. For example, in the Rushton Quality of Work Study (Goodman, 1979) we knew some of the planned social interventions, such as building effective intercrew communication. Prior to the intervention, we were able to describe the "before" state. Over time, we were able to trace the distribution of knowledge about this practice, growing acceptance, and eventually, the performance of intercrew communication. In addition, it was possible to catalog how deviancy from this norm was sanctioned. Over time, there were major changes in the behaviors used by group members to accomplish this function. Initially, each crew member communicated with his counterpart; later, only one representative from each crew communicated with each other, and then the representatives communicated within the crews. Three years into the intervention there was a noticeable decay in this normative behavior. A theoretical discussion of this process can be found in Goodman (1979), and Goodman and Dean (1982, appendix, pp. 268–276). The point of this discussion is that much of our discussion of norms in groups has been quite diffuse. Tracing the development of specific norms over time should provide a better understanding of their impact on groups.

• *Norms and group effectiveness.* Another approach to enhancing our understanding of norms is to trace their effect through a model of effectiveness. Simply looking at the relationship between norms and other indicators of effectiveness (the current approach in the literature) does not acknowledge the complicated set of processes that impact on different effectiveness criteria. The first place to start would be to focus on a single effectiveness criteria. We have already suggested that some norms (e.g., group standards) fit certain criteria (e.g., production), but not others. Next, we need to look at the technological and organizational context that provides constraints on group activity. If the technology provides little room for group effort or discretion to affect the production process, it is less likely that norms will develop that affect the production process. If the technology requires high levels of interdependence and there is no formal organizational coordinating mechanism, the condition for the development of norms is established. If the organizational environment is characterized by high levels of conflict and distrust between management and workers, we would expect to see the development of norms regarding effort, allocation, production, and pay. An analysis of the technological and organizational constraints in the context of a specific group setting may shed light on the emergence of norms and their impact.

Another way to trace the effects of norms may be to go back to the function of norms in a group. The basic function of norms is to reduce ambiguities. Norms provide programs for orienting group members' behaviors. In a sense they provide solutions for recurrent group activities. If this is true, then we should identify the major pockets of ambiguity or uncertainty in a group's production process, and look for the type of norms that have emerged to reduce ambiguity. In our coal mining example, there is a high degree of uncertainty at the beginning of each shift as to the nature of the equipment, problems in the mining cycle, problems with physical conditions, and so on. In the absence of any formal intershift communication mechanism (which does not seem to exist in the industry), the emergence of norms to improve communication between crews should be related to the effectiveness of those crews.

P. S. GOODMAN, E. RAVLIN and M. SCHMINKE

We can conclude this discussion of norms with the following observations. (1) We begin by assuming group-level norms are not a pervasive phenomenon in work groups. The task for the researcher is to prove rather than assume their existence. (2) We need to pay more attention to the prevalence of different types of norms in different group settings. The current literatures overemphasize the prevalence of norms that limit production. Too much emphasis is placed on a small number of early studies on output restriction. Our own prediction is that we would find many more norms about resource-allocation issues or social arrangements than about production goals or performance strategies. (3) The link between norms and effectiveness has not been explored theoretically or empirically. There is a prevailing belief that those two variables are related, but not in any precise way. Our own position is that norms are probably not major predictors of group effectiveness. In terms of group output, technology and organizational arrangements are probably the critical predictors.

METHODOLOGICAL ISSUES

We conclude this discussion of groups in organizations by highlighting a set of methodological issues. To some extent a number of these issues have already been raised in our discussions of definitions of groups, models of group effectiveness, and assumptions about critical concepts.

Good Theory and Good Methodology

A basic theme throughout this discussion is the need to improve our theoretical specification in at least two areas—the delineation of key concepts and the specification of critical processes that bear on work-group effectiveness. The loose conceptualization of concepts such as cohesiveness accounts in part for the mixed empirical results on the effect of cohesiveness on performance. The very general specification of models of group effectiveness precludes in most cases any serious tests of the confirmability of these models. We have suggested in this chapter some approaches for conceptual clarification and better model specification. For example, our discussion of three different levels of specification (e.g., heuristic, technological and organizational) points to a strategy for building models of effectiveness which will be testable, and which should increase our understanding of effectiveness. Unless these theoretical improvements are put in place, it is unlikely the quality of the methodological studies of groups will improve.

Level of Analysis

A problem in many of the empirical studies on groups is whether they are conducted at the appropriate level of analysis. Many of these studies view groups simply as an aggregation of individual response. In these studies, the group is simply the sum of the parts. A recent paper by McGrath (1985) states, "We need to ask: What goes on at the *group level?*" In our analysis of cohesiveness literature it seems that researchers simply aggregated individual responses of liking group members as a measure of group-level phenomena.

If one is to aggregate individual-level responses to some group-level phenomenon, then the variance of individual responses needs careful attention. Although there has been discussion that both mean and variance are important in constructing a cohesiveness scale (Evans & Jarvis, 1980), there is little indication that this idea has been translated into operational measures. A procedure sometimes used in cohesiveness studies is to do a one-way analysis of variance across groups. If the between-group variance exceeds the within-group variance, the researcher assumes aggregating individual responses is an appropriate procedure. However, even if a significant one-way analysis of variance is observed, there are still likely to be groups in the sample that have the same mean scores but very different scores among members. Given individual variability in responses, can one aggregate these responses to represent a group-level phenomenon?

A related issue is whether the referent in self-report questions is the group or the individual. Some of the questions seem to focus on individual preferences. "Do you feel you are really part of your work group?" (Seashore, 1954), or "How much warmth existed between members of your discussion group" (Fodor & Smith, 1982), or "Would you want to remain a member of this survey party on future projects? (Terborg et al., 1976) all represent individual-oriented questions. "How does your work group compare with other work groups . . . on each of the following points— the way the men stick together, the way the men help each other?" Holding constant our discussion about aggregating individual-level responses, items that refer to group-level phenomena seem more appropriate measures of cohesiveness. Unfortunately this point has not been discussed or reflected in the current literature.

One way to insure that the focus will be at the group level will be to select groups that produce a group output that is different from the simple aggregation of individual-member output. Consider the coal mining crews in our research. These crews are clearly identifiable (due to physical isolation). There is one final product—tons of coal. This output is a function of the interdependent activities of 8 to 10 crew members. The coal mining crew is very different from the Bank Wiring Room where the 9 wiremen independently worked on the same task. Group output in this case was the aggregation of individual work. The selection of the type of group, then, is critical.

Another way to insure the focus will be at the group level will be to insure that the measurement tools we select have referents at the group level. Many of the self-report measures in earlier studies really focus on individual-level phenomena.

If we use individual self-report measures, the problems in aggregation discussed earlier will persist. It might be useful to experiment with other approaches such as having group members collectively agree on the group score—that is, have the group members do the aggregation (Gladstein, 1985, personal communication). Another strategy is to move away from self-reports as a measurement approach to groups. During the 3 years that the senior author studied the development of autonomous work groups (Goodman, 1979), the most informative method for understanding work groups was through regular observations of group activities over time.

The last methodological problem related to level of analysis is not pervasive but is relevant to certain field studies. Cohesiveness is a problem of groups. If one wants to study cohesiveness in an organizational setting it is important to identify work groups as opposed to any other organizational unit (e.g., a section, department). Some field studies (e.g., Seashore, 1954; Schriesheim, 1980) survey organizational participants and then arrange the subjects by a common supervisor, department, and so on. It is not clear in these cases whether the data has been aggregated at the group level or at another level of social aggregation. People reporting to a common supervisor do not equal a group.

Designing Group Effectiveness Studies

A number of issues are related to designing studies of group effectiveness. We focus on two: the strategy of identifying causal connections, and the time frame for effectiveness studies. Our traditional scientific orientation is to identify and isolate causal variables that affect, in our discussion, group effectiveness. Given this orientation and the laboratory tradition that has dominated group studies, it is not surprising that much of the earlier research has tried to isolate the effect on group performance of factors such as size, group composition, etc. More recently, the research on redesigning groups in organizations to improve performance and quality of working life have reflected a different orientation. For example, in the introduction of autonomous work groups, a host of variables have been changed to improve group performance. There is no single causal agent, but rather a cluster of variables that will impact group performance. The broad issue is whether future designs should try to isolate specific causal variables, or whether they should acknowledge that there is a system of variables that bears on group effectiveness.

We have approached this design issue in the following way. First, we draw a sample of groups across firms that operate under the same technology. Then, we develop a model that predicts variation in group performance. Our objective is to begin with a very simple model, and then see whether more complicated models improve our understanding. In our work we started out with technology and a simple labor variable (see discussion, pp. 134–135). By estimating that model we can learn the relative contribution of different predictors. The next step is to introduce other theoretically relevant variables to examine their explanatory variables (e.g., organizational arrangements, group process). However, we have learned from our own work that within any organization there are multiple combinations of strategies (i.e., predictors) that groups can adopt that lead to similar effective performance. We need to learn about those configurations of variables. This type of investigation focuses on groups within the organization and tries to map out the configuration of exogenous and endogenous variables that affects group performance. The point is that at certain levels of aggregation it is possible to identify the relative importance of different determinants of group performance. However, it is also important to acknowledge that there is a complex configuration of variables that affects group performance and to adopt a more idiographic strategy to explore the nature of this configuration.

Another design issue concerns the time frame. There are many studies of group performance using ad hoc temporary groups. It is unclear whether those types of group studies are really informative. We are interested in groups in organizations that have a past, present and future. As the literature on group development suggests (e.g., Tuckman, 1965), groups vary in their focus at different times in their life cycle. A study by Terborg et al., (1976) clearly demonstrates that the relationship between cohesiveness and group performance varies over time. The relationships between cohesiveness and performance varied from significantly positive on the first trial, to neutral on four intermediate trials, to significantly negative on the last trial.

Another study (Goodman, 1979), on introducing autonomous work groups, also demonstrated the need for data over time. Initially, the groups were powerful mechanisms for changing behavior and affecting various performance criteria. However, over time other contextual factors led to the dissolution of the autonomous work groups. A single measurement of this change activity would not in any way portray the critical events of this change process. There is a clear need for designs that map the group's history over time. It is difficult to specify an appropriate time period. Access to the groups and to resources to conduct the research will determine the time period.

Describing Work Groups

Another major problem we reviewed in the section on tasks and technology is a method of describing what work groups do. Our analysis pointed to the weaknesses in the dimensional approach to describing groups. The use of dimensions such as task predictability, number of exceptions, and analyzability are based on an assumption that the work of a group is homogeneous. We have pointed out why this assumption may not be true. Also, these dimensions, with their focus on uncertainty, provide a very narrow view of technology. Most important, these dimensions provide us little insight on what groups actually do.

We need a new language to discuss groups. The language must shed some of the traditions of both the social–psychological laboratory, which dominate the descriptions of group tasks, and the structural contingency theory, which dominates the descriptions of technology. Although we do not know the eventual form of the language, we can specify some of its initial characteristics.

1.   We should return to describing what groups do, rather than using abstract concepts to summarize what groups do. Homans (1950) description of the Bank Wiring Room or Whyte's (1943)· description of "Street Corner Society" provide rich descriptions of what groups do. In these descriptions the reader is able to see the work and nonwork activities of the group unfold. These accounts are rich and complex but readable.

2.   It is difficult to describe complex phenomena without some organizing mechanisms. Researchers such as Homans, Whyte, and the social anthropologists of that period organized their descriptions around interactions, activities, and sentiments. This is a simple but powerful way to describe group phenomena. Another approach is to develop engineering-like process charts that trace the operations and flow of work through the work cycle. There is less theoretical organization to this approach but it does represent a method that has a long tradition in descriptions of work. Initially there does not appear to be a need to develop an elaborate coding system for describing groups. We simply want to know who does what? With whom? When? In what sequence? Where? How?

3.   The language should reflect the technological as well as the human aspects of work; it should be more interdisciplinary in nature. Most groups in organizations use some type of equipment (we use the word *equipment* broadly to refer to tools, machinery, and computers and their software), but we rarely find descriptions of the equipment as it bears on the group.

Characterizations of equipment in terms of the level of automation are not too instructive. However, there is an extensive engineering literature on machine reliability. Reliability is important because it deals with whether and when the machine may be available to the group. The concept of reliability in this context is engineering, not human-behavior talk, but it is important in describing and understanding groups that use equipment. This discussion of equipment can be expanded to how we characterize inventory, tooling, or maintenance policies that bear on how groups function.

4.   After we describe what groups do our focus should be on describing group-effectiveness levers. These levers represent factors that substantially change variation in selected effectiveness indicators. Our assumption is that in any work group there is a small set of levers that substantially determine what happens to group performance, group satisfaction, and so on. We need to develop descriptive methods that will uncover these levers. In the mining example, we noted that downtime of the continuous miner is a major factor affecting group performance. A variety of sources, some uncontrollable (for example, physical conditions), some controllable but exogenous to the group (age of machinery), and some controllable by the group (care of machinery), affect variations in downtime. The controllable sources are what we call *group performance levers*. They represent controllable points of intervention, exogenous or endogenous to the group, which affect group performance. There is no generic set of levers across all groups or any one way to identify levers. Our own experience is that an in-depth understanding of the group's technology will unfold the critical levers. (See Goodman, 1986a for more discussion on how to identify these levers.)

Sampling

In our review of the current literature, it appears that the type of group selected has an important bearing on what we learn about effectiveness, yet we found nothing in the literature that articulates a position about sampling work groups. Clearly there have been some interesting typologies of groups (cf. McGrath, 1984), but typologies do not articulate a strategy about sampling work groups. Our view is that many of the work groups studied were selected more out of convenience than for some strategic purpose.

We think the sampling strategy is important. Some factors to be considered include:

1.   The nature of group activities differs under different technologies. We do not think there are general models of group effectiveness that are

robust across different technologies. The initial sampling strategy is to concentrate on groups operating under a homogeneous strategy.

2.   We want to select homogeneous groups where the output is at the group level of analysis. In these groups, division of labor exists among members and the product of their efforts is group-level output.

3.   It has been argued here and elsewhere (Goodman, 1986a) that within a common technology there are a variety of combinations of equipment, materials, environment, and programs that will achieve the same production output. If this assumption is true and given that technology drives a lot of group activities, our next sampling strategy is to look at major configuration differences within the same technology. This position is consistent with a finding from our research that mining companies using the same technology generate different performance models. That is, the production function of the work groups differ between groups across companies, although they are all doing the same type of mining. Because our goal is to understand how work groups function, it is important to examine the impact of different configurations within a given technology. This is the only way we can move from some of the general models that characterize the literature to a more fine-grained understanding of work groups. The implication of this factor is to sample multiple firms using a similar technology.

4.   The organizational context is often cited (cf. McGrath, 1984) as an important constraint on work-group functions, but there is little evidence that variation in the organizational context is systematically considered in sampling work groups. The question is what contextual factors one should sample given the large number of possibilities. In our own work we have found manning policies and reward systems to be critical contextual factors.

For example, in the 26 mines in our study there are major differences in the use of indirect labor, that is, people who work outside the regular mining crews. We could look at two mines whose crews have exactly the same equipment, job configuration, and labor, but who differ greatly on the number of people who work in the mines, but not in the crews. We have seen 50% to 60% variation in the amount of indirect labor for mines having the same number of crews. The points of this illustration are as follows: (1) If we only look at the productive system for the group we would be unaware of other organizational policies that may influence group performance, such as this difference in manning policy. Efficient indirect labor may facilitate the work of the crews. (2) These policies that apply to all groups may be more important levers than a within-group intervention. That is, a change in the indirect labor policy may have more impact on some group-productivity indicators than might any change at the group level.

5. Once we have gained knowledge about work groups in a particular technology, various configurations within that technology, and variations within organizational context, the sampling plan should identify alternative forms of technology. The question is on what basis to select alternative technologies. Our position is to select technologies based on the extent to which they permit group effort and group discretion to impact on group effectiveness. These two dimensions are important because they will help unfold the relative contributions and interactions of technical and human factors on performance.

DISCUSSION AND CONCLUSION

The goal of this paper is to add to our understanding about groups in organizations. The strategy was to select a few concepts, critically examine the assumptions behind these concepts, and then provide some alternative views. Given the renewed interest in groups in organizations, it seems timely to review what we know and more importantly to examine our current strategy of thinking about groups.

The analysis of model specification introduced three levels of models—heuristic, technological, and organizational—that articulate a strategy for generating more precise and confirmable models of group performance. The examination of variable selection pointed to biases in the types of variables we use to explain work-group effectiveness. The origin of these biases can be traced to the powerful influence of the laboratory literature on groups and to the types of training experienced by many of the researchers in the field. An argument was made for paying more attention to technological and economic variables as well as rethinking whether group-process variables should play such a dominant role in models of group performance. The analysis of task, technology, cohesiveness, group norms concepts was presented to illustrate the need for reevaluating our conceptualization of these concepts. We could have subjected other concepts to that same type of analysis, but did not because of space constraints. The point is a set of central concepts about groups exists. These concepts were generated in the research arena, but are now fairly pervasive in the teaching or textbook arena. They seem to be freely transmitted, often without a basic review of the underlying assumptions and meanings of these concepts. In our analysis of norms we both challenged the pervasiveness of norms and their effects on group effectiveness, and posed some alternative ways to affirm the existence of norms and their impact on group performance. The discussion of the five methodological topics was presented to highlight some operational issues in studying groups. Of these topics, finding new ways to describe work groups seems to be the most critical. A breakthrough in this area would substantially change our body of knowledge about groups.

The strategy in this chapter has been to critically evaluate a few concepts. The focus on a few concepts was necessary because each analysis needed to be detailed. There are clearly other issues to be tackled and hopefully the form of analysis used in this paper will be generalizable to these issues and concepts. Some other topics for investigation might include the following. First, we have really concentrated on groups that produce something. (There are obviously other types of groups in organizations.) McGrath's work on typologies of groups may be a way to map out some of these groups and then begin to understand their differences and similarities. A comprehensive understanding of groups in organizations requires that we know how to utilize topics such as model specification, variable selection, and the role of norms across different types of groups. Second, our focus has been on groups and within group functions. Little attention has been paid to between-group transactions, yet these exchanges are critical to group functions (cf. Brett & Rognes, 1986). Third, the orientation of this chapter has been a research rather than a practice perspective. In groups literature a dichotomy has emerged between the research literature and the practice literature, yet there is new thinking (Lawler, Mohrman, Mohrman, Ledford, & Cummings, 1985) in our field about how to do research that affects both practice and theory. New work on groups in organizations probably should be more aware of creating new links between theory and practice. Fourth, an underlying theme in this chapter is that we should focus on designing effective work groups. That is, we carry an effectiveness bias in our analysis of groups in organizations. Although we feel effectiveness research is valuable for a variety of constituencies, it is clear it is only one lense to view groups in organizations (cf. Schwartzman, 1986).

In concluding, it is clear that interest in groups in organizations has followed a cyclical trend. We seem to be in a period of reemerging attention of groups. What is important is to approach this reemergence in a creative way. The area is exciting. The opportunities for new research are vast.

REFERENCES

Argot, L. (1982). Input uncertainty and organizational coordination in hospital emergency units. *Administrative Science Quarterly, 27,* 420–434.

Asch, S.E. (1951). Effects of group pressure upon the modification and distortion of judgments. In H. Guetzkow (Ed.), *Groups, leadership and men,* (pp. 177–190). Pittsburgh, PA: Carnegie Press.

Back, K. (1951). Influence through social communication. *Journal of Abnormal and Social Psychology, 46,* 9–23.

Brett, J. & Rognes, J. (1986). Intergroup relations in organizations. In P.S. Goodman (Ed.), *Designing effective work groups.* (pp.202–236). San Francisco: Jossey-Bass.

Carter, L.F., Haythorn, W.W., & Howell, M. (1950). A further investigation of the criteria of leadership. *Journal of Abnormal and Social Psychology, 45,* 350–358.

Cartwright, D. (1968). The nature of group cohesiveness. In D. Cartwright and A. Zander (Eds.), *Group dynamics* (3rd ed.) (pp. 91–109). New York: Harper & Row.

Cheng, J.L.C. (1984). Organizational coordinationa, uncertainty, and performance: An integrative study. *Human Relations, 37*(10), 829–851.

Coch, L., & French, J.R.P. (1968). Overcoming resistance to change. In D. Cartwright & A. Zander (Eds.), *Group dynamics* (3rd ed.) (pp. 336–350). New York: Harper & Row.

Collins, O., Dalton, M., & Roy, D. (1946). Restriction of output and social cleavage in industry. *Applied Anthropology, 5*(3), 1–14.

Comstock, D.E., & Scott, W.R. (1977). Technology and the structure of subunits: Distinguishing individual and workgroup effects. *Administrative Science Quarterly, 22,* 177–202.

Cummings, T. (1981). Designing Effective Work Groups. In. P.C. Nystrom III and W.H. Starbuck, *Handbook of organizational design: Vol. 2. Remodeling organizations and their environments* (pp. 250–271). Oxford, England: Oxford University Press.

Evans, N.J. & Jarvis, P.A. (1980). Group cohesion: A review and reevaluation. *Small Group Behavior, 11*(4), 359–370.

Festinger, L. (1950). Informal social communication. *Psychological Review, 57,* 271–282.

Festinger, L., Schachter, S., & Back K. (1950). *Social pressures in informal groups.* New York: Harper & Row.

Flowers, M.A. (1977). A laboratory test of some implications of Janis's groupthink hypothesis. *Journal of Personality and Social Psychology, 35,* 888–896.

Fodor, E.M., & Smith, T. (1982). The power motive as an influence on group decision-making. *Journal of Personality and Social Psychology, 41*(1), 178–185.

Fry, L.W., & Slocum, J.W. Jr. (1984). Technology, structure and workgroup effectiveness: A test of a contingency model. *Academy of Management Journal, 27*(2), 221–246.

Georgopoulous, B.S. (1965). Normative structure variables and organizational behavior. *Human Relations, 18,* 155–169.

Gladstein, D. (1984). A model of task group effectiveness. *Administrative Science Quarterly, 29*(4), 499–517.

Goodman, P.S. (1968a). Impact of task and technology on group performance. In P.S. Goodman (Ed.), *Designing effective work groups* (pp. 120–167). San Francisco: Jossey-Bass.

Goodman, P.S. (1979). *Assessing organizational change: The Rushton Quality of Work Experiment.* New York: Wiley.

Goodman, P.S. (Ed.). (1986b). *Designing effective work groups.* San Francisco: Jossey-Bass.

Goodman, P.S., & Dean, J.W. Jr. (1982). Creating long-term organizational change. In P.S. Goodman (Ed.), *Change in organizations* (pp. 226–279). San Francisco: Jossey-Bass.

Goodman, P.S., Ravlin, E., & Argote, L. (1986). Current thinking about groups: Setting the stage for new ideas. In P.S. Goodman (Ed.), *Designing effective work groups.* (pp. 1–33). San Francisco: Jossey-Bass.

Gross, N., & Martin, W.E. (1952). On group cohesiveness. *American Journal of Sociology, 57,* 546–554.

Guzzo, R.A. (1986). Group decision making and group effectiveness in organizations. In P.S. Goodman (Ed.), *Designing effective work groups.* (pp. 34–71). San Francisco: Jossey-Bass.

Hackman, J.R. (1976). Group influences on individuals. In M.D. Dunnette (Ed.), *Handbook of industrial and organizational psychology.* (pp. 1455–1525). Chicago: Rand McNally.

Hackman, J.R. (1983, November). A normative model of work team effectiveness (Tech. Rep. No. 2). New Haven, CT: Yale School of Organization and Management, Research Program on Groups Effectiveness.

Hackman, J.R., & Morris, C.G. (1975). Group tasks, group interaction process, and group performance effectiveness: A review and proposed integration. In. L. Berkowitz (Ed.), *Advances in experimental social psychology: Vol. 8*. (pp. 45–99). New York: Academic Press.

Hackman, J.R., & Oldham, G.R. (1980). *Work redesign*. Reading, MA: Addison-Wesley.

Hellriegel, D., Slocum, J.W. Jr., & Woodman, R.W. (1983). *Organizational behavior* (3rd ed.). St. Paul, MN: West.

Herold, D.M. (1978). Improving the performance effectiveness of groups through a task-contingency selection of intervention strategies. *Academy of Management Review, 3*(2), 315–325.

Hickson, D.J., Pugh, D.S., & Pheysey D.C. (1969). Operations technology and organizational structure: An empirical reappraisal. *Administrative Science Quarterly, 14*, 378–397.

Homans, G.C. (1950). *The human group*. New York: Harcourt Brace Jovanovich.

Horsfall, A.B., & Arensberg, C.M. (1949). Teamwork and productivity in a shoe factory. *Human Organization, 8*, 13–25.

Jackson, J. (1965). Structural characteristics of norms. In I.D. Steiner and M. Fishbein (Eds.), *Current studies in social psychology*. (pp. 301–309). New York: Holt, Rinehart and Winston.

Janis, I.L. (1972). *Victims of groupthink: A psychological study of foreign-policy decisions and fiascos*. Boston: Houghton Mifflin.

Kahn, R.L. (1977). Organizational effectiveness: An overview. In P.S. Goodman and J.M. Pennings (Eds.), *New perspectives on organizational effectiveness*. (pp. 235–248). San Francisco: Jossey-Bass.

Katz, D., & Kahn, R.L. (1978). *The social psychology of organizations* (2nd ed.), New York: Wiley.

Kiesler, C.A. (1971). *The psychology of commitment: Experiments linking behavior to belief*. New York: Academic Press.

Kolodny, H.F., & Kiggundu, M.N. (1980). Toward the development of a sociotechnical systems model in Woodlands Mechanical Harvesting. *Human Relations, 33*(9), 623–645.

Lawler, E., Mohrman, A., Mohrman, S., Ledford, G., & Cummings, T. (Eds.). (1985). *Doing research that is useful for theory and practice*. San Francisco: Jossey-Bass.

Libo, L. (1953). *Measuring group cohesiveness*. Ann Arbor: University of Michigan Press.

Lott, B.E. (1961). Group cohesiveness: A learning phenomenon. *Journal of Social Psychology, 55*, 275–286.

Lott, A.J., & Lott, B.E. (1965). Group cohesiveness as interpersonal attraction: A review of relationships with antecedent and consequent variables. *Psychological Bulletin, 64*(4), 259–309.

Manz, C.C., & Sims, H.P. Jr. (1982). The potential for "groupthink" in autonomous work groups. *Human Relations, 35*(9), 773–784.

March, J.G., & Simon, H.A. (1958). *Organizations*. New York: Wiley.

McGrath, J.E. (1984). *Groups: Interaction and performance*. Englewood Cliffs, NJ: Prentice-Hall.

McGrath, J.E. (1986). Studying groups at work: Ten critical needs for theory and practice. In P.S. Goodman (Ed.), *Designing effective work groups*. (pp. 362–392). San Francisco: Jossey-Bass.

Middlemist, R.D., & Hitt, M.A. (1981). Technology as a moderator of the relationship between perceived work environment and subunit effectiveness. *Human Relations, 34*(6), 517–532.

Mohr, L. (1971). Organizational technology and organization structure. *Administrative Science Quarterly, 16,* 444–459.

Organ D., & Hamner, W.C. (1982). *Organizational behavior.* Plano, TX: Business Publications.

Perrow, C. (1967). A framework for the comparative analysis of organizations. *American Sociological Review, 32,* 194–208.

Roy, D.F. (1960). Banana time: Job satisfaction and informal interaction. *Human Organization 18*(4), 80–102.

Salancik, G.R. (1977). Commitment and the control of organizational behavior and belief. In B.M. Staw and G.R. Salancik (Eds.), *New directions in organizational behavior* (pp. 1–54). Chicago: St. Clair Press.

Schoonhoven, C.B. (1981). Problems with contingency theory: Testing assumptions hidden within the language of contingency. *Administrative Science Quarterly, 26,* 349–377.

Schriesheim, J.F. (1980). The social context of leader-subordinate relations: An investigation of the effects of group cohesiveness. *Journal of Applied Psychology, 65*(2), 183–194.

Seashore, S.E. (1954). *Group cohesiveness in the industrial work group.* Ann Arbor, MI: Survey Research Center, Institute for Social Research.

Schwartzman, H. (1986). Research on work group effectiveness: An anthropological critique. In P.S. Goodman (Ed.), *Designing effective work groups.* (pp. 237–276). San Francisco: Jossey-Bass.

Shaw, M.E. (1981). *Group dynamics: The psychology of small group behavior* (3rd ed.). New York: McGraw-Hill.

Shea, G.P., & Guzzo, R.A. (1984). *A theory of work group effectiveness.* Unpublished manuscript, University of Pennsylvania.

Steers, R.M. (1981). *Introduction to organizational behavior.* Santa Monica, CA: Goodyear.

Steiner, I.D. (1972). *Group process and productivity.* New York: Academic Press.

Stogdill, R.M. (1972). Group productivity, drive, and cohesiveness. *Organizational Behavior and Human Performance, 8,* 36–43.

Terborg, J.R., Castore, C., & DeNinno, J.A. (1976). A longitudinal field investigation of the impact of group composition on group performance and cohesion. *Journal of Personality and Social Psychology, 34*(5), 782–790.

Thompson, J.D. (1965). *Organizations in action.* New York: McGraw-Hill.

Tuckman, B.W. (1965). Developmental sequence in small groups. *Psychological Bulletin, 63,* 384–399.

Tushman, M.L. (1979). Impacts of perceived environmental variability on patterns of work-related communication. *Academy of Management Journal, 22*(3), 482–500.

Tziner, A., & Vardi, Y. (1982). Effects of comment style and group cohesiveness of self-selected tank crews. *Journal of Applied Psychology, 67*(6), 769–775.

Whyte, W.F. (1943). *Street corner society.* Chicago: University of Chicago Press.

The Evolution and Adaptation of Organizations

Edited by **Barry M. Staw** and **L.L. Cummings**

CONTENTS: **Organizational Life Cycles and Natural Selection,** *John Freeman.* **Even Dwarfs Started Small: Liabilities of Age and Size and Their Strategic Implications,** *Howard Aldrich and Ellen R. Auster.* **The Political Environments of Organizations: An Ecological View,** *Glenn R. Carroll, Jacques Delacroix, and Jerry Goodstein.* **Managerial Discretion: A Bridge Between Polar Views of Organizational Outcomes,** *Donald C. Hambrick and Sidney Finkelstein.* **Organizational Evolution: A Metamorphosis Model of Convergence and Reorientation,** *Michael L. Tushman and Elaine Romanelli.* **Behavior in Escalation Situations: Antecedents, Prototypes, and Solutions,** *Barry M. Staw.* **A Model of Creativity and Innovation in Organizations,** *Teresa M. Amabileand Jerry Ross.* **When a Thousand Flowers Bloom: Structural, Collective, and Social Conditions for Innovation in Organization,** *Rosabeth Moss Kanter.*

1990   320 pp.   LC 90-4525   Paper $19.50
ISBN 1-55938-221-X

All articles are reprinted from: **Research in Organizational Behavior,** Edited by **Barry M. Staw,** *School of Business Administration, University of California, Berkeley* and **L.L. Cummings,** *Carlson School of Management, University of Minnesota*

JAI PRESS INC.

55 Old Post Road - No. 2
P.O. Box 1678
Greenwich, Connecticut 06836-1678
Tel: 203-661-7602

Evaluation and Employment in Organizations

Edited by **L.L. Cummings** and **Barry M. Staw**

CONTENTS: **Performance Appraisal: A Process Focus,** *Daniel R. Ilgen and Jack M. Feldman.* **Self-Assessments in Organizations: A Literature Review and Integrative Model. A Process Analysis of the Assessment Center Method,** *Sheldon Zedeck.* **Sex Bias in Work Settings: The Lack of Fit Model,** *Madaline E. Heilman.* **Understanding Comparable Worth: A Societal and Political Perspective,** *Thomas A. Mahoney.* **The Meanings of Absence: New Strategies for Theory and Research. Employee Turnover and Post Decision Accommodation,** *Richard M. Steers and Richard T. Mowday.* **The Effects of Work Layoffs in Survivors: Research Theory and Practice,** *Joel Brockner.*

1990   256 pp.   LC 90-4533   Paper $19.50
ISBN 1-55938-219-8

All articles are reprinted from: **Research in Organizational Behavior,** Edited by **Barry M. Staw,** *School of Business Administration, University of California, Berkeley* and **L.L. Cummings,** *Carlson School of Management, University of Minnesota*

JAI PRESS INC.

55 Old Post Road - No. 2
P.O. Box 1678
Greenwich, Connecticut 06836-1678
Tel: 203-661-7602

Personality and Organizational Influence

Edited by **Barry M. Staw** and **L.L. Cummings**

CONTENTS: Personality and Organizational Behavior, *Howard M. Weiss and Seymour Adler.* **Interactional Psychology and Organizational Behavior,** *Benjamin Schneider.* **Toward a Theory of Organizational Socialization,** *John Van Maanen and Edgar T. Schein.* **The Politics of Upward Influence in Organizations,** *Lyman W. Porter, Robert W. Allen, and Harold L. Angle.* **Principled Organizational Dissent: A Theoretical Essay,** *Jill W. Graham.* **Power and Personality in Complex Organizations,** *Robert J. House.* **Organizational Structure, Attitudes, and Behaviors,** *Chris J. Berger and L.L. Cummings.*

1990   326 pp.   LC 90-4524   Paper $19.50
ISBN 1-55938-217-1

All articles are reprinted from: **Research in Organizational Behavior,** Edited by **Barry M. Staw,** *School of Business Administration, University of California, Berkeley* and **L.L. Cummings,** *Carlson School of Management, University of Minnesota*

JAI PRESS INC.
55 Old Post Road - No. 2
P.O. Box 1678
Greenwich, Connecticut 06836-1678
Tel: 203-661-7602

Work in Organizations

Edited by **Barry M. Staw** and **L.L. Cummings**

CONTENTS: Motivation Theory Reconsidered, *Frank J. Landy and Wendy S. Becker.* **Activation Theory and Job Design: Review and Reconceptualization,** *Donald G. Gardner and L.L. Cummings.* **Toward an Integrated Theory of Task Design,** *Ricky W. Griffin.* **Of Art and Work: Aesthetics Experience, and the Psychology of Work Feelings,** *Lloyd E. Sandelands and Georgette C. Buckner.* **The Expression of Emotion in Organizational Life,** *Anat Rafaeli and Robert I. Sutton.* **"Real Feelings": Emotional Expression and Organizational Culture,** *John Van Maanen and Gideon Kunda.* **Work Values and the Conduct of Organizational Behavior,** *Walter R. Nord, Arthur P. Brief, Jennifer M. Atieh, and Elizabeth M. Doherty.*

1990   296 pp.   LC 90-4474   Paper $19.50
ISBN 1-55938-216-3

All articles are reprinted from: **Research in Organizational Behavior,** Edited by **Barry M. Staw,** *School of Business Administration, University of California, Berkeley* and **L.L. Cummings,** *Carlson School of Management, University of Minnesota*

JAI PRESS INC.
55 Old Post Road - No. 2
P.O. Box 1678
Greenwich, Connecticut 06836-1678
Tel: 203-661-7602

JAI PRESS

Information and Cognition in Organizations

Edited by **L.L. Cummings** and **Barry M. Staw**

CONTENTS: Management as Symbolic Action: The Creation and Maintenance of Organizational Paradigms, *Jeffrey Pfeffer.* **Rationality and Justification in Organizational Life,** *Barry M. Staw.* **The Use of Information in Organizational Decision Making: A Model and Some Propositions,** *Charles A. O'Reilly, III.* **Negotiator Cognition,** *Max H. Bazerman and John S. Carroll.* **Accountability: The Neglected Social Context of Judgment and Choice,** *Philip E. Tetlock.* **An Attributional Model of Leadership and the Poor Performing Subordinate: Development and Validation,** *Terence R. Mitchell, Steven G. Green, and Robert E. Wood.* **Information Richness: A New Approach to Managerial Behavior and Organization Design,** *Richard L. Daft and Robert H. Lengel.* **Cognitive Processes in Organizations,** *Karl E. Weick.*

1990   320pp.   LC 90-4523   Paper $19.50
ISBN 1-55938-218-X

All articles are reprinted from: **Research in Organizational Behavior,** Edited by **Barry M. Staw,** *School of Business Administration, University of California, Berkeley* and **L.L. Cummings,** *Carlson School of Management, University of Minnesota*

JAI PRESS INC.

55 Old Post Road - No. 2
P.O. Box 1678
Greenwich, Connecticut 06836-1678
Tel: 203-661-7602

DATE DUE